THE LUCKIEST MAN IN THE WORLD

An Autobiography
by
Carl W. Meisterlin

Azalea Art Press
Southern Pines, North Carolina

© **Carl W. Meisterlin, 2014.**
All rights reserved.

ISBN: 978-0-9899961-4-3

Cover Art:
Meisterlin Family Crest

Dedication

I dedicate this book to my immediate family and to all my good friends, dead or alive, who have made my life what it is today.

In particular, I would like to dedicate this book to my father, Carl, and to my mother, Edith.

Most of all I would like to dedicate this book to the most wonderful woman in the world, my wife Irene, who has made my life so happy, funny, and memorable.

CONTENTS

Preface   *i*

Chapter 1
Last of the Aristocrats   1

Chapter 2
The Early Years: Ages 5-17   22

Chapter 3
Earthquakes and Invasions   38

Chapter 4
Spaceships and Diamond Rings   54

Chapter 5
The Wedding, the Honeymoon and Anything Goes   66

Chapter 6
Opportunity Knocks   79

Chapter 7
The Big Break   90

Chapter 8
Beginnings with Soulé   99

Chapter 9
The Road to Success   114

Chapter 10
On to L.A.   142

Chapter 11
Further Adventures in L.A.   153

Chapter 12
Another Good Move   173

Chapter 13
New Ventures   188

Chapter 14
History in the Making   215

Chapter 15
Tragedies and Tribulations   228

Meisterlin Family Photos   247

Chapter 16
Dark Days   254

Chapter 17
Bogies and Birdies   278

Chapter 18
Ready for Love   307

Chapter 19
Life Gets Better					327

Chapter 20
Life is Wonderful				367

Chapter 21
The La Quinta Years				406

Chapter 22
Green Valley					432

Chapter 23
Trips and Travels				459

Chapter 24
All the Celebrities				481

Chapter 25
Timing and Dumb Luck				498

Chapter 26
The Natural, The Inspirational, The Adhesive,
   The Challenge, The Mother and The Sons	505

Chapter 27
The Attitude of Gratitude			517

Acknowledgments				*527*
About the Author				*528*
Contact Information				*530*

Preface

You may ask why I call myself the luckiest man in the world? It's simple: because out of all the negatives in life came eventually the positive things that have made me so happy to be here at the young age of eighty-six.

One of the most interesting life lessons I discovered was this—that to make the wrong decision at the right time is far better than making the right decision at the wrong time—and that either one is better than procrastination!

I have enjoyed many successes in my life, but I have also made many honest mistakes. I have also encountered a few unexpected tragedies. I think as you read my life story you will find instances that may parallel your own experiences.

Good reading and I hope you enjoy this memoir!

Carl Meisterlin
May 2014

THE LUCKIEST MAN
IN THE WORLD

Chapter 1

Last of the Aristocrats

I come from noble birth, the last of Norwegian aristocrats.

The Meisterlin family history traces as far back as 1158 in Strasbourg, France and then to Germany in the early 1500s. The first ancestor to appear in records is Siegmund Meisterlin, who reached a status entitling the family to a coat of arms in 1488. The family then appears in northwestern Germany in the city of Flensburg in 1828.

According to a heraldic report, it is not a common name. It is most likely a patronymic surname derived from "meisterlin," meaning 'son of a master.' The symbols on the Meisterlin coat of arms indicate that they fought in Spain against the Moors in the Middle Ages. Other symbols on the coat of arms stand for military fortitude, peace and serenity.

After 1828, the family splits, although we can only speculate why this occurred. One branch went to Rostov in northeastern Germany on the Baltic Sea. The other part of the family, from which I came, went to Trondheim, Norway. It was there that my grandmother, Ingrid Petterssen, and my grandfather, Wilhelm Peder Meisterlin, were married in 1886. It was an arranged marriage and we were a dysfunctional family right from the beginning.

Grandmother
Ingrid Petterssen

Grandfather
Wilhelm Peder Meisterlin

Granduncle
Wilhelm Meisterlin

Ingrid Petterssen (2nd from right)
Wilhelm Peder Meisterlin (on floor)

My great grandparents had three sons, two of whom went on to become very well known in Norway. The eldest son, Wilhelm Meisterlin, was a military colonel in the Boer War fighting for the British. This son was a much-decorated war hero, who became the King of Norway's closest friend and confidante. This granduncle became Secretary of State and Defense for Norway. My second granduncle, in the year 1911, started Norwegian Airlines, a two-aircraft mail service. After World War II, it merged with the German mail service and eventually became Lufthansa. The third son, my grandfather, Wilhelm Peder, never did anything of note. In fact, in my entire lifetime, my dad never once spoke of his own father.

The Meisterlin family was originally in the shipping business. Their company was a partner of the East India Shipping Company, which sailed to the Mediterranean. In the 1800s they made the trip from Iran (then called Persia) to Europe through the Mediterranean to Egypt, where today the Suez Canal stands. They then transported cargo over land to the Red Sea and sailed on to Persia. Supposedly, they were very active in the mid-1850s. In the year 1865, they lost three ships in a giant storm in the Mediterranean. There was a major loss of life. The economic loss to the Meisterlin family almost wiped them out, but they prevailed into the 20th century until World War I.

The Petterssen family also made their living from the sea. My maternal grandfather, Captain Petterssen, was a ship's captain who sailed across the top of the Arctic and down the coast of Alaska to San Francisco and back, weather permitting. Upon arrival in America, he changed his name to Petersen. During the time of the gold rush in Alaska, Captain Petersen relieved himself of his command and opened a bar and restaurant in the Skagway region. He was said to have made a fortune from renting rooms, and I suspect that he ran a very prosperous bar and hotel.

My father, Carl Bernhardt, was born in 1890 and graduated from grade school (equivalent to our high school) in 1908. He then went to work for my uncle in the State Department of Norway. For three years he was in the diplomatic service and traveled to 22 different European countries. He then followed the tradition of other male Meisterlin progeny and entered military school in Prussia in January 1912. After graduation from the Prussian Military Academy in 1914, he accepted a commission in the Prussian Army and was assigned to the Intelligence Corps. My guess is that this was because he spoke seven or eight different languages at this time, including Norwegian, Danish, Swedish, Spanish and Italian. He was particularly fluent in French, German and English.

My grandmother, Ingrid, divorced my grandfather for good reason. My grandfather had a mistress—a maid living in the house—which the family permitted . . . unbelievable! Divorce was highly unusual in those days. Sweden and Norway didn't permit divorce, but Denmark did. She couldn't return to her family in Sweden—that was verboten—so she obtained a divorce in Denmark and my grandmother came to New York City in 1896. She met a much younger man and they married in 1899. Later in life, they lived next door to the Roosevelts on Park Avenue. When my father arrived in the U.S., my grandmother introduced him as her younger brother. Earlier, when Harriet, my father's older sister, came to the U.S., Ingrid introduced her as her younger sister.

1899
Aunt Harriet Meisterlin
and Father Carl Bernhardt Meisterlin

My father sailed to New York City in 1919 on the Norwegian Steamship Line, of which his family was part owner. The ship was part sailing vessel and part steam-powered and regularly traveled between Trondheim and New York.

One of my father's favorite stories that I remember hearing repeatedly as a child was about his arrival in New York. He told the story this way:

Early one morning, I arrived in New York. There had been excellent sailing conditions. I only carried with me one huge trunk with all my personal belongings. As no one was there to pick me up or greet me at the harbor, I was forced to take a taxi.

Getting my trunk into the taxi was the first major chore. We then proceeded to the area called Greenwich Village. The neighborhood where my driver took me consisted of old three-story brownstones. After unloading the trunk, which again was extremely difficult, I dragged it over to a stairwell entrance.

The brownstones at this time were three-flat apartments. Unfortunately for me, my friend's flat was on the middle floor. The only way I could possibly get my trunk off the street was to drag it up the stairs one step at a time. When I was about halfway up the stairwell, with my back turned and leaning forward towards the street, I felt the presence of somebody behind me. I tried to make space for whomever it was to squeeze by and as I turned, I saw the most beautiful girl I had ever seen in my life. She was wearing nothing but a smile! As I admired her beautiful figure, she proceeded to enter the downstairs flat.

That evening when I told my friend about this encounter, he explained that this was a common occurrence. She was actually a professional model who posed and worked for the artist downstairs and another artist upstairs. I knew then that America was the country for me!

Dad never set foot in Norway again!

The following day my father started work at the Norwegian American Steamship Lines office. He married a young New York girl in 1920 and had a daughter, my half sister Patti Meisterlin. Patti Meisterlin had one son named Billy Peters, who had two children and now has grandchildren. We both caught the Petterssen gene. He acts like me, looks like me and has the same sense of humor.

In 1922, he divorced this lady—or she divorced him, I really don't know which—this subject was never discussed. In 1926, he married my birth mother, Catherine Wanda Paprocki. At this time my father was 36 years old and "Von," as he liked to call her, was 20. This marriage proved to be a disaster also.

**1925
Birth Mother
Catherine Wanda Paprocki**

Two years later, on February 16, 1928, I was born at Suffolk County Hospital on Long Island's south shore. By this time, my father was now a millionaire. He and a partner owned several gas stations in New Jersey—they were very successful as this business was growing hand over fist. He also invested very heavily in the stock market. Naturally, most of these millions were on paper. On October 27, 1929 my father lost all the money he had, including money he had invested for his wife's family, in the stock market crash. My mother Edith told me many years later that his partner committed suicide by jumping out a window.

My father and Von proceeded to San Francisco, with me as an eighteen-month-old toddler, and one month later my father got a job driving a truck selling coffee house-to-house. This was quite a come down from the lifestyle we enjoyed up until that point and my mother absolutely wouldn't accept it!

After a very short period of time, my mother packed up with me in tow and headed back to her mother's home on Long Island. For the next four years I lived in my maternal grandmother's house in Babylon, New York. My mother, who was all of 21 at the time, was a gorgeous woman—what they called in those days a "Flapper." Women in those days were finding a new sense of freedom from convention. They wore short skirts, bobbed their hair, smoked cigarettes and drove cars in "The Roaring Twenties"—all things that would have shocked the previous generation. My mother's lifestyle was even a little much for Grandma Paprocki, but the influence of my grandmother set the tone and future direction of my life.

**1951
Grandmother
Katherine Paprocki**

Grandmother Paprocki was a dark-haired, stocky, heavy-set Polish woman with warm brown eyes, whose family had come originally from Alsace-Lorraine. She was very strong and very loving. The four years spent living with my Grandmother Paprocki from the age of 18 months until five years old was the most fortunate happenstance I can imagine. It could very well be the key to the element of good timing throughout my life.

Grandmother Paprocki was born in 1880 and was only 50 when I came to live with her. By that time she was already a widow. Her husband died of unknown causes in 1926. Coincidentally, both of my grandfathers died that year.

1930
Long Island, New York
Katherine Paprocki, Carl Meisterlin
Catherine Wanda Paprocki Meisterlin

I would do anything my grandmother wanted—I was a very nice little boy I've been told. We especially had fun when my first cousin Walter Kelly, the only son of my mother's older sister Elizabeth, would come to visit. Late in the fourth year of my life, my grandmother taught me how to play Gin Rummy to help her pass the time. This was an immense learning experience for me. I have been excellent with anything to do with numbers my entire life, which I attribute to my Grandma.

Out of her seven children, two were lost to diabetes. My mother was clearly Grandmother Paprocki's favorite, and I was the favored grandchild. My mother came home only four or five times in my early childhood. When she did, she slept with me and I clearly recall her sleeping in the nude. My cousin Walter and his friends made a big deal of this.

When I was almost six years old my grandmother decided that I really needed to be raised by my father, who had remarried. This may have coincided with her own plans to remarry. And so, on January 4, 1934, my grandmother put me on a flight to San Francisco, California.

I did not want to leave my grandmother and did so only because I was bribed. My grandmother promised me that when I arrived in California my dad would be waiting for me with a cowboy suit and a gun belt with two pistols. That was one heck of a way to get me to go. On arrival, there was my father and my new mother and my cowboy suit and guns. Wow!

I honestly don't remember any of the flight, but I

found out later that I was the first child to fly unescorted across the United States. This flight was written up in the San Francisco Examiner on January 6, 1934. The flight was on a United Airlines DC-2, and the flight took 24 hours. After landing in San Francisco, all the passengers disembarked, except me. My parents were waiting at the Oakland airport. United Airlines flew me by myself across the Bay. Now that's service!

On starting school the next week I was placed in the first grade but after approximately ten days to two weeks, I was promoted to the second grade.

Here I should tell you of the other fabulous woman in my life—my mother Edith, who married my dad in 1931. Edith was born in 1896 in a suburb of St. Louis, Missouri. Her father John Palmer worked for the great Northern Railway Company. In 1906 he received a promotion to become the stationmaster in northwest Montana located in Whitefish. Mother said, "To go to school I rode my horse through the Indian reservation. The Indians were very friendly, but on some occasions they teased me by chasing me on their horses. I loved these early years growing up in such magnificent surroundings!"

Her father was again promoted in 1914 to become stationmaster at the end of the line in the west, about 25 miles north of Seattle. She finished high school in Everett, Washington, and began the University of Washington at that time, graduating in 1920. With her parents' blessing, she traveled by train from Seattle to her dream city of San Francisco.

My father's new wife, Edith, was a wonderful woman and was the one who really raised me. I never thought of her as a stepmother, but as my true mother. Edith (Palmer) Meisterlin, worked on Market Street for a well-known San Francisco retail firm named Schwabacker Fry. She worked there for almost ten years as the manager of the stationary department. Edith was an extremely intelligent woman who could hold her own with anybody when it came to business. She was an avid aviatrix and had a touch of daring in her personality.

1939
Edith Rose Palmer Meisterlin

She met my father in 1930; they fell in love, and were married in 1931. She was physically unable to have children and when my Grandmother Paprocki offered to send me to my father, according to my dad she was more than overjoyed. This was one of the many events that changed and influenced my life greatly. She was more than a woman or a mother: *she was a lady*. She was everything to me and I truly loved her.

According to Mother, the Palmer family traced their history to the time of Paul Revere in Boston, Massachusetts. Whether it's true or not, she told the story that it was a relative of her family that rang the bell and yelled, "The British are coming! The British are coming!" and then fell from the steeple because he was so inebriated. I feel that I was truly blessed by the powers above to have had such an interesting and loving mother.

In 1932, my father became very involved in politics, even though he was not yet a U.S. citizen and could not vote. He campaigned tirelessly to get Roosevelt elected, and thereafter hated himself for the rest of his life for having done so. In the late 1930s, when I was old enough to understand such things, I remember three occasions when my mother would stand and point at my father and say, "You wanted Roosevelt!" These were three powerful words. The color would drain from my father's face (he had a rather bad temper) and he would get up and leave the house and go for a walk until he cooled down.

In 1950 I traveled on business to Philadelphia, Pennsylvania and took a side trip to Bayshore, Long Island to visit my birth mother, Von, and her fourth husband. Honestly, in retrospect, I don't think she was overexcited to see me. I seldom heard from her or saw her until February of 1971, when I unexpectedly received a birthday card from my mother.

Irene was surprised, as she knew that Edith had died of injuries from a car accident on November 26th of 1967. This was and is another of the very significant dates in my life story, for although the accident was not my fault, I had been behind the wheel.

**Mother's Day 1965
Carl and Mother
Edith Rose Palmer Meisterlin**

When I told Irene about receiving this birthday card, her comment was: "I didn't think they sent birthday cards from up there!" Irene thought that I should get in touch with Von and she was responsible for bringing us back together. The return address on the card placed her living on the west coast of Florida in a small town named

Inglis. By then she had remarried for the sixth time to a much younger man by the name of Roy Hamblin.

In the year 1974, prior to Irene's and my marriage, we arranged to meet them on Long Island in Smithtown, New York. They were visiting her sister Elizabeth and her husband, who were celebrating their 50th wedding anniversary. On this trip I also met my cousin Walter Kelly, who had also been staying, off and on, with my Grandmother Paprocki during my four years with her. He helped fill me in on the Paprocki family history for the years 1860 until 1974. It seems that in the year 1896, great-grandfather Paprocki sold Fire Island and Jones Beach to the State of New York for $1 million in cash—a huge amount of money in those days. He kept the exclusive legal rights to the ferry business to travel to Fire Island and my mother's younger brother, John, later operated it. He became the recipient of those rights when my great-grandfather died in 1926. John was a big, handsome man and the baby of the family. He was a playboy and married two or three times—or maybe more.

In the year 1977, John moved on the river across the street from Roy and Von. All of Von's siblings, except for Elizabeth, had passed on long ago. While there, Walter Kelly gave me another little piece of Paprocki history—at one point the family name had changed to Parke.

Brothers Frank and William founded the Bank of Babylon in the 1920s. In the middle 1930s, they sold the bank to what would become Bank of America and retired. They were both avid golfers and belonged to the Southward Ho Country Club located near Hempstead, Long Island. At one time or another both of these men were presidents of the country club and their ashes were buried adjacent to the 16th tee.

While on our trip in 1974, Irene had a close friend named Bill Conway, who was active in the Bob Hope Desert Classic golf tournament. Bill was one heck of a guy. He invited me to play a round of golf at Southward Ho. As luck would have it, I had a very good round of golf that day and won Conway every bet. Afterwards, as club members usually do, we were sitting at the bar facing a row of ex-presidents' photographs. Conway pointed out photographs of my uncles William and Frank.

An elderly gentleman walking by was introduced to me as being a friend and golfing buddy of my uncles. The gentleman proceeded to tell me he did not remember William and Frank that much but did remember their younger sister, who had been wild and gorgeous. I told the gentleman, "You'd better be careful, because that's my mother you're talking about!" and we all had a good laugh.

Another small coincidence developed on this trip. By chance, I had a very close friend from La Quinta Country Club in the Palm Springs area, Jack Hewitt. Conway and Jack had offices in the same building at the corner of 46th and the Avenue of Americas in the heart of New York City. On this trip we gave each of them the other's address and phone number in the building. They went on to become close friends, golfing buddies and luncheon companions for several years until Jack became Assistant

Secretary of the Air Force in Washington, D.C. Later in this book I will discuss how each of these men played a part in my life history.

After completing this trip, Irene again became the go-between my mother and I. In 1978 we invited Von and Roy to San Diego where we had recently purchased a condo located on Shelter Island overlooking San Diego Bay. Everything went well on this get-together and they were very impressed with the condo and location. We again invited them to our new small residence we had purchased on the grounds of the La Quinta Country Club in 1979.

**1978
Catherine Paprocki Meisterlin Hamblin
with Husband Roy Hamblin**

The one thing I remember vividly about this visit was that we had a small, enclosed atrium patio where we had installed a Jacuzzi. One early evening we talked Roy and my mother into joining us in the Jacuzzi for fun and laughs. My mother made a very strong statement to the fact that there was no way that Roy would go into that Jacuzzi! Lo and behold, Roy did, and he was the first one in. We were surprised to find that Roy was totally covered from his feet to his shoulders with tattoos!

Roy was a very, very unusual man. He had run away from home and enlisted at the age of 15, lying about his age, and eventually was placed in the submarine service working as an electrician. The submarine to which he was assigned in 1937 was brand new. By the time World War II began, he had been promoted to be chief electrician. In 1944, the submarine's commander was promoted and given a new nuclear submarine to command. As chief electrician, Roy was promoted and commissioned to be the commander of his submarine. He patrolled the Eastern Pacific, but mostly on reconnaissance duty. He actually never saw any battle action or released a torpedo. At the end of the war his submarine was returned to Pearl Harbor for a complete overhaul.

During this period of time Roy had a very serious accident. In a very severe rainstorm, he slipped and fell down the conning tower ladder into the submarine and severely injured his spinal column. After approximately nine months in the hospital, he was given a medical discharge from the Navy, but was given a job in Philadelphia, Pennsylvania as a private citizen working for the Navy in the intelligence service, which was somewhat surprising. He had married by this time and in 1951 he and his wife moved to Florida so he could do exactly what he loved most in life—fish! Roy Hamblin will be mentioned many times in my life story because he relied on my economic expertise to improve my mother's and his retirement income. I also became Executor of his Will.

Basically, Roy was not very intelligent. It's hard to believe that he had been placed in the government intelligence service. My mother, on the other hand, had worked for the largest department store in Coral Gables, Florida for approximately 25 years and retired with a very adequate pension. For the last 20 years of her employment, she was the credit manager for Burdine's Department Store.

She met Roy, who was eight years younger, because he was married to one of her closest friends. When Roy's wife died in 1971, my mother tried to be of help and visited Roy and did some of the usual female duties. My mother also loved fishing and she and Roy began taking fishing trips together. Soon, they decided to get married. With their two pension incomes, they were economically sound. It was then that they moved and purchased a plot of land on a tributary to the large river that runs west through Yankee Town to the Gulf of Mexico, near the nuclear plant in Crystal River.

From 1974 until 2006, when Roy Hamblin died, some immediate members of my family, significantly Debbie, Claudia, Chuck and Scott, were active visitors to see Von and Roy. Debbie, in particular, was fancied by Von as a reincarnation of herself! This was not hard to believe as they had very similar physical characteristics and their personalities also resembled each other's.

My mother died in 1994 at the age of 88 in New Smyrna Beach, Florida. When she was put into hospice in 1993, she immediately got better! However, she succumbed to heart failure 11 months later. I really had very little feeling about her death. She didn't want to have children and couldn't have any after having me. She never really wanted me at all.

When she died, Irene and I were in the wilds of Colorado on a vacation. Communications were limited then. When we returned from our trip, she had already been buried. Claudia was the one who flew in to help and she handled everything!

Chapter 2

The Early Years
Ages 5-17

My good luck and good fortune started with being moved from the first to second grade in 1934. I did have one noteworthy failure, however, in May of 1934. Hollywood came calling, looking for a young boy to play opposite Shirley Temple. It seems that my second grade teacher had heard or read somewhere that they needed a smart young blondish new face to fill a role in Shirley Temple's next picture. Shirley Temple, who was then six years old, was already a huge child star. I actually had a screen test with five takes.

Shirley Temple

I didn't get the part and my father explained to me later that it was because of my Long Island accent.

I really didn't know or care about being in the movies. I had recently witnessed a Shirley Temple movie and for some reason I did not like her. Ah, Stupidity! That summer my parents moved to an area in East Oakland called the Diamond District. A very short two blocks away stood the Diamond Theater. On Saturdays they played children's matinees with either cowboy serials or *Our Gang* comedies, also known as *The Little Rascals*, which were short films that featured the adventures of a group of poor neighborhood children. Even though I was only six, I was allowed to go to the matinees at a cost of five cents. I was also given five cents to buy popcorn, a drink or candy. I liked cowboy movies the most!

I started third grade at Fruitvale Grammar School. We were to live in this home for four school years before moving again. The only meaningful thing that I can remember from this era was a fierce competition I had with a female student by the name of Patricia Smith. I competed with her scholastically for all four years. She was very smart and also very competitive! I remember Pat especially because we became close friends and business associates as adults.

In the summer of 1940 we moved to the East Oakland foothills and I started the seventh grade at Bret Harte Junior High School. On the very first day of school I was assigned to a homeroom class, which was a complete change in education from what I'd been used to. As I looked around at my fellow students, there, of course, was Patricia Smith and we proceeded for this year and two more to be in the same homeroom class. I just couldn't escape her but she did make a better student out of me. I owe her that compliment!

I enjoyed junior high much more than grammar school. I liked having five to six different subjects and teachers a day. There was more individual freedom and more opportunity to gain knowledge on my own. In my very first week in my social studies class, I met Ted Titus, who was part Indian and part Caucasian. Ted instantly became my idol. I was the youngest member of the seventh grade class and also the smallest boy in the class. Almost everybody was growing and maturing and at that time, I was not! I was about 4' 9" tall and perhaps 100 pounds soaking wet. Ted Titus was a head taller than I was, almost fully matured, and in my eyes, an Adonis. Ted indicated a liking for me and we sat next to each other.

I was not only the smallest, but also very much the most näive and immature student in the class. Fortunately, the teacher recognized this and gave me a homework assignment over the first weekend to study and present to the class on Monday a paper about heredity and environment and how they affect our lives and personalities. To this day, I remember how astonished I was with what I learned that weekend.

I had another teacher, J. P. O'Neill, who was my physical education teacher. He was also the afterschool playground director and coach. He announced there would be a signup for the school football team and on the designated date I showed up. Surprisingly, I was the only seventh grader to do so. All the other players were at least two years older, 6" taller and 50 pounds heavier. Coach O'Neill assigned me to be the second-string center. I did not understand, given my very little football knowledge, but I was on the team. Later on, I don't remember exactly when, I asked Coach O'Neill why he made me a center. He replied, "Carl, you have two things that every football team needs at the center position, guts and brains!"

Being so small, I got picked on quite a bit as young adolescent boys will do and I was stupid enough to physically retaliate, so I did get in a little bit of trouble in the seventh grade. My life totally changed on Christmas morning that year. My parents gave me a bicycle that was almost too big for me, but I was able to manage it. Now I could ride my bike to and from school.

At this time I was the family gardener. It was my job to cut the lawns and what I hated most—weed the same. We had two apricot trees and I was in charge of picking fruit, cleaning up, raking the leaves and doing whatever else in the yard that needed doing. My father paid me fifty cents a week for this, which I considered far too little, as it wouldn't cover my personal expenses. I asked dad for a raise to a dollar a week. He turned me down with an extremely crushing statement, saying, "You're not worth a dollar a week!" I then went to my mother, my ally at times like this, and pleaded my case. My mother wisely said, "This problem is between you and your dad."

As luck would have it, good timing (and here again

is the word 'timing' that means being in the right place at the right time) occurred. A ninth grader I had met in one of my classes mentioned he was giving up his paper route that afternoon. I asked him if they had a replacement for him. He said he didn't think so. I then asked if I could go with him to meet his boss that afternoon and apply for the job. He replied, "Of course, why not?" So we both left school on our bikes and proceeded down to the business district near Brett Harte. I applied and got the paper route and I started the next day. As I left my friend, I then asked how much he earned on his paper route per month. He said, "Between $13 to $15 a month, depending on tips! That night at dinner I told my dad that I quit as the gardener.

My dad said, "You can't quit!" I said, "I *do* quit! I've got another job starting tomorrow!" My mother started to laugh and quickly left the room leaving my father and I staring each other down. My father then asked what I was going to do. I said, "I have become a paperboy for the Oakland Inquirer where I can make more money than you would consider paying me."

My father just sat there speechless and the next day I began my first real job. Years later my mother told me that dad had to hire a gardener, which cost $19 a month because he wouldn't give me my fifty cents a week raise. She also said that my dad was so proud that evening of my standing up to him and for going out and taking the initiative to find a better job. He loved to tell that story to all his friends so they could all laugh together. He never told me this, however.

On Sundays after church I would make my monthly collections for my paper route. I chose to do this on a Sunday because the women who opened the door were always nice to me. Sometimes they would give me some cookies or candy. In contrast, the men who would come to the door were not so pleasant, but they would give tips. On the morning of December 7, 1941, Japan had attacked Pearl Harbor in Hawaii and I mentioned this as I went on my route. Over 50% of the customers I met that day had not heard the news. My feeling that evening was that I had served a purpose for my country! I was very proud of myself for being a paperboy and bringing people the latest news that December 7th.

From that day forward, World War II influenced at least 80% of my growing up. The war against the Axis and Japan changed the United States and the world forever. Because I was 13 at the time, not only did I have the usual maturing years to go through but my country to serve in any way possible—and this I did. When I was 14 and old enough to receive a Social Security card, I left my paper route and went to work as a stock boy for Walgreens Drug Company. I worked Saturdays only and was paid 50 cents an hour, which amounted to $4 a day, with no money taken out. When I was 14, I also started working for the Oakland YMCA at their summer camp in the Santa Cruz Mountains as a camp counselor, which I did for the next year also.

These part-time and summer jobs gave me more

time to be active in high school activities, which included after-school sports of every kind. I still was growing and maturing much more slowly and later than all my friends and classmates. At the age of 16, in the month of June, I was only 5' 2" tall and 115 pounds. Prior to this in January, with help of my father and mother, I purchased my first automobile—a 1937 Ford coupe. Again, this gave me more freedom and more time to accomplish whatever I so desired.

On my birthday on February 16th, I was hired by the downtown Oakland YMCA as the boys' department gym instructor, number two lifeguard and "go for" for the boys' department manager. My hiring at the downtown YMCA was no surprise, and I loved it for many reasons. I loved working with the young boys, which also included the underprivileged, 90% of which were black kids whose families had been moved from the southern states such as Alabama, Mississippi, Arkansas, Louisiana and Texas to work in the shipyards. From my underprivileged boys' classes came some of the most famous names in baseball history—Frank Robinson, Veda Pinson, and Curt Flood. One other young boy who was in the regular boys' gym class named Ron Tomsic went on to Stanford University and broke all the scoring records of, in my estimation, the greatest basketball player of all times, Hank Luisetti.

The war years completely changed the way we all lived. I was so proud of my father, who was appointed the head of the Office of Price Administration or OPA, the government agency that governed the use of all things that would affect the war effort. This was no small job and it was strictly a voluntary one that paid nothing except the satisfaction of doing your bit for America. The OPA governed everything from gas usage to being able to buy silk stockings. The gas rationing was allocated with stickers placed on the windshield of your car, marked "A," "B" or "C."

With an "A" sticker, you received the minimum amount of gas per week that would take your children to school and to the store to do your necessary shopping. It did not allow for pleasure driving. A "B" sticker would allow enough gas to get to work and back and again with no pleasure driving. When I was 16, I was issued a "B" sticker that gave me enough gas to get to school and to the downtown YMCA and back—that was it. A "C" sticker was for people who had critical administrative jobs in industry and the war effort, plus a few civilians who had no other way of performing their work without the use of a car that took them long distances.

My father had a "C" sticker because of his OPA position and job that took him all over Northern California, which was accessible only by automobile. He was very judicious in his use of gasoline! During these war years my dad also became president of the local Optimist Club and also president of a special salesmen's club called The Tip Club. Both of these clubs met once a month at Oakland's largest downtown hotel named the Coit-Ramsey. During the war years the Coit-Ramsey Hotel also became offices for some government agencies such as the OPA. One of the owners of the hotel was Robert "Bob" Ramsey. He also had a government appointment with no pay as a volunteer with another agency, which was located in his own hotel. During these years Bob and dad became each other's closest friends and later he also influenced my life going forward. Again, I must compliment my father for not only being a gentleman, but when the chips were down, also a great leader.

On entering Fremont High School in East Oakland as a 10th grade sophomore, again I found high school to be much more rewarding scholastically. My father insisted that I not take physical education, but that I take ROTC military training. I don't know why, but I was immediately given a commission in the unit. I was the only 10th grader to receive this honor, which I felt I didn't deserve, especially because of my size and stature. Frankly, I never did enjoy being a part of the ROTC program. I made no friends but I guess in the long run it made a difference when it came time for me to enlist a couple years hence. What I really wanted was to be in physical education where all of my friends and buddies were. During this time in conversations with my dad, he made a profound statement: "The Meisterlin family makes their living with their brains, not their bodies."

In my 10th grade year I, like all students at Fremont High School, had to take compulsory shots for various diseases that were common in 1942. As it happens I got in line directly behind this great big guy, an Adonis who the person behind me said was Fremont's star football player.

When he stepped up and the lady administered the shot in his upper arm, he fainted dead away to the floor! You can imagine how this little shrimp of a 10th grader that I was felt! Nobody seemed to make much of a fuss about his fainting and the nurse came back and took hold of my arm after pulling out a different needle and proceeded to jab me. I felt it, but it wasn't a big deal. I was totally amazed that I was still standing. I've mentioned this because you never know in life what can and will happen. In the 10th grade I rose to the top of my class in geometry, history and chemistry. During my 10th and 11th grades I was a very good student and by the end of the 11th grade I already had enough A's and B's to qualify to go to any college I desired. Things were a lot different scholastically speaking in 1944.

In the summer of 1944, a truly tragic event began affecting my thinking process and my future as far as World War II was concerned. In most high schools in America during the war years there were clubs named the "High Y" clubs, originally established in 1914 in association with the YMCA. Most students who were able to gain membership in the High Y clubs were athletes, student officers and a few outstanding and active regulars. I was the only ROTC student up to that time to ever attain membership at Fremont High School. In my senior year I actually became the ROTC Commanding Officer. After graduation in 1944, seven members of our High Y club went and joined the Marines together. The major Oakland newspaper, the Tribune, had a very large picture of my seven friends on the front page that June. At school the following fall, this was a big thing.

Unfortunately, the six students who had stayed together all through training were in the same landing craft at Iwo Jima in the invasion in late 1944. Their landing craft took a direct hit and they all perished without reaching shore. My High Y friends and I were totally devastated and the war then took on a completely different meaning. To this day, this event and the memories bring tears to my eyes. My senior year in high school, at least the first half of it, scholastically, was quite normal; but in my last six months of high school I totally goofed off. I cut classes, left early, arrived late and more important—I didn't study at all. I prefer to admit the truth—I'm not really proud of my actions during this period.

I would like to back up to the summer of 1944, because it was this summer in my young life that was both my most enjoyable but also the most painful. That summer started with my being able to drive on my own, in my own car, to my YMCA boys' camp with one of my close friends from the downtown YMCA. Otris Williams was an outstanding black man, student and athlete. Otris went on to become an all-American football player at Fresno State College.

On arriving at camp that year I was promoted to be the camp recreation director. My actual duties that I performed from daylight to the end of the campfire in the evening, were to conduct or at least organize, all recreation events—swimming in the river, being a lifeguard, teaching archery, organizing all religious services, and being the emcee at the campfire conducting singing, storytelling, skits and you name it. I became a hero while teaching archery because a rattlesnake appeared and was coiled and ready to strike. Fortunately, at that precise moment I had my bow and arrow ready to shoot. I was teaching a class of about one dozen boys. I shot the arrow at the snake and I got it right through the head. I thought I was really something, but later that evening the camp director shot me down. He had seen this happen before and also had heard from other people that it was a common occurrence. The rattlesnake is faster then the arrow and once he goes for the arrow the arrow goes right through his head. It wasn't until the last day of archery that I admitted this to my boys, but I did.

There was one other item that happened that summer and I still hope stands and is as beautiful today as it was then. It has to do with the building of the chapel where we conducted all our religious Christian services. On the hill above the camp there was a natural redwood grove. In the middle of the grove stood a majestic old redwood at least 200-feet-plus high. Surrounding it, in a near perfect circle, stood 24 redwoods all straight as an arrow looking up at the sky. All of the senior camp staff, of which I was included, took on the unbelievable endeavor of felling this majestic tree that stood in the middle of the grove without injuring the trees. The camp hired a gentleman who somehow organized us all into a team. He had all the equipment—saws, pulleys, chains, etc.—and we were 100% successful. After this, all of us joined in to extricate this huge tree from the circle without damaging the other trees. We began sawing the tree into log benches, which we then placed into the heart of the chapel. We then positioned these log benches so what we actually had created what was the most dramatic religious church and atmosphere I've ever entered in my lifetime.

    In the fall of 1944, in a class I was taking in public speaking, I told this story. Excuse me for bragging, but after I gave my little speech, somewhat more embellished than what I've just translated, the whole class stood and applauded me. High school juniors and seniors in my day didn't do that! After the class finished, my teacher asked me to stay on, which I did. He said to me, "Carl, that's the finest speech I've ever heard given in my classroom in my whole teaching career!" That year my grade in my public speaking class was an AA. As I've already noted, the rest of my high school scholastic career was terrible.

    There is one other story that took place in my trigonometry class that's significant. The teacher, who liked and listened every week to a radio program named *The Quiz Kids*, asked all of us in the class if they had listened to the program the night before. Nobody in the class, including myself, raised their hands. He asked the question again: "Who has listened to The Quiz Kids?" Again, nobody raised his or her hands, so he gave us a question. It had to do with a set of numbers being added, subtracted, divided and multiplied and it was quite complicated. No student raised their hand but me and I gave my answer.

I was correct! The teacher then accused me of lying! After hearing about my public speaking speech, this teacher came into my public speaking class and in front of the students in the class apologized to me. This man later on became the principal of Oakland High School. This is one of the ways in life you find out who the big men really are. It's important in life to show humility and ask forgiveness—never ever forget this!

On April 5, 1945, without consulting my mom and dad, I went to the recruiting station in downtown Oakland and signed papers to join the Army. My closest buddy at this time was Bob McDonald, who also accompanied me. We were given some paperwork to take home to be signed by one of our parents and dates for a physical and I.Q. tests. Oh yes, I also needed to present my birth certificate, which neither my parents nor I had at that time. My mother became extremely upset to the point of crying, which I had never witnessed before. I could tell that my dad was stunned! My dad said, "Well, let's get your birth certificate." When he couldn't find it, that helped soothe my mother, because waiting to get the birth certificate and taking my other tests would take a couple of weeks, which it did.

There is a funny part to this story. When the birth certificate arrived; my name was listed not as Bernhardt, but Walter. My birth mother had named me after my father and her father without my dad knowing. Later, we straightened this out. My father, while waiting for the birth certificate to arrive, spent the time placating mom and explaining that if they didn't sign and I got drafted and something horrible happened, they would never forgive themselves. Bob and I proceeded to the recruiting station and turned in our birth certificates, signed several other documents and then took our physical and I.Q. tests.

Passing the physical tests was very easy. My I.Q. tests results came as a complete surprise. The paperwork arrived in the mail, and of course my dad, who had signed my application, read it. I received an I.Q. grade of 140, which my father embarrassed me from that day on by telling all and everyone within earshot that his son was a genius! Being a genius was not the real me. I would rather have fun and just be myself. A couple of weeks later we received our orders to two different universities which were part of the Army Specialized Training Reserve Program or ASTRP. I was part of the last group of soldiers brought into the ASTRP (or Ass Trap as we liked to call it!). Bob was to report to Oregon State University and I was to report to the University of Utah on July 15, 1945.

There were two incidents in my life at this time, one good and one not so good. During the summer while working at the Oakland YMCA camp, I started growing so fast that all the joints, muscles, tendons and ligaments in my complete body were so painful that I couldn't sleep at night. It was actually easier to be doing any type of physical exertion then lying or sitting down. By the time school started in early September 1944, I had grown 6 1/2 inches and now weighed 140 pounds. I was no longer a plump little runt! In fact the girls were starting to notice me—actually for the last year or so, I'd been noticing them!

Around November 1944, I attended my first real dance party and shortly thereafter I had a girlfriend. At the same time as most young boys do at a much earlier age; I started having sexual urges and fantasies. I really was becoming a man, not a boy. "Hallelujah" is all I can say! The other story that occurred during my stay at camp that year was that another counselor and I planned a performance on our Saturday night off, the only night we received for the whole summer. Two other counselors joined us on this night and agreed to go along with our plan. That Saturday night we drove to the biggest drive-in restaurant in Santa Clara County, located between the cities of San Jose and Santa Clara.

What we did that night was very childish. It was immature and really not funny at all. We staged a fake fight right at the entrance to the restaurant, where one of the guys pulled out a real pistol loaded with a blank bullet. He faked shooting him and the victim had a capsule with catsup in his shirt, which appeared as blood. We then all ran for the car and skedaddled back to camp. Nothing ever happened to us, I don't even know how many people saw it. Nobody got in trouble, nobody got hurt, and we really thought we were so clever and funny.

I hate to admit it, but it took me years before I realized how stupid this was, but I am happy to tell the story here and get it off my chest. I was just a young, stupid kid.

Chapter 3

Earthquakes and Invasions

This part of my life story starts on a sour note. Two days before I was to leave from Oakland on the train to the University of Utah in Salt Lake City, I had a bad automobile accident. Three friends and I were traveling back from the beach in Santa Cruz, California on old Highway 9 when a car coming in the opposite direction crossed over and sideswiped my car. My car careened on a 45-degree angle to the right and hit a power pole located there. The car sustained a medium amount of damage but was visibly repairable.

Unfortunately, the police who arrived on the scene cited me for the accident. They did help me by phoning my father who had to come down from Oakland, a couple hours drive, to bring the four of us back to Oakland. But the Meisterlin luck prevailed! Nobody was hurt, not even bruised. The luckiest thing was that the only obstacle on the right side of the road running along the river, which was 50 feet below the road, was a single power pole. If we had not hit that one pole, chances are that we would've been very severely injured if not killed. That night, as you can imagine with my disciplinary dad, was not a very happy time for me. I'm sure it would've been a lot worse if I had not been leaving for the Army in two days. I left as scheduled from the depot in Oakland. The only other recruit heading for Salt Lake joining my unit was a young man from my rival high school, Castlemont High School. This young man was David McElhatton, who all Northern California TV news listeners will remember. Dave was the anchorman on Channel 5 CBS news in San Francisco for over 25 years.

On October 17, 1989, San Francisco-Oakland suffered a huge earthquake (later called the Loma Prieta Earthquake), where the Nimitz freeway in Oakland collapsed and a span of the Bay Bridge fell. A close friend of ours, Ann Hewitt, who was on the bridge and had passed the point of collapse before the bridge failed only a few minutes before, told us about the whole experience. It was Dave reporting the event live in San Francisco on Channel 5, powered by an in-house generator. I was privileged to be watching this coverage, which went nationwide on CBS and to almost every independent TV station in the country. This was the earthquake that occurred during a World Series at Candlestick Park in South San Francisco, commonly called by locals, "Candlestink!" The famous CBS commentator from New York City, Dan Rather, kept interrupting Dave. It was clear that Dan Rather didn't know anything about earthquakes. (Later in my story I'll have a lot to say about the Eastern and political Beltway news media.)

Dave McElhatton became my close friend for the

next eight months. On arriving in Salt Lake City, we were taken to the athletic field house overlooking the football and track and field stadium where the Utes play. The Fieldhouse was actually the basketball, volleyball, badminton and the inside sports Pavilion for the University. The ASTRP unit shared this facility with a Naval V-5 unit. The average age of the Naval cadets was approximately three years older than our program's cadets. All in all, there were approximately 250 people plus staff who lived, or I should say, existed, in the Fieldhouse.

1945
Carl Meisterlin at The Great Salt Lake

There were no beds. We all slept on cots with footlockers at the end. We were young, so this really wasn't that bad, but the bathing and toilet facilities were terrible. There were two phone booths in the lobby entrance. The morning after we arrived, the bugle blew to get up at 5:30 a.m. It was then announced that we had a half an hour to bathe, make our beds and stand ready for next instructions at 6:15 a.m. At that time we were ordered out onto the street, put in formation and marched for 30 minutes. We then had a five- to ten-minute break to again use the toilet facilities or finish making our beds, whatever we needed to do, but we were to be ready to go to breakfast at 6:55 a.m. and we did just that. We marched five minutes to the mess hall, which was the University's cafeteria, and we arrived exactly at 7:00 a.m. During breakfast we were all given a schedule of classes and diagrams to show us how to get there and when to get there, and I really should say report there, which we'd darn well better do—that was made very plain to us. We naturally did as we were told. We had no dummies in our unit.

We attended classes except for a lunch break from 11:30-1:00 p.m. at the cafeteria, and then attended afternoon classes. It you were lucky enough to get in line early and get your food quickly and consume it quickly; you had possibly 20 to 25 minutes to go back to the Fieldhouse for whatever reason. Or, you had time to actually go out into the park-like grounds in the middle of the University. At approximately 3:45-4:00 p.m. we finished classes and returned to the Fieldhouse on our own. At 4:30 we mustered again and we marched for another half hour. At approximately 5:30 p.m. we went again to the cafeteria for dinner. After dinner we were then sent to the University library to do any required homework. At 8:30 p.m., we were then marched back to the Fieldhouse where we had about an hour to ourselves. Taps blew at 9:30 p.m. Many, many years later I learned that we were being trained to invade Japan, just like Europe and Normandy Beach.

This schedule was adhered to for exactly 12 weeks, after which the program became much more flexible, livable, and enjoyable. During the first 12 weeks, Saturday was also a school day. Sundays there were no bugle calls, no marching, and the hours for eating at the cafeteria were extended. The second 12 weeks, the curriculum totally changed. We even had a class of physical education every afternoon that lasted from 3:30-5:00 p.m. All of the courses were completely changed and we had English, Spanish language, and all forms of social education. There were no more math, engineering and industrial-type studies.

In early July, President Truman's military advisors had calculated that there would be six to ten million American and 25 million Japanese casualties if we invaded Japan! He decided not to risk so many lives and on August 6, 1945, the atomic bomb was dropped on Hiroshima and then on August 9, 1945 on Nagasaki. August 15th marked the surrender of the Japanese, and upon signing The Instrument of Surrender on September 2nd; World War II was officially over.

I don't remember feeling fear regarding the war as I didn't have time to think those first 12 weeks. In general, I was proud to be a part of the Army! I didn't particularly enjoy the people in my unit, so I was overjoyed that the war was over and I could get out of the ASTRP. They didn't really know what to do with us at that point, so we were allowed to finish the semester. We became regular students. A few of the over 200,000 ASTP and ASTRP graduates later became quite well known. They included Henry Kissinger, newscaster Roger Mudd, author Gore Vidal, movie star Mel Brooks and four-star General James Harlinger.

When the war ended, we were excused from all studies on Fridays at 3:30 p.m. and all day Saturdays and Sundays. We were also allowed to leave campus and go into Salt Lake City or anywhere we wanted, as long as we reported back by 6:00 a.m. Monday morning. We were also allowed to participate in all campus activities after 5:30 p.m., seven nights a week.

It was during this period of time that Dave McElhatton and I became inseparable. Looking back, we really didn't have much in common with the balance of our unit. Physical education became almost a joke, as there were really no athletes. Our unit, in today's language, was made up mostly of nerds. In physical education they split the unit into six football teams. The teams were picked by random and Dave and I were placed on two different teams. There must not have been much talent in our whole unit as both Dave and I were picked to be captains of our teams. Neither of us was even close to being an average football player at that time or ever. With freedom and a normal life in hand we went to student dances up at the quad. We wore our best uniforms and we were very popular with the freshmen girls in particular. We even

43

went to the city and stayed overnight on a couple of weekends. We visited the Mormon Temple and grounds. On another occasion we traveled to the Great Salt Lake and floated on top of the water.

Up the hill to the east behind the University was the largest military installation in Utah, Fort Douglas, which also included a large army hospital. Like all military establishments, it had what is called a PX where you could shop and buy things, usually for about half of what it would cost normally. It also had as part of the PX a bar where you could buy beer. The 18-year-old cadets in our unit took care of us 17 year olds. This was the first time in my life that I had way too much to drink. I became sick enough during that night that I never touched any alcohol again for three years.

Approximately three weeks after I arrived in Salt Lake, I received a letter from my dad that might be to this day the very best letter I've received in my life. It read:

> Sonny (my dad's pet name for me when I was young), I've received notification from the Santa Cruz County Sheriff's Department that the citation issued you has been rescinded. Instead, the man driving the other car has received a citation and was the cause of the crash. I want you to know and I ask for forgiveness for talking to you the way I did and that I was wrong in doing so as you are not guilty of doing anything wrong and I

humbly apologize for my actions and words.

I believe this was the only time in my life that my father ever apologized to me.

**Christmas 1945
Carl Meisterlin and His Father
Carl Bernhardt Meisterlin**

The balance of the last 12 weeks in the ASTRP program was very uneventful. I really enjoyed going to college and having a lot of female company with no mother or father looking over my shoulder. I left on February 14, 1946, and arrived home on February 16th, my birthday. I decided not to go to OCS, but to take my chances on being returned to civilian life.

I reported to Basic Training at Fort Lewis, Washington on March 1, 1946. Basic Training was a snap compared to the first 12 weeks of ASTRP! We lived in barracks, which were better equipped than the Field House. Funny thing, next to our barrack was a POW camp of Italian soldiers. Their accommodations and lifestyle were 100% better than ours! Before I completed Basic, I was transferred to Fort Sam Houston in San Antonio, Texas.

It was very hot and humid. I had never experienced humidity like this before! Five days later I was in Brooke Army Hospital with a 104-degree temperature for no explainable reason. Two days later I had a 105-degree temperature and was in an iron lung. In the space of five days, I went from 150 to 130 pounds. Two days later I was put in an oxygen tent instead when my temperature dropped to 103 degrees. My weight kept dropping and the temperature persisted. I awoke one day to having my mom and dad with a minister alongside prepared to give my "last rites." The doctors had no idea what caused or what was wrong with me.

The government had flown mom and dad to San Antonio. My father told them to try any medicine or method possible to save me. That day I received a shot of penicillin every three hours and 36 hours later my fever broke and I had real food for the first time in nine days. My parents returned home immediately and I was in a regular hospital bed in a normal ward. I remained there for three weeks and the doctors decided going home would help me more than hospital care.

I was given a 30-day sick leave furlough and flew by commercial airline back to Oakland. Three weeks later I received an additional 30-day extension and airline tickets back to Beaumont General Hospital in El Paso, Texas. During my 60 days at home with my mom's excellent cooking, I was again 150 pounds. They weren't sure, but on my medical records, the doctors said that I'd had viral pneumonia.

During my stay I had a very unusual experience. My father received two tickets for me to attend the first professional football game played in San Francisco, pitting the San Francisco 49ers against the L.A. Dons (now the San Diego Chargers). The tickets were from one of his largest customers for his special Theirbach's Mocha and Java Coffee. The customer was the famous Sally Stanford, who at the height of World War II operated 52 brothels in the San Francisco Bay Area. In late 1947, the city took away her permit to legally operate. These were brothels my dad said operated 24/7 from 1942-1945! The military drank a lot of the best coffee that money could buy. When Sally retired, she opened a five-star restaurant across the Golden Gate Bridge in Sausalito on the water, which she operated herself. I met her years later at "Sally Stanford's" and thanked her and she told me what a great guy my dad was. In the early 1950s, Sally became the Mayor of Sausalito for well over a decade. In spite of her original business, she is still remembered today in San Francisco history as a wonderful lady, businesswoman and civic leader.

When I arrived in El Paso and reported for duty, my personal items from San Antonio were there. I was assigned to a very nice barracks—the best yet! My duties were to be a physical therapist working in the wards in the mental hospital, running the gymnasium and being one of several lifeguards at the hospital pool. Ninety percent of hospital use and patients were mental cases! El Paso is 4-5,000 feet in elevation—a high desert climate with dry air, perfect for my recuperation while doing the same work I performed at the YMCA.

Working with mental patients is extremely stressful. Those working the wards worked two weeks and then had a seven-day vacation to do whatever they wished to relax and enjoy. I was thankful that was not my duty as I'm not sure I could have coped with it on a daily basis. The hospital had football, basketball and baseball teams for hospital morale. I was asked to try out. As it was football and basketball season and they needed bodies, I was given uniforms for both. We traveled by air to San Antonio to play Fort Sam, which starred the future Hall of Fame player, Doak Walker! Late in the game, I was put in as a running back. Bad idea! I took a hand-off from the quarterback, got hit head on and woke up in the locker room. I was told on the flight back that I hadn't fumbled! We lost 35-0. I was definitely a better basketball player and I actually belonged on the team. I played shooting guard and I played over 20 minutes a game and was the fourth leading scorer!

The other high point was when we were driven by car into the northwestern mountains of New Mexico through a town named Silver City. We'd been driving for over ten hours when we approached a form of a guard's gate, but definitely different. We left our mini-bus and were led into a large room with tables against the walls and clothes baskets everywhere. The structure was solid concrete, including the roof, except for the air ducts. The other un-normal thing was that all the military personnel were wearing sidearms and some had machine guns. A loud speaker told us to disrobe and put our uniforms in one basket. We were then instructed to enter a door directly opposite the entrance and leave our baskets behind. We entered a corridor approximately 50-feet long and 10-feet wide. From the entry door to the exit door of the corridor were one-way mirrored glass walls. We had no idea what was going on, where we were or even our destination. On exiting we found our basket and over the loudspeaker were told to get dressed immediately. On command, we exited and were taken to our mini-bus by more weapon-carrying soldiers. Our bus was then led by a military escort for about 30 minutes to a mountain road further up the mountain until we came to an enclave of barracks, homes, buildings, a store or two and what appeared to be a large gymnasium, playing field, parks and assorted other structures. What appeared very unusual was that three barbed wire and chain link fences surrounded all the structures. We learned later that the middle fence was electrified.

The next morning, we were escorted to a military mess hall, treated with unusually good cuisine and learned we were in a place called "Los Alamos." After breakfast, we returned to our accommodations, which were not military. We were in large bedrooms for four, with chairs, decks, windows with beautiful views and super large bathrooms that could accommodate a man and a woman. Our coach came by to tell us our schedule for the day: lunch at 12:30, practice at 2:30 and rest until 5:30 when we would go back to the gym for the start of the game at 7:00 p.m. After the game and showering, we'd have a light supper.

Everything went as scheduled. The game was excellent. About 1500 fans crowded the gym and they were 100% partisan. We found out that night that the athletics games and the movie theater were the entire forms of entertainment for the inhabitants of Los Alamos. They could not leave in 1946! The game itself was very close and we lost in the last minute, but the crowd loved it. Our team and myself played well that night. I played more minutes than usual and scored in double digits. We left Los Alamos still not knowing what it was about.

On the way home, a few miles before arriving in Silver City, our mini-bus broke down. It was the middle of winter, freezing cold and with a little snow and not a good place to be, as we were not dressed properly. Help finally arrived and into Silver City we went on a Sunday. Silver City was a county seat with a courthouse and jail together. The people who rescued us said that there was no place to stay that night, but that they would turn on the heat at the courthouse. We headed straight for the jail. Alas, there were no prisoners or beds, just empty locked cells. I entered the courtroom and found the largest flat surface I could find. That night I slept on the judge's courtroom desk! It was warm, as promised, and the bathrooms worked. It turned out to be a good night.

One other thing happened in late November. The projectionist at the hospital was being discharged in about three days. My superior, a captain, said, "Carl, I need you to be the projectionist. You have three days to learn. Drop your other duties and get over to Sergeant Evans at the theater ASAP and learn to run the projector. That's an order!"

Sergeant Evans was a good guy, anxious to leave, but knew that until I could run the projector and the theater that the captain would withhold his discharge. We worked 12 hours a day. I could run the projector by the end of the first day—that's if nothing went wrong. By the end of the second day, I was prepared for anything that could go wrong except the machine breaking apart. The third day, I was taught how to clean up the theater, including mopping, sweeping, oiling seats and making sure it passed the captain's inspections. On that last day, I was the projectionist under Sergeant Evans' eye! He told the captain that I was great and he received his discharge.

In December I received our two movies to be shown titled "The Best Years of Our Lives" and "It's a Wonderful Life." We showed movies three times a day at 1:00 p.m., 3:30 p.m. and 7:30 p.m. I started the first day showing "It's a Wonderful Life" at 1:00 p.m., "The Best Years of Our Lives" at 3:30 and "It's a Wonderful Life" again at 7:30 p.m. That morning I ran both the movies for myself and to make sure the films were in perfect condition. They were! I didn't think after watching "The Best Years of Our Lives" that this was a very good movie for mental patients. After the first showing, I was positive that I assumed correctly. I started playing "It's a Wonderful Life" three times a day, five days a week and "The Best Years of Our Lives" two times a week at 3:30 when we had our poorest attendance. The captain never mentioned it.

I trained a replacement immediately. In January, through my father's connections, I received a letter from Walgreen Drug Company's top executive, Mr. Justin Dart, stating that I had a position waiting for me and asking for an early discharge. I took it to the captain and 30 days later, I was a civilian! I left El Paso late on February 15th and about a week later, I reported for work at Walgreen's.

I had many growing up experiences between late February and entering San Jose State College in early September of 1947. One particularly embarrassing moment occurred in June of that year when I ran away with a girl from my high school. I thought I was in love with her because I was unbelievably attracted to her physically. I believe to this day that her mother thought I was a pretty good catch and helped promote the romance.

My girlfriend and I headed to Reno, Nevada in my car. The laws in California stated at that time that you couldn't get married under the age of 21 without parental consent. Somehow, my father found out about this and alerted the highway patrol in Sacramento that governed the road to Reno. As we were entering the Sierra Mountains, a couple of patrol cars came blazing up behind us. They pulled me over and put me under arrest for running away with a minor. They took us all the way back to Sacramento and booked me. A half hour later, my father walked in, bailed me out and then took my girlfriend back home in his car, while I drove myself home. That ended the romance. By the time I arrived home, I was ready to kill my father.

In retrospect, if my father hadn't have had the guts and the experience and obviously the love he had for me, who knows what would have happened. He was truly the best father a son could have ever been born to. This is just another reason why I'm "The Luckiest Man in the World."

Chapter 4

Spaceships and Diamond Rings

A couple of days after my humiliation of having the trip with my girlfriend to get married in Reno interrupted, my father and I were not talking to one other. This was entirely my doing! I received a phone call from my buddy Bob McDonald inviting me for the next weekend with a group of veterans and High Y friends for a weekend at Clear Lake, California.

Clear Lake is a mid-sized lake approximately 40 miles northeast of Ukiah. It was used mostly as a recreational lake and had a couple of resorts, but mostly campgrounds where people could come and bring their boats and camp overnight. It was very beautiful and pristine. Bob said that there were seven or eight of the guys going. I accepted, as timing couldn't have been better because of my relationship, or lack of, with my father!

Two days later my boss at Walgreens asked me if I would help out by opening the store on the coming Sunday. I was used to opening on Sundays every fourth week, so this was nothing new to me. He said it was an emergency and he would be very grateful if I would help out. I was more than happy to do so, because I received double-time pay. That summer it was all about making money as I was entering San Jose State College in early September.

I called Bob and told him I couldn't make the trip and the reason why and to tell the guys I'd make it another time. It was providential that I didn't go. What happened on their trip to Clear Lake became a tragedy! In many areas of California we have what is called a Tule Fog—a ground fog so dense you can't see the hood ornament on your car—but you can look straight up and see the sky clearly. The two cars filled with my friends were trying to drive in this fog and the second car missed a turn and went over the bank! There were very severe injuries, one fatal, to the four friends in this vehicle. Fortunately for Bob he was a passenger in the first car. Here again, the Meisterlin luck was there for me! The other three passengers lived and had fine productive lives.

A few days later, it was my regular Sunday to open the store. Every Sunday we had a boy who was even younger than I was who worked part-time as a "soda jerk" as we used to call them. It was his job to open up the counter, make coffee and serve doughnuts, ice cream cones, milkshakes and malteds, but nothing that had to be cooked. (This was kind of like what a barista at Starbucks does in today's terms.) He was 18 years old and had just graduated a couple weeks earlier from high school.

I arrived at the store at 7:30 a.m., let myself in and proceeded to go through the exercises of getting the store ready for customers. About five minutes later the young man arrived. He was totally disheveled in appearance and told me the story of what had happened to him earlier at approximately 1:30-2:30 that morning.

Before I tell his story, I should also explain that on Sunday mornings at Walgreens we were lucky to have a customer before 9:00 a.m. The pharmacy was closed and only the lunch counter and the sundry departments were open for business. Here's the story he told me:

> I was parked high in the Oakland-Berkeley hills, which overlooked one of the great views in the world. We were looking over both the East Bay cities, the Bay Bridge, Treasure Island, San Francisco and the Golden Gate Bridge. My companion and girlfriend was a high school senior. We were at this very romantic spot, necking. In a second there appeared directly in front of us a tubular-shaped vehicle like I'd never seen before, nor had my companion!
>
> It was so large we really couldn't tell in the darkness how close it was to us. My guess is that it was 200-300 yards away and probably 100-150 feet long. Even though we were in complete darkness it had a green hue to the overall body and also had pattern of what look like portholes symmetrically along the middle of the tube.
>
> There was no doubt that this was a

flying spacecraft! We could see, but not identify, some type of bodies moving within the craft.

To say we were frightened is an understatement! I was actually fearful of turning on my headlights. The vehicle hung there in space without any movement for approximately 30 minutes and then, as instantly as it had arrived, it left. We sat stunned in the car for a while, and then we got out and walked around to see if we could see anything else. Then we got back in the car and went home. I couldn't sleep and I finally came the way I am to work.

He then asked me what I thought he should do. He was very confused. At this point in time, I wasn't sure that he was even telling the truth. I didn't know the young man that well. In opening the store I carried in several editions of the Oakland Tribune, the San Francisco Examiner, and the San Francisco Chronicle and put them in the newspaper rack near the front door. We both took copies of the newspapers and hurried through them. There was nothing at all about sightings of anything unusual. It was my suggestion that he call the local Oakland Tribune and the Oakland and Berkeley Police Departments and tell them what he had witnessed and to let them know that there was a second witness with him to verify his story. He liked that idea except he really didn't want to put the young lady into a situation by having her name possibly in the newspaper and/or on the radio, because of what her parents might think of her being up at Lover's Lane!

I then suggested that he mention when he called that there was a second witness to this, but she was not to be mentioned. It was just after 9:00 a.m. that he called both the Oakland Police Department and the Oakland Tribune newspaper. This actually ended our conversation and about this time we had our first customer of the day and we went back to work

Later that Sunday evening on the radio, and then in the newspapers on Monday morning, what he had witnessed were the headlines in all three newspapers! Evidently, the newspapers started receiving calls about 7:00 a.m. Sunday morning from people located in the San Francisco-Oakland area. Also, the authorities did have two or three calls in the 3:00 a.m. timeframe, but the main flow of calls started early Sunday morning. After the radio reports and the Monday papers hit the newsstands, again, there were several hundred more calls verifying that something unusual had been witnessed. This was a big story and it was rightly called a UFO sighting. The media reporters interviewed any and all of these people who were willing to tell their story, including my friend from Walgreens. He told me that the Oakland Tribune, the San Francisco Examiner as well as the Oakland Police Department interviewed him. He had told them almost exactly to the word what we had discussed that Sunday morning, with only one exception—he didn't give them the name of the second witness.

Two thirds of the calls came from people living in the Oakland-Berkeley hills, the balance coming from the San Francisco side of the Bay mostly to the north of the Golden Gate Bridge. There were approximately 1,500 calls verifying this sighting, but according to my associate, he might have been the one person who really saw this flying machine instantly appear and disappear after hovering for about a half hour right there in front of he and his girlfriend. Because of the timing that Sunday morning and the subsequent sightings and reporting, there is absolutely no doubt in my mind that there are UFOs and Beings with advanced technology out there. Here again I was lucky to be working that particular Sunday morning and I felt like I've been a part of history ever since.

The rest of the summer of 1947 was spent working at Walgreens and earning as much as possible for my starting college in September. In early September with my 32 units of college courses already earned, I entered San Jose State College as a sophomore. I was now a full 5' 10", weighing approximately 160 pounds and was quite popular with both sexes as I was and have always been very outgoing, fun-loving, and probably too loquacious! I found the courses at San Jose State to be very easy in comparison to my courses in Utah in the ASTRP. With my close friend Dick Goodison, we rented a room in a boarding house within walking distance from campus and downtown San Jose. It cost $75 a month, which included a breakfast and dinner five days a week. Dick had been a close friend of mine for over five years and we knew each other very well. He was taller than I, slim and very easy-going—a great guy for a roommate! We were very close in our thinking and actions. Dick was a police student at San Jose State. Years later, when Dick graduated, he made a career in police work and the last I heard of Dick he was a high officer in the California Highway Patrol.

Dick had entered the regular Army, enlisting in January of 1945. He had been placed in the Army's supply corps, and when discharged was a three-stripe sergeant. Two days prior to us parting ways, Dick received a telegram ordering him to report to Camp Roberts outside of Paso Robles, California, with a one-grade promotion to be the supply officer for thousands of vets being called back for action in Korea. Dick's specialty, it seems, was issuing uniforms, shoes, weapons and all pertinent equipment needed to be a soldier in 1948. This telegram came as a shock to both of us. Obviously, something was again a major problem in the Far East! I only saw Dick two more times in my life—at my wedding to the girl he introduced me to at San Jose State and at the 25th class reunion of Fremont High School held in the Directors Club at the Golden Gate Racetrack.

In mid-November 1947, I drove Dick to a boarding house on the opposites side of campus to meet his date for that night. I was not included. As we drove up to the boarding house, there on the steps was a young blonde girl who was absolutely the most beautiful girl I'd ever set eyes on! If there was ever love at first sight, this was it.

I said to Dick: "I've got to meet that girl!" Again, timing is everything. Dick's response was: "That's no problem. That's my date's roommate. Come on, get out and I'll introduce you to her."

I was then introduced to Mildred Gurrea. I remember making a date for after the Thanksgiving holidays—actually a double date with Dick and his lady friend, Mildred's roommate. This was probably, in my life story, the most significant thing that personally happened from that first date; to the day Mildred and I married on July 3, 1949. I had no idea then or for several weeks that Mildred was the daughter of a very successful agricultural industrial manufacturer. Her father had an article written about him for Life Magazine. I did see this magazine and read this story before we were married. For the rest of 1947 and until I left San Jose State in early June 1948, I didn't accomplish much in college. It was too easy, not stimulating and, truthfully, all I could think about was Mildred! I should mention here that my father and mother had supplied me while at college with $50 per month to augment my G.I. Bill money, which at the time was $90 per month. That extra $50 was a godsend.

Upon leaving San Jose, I returned home to live. Dad and I were back on speaking terms and my mom and I were closer then ever. Instead of working for Walgreens (the manager had told me that anytime I needed a job he would make a place for me, so I must have done something right), I had two jobs that summer in 1948. Thanks to my dad, who was a great thoroughbred horse lover, I worked for a handicapping service called Turfcraft in northern California. At this time Turfcraft was the number one tip sheet you could purchase on entering the racetrack, which hopefully would give you many winners and make your day!

I arrived every morning at Golden Gate Fields at 5:00 a.m. where the gentleman who owned Turfcraft would meet me and hand me a stopwatch and a pad and pencil. It was my job to clock the workouts of the horses and write down who was riding the horse, a professional jockey, the exercise boy or girl, and any unusual person—meaning young, old, heavy, and or perhaps totally unprofessional. I was also, if possible, told to speak with any and all people who seem to be involved with the horse, including stable boys and such.

In other words, I was supposed to poke my nose into any and everybody's business and see if I could find out some information. I loved doing this! I did this six days a week that summer until the meet at Golden Gate Fields ended. I received $10 in cash per day when I turned in all the information I had gathered that day. That was a lot of money to a 20-year-old student in 1948, equivalent to almost $200 or more in 2013 dollars.

At 9:00 a.m. I had a 9-5 job working for the Oakland City Recreation Department as a playground director. This job also was for the same six days a week that I worked at the racetrack and my pay was $1.25 per hour—also very good pay for something I enjoyed doing! When my first daughter Claudia was born, the birth certificate gave my employment as a playground director—which I think to many people is rather humorous.

Mildred and I, who were now boyfriend and girlfriend, managed to see each other about four times that summer. Twice I drove to her family's ranch in Gilroy and twice Mildred visited an aunt who lived in East Oakland, not far from my home. We were young, very religious Christians, and had a lot in common, including that we liked having fun and partying. We were both very athletic! One day at the beach in Santa Cruz we had a footrace. I barely won. At the end of summer, I was 20 years old and Mildred was 19, and we were both getting serious about our relationship. Looking back, we didn't want to be apart.

Starting in early September, I enrolled at the University of California, Berkeley. When Golden Gate Fields was open for racing, I still had my job with Turfcraft and with the recreation department. The only change was that the recreation department was kind enough to transfer me to Claremont Junior High School on College Boulevard, two miles directly south of the Sather Gate entrance to the university. I had moved into a boarding house on College Boulevard within walking distance to Sather Gate. Bob McDonald was my roommate. When the racetrack was open, I left the track at 8:00 a.m. I could make it to classes beginning at 8:30 a.m. and leave my last class for the day at 2:30 p.m. My racetrack pay was increased by $2 per day that year.

At the recreation department, my pay was $4 per hour, because my students were from the seventh, eighth and the ninth grades. Ninth grade was considered the freshman year of high school. I was in hog heaven! I had two jobs I loved, I was on my own, and I was in love! The only negative in my lifestyle was that I really was not enjoying going to college. For that first semester I did very well, but for the second semester I became, for the lack of a better word, distracted. I started, like the last semester of high school, going downhill in my study habits. I completed only three of the five courses I took that semester and my grades in those three were barely passing! My only reasonable excuse to this day is that I was in love.

On my birthday on February 16, 1949 at the Gurrea ranch in Gilroy, Mildred's mother and father hosted a dinner for my mom and dad. At this dinner, I presented Mildred with a ring and we announced our engagement! As I remember, both sets of parents got along famously. They ended up playing Bridge, which would happen between these four many, many times in the future. We all stayed overnight and my parents and I left the next morning. This was the first time in my recollection that our parents had met.

The only thing my father had to say was that Mildred was a nice beautiful young girl, but we were very young. My mother, on the other hand, was not thrilled at all. We were not only far too young, but the Gurrea's were Catholics! This became a very sticky problem in the Meisterlin house and took many twists and turns in my life.

Shortly after this engagement party, our parents decided that July 3, 1949 would be a perfect day for us to have a wedding in Gilroy at the local Catholic Church. I had no idea how grand and opulent this wedding and wedding reception would become. During the following four months, I rarely saw Mildred in person because between my two jobs and business school I had no time! I do remember a day at my playground that Mildred drove up unexpectedly and unannounced! She approached me on the playground and I could tell that things were not quite right. Out of her mouth jumped the following words: "Are you or are you not going to marry me?" All I could say was, "Of course I am, what's going on?" She then explained that I hadn't advised her of the wedding invitation list or who was going to be my best man, etc. I was very young, naïve, and I guess stupid when it came to weddings.

    I had no idea that this was to be the biggest wedding in what is now the heart of Silicon Valley. I did take one good thing from this conversation and Mildred's body language—that being, she really did want to marry me, no question about it!

Chapter 5

The Wedding, the Honeymoon and Anything Goes!

When we finally reached the wedding day of July 3, 1949, I found myself totally unprepared for what happened. The Catholic Church in Gilroy had a capacity of 400. The parking lot overflowed. We had standing room attendance and anything that could go wrong in the ceremony did so. The wedding, because I was not a Catholic, was held outside of the altar. Years later I was advised by my birth mother that in the years I was living with my grandmother, I was baptized as a Catholic. Actually, my father was unaware of this, but it would have made the wedding itself far better.

I'll never forget standing on the stoop just outside the entry where the groom and best man would enter the church and having my best man, Bob McDonald, say in all seriousness, "Carl, that's my car sitting right there and we can get the hell out of here!" I also remember a faux pas on my part when I could not get the ring on Mildred's finger and I uttered, "Goddammit!" The wedding finally ended after a good 45 minutes and Bob motored us down the road to the Gurrea's ranch.

The reception was held out on the grounds behind

the old house and lawns surrounding the large pool and pool house, bar, and game room. It was a gorgeous day and big Al had spared no expense. Again, the parking was a mess because over 500 people came. Even approximately 75 friends of my mom and dad's had come down from Oakland and San Francisco.

Thanks to my new in-laws attention to detail, the reception was fabulous. I might add that I've never seen to this day the number of wedding gifts, most of which ended up in the attic of the old house. I found out many years later that some of these presents were not opened for 20 years. Champagne flowed for everyone and the bar was open for those in need of something stronger. A couple of hours later, Mildred and I changed clothes and Bob drove us down to a little airstrip in Gilroy. We were followed by the wedding party, some family and several photographers.

Sitting on the runway ready to go, was Big Al's company plane. We exited Bob's car, the flashbulbs popping and the cameras rolling! (The wedding itself, the reception and now the flying away were all filmed for posterity and were just found in 2013 by my daughter Claudia in the attic of the old house with a couple of the wedding gifts. She made several copies, which she distributed to members of the family.)

Mildred and I climbed into the plane and we took off. We circled the crowd a couple of times and then headed for San Jose where we had stashed Mildred's car, given to her in honor of her 18th birthday. This car, a

1948 Studebaker Club Coupe had circular rear windows and became a classic as well as the most popular car ever produced by Studebaker.

We drove to Oakland where we spent the night and had dinner at a Hawaiian-style restaurant very similar to the famous Don the Beachcombers. We were seated at a very special table and Mildred was put in this beautiful big high-back wicker-style Hawaiian chair. She was absolutely gorgeous and really did look like a princess! Later that night we also enjoyed for the first time making love.

Early the next day we left Oakland for Portland, Oregon, where we were to stay with a member of Mildred's family. We drove for 12 or more hours that day and arrived in Portland the following afternoon. We left the next morning heading east on the Columbia River Highway. Something happened here, which had an effect on our honeymoon. Mildred was driving for a stretch and there was in the middle of the highway a small boulder, or a very large rock, which she proceeded to run over! We did not have enough clearance for the undercarriage of the Studebaker! So we stopped and examined what we could see, which was nothing. We restarted the car and went on without a problem.

We headed east until we reached a major intersection to the north taking us through Pasco, Washington to Spokane. We then headed to Coeur d'Alene, Idaho. From there we headed north through Sandpoint, Idaho to the Canadian border. The weather was beautiful and the scenery from Spokane to Canada was breathtaking. On entering Canada we immediately were detoured off the main road about one half a mile on to a logging camp road which had tree stumps in the middle and no turn-out shoulders to use. After the incident on the Columbia River Highway, I actually got out of the car and got underneath and examined exactly where the high point of the undercarriage would be so I could aim that part of the car to hopefully go over the stumps.

The unexpected then happened! The largest moose I've ever seen didn't like our intruding on his territory and started chasing us! He was larger than the Studebaker! I accelerated to about 15 miles per hour, but he was right there in my rearview mirror, and gaining. I accelerated to 20 miles per hour and was very careful to keep the car in the right position for the undercarriage. That darn Moose chased us for over a mile. That was probably one of the best bits of driving in my life. About the time the moose gave up, the detour ended and we were directed back to the main highway. This really was an event Mildred and I remembered for years when we discussed our honeymoon.

We then proceeded north through Banff on to Lake Louise where we had reservations for three nights at the very famous Château Lake Louise. When we finally reached our destination, we were exhausted but the Château, the magnificent lake and the glacier behind were spectacular!

As we perused the surroundings, it became quite evident that we were the only young people there. The average age I would guess, was what we at that time in our lives considered ancient, about 60 years of age plus or minus a few years. There were a few very young children who we thought were probably grandchildren. At dinner that evening I wore my one and only dark suit. I was the only one in a suit. All of the men present were wearing tuxedos and/or dinner jackets. What Mildred wore was more than appropriate, as she was by far the most beautiful female in the dining room. As I have already indicated we retired immediately after dinner and for the next three days we did very little or nothing at all except sleep and get our energy restored. All in all, Lake Louise was everything we had thought it would be—beautiful, pristine, quiet and educational in that it showed us another side of life.

On leaving Lake Louise, we headed directly west to Vancouver British Columbia, where we reentered the United States and headed to Seattle. Then next afternoon we boarded an auto ferry that shuttled back and forth daily overnight to Victoria, British Columbia. The weather was excellent, and we had a clear starry night. Something happened there that still today, 60 years later I still don't understand. We were standing by the ship's railing admiring the stars, the moon and the calm seas. It was a truly romantic night. For no reason, all of a sudden Mildred started yelling at me, in fact screaming, "I hate you! I hate you!" We immediately retired to our stateroom and went to bed without any conversation. The following morning upon rising and going to breakfast, everything couldn't have been nicer. It was as if nothing had happened the night before. I really didn't know what to make of it!

On disembarking in Seattle, we headed directly for Gilroy. We spent about three days there while Mildred went through wedding presents and packed her personal belongings that she needed to start housekeeping in Oakland. We arrived in Oakland and moved in to our first apartment on August 1, 1949. Our apartment was not in an ordinary apartment house. The apartment was on the second story of a late 1800s mansion built in Oakland by the Hills Brothers Coffee Company family. It was very different but spacious, comfortable and had a magnificent view overlooking the San Francisco Bay. In my opinion it was a great place to start a marriage. For the next month Mildred was busy making our apartment into a home and getting settled. I, in turn, worked at Walgreens and the recreation department part-time. What I enjoyed most was coming home to my own house, the beautiful surroundings and a beautiful wife!

I entered the University of California in early September. It was to be my junior year and unfortunately my last year of college. I was taking classes and still working from 3:00-6:00 p.m. for the recreation department. In late November, Mildred advised me she was pregnant! To be honest, I was totally unprepared for this news and I'm not sure how my reaction came across. I was so young, so naïve and completely unprepared to start a family. Here again the Meisterlin luck prevailed. On June 15, 1950, the good Lord presented us with a beautiful daughter we named Claudia Louise. I must add right here that I don't know where my life would have led without Claudia, as you will hear in the balance of my life story. I honestly think of her as "St. Claudia." She has always put our family first!

From that November announcement until dropping out of school and getting a regular job, moving, starting with a new business (with Al's help), my life was a blur. I dropped out of school shortly after Thanksgiving at the end of the first half semester. With the extra credits I had earned at Utah and San Jose State I actually had 3 3/4 years of college. This was not the end of my education, however, as I have attended many management seminars and even a four-week corporate management school. I'm still learning today as our world we live in is changing at an unbelievable pace! A bit of advice—you're never too old to learn!

During the Christmas holidays, Al came to me with an idea about starting a company that he'd heard about that was brand-new and thought would be very successful. It was an automatic coffee vending machine that would be placed in industrial factories. He had researched the manufacturing company that produced the machines, Kwik Kafe. He had all the statistics, including actual earnings from several machines in several factories in the east, all of which were very positive. Al said he'd like to start out with one and if it would be as successful as the research indicated, we would order three more machines to be delivered as we needed them over the next six months.

If successful, we could then probably go to the bank and borrow money to expand. He then offered me the opportunity of running the company and being a part owner or even being the owner once it really got going. After studying the facts and figures for a whole one night, I accepted.

Al and I decided that what I should do would be to go to Philadelphia where Kwik Kafe was located and take two associates along with me who I would need if the business were to grow as we hoped. I then asked my close friend George Alexander and another brilliant young man from Oakland High School, Blair Fountain, if they would be interested and willing to take a chance. They both accepted after I explained that we would drive in my car from Oakland to Philadelphia and back completely at my expense. We left in the first week of January 1950 and the trip was routine. On arriving in Philadelphia, we went directly to Kwik Kafe where they were expecting us and directed us to a hotel. The next morning we started our learning course on how the coffee machines were built, how they worked and were maintained, etc. The second day was spent more explicitly on the maintenance and workings of how a cup of coffee with cream and sugar would fall in place so that the customer had a good cup of coffee. Of course during the first two days we were told that we had to buy our coffee from them and what was in their coffee that made it better for a vending machine than a normal coffee maker. The third day was spent visiting various factories in the immediate Philadelphia area. We visited three factories and each one had a delegate who showed us and told us how and when the machines did the maximum amount of business and what we should look for in the type of factories that would be favorable to installing our machines. That evening they had a small cocktail party at which, with Al's permission, I ordered the first machine, which they would deliver to Oakland within 10 to 14 days.

We had allowed five to seven days in Philadelphia. New York City and Long Island were not that far away. The three of us had never been to New York City or Long Island. We all agreed, because we had money left to use, that this side trip would be great. The next morning we headed for New York City. The highway we took was unlike anything we had ever seen in the western United States and had six lanes or more. New York City was nothing more than a huge concrete jungle!

Driving a car through New York City was not something a person with any brains at all would do. As soon as we could find an exit to take us to the South Shore of Long Island, we took it. Long Island was the last address I had where my mother lived. We arrived in Hempstead that evening and stopped at a gas station, where I made a call to my mother from a phone booth. (In those days there were no portable or cell phones.) My mother answered the phone and I asked her if I could drop by with a couple of my associates. She agreed and gave me directions to her house and we were there in a few minutes.

Frankly, she and her fourth husband were not very

happy to see us. It was late afternoon, but light enough to take a picture. For some reason she didn't want her picture taken with me. We did have a picture taken of Blair, George and I to show that we had been on Long Island. We started home the next morning early and because we were in the month of January we did have an extremely unusual happenstance.

1950
Long Island, New York
George Alexander, Carl Meisterlin
and Blair Fountain

The fastest way home, as well is the safest instead of heading directly west, was to take the highway to St. Louis, Missouri on the famous Route 66. The trip was going excellently until we entered New Mexico. It started to snow lightly and steadily got worse. We were lucky in that

I had a set of chains, which we stopped and put on the tires. We continued on until we were in a blizzard and it was impossible to drive. We went safely as far to the side of the road behind a car a few feet ahead. On getting out of the car we discovered that we were trapped with about ten other cars, of which we were more or less in the middle. It seemed a lot longer than it was, but a New Mexico state patrol car pulled up, advised us to follow him and stay as close to the car ahead of us as possible. He told us to position our car between the taillights of the car in front of us and not lose sight of those taillights! This meant, of course, that we all had to put our headlights on—another lesson to learn if you ever get caught in a blizzard! The officer advised us that we were only about six miles east of Gallup, New Mexico. It was just turning dark and it took our caravan a good hour to reach the small town of Gallup.

On arriving in Gallup, our savior, the patrolman, recommended that we try and get lodging at The Lodge in the middle of town. We were finally able to find a place to park our car in order that we could physically get into the building. This was not an easy task! When we entered The Lodge it was apparent that there were many more people in our predicament! The place was loaded with people already on the floor wrapped up in blankets. The Lodge had a massive fireplace with a wonderful fire going, and it felt like heaven on earth! There were no rooms available.

There were a few cots being brought in, but not near enough to take care of us travelers. The bar was open and, a few hot brandy drinks later, life could not be better! For the next three to four hours, people continued entering The Lodge, but not travelers. The people who entered were locals—all of whom had their arms filled with pillows and blankets! There are many thoughtful wonderful Good Samaritans in this world, particularly in Gallup!

I was lucky that night to have a pillow and two blankets and a place on the floor that I could stretch out. Believe it or not, that night continued to get more fantastic by the hour! There were about 75 people on cots and under blankets on the floor in the lobby that night. The bar stayed open I would guess far past legal closing hours. But what happened then was that three or four people had musical instruments. Also, there was an old upright piano against one of the walls. All of a sudden we had a band! The music started playing, the people started singing, some people cleared a space in front of the bar and people started dancing. When the music stopped, occasionally then some people got up and started telling all sorts of stories—not jokes, but funny stories about their lives, or the lives of somebody else they knew or had read about. In some cases, these were hysterically funny and in the early morning becoming funnier by the hour. About 4:00 a.m., we all finally went to sleep from sheer delight. I have never seen or heard so much talent or companionship among strangers and all around good spirit than on that night. It was a wonderful lesson in life!

We were able to leave the next morning, escorted by the same patrolman, for about 20 miles. The storm had dissipated and we were able to take our chains off and head for home. The rest of the trip was totally uneventful, but the night in Gallup lives with me still today. The lesson learned is that no matter how miserable and terrible life can be, it brings people together and somehow always shows the good side of human nature!

    Don't ever give up on humanity!

Chapter 6

Opportunity Knocks

We arrived back in Oakland safely, a couple of days early, without being charged for lodging in Gallup.

We were allotted 40 meals, 14 nights lodging and over 750 gallons of gas whether we used them or not. The meals counted for approximately $400. The lodging accounted for $600 and the gasoline expense was the same. As we had not used up our budget due to being very penurious, I made my first executive decision. I decided that both Blair and George were entitled monetarily to something. I thought it would be very fair if we split the monies three ways. I gave Blair $250 and George likewise. My share I left in the company with the rest of the budgeted residue. They were extremely pleased at receiving this money. George needed that money badly. Unfortunately, Blair would never see another dollar.

The coffee machine arrived in the 14 days as promised and I had procured a major industrial manufacturer of typewriters, adding machines and calculators for its use. This plant was open from 6:00-1:00 in the morning. From what we had learned in Philadelphia, it appeared to be a perfect fit. The manufacturing company had found a perfect place to install it, which George and I did immediately and without a problem.

The next day everything went well until I received a phone call about 7:00 p.m. The caller said the machine flooded, had turned off and was ejecting cups and liquid all over the place and that he had unplugged the machine to get it stopped. I immediately jumped in my car and was there at the plant within 30 minutes. Upon opening the machine (thanks to my training in Philadelphia), I saw what the problem was immediately and fixed it. This particular problem was one of many that we had been warned about—it was caused by the customers pushing and/or shoving the machines—in other words, rough handling!

The next morning we received another call and this time George went to the plant and again was able to correct the problem. He did so, but by dinner hour we had another call, which we both answered and went together. Again the problem was fixable. We handled it and went home to dinner. The next day, another call from the plant —another problem—and again we were able to return the machine to duty.

It appeared to both George and I that the people using the machine must be leaning on it and pushing it and the machine was too sensitive to these physical attacks. The next couple of days we received two or three phone calls and complaints, which we did our best to satisfy. I had phoned Big Al earlier in the week and told him of our problems with the machine. On the last phone call both of us went to the plant and were unable to get the machine to work at all. I called Big Al and explained our predicament. Al replied, "I have a maintenance mechanic foreman who has worked for me for years who can fix anything!" He further said, "If this man can't fix that machine then the machine probably isn't worth fixing! I'll have him meet you and George at the plant at 8:00 a.m. tomorrow and we'll see what he can accomplish."

For the previous 48 hours I had been on the telephone with the man in Philadelphia several times about our many various problems. The next morning when we arrived, Al's Mr. Fix-it was waiting for us. By noon he had not been able to get the machine working. By now the factory's mechanical guru was also involved. He too, wanted to be the individual to solve the problem. Late in the afternoon after much swearing, cussing, waving of arms and stamping of feet, both of these gentlemen pronounced that this machine was poorly conceived and even worse, poorly built! They both let us know, along with the plant manager who had joined us by this time, that this piece of equipment was a piece of junk! Al's man from Gilroy then called Big Al and in words that I can't use in this book, told us not to waste our time and money. We unplugged the machine, said good night, and went home. Later that night I called Al to find out what he thought we should do. After all, it was 100% his money. Al's reply was very candid: "You win some and you lose some! Carl, get rid of the machine. If there is any way you can sell it and get some money for it, it's yours for all your effort.

If not, take it to the junkyard." The next day I met with the factory manager and we discussed both his and our options. He called in his plant guru again and asked if there was any way to salvage the machine? The man said, "I don't think the way the machine is built is on a sound principle, but I think that the concept is excellent because the coffee that came from the machine when it was working was one hell of a cup! Personally, when we have a little time on our hands, I'd like for us in the maintenance department, to experiment in rebuilding it." He then said, "But if it's going to cost us any money, then forget it!" The plant manager looked at me and simply said, "Well, Carl, what do you say to this?" I said, "If you'll keep the machine and I don't have to move it, we've got a deal, it's yours!" We shook hands and Kwik-Kafe of California was out of business!

The next day I was at about as low spirited as one soon-to-be 23-year-old young man could be. First I called George and told him of Al's decision and that we were both out of work. George remained one of my closest friends my entire life, even though we rarely were to see each other.

I now, however, had a wife who was five-months pregnant and no real means of support other than the part-time Walgreens and Oakland Recreation Department jobs. The next day I completed my first job-seeking resume. In the newspaper want ads I found an ad placed by Montgomery Ward. I thought my educational background of 3 3/4 years of college and work record with the recreation department and Walgreens might be a fit. I called the personnel department and made an appointment for two days later. I must have guessed correctly, as after the first interview I was called in for a second with a department head. After that I was called again to meet with some executive who would be in Oakland three to four weeks hence and that they would contact me if I were still interested, with the time and place. During this period of time, approximately six weeks, I was busy with my two part-time jobs and Mildred.

We were busy shopping for a new home because I was lucky enough to be a Cal veteran. In 1950 a Cal veteran could obtain a mortgage with only 10% down for 30 years at 3%. This loan actually was "too good to be true." Even with this great incentive loan, the cost of housing in decent neighborhoods of Oakland were far greater than we could afford. We heard of a new development 20 miles directly east of Oakland proper through a newly-completed tunnel where the main highway ran directly through the beautiful Moraga Valley to Walnut Creek. We then drove north on the main highway about three miles to the very southwest corner of Concord. There we found Gregory Gardens, the new development that was heavily advertised. The homes were three bedroom, one bath, cement slab, slate roof, one-story dwellings. We found a particular floor plan that we liked and a future location in the next phase to be built, as the phase currently was sold out. The next phase, in which we could get the floor plan we wanted, had several lots left. Better yet, they would definitely accept my Cal vet loan application.

The cost for the home we wanted and the lot we desired was exactly $8,000 with an $800 down payment and payments to be $72 per month. This, with me working only part-time jobs, was well within our budget. We left a $100 deposit and were given a completion date of between three to four months. Everything looked much brighter that evening!

We now figured that our home would be finished, allowing for a slight error in time, before July 1. Our new baby was expected early to mid-June. That was cutting things mighty close, but we were young, in love and thought we were invincible. I then decided that if I were to be living in Concord, which was in Contra Costa County, that it would be wise to find a job in that area. We were still living in the Hills Brothers apartment in central Oakland. At that time if the Montgomery Ward job were to pan out, that location was perfect. But now we both agreed that Gregory Gardens was for us.

Two weeks later I received the call from Montgomery Ward. I went on the interview, which went very well. Upon leaving, the gentleman said he would be in touch. A week later I did receive an offer for a training position in the Oakland store with a salary of $250. That was very tempting but the time and cost of driving from Concord to southeast Oakland was too much of an obstacle. Not wanting to burn my bridges, I wrote the last gentleman who interviewed me a personal letter thanking him for his time and trouble and explained to him my reasons for not accepting his job offer. I received a short note back from him, which said, "If I were in your shoes, I'd make the same decision."

My father suggested I should call his banker at Central Bank, which was in the midst of a very large expansion into the surrounding areas, including Contra Costa County. The corporate offices for Central Bank were just one block down Broadway from Walgreens, so after work one day I walked down and asked for the gentleman my father had advised me to contact. I made an appointment to meet with him the following day. Central Bank was indeed expanding and again as luck would have it they were opening a new branch in Concord sometime in late June or hopefully after the July 4th holiday. I immediately qualified to be hired as a teller. The salary would be $175 a month to start. I said I would be interested but I was not available until my new house was finished in Concord, which I hoped would be at the same time as the new branch opening. He said to call him when I was ready to go to work. Mildred and I discussed it and agreed that this was probably a good temporary move. That week we gave notice to our landlord that we would be vacating our apartment on June 30th, the day our lease expired.

The next few months were very hectic. Mildred was handling her pregnancy very well except for gaining more weight than she desired. I returned to work at my two part-time jobs and found time to take two courses at a local business school. Finally on June 15, 1950, our first child, Claudia Louise Meisterlin, was born and our lives changed for the better and forever! Our new home was finished and we were able to move in just before July 1st. We spent the July 4th celebration moving into our new home. This was really tough on Mildred both mentally and physically! She never complained, but I felt very guilty for putting her through this move at this particular time.

I started work the following Monday as a teller at the bank. After only two to three weeks, I knew for certain that I was not cut out to be a banker, nor did I enjoy the people surrounding me. Maybe I was too ambitious, but there was no challenge in this profession. In perusing the local paper, I noticed that the largest company in Contra Costa County, the United States Steel Corporation, was hiring in all categories. The next day I left the bank feigning sickness, and headed for Pittsburgh where the Mill was located. The personnel manager himself subsequently interviewed me. Lucky, lucky, lucky! After presenting my brief resume and being interviewed, he asked me to return the following Monday for an interview with his superior. That Monday I called in sick again and proceeded to Pittsburgh. I was taken to the plant manager's office where I was interviewed for well over one hour. The plant manager then offered me a training position job as an expediter paying $215 per month, starting as soon as possible. I drove directly back to the bank and told the bank manager that I was leaving for what I felt was a better opportunity. Of course, I could have been wrong.
I asked him how soon I could be relieved of my duties. He told me to finish the week in order to train a replace-

ment, which I did. That afternoon I placed a call to the plant manager at U.S. Steel and informed him that I would be at the plant the following Monday morning. I was to arrive at 8:00 a.m. at the west gate where the expediter office was located and report to Peter Tew, my mentor.

The following Monday I was directed to Mr. Tew's desk. Peter was already there waiting for me and seemingly anxious to begin. For the next two weeks Peter and I were like one person. The Pittsburgh Steel Mill covered approximately 50 acres of land. It was completely surrounded with chain-link fencing and topped off with barbed wire. There were six entry gates that could be entered at any time for parking. The entry doors to the Mill and offices within were all locked with a coded entry box, which were recoded frequently. To walk from one corner to the opposite corner of the Mill took over 30 minutes. I walked many miles to deliver production orders to the many various departments. I was constantly in motion. In the first month I lost almost ten pounds, which made Mildred very happy, as well as myself!

My two weeks shadowing Peter were awesome. Peter was not only a superb mentor; he was a remarkable, inspirational human being. Peter was only two to three years older than myself in age, but he was decades ahead in understanding what life was all about. Physically, Peter was also impressive. He was handsome and perfectly proportioned and stood 6' 1" and weighed 195 pounds. He was a British citizen here in the United States on a three-year visa to work for the U.S. Steel Corporation and also to play soccer for, at that time, the number one United States amateur soccer club located in San Francisco, the Olympic Club. What made Peter fascinating was the life he lived during World War II. In 1939, Peter joined the British Intelligence Corps at the age of 14—yes, 14!

As Peter told it, he had spent two years at a military school in England prior to being recruited and accepted into the intelligence division. After being specifically trained on how to spy and conduct himself like a typical 14-year-old boy behind enemy lines, he was taken by submarine to the coast of Holland and dropped off in the middle of the night and picked up by the Dutch underground. He did this spying for over a year. He then left the Netherlands, again by submarine, and returned to England. After a fun-filled furlough of a couple of months, he was reassigned to be an assistant to a full colonel in India. In late 1944, he was reassigned to be an assistant to the commander of the English expedition forces in Burma. He actually served under Prince Philip in Burma, who is today married to Queen Elizabeth. I have no idea what became of Peter Tew, but I owe him immense gratitude for teaching and inspiring me!

The same week I became an expediter, another young man joined the U.S. Steel Corporation Mill at Pittsburgh, California. His name was Bill Black. Bill also became an expediter, but had a different mentor in another part of the Mill. I've mentioned Bill because he was the youngest son of Charles Black, Sr. who was the owner of the Matson Lines, Ampex Corporation and on the board of directors of Bethlehem Steel Company. Although Bill and I started at the same time, due to his connections, he was placed on a much faster career track. Bill was also the younger brother of Charles Black, Jr., who later married Shirley Temple. This was the second time Shirley Temple had crossed my path. She became a beautiful lady that I greatly admired. In addition to being a world-famous actress, she served as ambassador to Ghana and to Czechoslovakia as well as our country's first Chief of Protocol.

The weeks and months rolled by for both Mildred and I with our new baby Claudia and our new home. We were very happy, at least I was, and the time flew by. Being an expediter, I learned something new every day about the making of steel, labor unions, social conduct, people management, and business finance. I credit Peter Tew for this. Even then, I counted my blessings and knew I was, as usual, extremely lucky!

Chapter 7

The Big Break

Seven months after beginning at the Mill in Pittsburgh, I was called into my big boss's office. I had no idea why I was being called in, as I had probably not talked to this gentleman four times since I had begun working. As I walked through the plant all sorts of thoughts went through my head, even that maybe I was going to be fired. As I entered his large office he stood up and greeted me with a handshake. He said, "Carl, you've done a fine job at the many things we've asked of you. The company wants to promote you to a management-training program. This is a very special program that only accepts two trainees per year. If you accept, your new position as a trainee will be in the southwestern division office located in Los Angeles. This is the largest population growth area in the United States and the territory extends from Santa Barbara on the Pacific Ocean; south to the Mexican border, then East to Yuma, Arizona; then north to Phoenix, west to Las Vegas, across to Bakersfield and west to Santa Barbara. This division also includes the Hawaiian Islands. You would be transferred with all costs of moving to be paid for by the company. Also included will be 30 days lodging and food allowance until you find a place to live for you and your family and a $40 per month salary increase that will make your pay $275 per month."

I really wanted to say yes right there and then, but before doing so, I thought Mildred should have a say in our decision. Without hesitation Mildred agreed. Two weeks later I presented myself to the vice president of the southwestern division of the United States Steel Corporation, who was to be my overall boss. His secretary led me to his office, the grandest walnut-paneled office with the largest desk I'd ever set eyes on. This extremely large man rose to his feet, circled the desk, shook my hand and welcomed me to Los Angeles. He asked personal questions about my wife and family and about how I liked my days learning the steel business from the ground up in Pittsburgh. He then called in the head of the internal sales and marketing department who was to be my supervisor for the following three years.

This move took place in mid-March of 1951. The corporate office was located in the middle of the industrial area directly south of downtown Los Angeles. It was a fairly large two-story building. Downstairs consisted of four major executive officers plus secretarial offices for each of these. (The executive secretaries were making salaries considerably greater than mine.) There were also three meeting rooms—small, medium and large—and beautiful lavatories for the men and women. The upstairs was divided by the work to be performed, which was basically taking production orders for the manufacture of all types of steel.

There were three divisions of steel production: the wire and cable division, the sheet and tin division, and the structural steel division. There were also some specialty steels, but they represented only about 3% of what U.S. Steel produced. Each division had seven career salesmen who specialized in the types of steel produced by their division. The next level of employees were the inside salesmen. The next lower level was the order takers. That's where I started. There were no women in the above categories. But, there was a secretarial pool on the second floor with 20 very pretty, if not beautiful women. They were all handsomely dressed.

During my stay at the Pittsburgh Mill, on two occasions I had been sent with documents to the northwestern division in San Francisco. The first thing I noticed there was that the female employees even wore hats and gloves to and from the office. In Los Angeles it was not quite so formal, but they dressed far nicer than any other offices I visited. Looking back, my guess is that half were married and half were unmarried. There were 80+ people working in the building and even two very young men who were errand boys who carried paperwork to and from the various internal departments. Lastly, there was a single janitorial employee whose main job was to keep the bathrooms spick and span.

Before leaving Concord, we had been booked by the company into our motel on Firestone Boulevard near the large Firestone plant, and across the street from the famous Trianon Ballroom. We were only a five-minute drive from where I would work and surrounded by restaurants, and movie theaters. The first day at work, I was escorted by my new supervisor and introduced to the personnel who were working in the office. At lunchtime the supervisor kindly told me that I could return to my family at the motel and make them comfortable

After lunch I called our real estate broker in Concord to give him our temporary phone number. After accepting my promotion, we had put our home up for sale. Surprisingly, he stated that he had an offer for our home! The offer was a good clean deal with no contingencies. It was for a 30-day escrow and we would receive cash to our loan minus commission, escrow fees and a few very minor governmental fees. I countered, asking for 4% more or $500. The final sum was $11,000. The broker was very happy with our counter offer and two hours later he called back and said we had a deal. Were we lucky! Soon after, we found an apartment in West Los Angeles in a nice neighborhood with beautiful surroundings and only a 20-minute drive straight east on Slauson Boulevard where the office stood—a very short, pleasant commute.

All things considered, with a career change and the selling of the house at an unbelievable profit, happiness prevailed. One afternoon around April 1st, while Mildred and Claudia were back in Concord, the supervisor asked me if I was a baseball fan? I replied, "Yes, I'm a big baseball fan. I follow the Pacific Coast League baseball, not the major leagues." He said, "If you haven't anything better to do tonight, would you like to attend the opening game between our Los Angeles Angels and their crosstown rivals the Hollywood Stars?" It was being played at the old Wrigley Field just a couple of miles away. I accepted. He then handed me a box seat ticket and instructed me that when entering the box I should sit in the back row on the furthest seat from the entrance. He stated that there would be a couple of our stellar salesman with their customers who would fill our box of six seats.

I arrived at the ballpark 30-40 minutes early and proceeded to the company box, which was located just left of home plate in row five and six—an absolute perfect position to watch a ballgame. I took my seat as instructed with no problem, because the others sharing the box had yet to arrive.

I noticed that coming down the stairs on the aisle to my left there was a slight commotion. There were two very young beautifully dressed young ladies with two handsome young men surrounded by three to four photographers. The photographers were shooting pictures from any and all angles. The whole group proceeded all the way down onto the playing field. They then started filming the four walking up the aisle. After that they started taking single photographs of the girls, the men, the girls by themselves and the men by themselves and so on and so forth. This all took about 15 minutes and there was no question in my mind that these were Hollywood actors and actresses.

When they finished their shoot, the photographers

disappeared and the actors proceeded to sit down in what was evidently their box. The two girls stayed together and sat in the back row furthest from the aisle and the young men directly in front of them. One young lady, the blonde, I thought was a slight bit pudgy, but still very attractive. The other young lady was truly gorgeous! She was elegantly dressed and her clothes flowed over what I guess was probably a perfect body. Upon entering their box, the blonde girl sat down next to the rail that separated the two boxes. Actually she was sitting less then two feet from my left shoulder. About then our box and the box next to us began to fill. The opening night festivities started almost immediately and I was introduced to everybody in our box. Early in the game I caught the eye of the blonde girl and asked, "Are you a baseball fan?" She answered, "Not really, but I do understand the game and I root for the Hollywood Stars."

During the game I asked the man sitting next to me "Who's in the box next to me?" He replied, "All I know is that it's one of the very big studios and they have had that box as long as I can remember." I asked if he recognized the actors and actresses. He replied, "The gorgeous brunette is Jean Peters." One might remember that Jean Peters retired very early in her career because she married Howard Hughes. The pudgy blonde's name was Marilyn Monroe. Here again I was in the right place at the right time. I don't remember who won the game or anything else about that evening, but I did ask a question of the very famous Marilyn Monroe and she answered me!

Those first few weeks in the office were completely different then I expected. I was one of eight order writers who received factory orders from the inside salesmen and placed orders for the various types and grades of steel with the producing steel mills. We then initialed the order and passed it on to another order writer to be rechecked, insuring accuracy. Once done rechecking, there was a box to be initialed also. This was very arduous and exacting work. Luckily all of the order writers were young with excellent eyesight and good demeanor. I fit in with all of the order writers and was accepted on a one-for-all basis. This was not true with the inside salesmen contingent. They were considerably older, on the average ten years or so, and their aspirations for their future with U.S. Steel were to become, at best, a salesman! Because of my reputation for being a corporate management trainee, I had no ceiling on where I was headed in the corporation. I instinctively felt some jealousy towards me.

On the home front, Mildred and I settled into our apartment in West Los Angeles and remained there for six months. We then found a small home for rent in the South Paramount area where some associates from work lived. The house was larger than the apartment and had a front and back yard and Mildred was pregnant again. My work as an order writer was not really my cup of tea, but I fought my way through it. Before we moved to the Paramount house I took half of the profit we made on selling the home and bought a new Pontiac and we became a two-car family from then on. Although the Paramount home was larger and less expensive, neither of us had anything in common with anyone in our neighborhood. We found a three-bedroom, two-bath home on the border of Lakewood, Bellflower and Paramount, which Mildred liked. We had cash in the bank and I had received a $25 a week raise and we could afford it. The house had been built in 1939 and needed some rehabbing. We repainted the kitchen, bathrooms, and all three bedrooms, which also included ceilings. We did it all ourselves.

On January 2, 1952, I received a promotion to the rank of inside salesman. This position was much better suited to my personality and loquaciousness? I remained an inside salesman until I left U.S. Steel. During this stay in Paramount and Bellflower, my daughters Cynthia and Debbie were born. Cynthia was born at Queen of Angels Hospital in Los Angeles and Debbie was born at St. Mary's Hospital in Long Beach.

In March of 1953, we had a terrible earthquake that was centered near Tehachapi and was felt and caused damage all the way through Los Angeles and south to Long Beach. As we were not near the epicenter, but out on the fingertips, our home rolled but somehow stayed on its foundation. The next day we couldn't find any cracks or damage anywhere.

With a wife and three beautiful little girls, I needed to move up the ladder. We weren't doing badly monetarily as I had received on January 2nd another $25 raise and I was now earning $350 per month. In addition, starting in the winter of 1952 there were four associates including myself who were carpooling to the office—three men and one girl. She was married and her husband required their car. The three men took turns driving one week at a time. The girl was very nice, but she was always late. She would come running out the door almost every morning with her hands and arms full of clothes and proceed to get dressed in the backseat. She was not at all embarrassed or ashamed to show her body. We men kind of looked forward to this break from the monotony of driving a half hour to work!

In the summer of 1953, I asked for an appointment with the senior vice president. We met the next morning and he greeted me the same as usual by getting up, coming over shaking my hand and then asking, "What's on your mind Carl?" My question to him was, "When do I make my next move? I now have three daughters. I honestly feel that I haven't learned much in the past six months." He waited for a while and then looked me straight in the eye said, "When you mature!" With that, and no other words but a handshake, I left his office. Approximately 45 days later I gave my 30-day notice, which they accepted and I was released ten days later. They made no effort to persuade me otherwise.

One of the reasons I decided to resign was because Mildred and I had come into an inheritance early in 1953. I got really lucky and invested the money and in the next six months basically doubled our money. I was young, impatient, with a growing family, and possibly foolish to quit my job, but the Meisterlin luck prevailed.

Chapter 8

Beginnings with Soulé

Immediately upon leaving U.S. Steel in Los Angeles, Mildred and I made the decision to return to our home territory in the San Francisco area. We decided that I should go to the ranch in Gilroy, where they had plenty of room for me to stay while searching for work. We called Emily and Big Al and advised them of what we were planning and asked if I could board with them while searching. The answer was yes and I could tell from Emily's voice that she was pleased!

The following day being a Sunday I drove to Gilroy with a suitcase and a couple of business suits to start my quest. The next morning I called a company I had visited during the Kwik Kafe fiasco, Gilmore Steel in Oakland, to speak to Mr. Al Zeller, their regional vice president, whom I had been very impressed with! When I phoned Gilmore, thankfully Mr. Zeller remembered me. "What's on your mind Carl," he said. "Don't tell me your going to try and put a coffee machine in my plant again?" I replied, "No, Mr. Zeller, I'm calling for an interview for employment." He told me he had an opening between 9:30 to 11:00 a.m. the next day, but warned me that he needed to leave for an appointment in San Francisco at noon.

I replied, "I'll be there at 9:30 a.m. and thank you very much." It always pays to be polite when you're asking for something!

I arrived on time and was ushered into Mr. Zeller's office and his first words after greeting me were, "Please call me Al." I then handed Al my resume and a list of references, which included the Oakland YMCA Director and the two top men at the Oakland Recreation Department as well as the manager at the local Walgreens drugstore. Al took some time to peruse these papers and exclaimed, "You certainly have a wonderful steel industry background and your references are even better. I had no idea what happened to you since last time we talked and I'm even more impressed now. Unfortunately right now I don't have anything that I could offer you that would be good enough and pay enough for you and your family." He asked, "Have you talked with anybody else?" I replied, "No, but if you weren't interested I thought I'd stop by Kaiser corporate offices later." He agreed that would be as smart thing to do as they were continually expanding.

All of a sudden his expression changed and he said, "Carl, I'm having lunch today in San Francisco with the manager of purchasing for Soulé Steel, Mr. George Ford, who is also one of my very best friends in the metals industry. I happen to know that he has been searching for the right person to fit a new position he's creating in management at Soulé's San Francisco corporate division! Would you like me to take your paperwork and present it to Mr. Ford? You're a little younger man then he was seeking, but your educational background plus your impeccable references might outweigh your youth! I'll have my secretary make a couple of copies—one to keep for myself, one for George, and one in case somebody I know happens to be looking for a young family man like you. Frankly Carl, I wish I had a job for you, but I don't. Give me your phone number where you can be reached and prepare whoever answers the phone that if it's a Mr. George Ford of Soulé Steel that you receive that message!" He handed me a business card of Mr. Ford's with the suggestion that if I didn't hear from Mr. Ford within 48 hours, it would be wise to be aggressive and call him. We shook hands and I left and headed for Kaiser.

    I arrived at Kaiser and went to the personnel department. I knew nobody at Kaiser in spite of the fact that my mom and dad were on personal talking terms with Henry Kaiser and his wife. The lady at the front desk asked about what type of employment I was looking for. I handed her my resume and after a few minutes she said that I should talk to a Mr. McConnell who would return after lunch.

    At 12:30 p.m. Mr. McConnell presented himself and walked me into his small office. My resume and references were already on his desk and appeared to already have been read. Being that I was so young; Mr. McConnell took the liberty of calling me by my first name. He said, "Your resume and references make you an ideal candidate for many future positions in Kaiser, as well as your being a local boy. The Kaiser organization likes helping worthy local men and women! I already have placed a call to divisions in Kaiser that I think would be very interested in meeting with you—one in particular in the steel division. Would a position that might be available outside of the Oakland area interest you?" I told him, "Mr. McConnell I have a wife and family, I need a job that allows me growth and opportunity for the future! I'll listen to any offer!" He replied, "If you'll leave a phone number where I can reach you, I'll phone you as soon as I hear from my superiors." That ended the interview and I headed directly back for the ranch in Gilroy with high hopes.

    I arrived at the ranch just before 3:00 p.m. and told Emily about my two interviews and that although I didn't receive any offers, I did receive excellent possibilities. Emily responded that she'd had a call from a Mr. McConnell at Kaiser. I phoned immediately and Mr. McConnell responded that the best offer from Kaiser based on an interview with the general manager of the Fontana Steel Mill appeared to be my best opportunity to get started and go forward rapidly in the Kaiser steel division. If I was interested he asked me to return his call and he would arrange an interview with the general manager/vice president at Fontana!

    Minutes later the telephone rang again, Emily answered and called to me saying, "Mr. Ford is on the line, Carl." I picked up my extension and politely and clearly said, "Carl Meisterlin." Mr. Ford responded, "Carl I'd like to meet you in person as soon as possible. I've read your resume and your references carefully and I've listened to

my friend Al Zeller for over an hour at lunch raving about you! I understood from Al that when you left his office you were headed for Kaiser. I'm hoping that you'll give Soulé Steel and myself an opportunity to meet you personally and let you witness what we're accomplishing!"
I responded, "Kaiser was very encouraging, but I haven't made any decision yet as I have a wife and children to plan for. I'm available tomorrow all day. Set the time and I'll be there, but I'll need directions as I'm not that well acquainted with San Francisco." Mr. Ford replied, "How about 9:30 a.m., as I would like possibly to have you meet a couple of other Soulé employees and tour our operation?" I agreed and he gave me instructions to locate Soulé Steel, which would take about two hours of driving time from Gilroy.

As I hung up the telephone, I noticed that Emily was listening to every word. There are not enough good words that can express my love for and friendship with my mother-in-law, Emily. She was a very, very special and loving lady and in my heart I've always thought that our relationship was based on mutual respect for each other. That night Emily fixed leg of lamb for dinner, which was my favorite meal, and later we went a couple of miles down the road to Gilroy's drive-in movie. Al chose to stay home. I'd don't remember if either one of us really saw the movie itself, as we talked during that complete show about Mildred and our future plans. We also discussed her grandchildren Claudia, Cynthia and Debbie, whom she seemed to favor over other family grandchildren. I have no idea why!

The next morning, Emily was up and my breakfast of cereal, ham and eggs was waiting for me in the kitchen at 7:00 a.m. I had brought my very best business suit, white shirt and matching tie, socks and polished black shoes. I entered the kitchen and Emily immediately complimented me on my appearance. I had breakfast, thanked Emily, gave her a kiss and away I went, future in hand! The road traffic to San Jose was the same but at the turn in the road to go to San Francisco the road was significantly busier! Fortunately, I had left about 15 minutes earlier than I anticipated and arrived barely on time. Lucky, lucky, lucky!

On entering Mr. Ford's very nice executive office, Mr. Ford said, "Welcome to Soulé! I hope you'll like it here." "Thank you," I replied and mentioned that the instructions he gave me were perfect; otherwise I wouldn't have arrived on time. Mr. Ford sized me up and I did the same to Mr. Ford. Mr. Ford was of identical size and build as myself, but my guess was he was very close to 40 years of age, plus or minus a couple of years. Mr. Ford observed, "You're young, but you give a great impression of being a very astute successful businessman!" I sat down and we talked mostly about my background at U.S. Steel, both in Pittsburgh at the Mill and Los Angeles in the sales and marketing division. After answering all sorts of questions about my background, the war years, my father and mother, my wife and children and where I possibly would be living, he picked up the phone and told somebody,

"Are you ready to give Carl the grand tour?" A minute later, Mr. Ford's door opened and a man over twice my age entered. Mr. Ford introduced me to Mr. Heinz Steinman, Soulé's head of engineering and research. We all headed for the tour of the plant. There was nothing really spectacular, but it was clean and the machinery was extremely well placed and very efficient looking. We walked the complete property, which contained a couple of empty acres in the rear and about 300 feet (the length of the building to the west), which Mr. Steinman said was for future already-approved expansion. Obviously Mr. Steinman hadn't been speaking English very long. He had a very heavy German accent and was searching for the correct words. He was very nice and polite to me. On returning to the offices, Mr. Ford and I went to his office and Mr. Steinman disappeared up the stairway.

Mr. Ford then said, "Carl I want you to come to work for Soulé as a purchasing agent. I've already talked with Mr. Reinheimer, our chief executive and showed him your resume and references. After reading your material, Reinheimer told me if I wanted to hire you to go ahead and do so!" He then outlined the terms of the offer to start with an automatic 120-day escalation if we both were happy working together. I would be the purchasing agent with an assistant and secretary that I would share with my assistant. The salary offered was $50 a month higher than I made at U.S. Steel and after 120 days it would be increased by $25. Mr. Ford said, "If you accept, you'll need to be here at 11:00 a.m. next Monday to meet the founder

105

of our company, Mr. Soulé, Sr. Although Reinheimer and myself have the complete authority to hire people without Mr. Soulé's approval, as the founder of Soulé we always present our new executives for his approval. In my eight years at Soulé every person we've hired has been approved! I expect you to go home and talk to your family and I would ask for your acceptance as purchasing agent within 48 hours. I almost forgot, Carl, that following the meeting with Mr. Soulé that you and I will have a celebration lunch and I'll do my best to help you with ideas as to where to look for housing and transportation. It makes a difference when you work, not only in cost, but in your time spent traveling. I drive in from Menlo Park every day because my job requires that I have a car here. To start with, your job should not require one. Also we'll take the time to introduce you to all the people who you will be working with. From now on please call me George. I expect we'll succeed and have fun together!"

  I drove straight to the ranch and told Emily and Al my good fortune and phoned Mildred. She was delighted and agreed that I should take the job. She also suggested that I take the time until Monday to find some homes that we could look at together the following weekend when she would drive with the kids to the ranch. I then talked to Emily and Al and explained the offer and my new position as a purchasing agent. Big Al wasn't excited at all, but Emily was! I called George Ford the next day and accepted the position. I then asked George where I should possibly be looking for a dwelling to rent. He mentioned that

Mountain View had a commuter train that arrived at San Francisco train station at 8:00 a.m. every morning Monday through Saturday and was an express service when you boarded in Mountain View. The next few days I shopped around Mountain View and found a couple of nice rentals. On Monday at 11:00 a.m., I met with Mr. Soulé, Sr., Mr. Reinheimer, Mr. Steinman and George and I was officially hired. George and I went to lunch. That afternoon I met my staff, talked with George, and rented a motel until Saturday.

My first morning at Soulé was very hectic, but rewarding. My assistant and both the girl secretaries reported on time almost to the minute. I found this to be true every day from then on. Mr. Ford arrived approximately 30 minutes later, which I also counted on. The difference between George's and my arrival was that I took the commuter train and George drove to work because he needed a car in San Francisco almost every day.

On my first day immediately after George's arrival I was called to his office. "Carl," he said, "I want you to settle in with your assistant and secretary, but you're to be in charge of building an anodizing plant on the back lot." Anodizing is a form of rust proofing and giving color to sidings and roofs of industrial buildings. It brought a new dimension to the old corrugated steel buildings and certainly made them more attractive. While in Europe, Mr. Soulé had witnessed anodizing of sheets of steel, but primarily aluminum. He said, "There's no one at Soulé at this time who has the qualifications to manage this project.

I think to get started you should collaborate with Heinz Steinman—the German engineer you met earlier—his office is directly upstairs over my office. Don't worry, he's expecting you to drop by." George then said, "Everybody in the company from Mr. Soulé, Sr. on down is excited about the future growth anodizing will bring and frankly that was one reason for your being hired in spite of your youth."

I knew a great deal about steel products, aluminum and another new metal called titanium, but anodizing was really new to me. I spent a little time with my assistant, Hilda, and my secretary, Pat. They acquainted me with our physical space, equipment and most things pertinent to running a purchasing department. I told Hilda that she was to continue meeting and seeing any and all of the salespeople she dealt with. The only people that I would meet with for the time being would be people that asked for me specifically, but she was to screen them first and if possible satisfy their needs and/or requirements. I noticed from her body and facial language that she seemingly relaxed a little.

At lunchtime, I took the time to again traverse the factory and went out to the back lot, as they called it, and found it to be large enough for a building of approximately 7,500 square feet. After lunch, I went upstairs to the engineering department, which was not overly large and filled with several drafting tables and a couple of the usual stools and chairs. It was not a very imposing office, but it was adequate. As I entered, I noticed there were three men at drafting tables and one man at a desk. Chief engineer Steinman was at a table with his back to me. I approached him from the rear and stood and waited, and waited and then did something really stupid! I said, "Herr Steinman!" instead of being businesslike and polite in talking to an older superior officer. He whipped around, took a look at me and started laughing. His face lighted up, he exited his stool and came over to me put his arm around me and said, "Carl, nobody has called me that since I left Germany five years ago. Thank you." He spoke with a very heavy German accent and I found out later that his command of the English language was still in the learning stage. He then said that he was sure that our joint relationship was not only going to be productive, but also fun! A short discussion about building the new anodizing facility ensued.

Thankfully, Heinz, which he wanted me to call him by, was knowledgeable about what it took to build our new plant. He gave me some leads on information pertaining to anodizing to bone up on. He also stated that he would take the responsibility for building the structure itself and made a list of equipment necessary for anodizing. We also talked about personal issues, his and mine both, and how to get along with the other management employees within Soulé. Heinz was not on the board of directors but he, like George Ford and Bill Reinheimer, had complete authority from Mr. Soulé, Sr. to do whatever they deemed necessary for the success of the company.

During my career with Soulé, I learned from

Mr. Soulé, Sr. maybe the greatest leadership quality for success—which is surrounding oneself with men (talent) better than yourself and then having the humility to allow them to do their jobs. I left the engineering department knowing that I had made a friend and that I was with a brilliant man as a mentor again.

After leaving Heinz, I went directly to Pat and asked her if there were any messages and/or was there anything I could help her with? The answer was no, but I could tell that here again was another person who was professional and liked having me in my new position. I went to Hilda's office and asked the same question and received the same answer. I thought to myself that it was really unfair on the surface of things that Hilda, who I found out that week was 52 years old and a consummate purchasing professional, was passed over seemingly without reason. After this, I asked to see George and he waved me into his office. I told him of my long conversation with Heinz and my feelings businesswise about our departments working together. George echoed my first impressions and proclaimed that Heinz was without a peer. The balance of my first week each day was the same as the first day, but I was learning from George and Heinz daily.

On Monday of my second week, I had my first visitor to my office, who did not enter unannounced but asked Pat if I would see him. Bill Reinheimer sat down across from my desk and politely said, "Carl, how's it going?" I replied, "I'm learning as quickly as possible and

I'm really enjoying myself!" Before letting Mr. Reinheimer talk further, I said that every person within my department plus all the other departments had been more than cordial and helpful.

Mr. Reinheimer was the only Soulé employee who sat on the board of directors, which consisted of seven members, including the Soulé family. The chairman of the board was Mr. Soulé, Sr.; the associate chairman was his eldest son, Edwin Jr.; and his youngest son, Stanley, was the vice president of sales and marketing. He then asked what I had planned for the next day and if I could free up an hour. He wanted to personally introduce me to the younger Soulés.

The next day I had a phone call early from Mr. Reinheimer who said our meeting with the Soulés would be late morning and he would call me when everybody was available. We then talked about my duties as purchasing agent here at the San Francisco facility. I was astonished when he told me that I would be responsible for procuring all goods and services in the amount of over $50 million a year (goods and services would amount to approximately 50% of the money earned by this division of Soulé.)

We chatted about a few personal matters. Mr. Reinheimer was exactly 50 years old and had been with Soulé for 16 years as manager of finance and for the last six years as financial vice president and a member of the board of directors. He lived in San Francisco in a very prestigious high-rise that overlooked the Golden Gate

Bridge, Alcatraz, Tiburon, and the Bay Bridge. Because of the height of his home, he could even see to the Pacific Ocean! Mildred and I were never invited there, but neither George nor Heinz had ever been invited either.

As he left my office he turned and said that he had heard some very good things from Ford and Steinman and a couple others that I was fitting in very well. Midmorning the next day, Mr. Reinheimer called and said to meet him in Mr. Edwin, Jr.'s office in five minutes. I entered the office and they were obviously waiting for me. Mr. Soulé stood up reached over the desk and we shook hands. Absolutely nothing happened during this meeting except my meeting him and him welcoming me to Soulé. Mr. Reinheimer and I went to the next office and there was Stanley Soulé. He was a little bit smaller than his older brother and I would guess five years younger. As you would expect from a sales manager, Stanley rose from his desk, walked around and met me halfway and we shook hands. He was much easier going than his older brother and actually made a humorous quip. He said, "I've been waiting to meet the guy who I hear is really shaking up the purchasing department!" I chose not to reply other than to stick to the truth. I told him, "I'm getting a lot of help and cooperation and I am doing my best to assimilate all the knowledge and learning coming from all directions. I couldn't be happier at this moment."

Stanley talked about the new anodizing plant and all the new products we would be able to market and sell. Thanks to Heinz, I was able to carry on a somewhat intelligent conversation on the subject. We left shortly after, but as we parted in the hallway Mr. Reinheimer patted me on the back and said, "That went very well!"

The following week Heinz called and told me I was spending the day with him the next day and to wear workmen's clothes and walking shoes. He was taking me on a field trip to building sites where Soulé was the contractor. He said, "It's about time you learn the steel building business through an engineer's eyes rather than a steel worker's." I must admit the day in the field did more good for both Heinz and myself than either of us could have imagined.

Chapter 9

The Road to Success

During my on-site lesson from Heinz, I was watching the erection crew sheeting the structural frame of the buildings. It took two men—one on the outside and one on the inside placing the nut on the bolt—both using a heavy washer to prevent leakage and both also using power tools, to tighten them. I asked Heinz, "Approximately how many of these fasteners per building are needed?" He answered, "On the standard size building, probably close to 1,000 nut and bolt combinations." I asked if he had ever used a self-tapping screw? His answer was that he'd never seen one.

From my experience in the wire mill in Pittsburgh, plus being in Los Angeles and having visited the Cherry Rivet division in Santa Ana of the Townsend Company, I was familiar with self-tapping screws. Cherry rivets were a form of a self-tapping screw specially designed and manufactured to hold the skin on aircraft. My next question to Heinz was, "How much would we save if we could eliminate the man on the inside of the building?" His answer was: "Over half the labor cost, plus it would improve the safety factor immensely!" When I asked what it was costing us to purchase the bolts, nuts and washers, which were all standard, his reply was, with a grin on his face, "I don't know! That's your job!"

The very next morning I placed a call to Santa Ana and was directed to their sales engineering department to William Nicolay. I asked Bill if, in his infinite knowledge, could we take a self-tapping screw, upset the head into an umbrella shape (taking the place of a washer), and then use a neoprene rubber spray coat under the umbrella head, which would seal the hole made by the screw? Bill replied, "That really is an interesting problem, or I should say, challenge. Before we spend a lot of money, what kinds of volume could we expect per year?" I replied, "Soulé alone would use well over $1 million of these self-tapping screws and I'm sure our competitors nationwide would be using three to four times that amount. I'm equally sure that there would be many other users for a self-tapping screw that sealed itself!"

Bill said that he would get back to me by phone in 48 hours and if he received a positive decision he would be in San Francisco in a week's time. The very next afternoon I received a call from Bill stating that they were actually working on my request—and challenges such as our request were what the Cherry Rivet Company was built on. The following Monday morning I received a phone call from Bill. "What day is convenient to spend with you and your engineering and erection people?" he asked. "I already have in my hand a product exactly as you described and I am as excited as I can be. The only thing I don't have is what it actually is going to cost to mass produce this screw if it's acceptable, but I should have that within 48 hours." I told him I would talk to the engineering and erection managers and be back to him before the day concluded.

I called Heinz and told him of my conversation with Cherry Rivet. I could tell from the tone in Heinz's voice that he was more than somewhat skeptical. He said he would contact the erection manager and get right back to me. Within minutes I had a call back saying that Thursday late morning on would be perfect for them both. I arranged to meet Bill at San Francisco Airport, asking him to just call and leave a message with my girl Pat and I'd be there waiting holding a placard with his name on it at the gate. Within an hour, Pat received our instructions and Thursday was the day that I hoped would be the day that would become famous for the fastener industry.

On my arrival Thursday morning, Heinz was in my office waiting for me, all excited. All the power, electricity and gas in the new building were in and working! In addition, the new style Cookson overhead doors were being installed that morning and we had a steel building ready for the installation of all of the big tanks and tubs to be delivered starting tomorrow. As the three huge pieces of equipment had to be accurately placed in their prominent positions on arrival and not wanting any SNAFU's (situation normal all f----- up!), I told Heinz I would do my best to get the major equipment delivered on Saturday and gave him my reasons. He readily agreed!

With that and no mention of our 1:30 meeting with our erection chief, Bill from Cherry Rivet and myself, out he went. I told Pat to call the airline Bill was using and track the flight as to arrival time. I talked with Hilda about releasing for delivery immediately all of the other equipment and parts of all kinds that were needed to put us in the anodizing business, with the exception of the three major pieces, which I would personally take care of. These three custom-made tanks, or tubs, two of which weighed well over two tons, were ready for delivery. I called the tank manufacturer's number and spoke to the man in charge of our order. I specifically requested that I wanted delivery on Saturday morning of these three tanks per Heinz's request to be delivered about an hour and a half apart, giving us time for placement. We were lucky—the manufacturer was very agreeable.

I walked back to the new building to witness the installation of the new type of warehouse entry doors! This was a very large door that went up and down electronically. This was a big improvement to our buildings and Heinz was glowing. I reminded him of our meeting at 1:30 and asked him to remind the erection superintendent. I then talked to Hilda and asked how the anodizing equipment and such was proceeding? The answer was clearly affirmative and she expected it to be done that day. She had encountered no problems in filling our orders so far!

Bill Nicolay's plane arrived on time. Bill was carrying a large satchel-style bag, which contained a power tool and cords, plus several bags of our specially made self-tapping screws. On the way from the airport Bill and I discussed our joint accomplishment. By the time we reached Soulé I was certain that Bill was every bit as excited as I was! On entering my office, Bill took from his bag a few of the screws, which appeared to the naked eye to be the same. They were not, of course. They were made from different types of metal, mostly steel, but a couple of aluminum and titanium ones were also on my desk.

We discussed the merits and cost analysis of each type of screw. We also discussed the tensile strength of the different screws and the possibility that the titanium screws with the highest strength might not require the volume of fasteners needed per building. We were so enthusiastic talking about our newly created product, with questions back and forth, pro and con, and from left field, that we did not notice Heinz enter. We showed Heinz the fasteners on my desk, but there was obviously something else on his mind and he wanted to get back out to the new building and meet with the erection superintendent. As I walked out with Bill and Heinz I thought to myself, 'Heinz is going to be a tough sell . . .'

The erection supervisor was more than ready for us. He had set up two stands of our regular galvanized corrugated steel siding ready to be tested with our new self-tapping screw. After introductions, we wasted no time in starting our first big test. Bill plugged in his power tool. He placed a specially-made socket on one end and inserted one of the standard galvanized steel screws. "Where do you want me to insert the screw?" he asked. The point was established and Bill pulled the trigger. In less than five seconds it was over. Bill then handed the power tool to the erection supervisor and said, "Would it save time for you to do it rather than you pointing out where I should be doing it?" The erection man then loaded the socket with the screw and drilled the hole in less than ten seconds. Heinz finally got involved saying, "Well, you better put enough screws in that so we can turn the sheets over and examine the underside. Our erection man Joe then drilled a dozen more holes and said, "That ought to do it." This whole drilling exercise consumed less than five minutes!

Before we turned the sheets, Bill wanted to examine how the umbrella heads on the screws held up. We all looked at the different screws for any cracks or fissures. There were none, plus we could see that the neoprene washers had spread out perfectly under the umbrella head. It took all four of us to turn over our test sheets. On the inside hole, we had approximately one inch of screw showing. But even better, we could see the neoprene filling the threads of the screw all the way down and through to the inside! The first test was absolutely 100% perfect. Heinz suggested that we finish our first two sheets and then time one of his actual erection siding men to do the other sheet—testing and timing the sample fully.

Joe stepped out and returned with two men, stating, "This is what these men do for a living and they are the best men we have!" The two men, plus the rest of us except for Heinz, then returned the test sheets to their original position. Joe then took a couple of the screws and drilled a couple holes showing one man how it was done. He instructed him to finish the wall for practice and that we would time him on the next two sheets. The man completed the first test in a very short time, but it was apparent to all present that he improved as he went along.

"Ready, set and go!" Everybody in the room was looking at their stopwatches, except for our man with the power drill. With absolutely no help in any way, from anybody, he finished the test in less than 15 minutes! He apologized because he evidently felt he lost some time because he got so excited! I asked Joe how much time it took two men (one outside, one inside using our standard equipment bolt nut and washers) and the answer was 30 minutes each. Joe told Heinz, "Send a man from your department with these two men to time them tomorrow on the jobsite using our bolt and nut assembly to make sure that the timing is correct and unbiased." San Francisco in 1953 was a very heavily steel union city! The unions were known to slow down or speed up depending on what was good for the union and in this case, not for Soulé.

On completion of the timed test, Joe uttered, "My God!" Heinz scowled and stated, "Well, we still have a lot of testing to do. We all helped and turned over the second test sheet. The erection man as well as everybody in the room then proceeded to inspect the underside. Just like the first test, there was uniformity and neoprene in each and every thread identically. "Wait," Joe said, "let's give it one more test with water to see if we can dislodge the umbrella head with the neoprene. They moved the first test panel into the new structure near a very large drain. They stood the test panel upright and Bill got on one side and I on the other and we held it while they hooked up a large hose to a water outlet. Joe, on the other hand, had brought in some type of water gun that supposedly had great water pressure. Joe said to Bill and I, "You'd better get away from there as you'll probably get soaking wet!" He then turned on the water and kept increasing the pressure.

Again I thought to myself, 'this is ridiculous—there would never be a storm of this magnitude.' Nevertheless, Joe kept increasing the pressure to its maximum and then shut it down. This probably only took a little over ten minutes. We proceeded to drag the first panel back into the office and place it in position to be examined. We then dragged the second panel to the same position and performed the same test, which again lasted less than ten minutes. We all gathered, including the workmen, examining the screws for any possible problems.

This time to inspect, Heinz had produced several magnifying glasses and everybody in the room except Heinz, Bill and I inspected each and every screw. This included turning the sheets over again, underside up. There was not one flaw discovered! Another thing that I learned during these tests was that the man handling the washer and nut on the inside during the erection was in a very precarious, dangerous and unsafe position at times. I was told that there had been an accident or two because the inside worker had lost his balance! By now we had used most of our allotted time together. Bill and I both thanked Joe and his men for being so cooperative and professional and promised them that we'd make sure that they would know the outcome of their efforts.

On the way back to our offices Heinz asked me about the cost comparisons of this new self-tapping screw. Bill said, "I think even in the smallest quantities it would be less than half of what you're spending now, but by Monday I'll give you a cost per gross for several quantity levels." I told Heinz that I would have our exact costs for the past year on his desk in the morning. I could tell from Herr Heinz's demeanor that he might believe in this new cost and labor saver after all! Before Bill and I left for the airport, I asked Hilda and if it was possible to run a cost analysis on our steel building nut and washers for the last 12 months. She said, "No problem. I'll have it ready tomorrow morning early for you." I responded affirmatively that the two of us would study them together and she could fill me in on anything that might be unusual, including our relationships with their suppliers, cooperation, and length of service—even family ties if they existed.

Bill and I left for the airport and arrived about an hour before his departure time. We were both on cloud nine! Bill decided that I should wait and have a pre-celebration cocktail together. I ordered my drink and then found the closest telephone booth and called Mildred to explain that I was at the airport and as soon as Bill entered the gate I'd be heading home with what I honestly believed was good news!

While Bill and I were sipping our drinks, Bill gave me another bit of positive news. "Carl," he told me, "our research and development department put the sample screws through considerably tougher tests than what we just witnessed. They tested and retested and retested over 2,500 umbrella head, neoprene coated self-tapping screws and didn't have a single failure of any kind. I really think we have something that's going to turn the fastener industry on its ear!" This was either true or Bill Nicolay was one heck of a salesman!

The next morning the engineering department disassembled the sheets from yesterday and took 90% of them plus some of the unused samples including the aluminum and sent them to a private testing laboratory. The following day, the three major pieces of anodizing equipment would be delivered and installed in precise position according to Heinz. The engineer said he and his fellow engineers would all be there to oversee this very delicate installation. He told me to take the day off as I had done my job perfectly!

The new building and the anodizing process itself were now within two weeks of completion, testing and operation. Everybody in the company was in high spirits, as we already had received numerous orders for anodizing. At this time, Soulé had a fleet of pickup trucks but only three major trucks, one each at all three manufacturing plants located in Portland, San Francisco and Los

Angeles. That day George told me that we manufactured and furnished labor to our customers with 20% for Portland, 35% for San Francisco and 45% for Los Angeles. George asked if we had a major tie-in with any trucking company? I told him I really didn't know, but to give me a few minutes and if I did find we had a connection, I'd get some prices right back to him. I went to Hilda and relayed the question. Hilda went to the file cabinet and pulled out a large file of a company that we've been using for extra hauling for years. In the file were work copies and invoices of orders. George and I both looked at the invoices and George asked what I thought? I said, "I think we should be in the trucking business!" George had a surprised look on his face and said, "Why?" My answer was simply, "At the prices we're now paying, there is a very big margin of profit! But the main reason is that between Los Angeles and San Francisco we could give one-day service, thereby serving our customers better and making a bigger buck. George replied, "That makes sense." A few days later it was announced that we had a new transportation division! George, a few more days later, presented me with an order for two specific types of long-range trucks to be purchased immediately.

Back on the home front, our home in Bellflower had sold quickly. Mildred, as usual, had performed another superb job of preparing the house for sale. We were very fortunate again in that after all costs we had cleared in excess of 25% profit. We were renting a small house in Mountain View close to the famous 101 Highway. There was an empty building lot available within one block of our rental that had a builder's for sale sign. The particular lot was the last house on the north edge of Mountain View. The very next house was in prestigious Los Altos. It appeared to be approximately a 12,000 square foot lot. On calling the builder, he said that the lot had a 100-foot frontage and ran 120 feet deep, without any easements or deterring factors. The price for the lot was $2,500 and he also said that his company needed work right now. He further stated that he had approximately 12 different floor plans he specialized in constructing. If we would choose one of these plans, he would customize the plan to our needs and wants. In addition, to be able to retain his top employees, he would give us a 20% plus discount. He would show us past invoices and give us the names of people locally we could call for recommendations. In two weeks time our escrow in Bellflower had closed, we had a check in hand, and I had arranged for financing. We had made a couple of phone calls and the owners were extremely happy and affirmative about our builder. With his help, we customized a home of 1,875 square feet, with three bedrooms and two baths. It also included a large fenced-in yard for the children to play in. Timing is everything! All of this was happening within ten weeks of my employment with Soulé.

In less than one week, Heinz received the report from the testing lab. Our custom self-tapping screw had passed every test and without exception there were no failures! All I know is that Heinz came into my office, gave me the printed test results and told me to order the minimum amount that Cherry Rivet would produce, enough for two structures. He then walked over, put an arm around my shoulder, gave me a fatherly hug and said, "Young man, you're something!" I picked up the test results and went to George's office. George looked at them and uttered, "Incredible!" I called Bill Nicolay and requested a quote on a minimum production order. Within a couple of hours, Bill quoted a price for a minimum testing order, which would include 40,000 steel self-tapping screws and 10,000 aluminum screws. He also stated that it would be less expensive if we could order 200,000+ for production in the future and that figure was 18% less than the test order. Bill was smarter than I, because I said I didn't want the aluminum screw. Bill said, "Carl, your anodizing plant is going to be operating in a week. Anodizing is far more important to aluminum use than steel. I'll bet that the orders, especially those from the Los Angeles area, are going to be for anodized aluminum. That made sense to me. I placed the order and we were in business using self-tapping screws! Before hanging up on Bill I said, "I think we should be patenting our custom screw. Should we share the patent, or is that your prerogative as the manufacturer?" Bill replied, "No, it was your and Soulé's concept and the patent rights should be yours!"

  I went to George's office and gave him all the information about the quantities, the costs and why we should have the 10,000 aluminum screws, and George was extremely pleased. I repeated Bill's and my conversation about the patent rights. Unfortunately, the issue was put on the back burner until the completion of the two test buildings. Somebody in the top office overruled George and I.

Now the word was out that the kid in the purchasing agent's office looked to be successful! In the following week a couple of strange things happened. I know because I felt guilty that George, Heinz and Mr. Reinheimer had been spreading good words about my performance and progress as purchasing agent, but the following happenstances were unique and somewhat humorous.

The door to my office was always open and early every morning I would see Mr. Soulé, Sr. pass my door and take the hallway into the plant itself. Always going, never returning. But starting just a couple days before the anodizing plant was placed in production, Mr. Soulé, Sr. poked his head into my office and greeted me and reminded me that he was at my beck and call! This now became a daily happening! From then on I knew if and when Mr. Soulé was in town without asking.

The next odd happening was that Mr. Reinheimer would visit me whenever he saw fit. He would come in my office at any time of day and if I had people with me and/or I looked busy he would leave. If I didn't appear busy he would come in and sit down and proceed mostly to use me as a sounding board for whatever was on his mind. It became a regular unscheduled meeting. Like Mr. Soulé, Sr., this became a regular part of my employment. I should add at this point in my story that I was now 26 years old. The next occurrence without a doubt sealed my relationship with this Soulé hierarchy! Into my office came Edgar L. Soulé, Jr., the president of the company, with whom I'd had very little contact. He stated, "Carl, I'd appreciate it if in the future you would call me Lee, that's what my friends and associates call me by!" He walked over, we shook hands, and said that his office was always open and to feel free to come on in and talk whenever I wanted.

  By coincidence, on the very first day the anodizing began with the first legitimate order, the self-tapping screws from Cherry Rivet arrived. But what will always make this day so special was a people occurrence. Hilda, who rarely smiled and was all business, (and damned good at it) entered my office just before closing time. She had the biggest smile on her face that I had ever witnessed to date and stated, "Carl Meisterlin, I understand now why you were hired and I'm truly enjoying working with you!" I jumped from my chair, literally ran to her, gave her a hug and said what was honestly speaking from my heart: "Hilda, I think—no, I know—that together we make a great team and I also am having a whole lot of fun!" In my years with Soulé, this never changed.

  The anodizing and new trucking division had an immediate effect on Soulé, particularly the San Francisco plant. The anodizing operation, the only one west of the Mississippi, was flooded with orders once the word got out that we were successfully operating. Kaiser Corporation was one of the largest in the United States, a conglomerate of manufacturers and producers of basic materials such as iron, steel, aluminum, titanium and several other specialty metals, plus shipbuilding, shipping and resort hotels. They called a customer of theirs, Gilmore Steel in Oakland, and asked the head man, Al Zeller, who they should talk to at Soulé about a joint venture that included selling siding as well as using the anodizing facilities? Al Zeller gave the gentleman from Kaiser Corporation George Ford's name and phone number.

A man named Carlson called George for an appointment. When George returned the call and Mr. Carlson stated what he was calling about, George, who was very, very busy at the time with the Los Angeles and Portland operations, told Mr. Carlson that in actuality Carl Meisterlin would be the right person to talk to and he was sure that any proposal from Kaiser Corporation would receive an affirmative response. Before George could get to my office, I received a call from Mr. Carlson explaining that he had just talked to George and George said that I was the person he should be speaking with. He introduced himself as the general sales manager located in the corporate office in Oakland for Kaiser Corporation. By now, George was standing by my desk and also listening to the conversation. Mr. Carlson then said that when he came to San Francisco he liked to have lunch at the men's-only dining room at the Fairmont Hotel. He would be more than happy to buy the lunch, if I would accept. George was nodding up and down with a big smile on his face to say yes, which I did.

We made an appointment for a week from that day to meet at 11:45 p.m. in the men's dining room and I was to ask on entering for Mr. Jack Carlson. I asked was there anything that I needed to bring with me to enhance our meeting. Humorously, his answer was, "Just a brain!" George exclaimed, "Great! I'm on the road all next week. Unless something unforeseen happens, you and Hilda can make all the decisions unless there is something so important that you need to consult me, then call me and I'll get back to you." For the first time in my Soulé career, I didn't see or speak to George for ten days. From then on, George seemingly was very happy to let the San Francisco purchasing department be run by Hilda and I. He started spending a great deal of time in Los Angeles and about a trip a month to Portland. While George would be away, I gained another employee, Sam, who was George's secretary. Sam was younger then Hilda and five or six years older than Pat. She was an excellent secretary and extremely professional in any duties assigned to her, and with a wonderful attitude! She fit in perfectly with the three of us and verbally admitted one day how enjoyable it was to be doing something different and challenging!

The meeting the next week with Mr. Carlson of Kaiser Aluminum not only began another win-win situation for Soulé and Kaiser, but also initiated a major change that would affect my family's lives forever. On arriving at the Fairmont Hotel and finding the men's-only grill, I was led by the maître d' to a small but very private booth where Jack Carlson was waiting. I guess that Al

Zeller had forewarned Jack about my youth. His first words were, "I guess you and I are the two youngest executives in our respective companies." He was right. Jack, before getting down to hard business conversation, told me of his accelerated rise within Kaiser. He had been given the position of general sales manager of the aluminum division only seven months prior. He was still trying to get his feet on the ground, as he was not certain yet how much authority he had. The main reason for meeting with Soulé was location. We were the only anodizers on the west coast and they had a great need for anodizing their various aluminum products. In turn, because of our position in the western industrial building market, we were potential customers for their steel and aluminum sidings. This did not surprise me, as George and I had discussed the possibilities the week before. It made sense to Jack and myself, but where to begin? Logically, we decided that Kaiser's sales department should call on me with samples and price sheets tailored for reciprocal business. In turn it would be well for he and his project engineers to visit with our engineering department and Mr. Stan Soulé, our vice president of sales. We agreed and our lunch hadn't even arrived yet.

  Jack, I found out, was 38 years old and a family man such as myself with California roots. Although I was 12 years younger, he accepted me on an equal basis. He started talking about what he thought was going to be the biggest monetary gains in his young life going forward, whether he finished his career with Kaiser or not. I almost thought as he talked that he was trying to get me to go to work for Kaiser. In only ten days from our lunch there was to be a new stock program for not only Kaiser employees but also anybody who thought Kaiser would be a successful growing company. He didn't give me any what they call insider information. He did say an outsider could go to Sutro and Company, a large investment brokerage company in San Francisco, and buy the same stock that he was being offered. His optimism was because all of the Kaiser companies were going to be operated under one new company called Kaiser Industries, which would greatly enhance their growth and earnings in his estimation. We talked about the individual divisions of Kaiser and how they were doing and where they were going and from what he said I understood that Kaiser was enjoying too much growth and far too quickly, the same as Soulé. If you have to have a problem in business this problem is by far the best! We parted company shortly thereafter.

    The following Monday I asked Mr. Reinheimer's advice as to what Jack Carlson had talked about at lunch. Initially I talked about the reciprocal arrangement for dealing with Kaiser Corporation. Mr. Reinheimer's response was to go ahead and set up the meetings and he would appreciate sitting in with the salesmen, but he thought that Heinz, Stan and I were more than enough to meet with their raw material people for which we would be performing the anodizing. I asked if he had a little extra time for a personal investment situation I was contemplating. I then told him of the new Kaiser stock encompassing all of the Kaiser companies as explained to me by Jack Carlson. I told him that my wife and I had been very fortunate recently with a small inheritance as well as in a few stocks that I had invested in some nine months previously and had gotten lucky! I also said that Jack was using an investment company here in San Francisco named Sutro. Mr. Reinheimer without hesitation replied that he had a very close personal friend who was a top executive with the local office of Sutro and Company! I explained that Mr. Carlson was not only receiving stock and stock options, but he was buying as much as he could afford on the open market through Sutro. Mr. Reinheimer replied, "We don't have much time. I'll get on the phone immediately and find out from my friend at Sutro what his recommendation would be."

On arriving the next morning, I had a message to see Mr. Reinheimer immediately. We went outside the building to talk and Mr. Reinheimer said, "I already have an offer in for myself at the opening of the market this morning. My friend at Sutro was not advertising this new offering except to his priority investors. He was very surprised that I had any knowledge of this whatsoever. Carl, I think this is a great opportunity for a young family man such as you. I don't think that you or I should mention this around here! We're not doing anything wrong or illegal, but my friend at Sutro would like to satisfy his clients while the new stock is still available. He's expecting your phone call right now." He gave me the gentleman's business card with Sutro's address and phone number. The title under the name was 'president of investments.'

I immediately called him. He said something to the effect that Reinheimer was not only a client of his, but a friend and confidant for almost 15 years, and he would be very happy to meet me and start an investment relationship. I advised him that I could only afford to buy $10,000 worth of the new stock. He said, "That's fine, but I'll need a check within 72 hours. I can't hold the stock any longer than that!" I asked him if he could possibly fill a large offer. "How large?" he asked. I said, "A member of my family might like to purchase the stock and spend $100-$200,000." His reply was, "Well, after taking care of Bill Reinheimer and yourself, Sutro has $470,000 worth left to sell. If you're serious, I suggest you call your man and give him my name and number and I'll do my best to fulfill his request, but I can't promise. Be sure, Carl, that if he calls Sutro, he only talks with me!"

That evening I called Big Al and told him of my meetings with Kaiser and my conversation with Mr. Reinheimer. I also told him about my own gut feeling and that Mr. Reinheimer also agreed that was this would be a very, very successful company. I then told him that Mr. Reinheimer purchased the Kaiser Industries stock today and that I opened an account with Sutro and placed an order for $10,000. I told him of my conversation with the president of Sutro. Big Al was a terrific businessman! He kept asking me extremely pertinent questions about all the people from Kaiser, of which I knew only a few.

My own dad in 1953 lost his patent on his special

Mocha and Java Coffee. His coffee business was then heading in the wrong direction. But during the days of World War II, he and my mother both had become friends of Henry Kaiser and his wife. He knew several of the Kaiser executives because of the war years and I was aware that in the early years around 1950 he had bought a small amount of Kaiser steel stock, and done very well by it in a bear market. The only thing I mentioned while I gave Al the Sutro man's name and number was to be sure not to talk to anybody else. If he couldn't get the right man, he should hang up and try again! Also, time was of the essence, as the offer expired in 48 hours. I told him that I hoped my phone call served to repay he and Emily for all the wonderful things they had done for Mildred and I and the kids! The call lasted an hour. I think this was the longest single conversation I ever enjoyed with my father-in-law.

    The following day I went to Jim's office at Sutro, signed documents opening an account, and gave him $10,000 to buy shares in the new company. Jim was considerably older then myself and surprisingly older than Mr. Reinheimer. He had always worked as a financial advisor and only for Sutro for almost 40 years. He thanked me for my order that would hopefully make me a new client. As I was leaving, he said, "Thank you for sending me a great client this morning!" Then laughingly he proclaimed, "Thanks to you, I am indebted to Bill Reinheimer for many drinks and lunches." This was the penultimate conversation I had with Jim.

I had written a check from our personal house checking account, which was now close to zero. One of the four stocks I had bought nine months ago was Kaiser Steel. I had bought $5,000 worth at that time. I called my local broker in Palo Alto and asked what was it selling for today. The market had already closed for the day, but my Kaiser Steel stock was worth slightly over $8,000. I gave him instructions to sell at the opening and send the check to my address in Mountain View. Once things are going well, it seems everything goes well. The stock was up over $100 in price when sold, enough to pay the commission. That night I recounted to Mildred all of the day's conversations and occurrences. She was disinterested, but I was ecstatic! I had no reason to call Big Al and I decided that it was no business of mine what he did. Many weeks later, Big Al did mention that he was doing some business with Jim at Sutro. We never once mentioned to each other what took place, nor did I question Mr. Reinheimer.

When Big Al sold his company for all cash and retired, in the sales agreement there was a non-competing clause which stated that Al could not enter the agricultural machinery manufacturing business in any way that could be deemed competitive for the period of three years. Al had a new idea for manufacturing a Land Plane that could be used for leveling farmland and possibly roadbeds. His oldest son, Raymond, who had also quit the company along with his dad, was going to move to Reno, Nevada, a state with no income tax. In Reno, Ray was to start a new company to manufacture the Land Planes and some companion pieces of equipment. Al, who by law was unable to monetarily help in the creation of this new enterprise, then asked us to return every dollar we had inherited. Actually, Big Al ordered us to return the money saying after the three years he would repay the original amount. In addition, Raymond would also give us a share of the new company. Subsequently, we were advised that each of the four of us, excluding Ray and possibly Big Al, were to receive 5% each. Mildred and I questioned the logic. For giving up $30,000 immediately that was earning us money at the rate of over 20% per annum, it didn't seem fair to us at all.

One of the reasons that also came into play was that Ray, "daddy's favorite," was in our eyes a playboy and a terrible businessman. Without Big Al at his side, and Al having by law to stay in a hands-off business relationship, we were not confident of success. In fact, we both agreed it had less than a 25% chance for a successful conclusion. Unfortunately, Mildred and I were the only ones who didn't think it was a fair deal. Anyway, I called Ray and let him know our feelings. I could tell he was furious, and he became very insulting personally, telling me I had no right to be interfering with the Gurrea family business. He then hung up on me! A few days later I got a telephone call from Raymond in which he asked if our getting 8% would make us happy? I thanked him, and I hung up on him! I only saw Ray one more time in my life, and unfortunately for the family exactly what Mildred and I predicted over time became a reality. This subject was never discussed between Big Al and I.

In 1954, a year that truly becomes one of the cornerstones in the foundation of the Meisterlin family future, most everything was going fabulously at Soulé; almost too well as it seemed—I was asked to attend every petty meeting in other departments and felt obligated to do so! George, in the meantime, started spending considerably less time in San Francisco. The anodizing operation was booked solid and was working 24/7. Stan Soulé, Heinz, Reinheimer and Mr. Soulé, Sr. were entering into a contract with Kaiser Aluminum. I found this a little humorous: on the day Mr. Soulé, Sr. signed the contract, he entered my office and asked me to examine and approve it before he affixed his signature!

Family-wise, I came down to earth when we received the orders from Big Al to finance the Land Plane business by returning the $30,000. After the bickering and bad feelings that took almost a lifetime for Mildred and Ray to overcome, we now had a problem as to where the $30,000 was going to come from? We were not broke by any means because of the bull market affect on the $20,000 of investments that we had luckily made, but in addition to the money for Raymond, we were almost ready to close escrow and move into our new custom home. We had to make a very tough decision. We decided we must sell two of our investments. It was barely six months from the purchase of the Kaiser Industries stock, and we decided because of the money involved at that exact time, that it made sense. The day I called Jim at Sutro.

Our Kaiser stock was worth over $18,400 and I sold it immediately. Jim thanked me for the business and said he hoped I might still have use for his services in the future. He never mentioned Big Al. We also needed to sell one of our $5,000 investments that we had owned for a year, and this sold for right at $7,500. With the two sales and some money from both our checking and savings account, we purchased a cashier's check for $30,000 and sent it on to Raymond. Ray put nothing in writing and Mildred and I never saw a dollar of this money again. I estimated that in the short period of time that we had the $30,000 inheritance, mostly thanks to luck, I had earned $18,000. A lesson in life—what is given can be taken away!

Late in 1954, George came to me and stated, "Carl, I've fired the purchasing agent in Los Angeles. He gave no reason but said that he and the rest of top management would like my family and I to move back to L.A. The company felt that the Los Angeles operation, which was our largest fastest-growing manufacturing and construction part of Soulé business, really needed to have one of their people there. All the costs of moving my family and the costs in selling our new home, if for a loss, would be reimbursed. In addition, there would be a raise of $60 per month and I would have complete authority in Los Angeles, exactly the same as I had in San Francisco. I was told that the only individual in Los Angeles that I should listen to and confide in was the vice president in charge of the complete Los Angeles operation; however, he would still be my boss. "Carl," he told me, "I'm sure you'll learn and get along with E. P. McClure famously, as he is a great guy and a great executive. Talk to your wife and give me a decision ASAP."

Mildred understandably wasn't thrilled about giving up her beautiful new home and moving back to L.A. With three children, it really wasn't fair to ask this of her! I talked to my father who without hesitation said, "You have to go! You can't pass up an opportunity like this at your age. If you don't take a promotion like this your future with Soulé is zero!" At work in San Francisco the next couple of days, I sought the counsel of my three peers, George, Heinz and Mr. Reinheimer. I explained to all of them Mildred's feelings, and that we were both more comfortable living in the Bay Area. They all concurred that this would be a great move in my career with Soulé and top management. Mr. Soulé, Sr. on down wanted me in Los Angeles for many reasons.

Mr. Reinheimer, who by now I realized was by far the brains of Soulé, was the last of the triumvirate that I spoke with. He suggested we step outside. I thought Mr. Reinheimer wanted to talk about our Kaiser venture and I told him that I had been forced to sell my stock to satisfy some family problems, but at more than an 80% profit. Mr. Reinheimer then replied, "Great! But that's not what I want to talk about. Carl, Soulé expects Mr. McClure, the only really excellent man we have in L.A., to retire in five to seven years. Unless there's some unbelievably unexpected occurrence during this period of time, you're the chosen candidate for his position, as none of our top echelon will leave the Bay Area. Read the writing on the wall!" That ended our conversation.

That night, although Mildred and I talked as seriously as we two could ever do (we'd rather laugh and tease each other and play with the kids), I tried to be as fair and honest in explaining what my father had suggested and what the real top management of Soulé had expressed, particularly the last comment by Mr. Reinheimer. The following morning she agreed that we had to seize this opportunity and that we really didn't have a choice. That morning I accepted the promotion.

Chapter 10

On to L.A.

I had no idea of what to expect on my arrival at Soulé's Los Angeles division. The factory and facilities (including a large construction yard) were more than twice the size of the San Francisco operation! In contrast, the office building was a one story fairly modern building of 6,000+ square feet. I was overwhelmed as it was by far the most luxurious office suite I had ever seen, even in San Francisco. Upon entering the building there was a small reception lobby with a receptionist seated directly in front of the entrance.

On entering the purchasing department, the first office was approximately 12' x 16' and held two desks, which gave the appearance of being the secretary's and purchasing agent's desks. The next door opened into a modest but very adequate office space of 12' x 13' and contained an executive desk with chair (and matching chairs in front) as well as two extra chairs against the far wall with a small table in between. There was no paneling, but three walls were covered with beautiful paintings. The outside wall had large windows covered by wooden shutters. It was truly first class and appeared to be very recently decorated.

When I entered the lobby I said, "I'm Carl Meisterlin and I am reporting for my first day at work here in Los Angeles." She replied, "Your offices are to the right, Mr. Meisterlin. I'll call Mr. McClure and let him know you're here." As I was perusing the purchasing department, the receptionist entered saying that Mr. McClure would see me now. She led me to Mr. McClure's door, I knocked and heard a voice say, "Come in!"

I literally went into shock. Directly in front of me sat the great actor, Sidney Greenstreet! It wasn't Sidney Greenstreet, of course, but Mr. McClure did have a part-time job occasionally being Sidney Greenstreet's stand-in. Later in our relationship, Mr. McClure shared with me many stories of his movie career and his position in the movie Screen Actors Guild.

Mr. McClure gave me a local employment agency's phone number. He said, "It always helps to have a pretty secretary!" I called, and that day the lady sent me Gayle—young, eager, with great business school records, references and who was extraordinarily intelligent!

I took her school records and references and headed for Mac's office. He gave the documents a quick look saying that her qualifications seemed excellent but also that she was quite young. I replied, "I agree that she's young, but she's sharp as a tack, meets all your requirements and has a sense of humor. Before I make any commitment would you like to meet her? She'll make herself available to you tomorrow morning if you wish."

Mac asked what salary I offered her. I told him the figure and his answer was another lesson in my education as a top executive. Mac exclaimed, "That's more than we were paying her predecessor who worked here for over ten years!" Mac was surprised by my answer. I told him that the figure I offered was 10% below what I paid my secretary in San Francisco. Together, we started looking at the other clerical and office help, estimating costs. To our surprise, we found the pay scale in Los Angeles was as much as 30% lower for certain positions. Mac was very gracious and said, "That's very interesting!" We both learned something that day! He added, "I guess if we're paying this young lady that much money at her age, I should at least meet her before you put her on our team!"

The next morning Gayle arrived and I took her to Mac's office. Mac was stunned. A minute later she had Mac eating out of her hand. He did ask a few personal questions such as was she a native Los Angeles girl, where she lived and what schools had she attended, etc. As we were exiting the office, Mac gave me the 'yes' nod! I asked Gayle when could she start work and tomorrow morning was her answer. I asked her to report to the receptionist early the next morning to our personnel manager. It turned out we had no personnel manager and that Bill Tedford's secretary took care of all the paperwork.

After Gayle left, I couldn't help myself—I had to go to Mac's office. I said to him, "Well?" Mac's answer was priceless. He said, "Carl, I would've paid her more!" And we both had a wonderful, bonding laugh together.

That day, I called the employment agency to advise them that we had hired Gayle. I asked them for a young local college graduate for a position of assistant purchasing agent, preferably married, which I thought indicated stability. Again, luck was with me. She had interviewed a young man named Bob Moore that morning who had just been discharged from the Army, who had attended the University of Southern California and was captain of the USC basketball team. He was married to his college sweetheart and had one little girl and another child on the way. Before closing time I had a call back from the employment agency setting an interview for 10:00 a.m. the following morning.

The next morning when Mac appeared at his usual arrival time, I told him I was interviewing Bob Moore who used to play basketball for USC. Mac replied, "No kidding! He's a big red-headed kid who was the team captain." I then asked Mac if when I finished my interview would he take the time to talk to Bob Moore if I really liked what I heard and saw during my interview and he agreed.

This time, because of the wage fiasco of the day before, I placed a call to Hilda in San Francisco to find out what they would be offering a new candidate for assistant purchasing agent. George hadn't yet advised me that Hilda was made purchasing agent, replacing me. I was delighted when she told me the news! She deserved it. After a few kudos back and forth, I finally asked her the salary they were offering for her new replacement. I immediately subtracted 20% to arrive at a starting salary, but then thought that if I really liked Bob Moore and wanted him to join our team, I'd better only subtract 15% and be prepared to go higher with Mac's approval.

The next morning, right on time, Bob Moore came into my office. He was huge! In fact, he was taller and larger than Mac, but slimmer. His degree from USC was in business administration. He'd spent his two-year enlistment in the Army as an infantry officer, rising to the rank of first lieutenant. Bob wasn't what you call a handsome man, but he had presence. He was very aware and knowledgeable in regard to the steel industry and Soulé in particular. He also mentioned that he was a member of the Trojan Club, the very elite of the USC alumni. After talking sports of all kinds and getting Bob to relax and be himself, we discussed all the normal subjects that young men in our age bracket discuss. He even made a humorous statement to the effect that who wouldn't want to share an office with your secretary! That did it. I picked up the phone and called Mac, who told us to come on in.

Mac was already heading our way ready to shake hands when we arrived. I felt like a dwarf standing between two redwood trees. Through the media Mac already knew everything about Bob's athletic career. Within a couple of minutes these two men took a liking to each other. It was very, very obvious—to the point that I had a hard time breaking up the conversation and getting Bob out of Mac's office! On returning to my office, I offered Bob the position at a salary that was 15% less than San

Francisco offered. Before he answered, I added: "Bob, this is a big decision in your life, not only for you, but for your wife and family. You might want to spend the weekend thinking it over and talking to other members and friends." I felt very confident that on all issues except maybe the salary that Bob wanted to accept right then and there, but I took that chance remembering my own experiences.

Monday morning Bob called to accept the job at the salary offered. When his paperwork was signed, he was to come over to the purchasing department and officially meet Gayle, his office mate, and come into my office. I let him know how pleased I was with his decision and that I was really looking forward to our working together. I called Mac and gave him Bob's decision, which pleased Mac no end! He asked, "What salary did he accept?" Proudly, I told him 15% less than San Francisco offered for the same position, and gave him the figure. Mac then replied, "Well, Carl, we really learned something last week didn't we?" We both laughed.

Now that I had a secretary to greet our suppliers and whoever wanted to see the purchasing agent, I started meeting people, mostly salesman that Pat directed to our department. It was a relief actually to return to the normal purchasing agent's duties! That afternoon I met with Bill Javier, a salesman from L.A. Stationers, Inc., our sole supplier of stationery, all paper goods and office supplies from pencils to paperclips. Bill Javier became the closest friend I had until he died in the year 2,000. I liked Bill's demeanor from the very beginning! Businesswise, he was a no-bullshit salesman. Socially, he was all bullshit! Actually, as I sat there talking that afternoon getting acquainted, like Mac and Bill Tedford, I thought I had possibly met a gentleman that would become a friend. More than just a salesman, he was special. Bill was nine years older than I, bald, tall and slim. In years to come, we nicknamed him "The Naked Fox"!

**Circa 1967
Mike Flick and Bill Garvai**

The next morning Bob arrived and we held our first purchasing department meeting in which I gave Gayle and Bob the agenda for how we would operate for the next two weeks. Gayle was to show all people, suppliers and others who came to the purchasing department into my office where Bob and I together would listen and respond to what they asked and/or offered. In turn, Gayle was to be more than just our secretary. She was to be our 'Girl Friday,' running errands and being our PR girl! She loved this part of her new position as it gave her an opportunity to learn what Soulé was all about. Bob, in turn being joined at the hip with me for the two weeks, learned how and what to do and say to the salesmen who entered our offices. The very first lesson was that we treat our visitors with respect. Nothing was too trivial to consider! With that, the meeting ended and the purchasing department went to work. In my entire business career I never believed in meetings on a regular basis, only when emergencies made them necessary. If you've hired good professional people to perform a function, then you have to let them do it, not waste their time with meetings.

The next two weeks flew by and the three of us worked together better than I imagined. On the home front, things were even better than I had hoped, although I missed Mildred and the kids more than I expected. Mildred and the kids were all healthy and I talked to them every night. Because of the special deal I'd made with our builder, our total investment in our home was $16,500, which included the lot. We had listed the home with a local real estate broker, who thought we should place a sales figure of $26,900. I thought this was too high, but he was the professional and working for us on a commission basis. That evening, the first thing out of Mildred's mouth was that they were preparing an offer for the house, but before they presented the offer the financing for the purchase and all other small paper problems had to be satisfied. Our broker had told her that these problems were very routine and minor and expected to have the offer in hand within 48 hours.

    Mildred, not being a businesswoman, had forgotten to ask the amount of the offer. I laughed and told her to call me as soon as we received the offer and we'd discuss it. What I should have done was to have the broker call me in Los Angeles in the first place. Mildred called before lunch on the second day and said the offer was for $25,000. I said, "That's great. Let me take it from here and I'll call the broker immediately. I then called our broker and asked if the buyer was open to a counter offer. His reply was that the offer was predicated on special financing that the buyer had arranged in order for the purchase price to be $25,000 and he was pretty certain that was the buyer's limit. As all salesmen will do, he added, "I think the offer is a very, very fair one and the buyers are an excellent family with two young children." I told him to give the papers to Mildred to bring to L.A. this weekend, as we had to find a new home to live in and that we would have the papers to him no later than Monday. I could tell he was disappointed and that he wanted to papers back today. I assured him that we weren't playing games—he could mail them to me if that would help. The next day I received the offer at the office special delivery! Our salesman forgot one thing, he didn't have Mildred sign the document prior to mailing it, and California being a community property state needed both of our signatures. He did receive the papers on Monday as promised. At the sale of the house, we had made over $8,000 in eight months—75% more than I made in a year working for

Soulé!

    Mildred and the kids arrived Friday night and Saturday morning after breakfast we began house hunting. Bill Tedford had told me of a new housing development being built on the very west end of Anaheim, two miles south of Buena Park and Knotts Berry Farm and seven miles north of Huntington Beach pier. He and his wife had looked through the model homes and he thought they were great and a hell of a deal. The name of the project was Cinderella Homes. That morning we headed there. Upon turning into the development there was a model home complex of four homes, with the first home's garage made into a sales office. The first thing that caught my eye as I entered the sales office was the back wall, covered by a tract map of the complete project. Sticking on the individual lots on the map were red pins saying sold! The map was divided into four phases. Phase 4 had no pins and Phase 3 appeared to be 80% sold. We were early and there was a salesman who told us that they were just beginning Phase 3 and that the delivery time on the very first homes was approximately four to six weeks. The last would take approximately three months. Claudia listened intently to every word.

    The exteriors were beautiful, but none of the models came close to matching the quality and the size of either the land or the home we had just sold. I assured Mildred and the kids that this home would be temporary until we could find and agree upon a location that fit our family's needs and would be "special." I made a promise that this period of time would be less than five years.

We both agreed on Plan B—a three-bedroom, two-bath home with a base price of $13,500, plus all sorts of extras for upgrades in carpeting, wall coverings and kitchen appliances. The houses were all built on fenced lots of 72' x 100' or 7,200 square feet. The front yards and garage setback were minimal, leaving a backyard that was plenty large enough for the kids to play in and/or a swimming pool installed if one so desired, which they were also offering for the sum of $3,500.

Our salesman back at the office was there and ready. We advised him of our interest in Plan B and asked about the terms and conditions, including did they have in-house financing? He said, "Yes, we have a special low-cost financing program you won't find elsewhere. Frankly, we're not selling these units, we're taking orders." What a sales pitch! Here again our luck prevailed. He had a cancellation late yesterday on the second street to be built in Phase 3 of Plan B. It was to be finished in about 35 days. Our escrow in Mountain View was a 30-day escrow, with a one-week extension for our moving out. That meant we would have only seven days to move! I asked the salesman if I could reserve that particular Plan B for a period of one week. He agreed. With down payment of $175, to be applied to the purchase agreement, we sealed the deal.

Chapter 11

Further Adventures in L.A.

It became very evident throughout the entire Los Angeles division that there was a complete change in attitude and direction. Bill Tedford was a wonderful surprise, a man with great leadership abilities and even better sales and marketing talent. Soulé was very lucky to have Bill— he was the right man in the right place at the right time! I was personally very fortunate in that Tedford and I saw eye-to-eye 98% of the time. Working together with Mac and Bill wasn't work, it was fun, and I looked forward to it every day.

Gayle became the Soulé Los Angeles division Joan of Arc! She was not only physically beautiful, but was so willing, bright and quick to learn, that Mac, Tedford and the complete office department staff, man or woman, were using her talents. She was tireless. Bob Moore was an equally tireless, educated, intelligent young man with a desire to learn. Bob's sports background from USC had already made him extremely well known. His affiliation with their Trojan Club opened doors that enhanced Soulé's opportunities. Thirty days after forming the new purchasing department, I was receiving phone calls from some of my old buddies at the U.S. Steel office in Los Angeles. The phone calls basically asked, "Carl, what the heck are you doing over there at Soulé? It's the number one subject of conversation not only here in our office, but according to our sales staff, the whole metals industry! Plus, the word is very positive about Soulé's new leadership team; which includes you, your new assistant Bob Moore and your very beautiful and accommodating Girl Friday."

During this acute steel shortage, my connections with U.S. Steel became very valuable, because I received calls from their office when a steel order would be canceled and Soulé had first chance to replace the order. Bob Moore had a connection through the Trojan Club with Bethlehem Steel and one small local rolling mill named Finkelstein Steel that made Rebar. Bob was able to take advantage of his contacts with these two companies in the same manner as I was with U.S. Steel. Again, we were the right people at the right time in the right place!

This extra steel made the company much stronger, as we were able to keep our employees working and the cash registers ringing. This did not go unnoticed, as I heard this for the next full year from Mac and Bill Tedford. Six months after my move to L.A., I received a call from my boss, Heinz, in San Francisco, letting me know that the corporate officers were very aware of our accomplishments. We chatted briefly about the usual things and he told me that he had bought a piece of property in Marin County across the Golden Gate Bridge that stood on the side of a small wooded mountain about 1,000 feet above sea level and that he was designing a home for he and his wife. Approximately 18 months later, Heinz's home appeared on the cover of Architectural Digest! It was a cantilevered structure, almost all glass with a 270-degree view of the Golden Gate Bridge, San Francisco and Oakland, Treasure Island, Alcatraz, Tiburon, and a little further northeast. It must have been magnificent!

Time was flying by, as it always does when you're enjoying yourself. I was! About 90 days after my start in L.A., I received a call from Mr. Howard McBurney, the top executive for National Screw and Manufacturing, another large fastener manufacturer, asking for an appointment. We set a date and when that time came I met another mentor who would again help to shape my career and life forever, including my family life.

Gayle led Mr. McBurney into my office and when she closed the door he exclaimed with a big grin on his face, "Wow! What a gorgeous young lady!" To which I replied, "Believe it or not, her professionalism, talent and attitude exceed her good looks!" Mr. McBurney said, "How about you calling me Mac, and I call you Carl." As Mac was a very handsome 50+-year-old gentleman, I was flattered and at ease. He shifted the conversation around to the new umbrella neoprene self-tapping screw. In his words, I had revolutionized the fastener industry with my concept. Because of our new fastener, National Screw and Manufacturing was now producing a new washer with a bonded neoprene undercoating to use not only with self-tapping screws, but a full line of regular bolts and screws and had increased their sales of these standard items by over 30%. He thanked me for not only for opening their eyes, but to let me know that they would supply all of our other fastening products with a special 20% discount after our usual discount as a thank you!

We then discussed the business climate and how my wife and family were readjusting to L.A. He told me some of his background and how he got started in business. He now lived in a home on Ocean Avenue on the bay in Long Beach within walking distance to the famous Pacific Club. He started asking me questions about the special corporate training program that I was so lucky to be a part of at U.S. Steel. I told him about the training at the ground level in the various stages of producing iron and steel. He was intrigued by how I had worked everywhere from the blast furnaces, open hearths, annealing, wire mills, rolling mills, sheet and tin departments and even training in structural steel, for which I was sent for a three-day, two-night education at the mill in Geneva, Utah. I admitted to Mr. McBurney that I had no idea why and how I was selected for the program except being in the right place at the right time! I admitted that I was not a college graduate, but that I did have an extremely intelligent and wise father.

Mr. McBurney's reply was, "That's the same as my own personal history. Carl, you're obviously a very special young executive, even younger than I expected. That's not meant to be negative but to be complimentary! I think that I know of two possibilities that are available at this very moment for a young executive that you should look into immediately. There's a very prestigious men's-only club in downtown Los Angeles called the Jonathan Club, which is having a junior membership drive until the end of this month. It's an absolutely wonderful businessman's club that is ideal for eating and entertaining; has a spa facility, physical therapy, swimming; and holds all sorts of business educational seminars on a regular basis. To qualify you must be under 30 years of age, be recommended for membership by two present members and pay $250 total. I'll have two of my junior executives who are members sign an application which I will send to you and then it's up to you. I'm also an officer in the American Management Association, which costs next to nothing. This organization is strictly for meeting other executives, having lunch and listening to outstanding educational speakers. This organization meets quarterly and the cost depends on where it's held and the lunch. It's usually about $20 per lunch. It's outstanding and I'll send you the application for that plus a calendar of the meetings for the balance of 1955."

    On the way out the door I introduced Mac to Bob Moore. Mac, being a USC fan, was very familiar with him. We stood and talked together (actually they did all the talking and I listened until they stopped), at which time I told Mac that National Screw would be dealing with Bob directly as fasteners were his responsibility. Mac seemed to like that arrangement and as he left our offices he told me he thought we'd be seeing a lot of each other—and for many years we did.

In the afternoon, the other Mac was in, and I spoke to him about the junior membership at the Jonathan Club and what he thought of my possibly joining, as I had two sponsors and met all the requirements. He said "I think that's a great opportunity not only for you, Carl, but for the Southern California division of Soulé!" He went on to say that Soulé was not represented in the membership of the Jonathan Club and he had always thought that we should be. In fact, he said he'd always thought that he should probably be a member. The problem was that the location was not convenient. He lived in the San Gabriel foothills and spent most of his time at Soulé or in Santa Monica at the studio, or San Gabriel at Santa Anita Racetrack. Of course he asked me not to advertise the latter! He asked what a junior membership would cost. I repeated what Mr. McBurney had quoted, that the total cost was $250 until the member reached the age of 30, at which time it was applicable to the full $1,500 lifetime membership! Mac thought it was very inexpensive. He said, "Carl, you join the Jonathan club ASAP. I have enough money in my budget for things such as your membership and I'll just pay it out of my budget." Within ten days I was a junior member of the Jonathan Club, which did help the Soulé organization as well as myself.

On the home front in March Mildred announced that she was pregnant! She was happy, as she wanted to present Big Al and me with a son and a grandson. Our

Cinderella Home was finished right on time and the physical move was easy, as we spent every dollar necessary to make it effortless. As Mac ordered, "Soulé's paying for it and your family deserves the best service available!" Mildred and the children seemingly were happy with their new home, especially when the first thing we bought was a playhouse for the girls.

Two negative problems appeared at this time regarding both my family and the relationship between Mildred's family and mine. My father was a very, very proud man. He had never told me the exact details of he and Leon's purchase of the Theirbach Coffee Company from George's estate in January 1, 1948. George's Will stated that either Leon or my father or both equally had first option to purchase the company at a price he established dating back to pre-World War II. The price was extremely low. Leon and my dad both took advantage of this opportunity equally. There never was a problem between these two that ever reached my mother's ears. What I didn't realize was that the property itself was not included in the sale but was on a lease, which was also very favorable to the lessees, Leon and dad. In February 1953, the company's patents expired on the Mocha and Java Blend, the only coffee Theirbachs ever sold!

All of their competitors west of the Mississippi (Hills Brothers, Folgers and Peerless Coffee, a direct competitor who also only sold to restaurants, hotels and repacking for small market chain stores) immediately were offering a mocha and java blend on the open market! Initially their mocha and java blends were not the quality of dad's, but the price was 20-30% lower, and as the competition between these four companies intensified the prices deteriorated even further. The company's top restaurants and hotel customers who insisted on quality started asking for price breaks and worst of all they lost their one and only repacking customer, A & P Markets, who accounted for almost 40% of their production. By the end of 1953, the company was now unprofitable and unbeknownst to me was up for sale.

Both my mom and dad took and passed the California Real Estate Exam and became realtors—dad a broker and mom a salesperson. Interestingly, they took exactly the same test on the same day. The difference between the sales and brokers license was $10. During this time mom and dad had become good friends with Emily and Big Al and they played Bridge together whenever possible. My mother, years later after dad had passed on, said that during some of the Bridge games Al and my dad openly discussed where to invest money.

According to my mother, it was in late 1953 to early 1954 when dad's closest friend Bob Ramsey asked him if he had a source of capital in order to expand his most treasured property, the Highlands Inn located in Carmel Highlands, where both mom and dad had stayed occasionally. Ramsey wanted to expand by adding a dozen suites above the swimming pool facing the Pacific Ocean with an unobstructed view. He was willing to pay 8% interest on the $400,000 needed, double or more what banks and commercial lenders were offering at the time, for a period of three years. As collateral, he would put up the Highlands Inn land and hotel.

Dad took this offer to Big Al, they met with Ramsey the following week, and both Ramsey and Big Al were extremely satisfied. According to my mother, they became friends for life. Shortly thereafter, mom and dad received a check from Ramsey in the amount of $5,000 as a finder's fee—the amount of money necessary for mom and dad to live comfortably for a year. The architectural plans for the expansion were finished prior and within a week construction started and was finished in less than five months.

The suites were a smashing success and Ramsey told Big Al and dad they had increased the total profit margin of the hotel 40% in just seven months. Ramsey paid off the loan six months early. Ramsey said that on the adjoining property up the road past the swimming pool suites sat a pristine cottage with a gorgeous guesthouse down the hill, both overlooking the ocean. They were up for sale by the estate of a state senator named Tickle. The problem was Senator Tickle and Ramsey had not been on speaking terms for 20 years. In Senator Tickler's Will there was a stipulation that his property, called The Tickle Pink, was not to be sold to Bob Ramsey or the Highlands Inn. What Ramsey wanted was for Big Al and dad to pursue the purchase of The Tickle Pink. Big Al, who was a well-known retired industrialist with means; and my dad, acting as his real estate broker, would buy, build and operate a motor inn for a period not to exceed two years, built to the specifications of the Highlands Inn, which later would become another addition to the inn. The architectural plans would be given to Al at no cost to give the builder, who was to be the same builder who had constructed the swimming pool suites. Nowhere in the agreement between Ramsey and Big Al was a stipulation that Big Al had to sell the finished Tickle Pink to Ramsey and/or the Highlands Inn. Let me make this clear—Bob Ramsey had the contractual commitment to buy the property and buildings thereon, but Big Al had no obligation to sell.

The next week my dad, acting as a real estate broker representing a client interested in purchasing The Tickle Pink property, phoned the real estate broker, Rose, who represented the estate, for an appointment for he and his client ASAP. Two days later, dad and Big Al met with Rose and inspected the property. Rose lived for over 50 years on the first residential lot next to the Highlands Inn Wedding Chapel. After bringing all the detailed estate information back to Bob Ramsey, the three began negotiations. My dad said he had very little to do with the negotiations except to question and recommend some bargaining practices. His position was strictly the potential buyer's real estate agent. Ninety percent of the bargaining was dictated by Ramsey, and the remainder by Big Al. An offer was made and rejected by the estate, but they counter offered. Big Al, based on Ramsey's instructions, re-countered. This bargaining went on for another week until they struck the deal that satisfied both parties.

Escrow closed 30 days later on an all-cash transaction. My father received $10,000 as his brokerage and finder fee commission. According to my mother, half of the fee was paid by Big Al, and half by Bob Ramsey. I knew absolutely nothing about my father's involvement as a paid real estate broker. I thought he was doing this strictly on a friendship basis. Ramsey hired for Al a few local workers who started site cleaning immediately. This meant clearing and leveling a plot of land of approximately an acre. It also entailed the removal of three or four trees for which they received permission from the local planning commission. The property was zoned commercial, the penultimate commercial building site on Highway 1, for a stretch of 10 miles south to famous Big Sur.

The first architectural drawings were taken to the local planning department for expedited approval, and as the property involved was commercially zoned, this was a routine matter at that time in history. The approval came about four to five weeks later, and the completed architectural and working drawings almost the same time. We were visiting the ranch in Gilroy on a long weekend then and I remember Big Al's saying, "Come on, Carl, let's go see what's happening down at the building site."

We were driving up the road to the entrance to the Highlands Inn when Big Al spied a car sitting behind a small chapel. He stopped, backed up and took the road up to the parked car. As we were getting out of the car, Al stated, "I want you to meet Rose, the lady who helped me put this deal together." A lady about Al's age appeared in the doorway and Al introduced me to Rose, who showed no interest in me. Rose invited us in but Al said, "I wanted you to meet my son-in-law." He asked her if there was anything she needed. She answered no and we left.

One minute later we were in the parking lot for the new inn. It looked great from the front, but as we made our way around this structure to the rooms, which all had balconies overlooking the Pacific Ocean, the view was unbelievably magnificent! It was a perfect day, but I was totally overwhelmed by the view, as was Big Al!

Nothing unusual happened on the way home other than conversation pertaining to the magnificent view we had just encountered and Al answering some economic questions I had for personal use in my career. I never asked what he paid for the land nor did Al ever tell me! But I was very interested in what the building costs on a square foot basis were. The building itself was to contain 35 total rooms, including approximately 10 suites. The building had three floors. There were two suites downstairs, one of which was to be called the owner's suite. On the middle and top floor there were four suites. The middle and top floors held 12 rooms and/or suites. The nine rooms downstairs were slightly different. Each suite had an adjoining small bedroom with bath making the suite basically three bedrooms three baths! The two extra rooms could also be entered from the balcony and locked off from the suites thereby providing 35 rentable rooms. He said that the total contract costs for the building itself plus the parking and land site preparation would be just under $500,000. I remarked that I thought that was very inexpensive. His response was that they got very lucky as their prime contractor was in need of work and we were paying cash. From his experience building the swimming pool suites, the contractor was very happy to have the work at the negotiated price. I then asked about the furnishings, which I presumed would be ultra first-class to go along with the phenomenal views. Big Al assured me that the same decorator who did the swimming pool suites would do the work and for under $100,000. I'm not sure why, but I had the feeling that the total cost was going to be under $1 million.

As The Tickle Pink was nearing completion, the manager of the Highlands Inn for the past decade applied to Al for the management position for he and his wife. I thought this was rather odd, but I never asked my dad, Bob Ramsey or Big Al what was going on. The Tickle Pink opened and it was immediately successful! Not only did it bring curious people who'd heard about it, but on Friday and Saturday nights they were booked solid from overflow from the Highlands Inn.

From day one I learned from my dad that it was making money hand-over-fist—he referred to it as a cash cow. But after five to six months Big Al thought that something was wrong because after four weeks in a row they were not selling out on weekends during the peak tourist season. Al and Emily turned detective. For two Fridays and Saturdays they literally snuck into the parking lot. The Tickle Pink's parking lot was barely large enough for one car per room and only had room for six or seven extra cars. So when they were sold out, there were no parking places available. On all four nights that they sat in their car, Al and Emily observed that there was not only no parking places available, but people were parking in the trees above The Tickle Pink and carrying their luggage back. The following Monday morning, Al presented himself to his manager and asked to see the books for the weekend. The books indicated five vacancies on Friday, six vacancies on Saturday and ten vacancies on Sunday. At this time the regular rooms were renting for $165 per night and the suites for $215 per night. Both Fridays indicated two suites and three rooms not rented and were exactly the same rooms for both Fridays. The same thing prevailed on Saturday nights—two suites and four regular rooms not rented, and exactly the same rooms.

Big Al liked telling this story! "On that Monday morning I examined the books, and then said to the German manager, 'my wife and I were here both last Friday and Saturday and this Friday and Saturday, and I happen to know that you were sold out and there were no vacancies. Now, do you want me to get the police or are you vacating by noon?'" He and his wife disappeared shortly thereafter. Al also said that nobody had seen or heard of them since!

Big Al also had an ace in the hole. His loyal sales manager at the farming equipment company in Gilroy and his wife, a bookkeeper, were both recently out of work.

Mr. and Mrs. Byde arrived at noon and started work immediately. Directly under the ground-level office were very nice manager quarters, which contained a small living room, eating area, standard kitchen area a fairly large bedroom with a beautiful bathroom with a walk-in tub and shower. Big Al said he told Mr. Byde to try running the place for a week and if he and Mrs. Byde wanted a full-time job, they'd work something out. Before the week was over they accepted the positions at a salary of $40,000 a year—$30,000 for the manager's job and $10,000 for a bookkeeper clerk. This was more than they had earned while working for big Al previously. Everyone, including all family members who knew the Bydes, was happy.

After a couple weeks, they hired (with Al's permission) two part-time employees to work the front desk and do odd jobs. Big Al stated that the income per week increased by over $2,500. Al and Emily were darn good detectives! From then on the monies rolled in far greater than the monies earned in the farm industry business and those words came to me from Big Al's mouth.

On the home front everything was fine, except Mildred was having some trouble carrying the baby. We decided that when we got close to delivery time, which was August, that Mildred would go to the ranch and prepare to have the baby at the Stanford Hospital in Palo Alto. All was well with me and with our home in Anaheim, but with a new baby on the way I realized that we needed more space. On weekends we again occasionally started searching for a new location to build more than just a house, but something on the order of a mini-ranch. Financially, though we weren't rich, we were living comfortably and earning and saving more money then we spent.

Things at Soulé in L.A. were going well and I was making some extremely good friends, particularly Bill Garvai, Bill Tedford and several people from the Jonathan Club and the American Management Association. Garvai was an avid golfer and belonged to the Palos Verde Golf Club. Bill invited me to play as his guest at his club at least once a month and I reciprocated by meeting him at the Jonathan Club downtown, which was less than five minutes away from his office. Bill and I were each other's best friends for the rest of his life, but it was he who really got me hooked and addicted to golf!

My business and social life were almost meteoric, as nothing would go wrong. The AMA, in only the space of two lunches, I found to be inspirational. There was so much that I learned! I realize that my success to this point was entirely due to my father's training and people I've already mentioned, but mostly due to being in the right place, with the right knowledge, at the right time.

During the months waiting for the baby to be born, I noticed that I not only was I not hearing from my direct boss and mentor, George Ford, but that he hadn't made a trip to L.A. that I was aware of. Nor had I heard from Mr. Reinheimer! I called Ford and asked him if I had the plague. He laughed and said, "Carl, you obviously don't need any help down there, as the word here is why can't we do things the way L.A. is doing it? Unfortunately,

Hilda and I haven't been able to pull off the miracle of obtaining extra steel and aluminum needed to keep the factory running satisfactorily. We're working day and night. In fact, I've been traveling all over the country attempting to find allotments of materials and they are at exorbitant prices. I just haven't had the time to spend with you when you don't need me!" Two weeks later I received a phone call from George from St. Louis, Missouri and he said he'd be in my office tomorrow morning at 9:00 a.m. if I was available. George arrived on time as usual, and I had alerted Mac and Tedford of George's plans. It was no secret that George was the favorite man in San Francisco with these two!

When George arrived, the first thing I asked him was when he had to leave and found out it was 3:00 p.m. that day. I introduced George first to Gayle and then to Bob Moore and as usual George made the time to talk, asked questions and made attempts to put them at ease; but let them know that it was he who was my direct superior! He also encouraged them that if something happened and I wasn't available, that they should phone him directly. His last remark was that the work all three of us were doing great, not only in purchasing, but for the morale of all Soulé.

When we arrived at Mac's office, Tedford was already there. Mac and Tedford were ready for George with several inter-divisional questions—nothing serious, but questions that needed a San Francisco insider's answer. I was surprised that Mac had a couple of pertinent questions, mainly about Mr. Soulé, Sr.'s health and managerial ability. I'd never given that a thought! George wanted to tour the plant and see the new Electrolytic Paint Line (EPL) that we had installed, plus the new type of truck we were now using to service Arizona, Nevada and Santa Barbara. Before leaving Mac's office I invited all three to lunch at the Jonathan Club. Tedford and Mac had previous engagements, but George said he'd heard of the club but never been there and would enjoy it very much. We could go from there directly to the airport.

He liked the Jonathan Club and mentioned that he should probably join the Olympic Club in San Francisco. We talked without stopping through lunch and to the airport about Soulé and where it was headed. We also discussed Mr. Soulé, Sr.'s health and managerial capacity in reference to Mac's earlier question. George let me know that since I had left San Francisco, that Mr. Soulé, Sr. was slowing down quite a bit, both physically and mentally. After all, he was 75 years old. He was making a very concerted effort to turn over his responsibilities to Lee, the president. We both liked the Soulé's very much—they all were gentleman and treated us as such. We agreed there was nothing negative you could say about Lee or Stan, but that they lacked Mr. Soule, Sr.'s spark! I asked George pointedly about Mr. Reinheimer and Heinz. He surprised me when he said that he would not be surprised if Heinz retired soon or possibly took another direction in his career, due to the notoriety he was receiving nationwide over his new home. He was the toast of the northern California architectural engineering profession, as well as being almost 60 years old!

Reinheimer, on the other hand, was much busier than usual. Because of the crippling steel shortage, we were experiencing hard times. Profit was down in all divisions, except L.A. Reinheimer estimated that in 1956, the Los Angeles division would earn 80% of the profit in the company. George said, "You need not be concerned, Carl, because the board of directors credit you, Tedford and McClure for the success. Lee Soulé, in particular, is taking a hands-off position regarding L.A. The company, in spite of the economy, increased both sales and earnings just under 20% last year and at the rate we're going, it should improve this year. Reinheimer, Heinz and myself believe that much of Soulé's success recently has come due to your energy, enthusiasm, contacts, management training and people skills. Reinheimer likes to say that you make the people surrounding you more competent, productive and even happier. But he did warn me to not ever get complacent." I thanked George for all the kind words and praise. But again, I repeat, I had just happened to be the right person in the right place at the right time.

George didn't visit L.A. again for over a year. About six months after his visit, Mac asked me if I'd heard about George getting into politics? He was running for Mayor of Menlo Park and had started campaigning the previous week. He told both Lee Soulé and Reinheimer that he would be curtailing his duties at Soulé until the election, which was two months away. I did phone

George and congratulate him and wished him well. Two months later he became mayor of Menlo Park and never really worked full-time for Soulé again.

I actually never saw or heard from Mr. Soulé, Sr., seldom from George, and received only one phone call from Heinz telling me he was retiring in a few months and that he was not positive where he and his wife's lives would lead. Maybe back to Germany! There's always two sides to a coin and the good thing for Soulé was because of George's, Bob Moore's and my efforts, we were finally getting all the steel products we needed at all our production facilities. In 1956, our L.A. division spent $125 million through our purchasing department—almost double what was spent in 1953!

On August 23, 1955, my son Carl Albert Meisterlin was born at Stanford Hospital and I almost lost Mildred in childbirth. My life was beginning to change and I was finding that I was enjoying life from my position at Soulé. Playing golf, in particular, became an addiction, but as long as Mildred was happy at home I started playing golf every chance I got. I played every Sunday morning at the crack of dawn almost always in the fog at a little course in North Long Beach across the street from Douglas Aircraft called Lakewood Golf Club. It was a public course, and at least one afternoon a week I played with whoever would join me and wherever we could obtain a starting time. I continued receiving wage increases and Mildred and I were definitely able to be on our own with no help from family.

Chapter 12

Another Good Move

On George's departure I took the time to return to the EPL operation. It rang a bell in my memory of a conversation I'd had with my new friend Bill Garvai about a customer of his who for several years was going through an ownership and management problem.

The company's name was Diamond Perforated Metals of California, a division of a parent company named Diamond Perforated Metals. I asked Pete whether we had ever done any work for Diamond Perforated. "Not that I remember," he answered. On going back to the main offices, I went directly to Bill Tedford's office. "Bill, has Soulé ever performed any work whatsoever for a company named Diamond Perforated Metals?" He made a call, which confirmed that we had no record of any activity with a Diamond Perforated.

"Bill, I have a friend who has called on this firm on a regular basis for many years. Without getting anybody excited, would you personally (not your staff) do some financial sleuthing and see if they're for real? I believe we're missing the boat! Don't do any more than check their financials and let me know ASAP. In the meantime,

I'll be in touch with my buddy Garvai and if both of you come up with positive info, I'll arrange a meeting with them for you and I. As you're the general sales manager here in L.A., you'll be the lead man and I'll be the sales engineer you're bringing along for an analysis of how our two firms will coordinate."

I placed a call to Garvai and asked how I could arrange a meeting with the head man at Diamond Perforated. Bill responded that the new owner had arrived yesterday and stated that he made his monthly sales call on Thursday with his man. "I'll phone you immediately after my appointment at 9:00 a.m.," Bill said. He reminded me that we had a starting time at Palos Verdes Golf Club on Saturday at 8:40 a.m.

Late the following day, Tedford walked into my office with good news. "Diamond Perforated Metals is located in Gardena just off the intersection of the Harbor and 405 freeways. For the past six years they have had an excellent credit rating." I inquired if anything was said about a change in ownership. Tedford replied that nobody had mentioned anything negative about the company. On Thursday morning, right on time, I received my phone call from Garvai saying that the new owner was going to be a hands-on owner who would be working daily with the present staff. Bill went on to say that Mr. Dave Hall was going to be a huge improvement for the employees because they had received no direction from the home office for over three years. Bill said that the man was expecting my phone call and already knew about our friendship both in business and on the golf course! "If I were you, Carl, I'd hang up and call him immediately for further instructions to obtain a meeting with Mr. Hall. See you in the locker room around 8:00 a.m. Saturday."

I went to Tedford's office. I frankly didn't want the rest of the sales force aware of our actions regarding Diamond Perforated yet! I told Tedford word-for-word what Garvai recommended. Tedford handed me his phone and I dialed Diamond Perforated and asked for the man on my notepad. We set a time to meet on Monday. I told Tedford, "Frankly, I don't care what's on your calendar, you and I are going to be there!" Bill gave me a very questioning look. "Okay! I'm available, seeing as you put it that way!"

Garvai and I played golf and I thoroughly enjoyed my day as Bill was giving me some good instructions, which were improving my game. We also talked about Diamond Perforated and how Joe, who was the plant manager, and all the employees, liked their new owner and boss. Garvai mentioned in his short meeting with Joe that he noticed a significant change in morale. He also stated that Joe had made a special 9:00 a.m. appointment on Wednesday for him with Mr. Hall. He asked if I would call him Monday after our meeting to help prepare. Like Soulé, Bill received all of Diamond Perforated's stationary, pencil and paper business, etc.

On Monday we were led directly into an office with no name on it where two men, approximately Tedford's age, were standing. Bill spoke first, introducing himself, and then introduced me. The larger of the two men stepped forward, hand outstretched. "I'm Dave Hall, Dave for short, and this is my plant manager Joe Phillips." Dave asked what he could do for us and for Soulé? Tedford replied, "We have a great deal of specialized equipment that my sales engineer purchasing manager Carl believes will be very important to Diamond Perforated both now and in the future." Dave replied, "That does sound interesting. I think that possibly the best thing we four should do is witness our operation. Joe, lead the way."

We followed Joe into the plant. Dave instantly asked why I was certain that our companies needed each other. I answered, "Dave, it comes from being a steel worker, a U.S. Steel L.A. sales department employee and a purchasing agent for Soulé in both San Francisco and L.A."

My most notable impression of the plant was the enormity of the machines required to manufacture perforated, expanded metals and other specialized products made from steel, aluminum, titanium, copper and even an unfamiliar form of plastic. Joe and Tedford were in serious conversation and I could tell from Bill's body language he was on to something! Dave and I continued our conversation pertaining to Soulé, which Dave had no knowledge of whatsoever. He admitted that he had only arrived ten days ago in L.A. With Joe's help, he and his wife Catherine had been looking at homes to purchase in the Palos Verdes Estates area, which was less than a 15-minute drive to work. In fact they had found a home that was perfect for them in an area called Rolling Hills and they were making an offer that afternoon! I responded that I had been in Rolling Hills Estates only once, but in my estimation, it was one of the finest areas in Southern California. I told Dave that I thought he should check Soulé financially and tour our property, plant and newly completed EPL. Dave's facial expression changed. "Did I hear you correctly Carl? You have an EPL facility?"

I replied, "Yes, and I would like you to visit and bring Joe if you desire." Dave said, "Carl, I'd be there this afternoon if Catherine and I weren't making the offer on the house. I can be there in the morning as early as you can give me the tour and, yes, I'll bring Joe." It was decided that between 8:45 a.m. and 9:00 a.m. they would be at Soulé. We then asked Joe and Bill if they would join us tomorrow. Joe and Dave agreed, as did Bill.

As Bill was driving us back to Soulé, he said, "Carl, you were correct, there's a great deal of materials they should be purchasing from Soulé and an equal amount of cutting and fabricating that we could save them lots of money over the methods they're now using." I replied enthusiastically, "I'll bet money that our EPL operation will save and make them more money! Tomorrow we'll get an even better idea, as I believe that Dave was completely astounded that Soulé had an EPL."

The next morning Dave and Joe arrived early. From the questions, facial expressions and side trips to view certain specialized machinery, I could tell that they were very impressed. When we entered the plant, Pete, our plant manager, joined us and answered 98% of the questions. Dave was almost speechless as he stood looking at the EPL. I thought to myself for a moment that Dave was going to cry. All of a sudden he started laughing, loudly laughing to the point that he visibly embarrassed himself. Finally he said, "Please accept my apologies for being somewhat out of order, but seeing your new EPL operation, I don't know whether you're aware that your EPL is the finest in the country! Carl, Bill and Pete—we've seen everything we need to. And, by the way Carl, your prediction was understated."

As the four of us walked back to the offices, Dave said, "I'm going to have Joe make out a list and research all of the products and services that we saw today as a total estimation other than the EPL, which I'll handle myself. If Tedford and you will do the same, I'd like to continue this meeting later this week if possible. Believe it or not Catherine and I plan to move in to our new home next weekend. Oh, and yes Carl, someday remember to ask me why I started laughing, it's a great story you will never forget. In the meantime, hopefully I'll see you later this week. Also I think from now on Joe will probably be in touch mostly with Pete, but maybe Tedford on occasion."

I phoned Garvai immediately and told him that Dave Hall was one hell of a guy and that he was going to like him. "He has a great sense of humor, is very intelligent, well-educated and knows nothing about Southern California; consequently, I think you can make, hopefully for both your sakes, a friend for life!"

Garvai asked a few pertinent questions, one of which was, "How does he get along with Joe?" I replied, "From what I saw, Bill, they make a great team and seem to enjoy working together. My guess is that Joe's employment status is far, far better now than previously." Late that afternoon, Tedford contacted both Stan Soulé and Reinheimer in San Francisco and repeated our successful meeting with DPM. He asked for financial assistance in forming a mutual alliance similar to the Kaiser arrangement. Bill also told me that he told both Stan and Reinheimer that it was all my doing, which it wasn't. It was, as always, a person with the right amount of knowledge being in the right place at the right time with a solution. That's what luck is all about! I went back into the plant and found Pete and suggested that he contact Joe at DPM and even possibly visit Joe ASAP so that we could estimate what we could do for one another. Two days later Pete called and stated that he had visited DPM and he and Joe were working together diligently. He said he really liked Joe, whom he proclaimed was no ordinary plant manager. We didn't have all our figures together from San Francisco, Tedford, Pete and DPM until closing time Friday. On Monday, Soulé and DPM agreed to terms and conditions for a mutual alliance benefiting both companies.

After the Monday meeting, Dave phoned me and thanked me for what I had done for he and Catherine and he had talked so much about me that they would like to invite us to dinner at a mutual restaurant. I said, "I'm sure Mildred and I would accept, but she always has the last word." I asked him if he would meet us at my private club, the Jonathan Club, which he was not acquainted with, but we would let them pick up the check if they wished. I added that I very seldom got to take Mildred to the club, and was forever talking about it. Dave said, "Well, I'll have to talk to Catherine about the Jonathan Club idea, but it sounds great to me." I let him know that one of our big problems was getting a babysitter. Dave said, "Been there!"

    A lady across the street had been kind enough to babysit for us occasionally and she stated she was available almost any time for the next two weeks. I phoned Dave the next day and we set a date for dinner and getting acquainted. The evening was a complete success—the ambience, and the delicious food and fantastic service at the Jonathan Club was superb. Actually, what really made the evening were the four people sitting around the table, all different in age and maturity, who instantly became friends for years. At that time, Catherine was 42, Dave 32, myself 27, and Mildred 25. Unbelievably, we had everything in common—mostly a sense of humor!

    During dinner, Dave and I started discussing golf. Dave was an excellent single-digit golfer in Pennsylvania, where he used to play three days a week, also at a private club. He also mentioned that my friend Garvai had invited him to play Palos Verdes Golf Club on a Saturday that I would play, which he was looking forward to. I replied,

"That wouldn't be this Saturday would it?" "Yes I hope it is," Dave replied. I asked Mildred if it were all right if I joined Garvai and Dave that day. It wasn't a fair question, as under the conditions, she could hardly say no. The evening ended on a high note, with dual invitations for dinner and cards at each other's homes in the near future.

On Saturday I arrived on time, as did Bill and Dave. We changed shoes and proceeded to the driving range to warm up. Bill was to ride with Dave in one golf cart and I was to ride with a General James Walsh, a retired Marine Air Force commanding officer who had served in four wars starting with World War II. It was another spectacular Palos Verdes day on a great golf course with three men I truly enjoyed. The lunch and the splendor of the clubhouse with its view of "The Necklace," as it was called, were equally enjoyable. The only negative was my inability on the golf course. It was evident after the golf and lunch that Dave really enjoyed everything about the Palos Verdes Golf Club! After lunch, Dave, Bill and I made a date for lunch at the Jonathan Club later the following week and a golf game back at the club in two weeks.

The following months flew by as Bob Moore and Gayle continued taking on more responsibilities and receiving most of the credit for the continuing improvement in morale. Mac, Tedford and I continued to be applauded for the accomplishments and the profit and loss columns of Soulé; particularly L.A., the most profitable division by far in the company. As Mac was now our direct-in-line superior, we were able to accomplish our goals quicker and more efficiently. It gave me more time for my family and golf.

The summer of 1956 was very tumultuous for the Soulés and the company. Heinz had retired completely and George was gone most of the time being a mayor and I had no contact I can remember with Reinheimer, the brains of the company. Mac wasn't avoiding me, but I had the feeling that he thought I didn't need him bothering me, so he left me alone to do my thing, whatever that might be. He preferred not going to the Jonathan Club for lunch but to the same local deli lunch restaurant down the street, but these most enjoyable lunches were starting to become less frequent. Mac was also using Gayle's services increasingly, both as a secretary and a Girl Friday. I attributed this to his newfound duties as a line executive again. I asked Gayle one day, off the record, whether she thought Mac was dodging me or had other things on his mind? I was still Mr. Meisterlin to Gayle when she replied, "Anything but! He thinks you're the best young executive he's ever known. One day he even said he'd wished he'd had a son like Carl." I was still Gayle's direct superior, but there was no doubt that Mac enjoyed being a line officer again and he did need Gayle, so Bob Moore and I managed.

It was near Easter that Mildred announced that she was pregnant and that the baby was probably due in mid-November! Thus began another chapter in our lives. There was no way we could live in our little home in Anaheim. I was doing well monetarily at Soulé, we had made many good friends during our two stays in Los Angeles, and we liked being on our own and not dependent on our parents. We both decided that our future was here in Southern California. I had promised Mildred when we purchased our home at Cinderella that our next home would be a mini-ranch. While we were looking at homes a couple years earlier in Los Altos, we had looked at a floor plan that contained five bedrooms and three baths and would fit comfortably on a 12,000-square-foot site. We had money enough, plus we had a very potential gain in the equity of our Cinderella Home.

Starting the next weekend we went looking for land as far east as Yorba Linda and north to Diamond Bar. We were looking in basically wooded terrain. We found a couple of parcels—one in East Anaheim, now known as Anaheim Hills—and another in an eastern section of Diamond Bar, but they didn't quite fit our game plan. The months went by, and Garvai called and said that instead of playing Palos Verdes next Saturday he'd gotten us a free pass at Hacienda Golf Club, a private club directly north of my house, about eight miles in La Habra Heights.

I thought that was a great idea, as I didn't have to make that one-hour-plus drive to Palos Verdes. I met Bill in the parking lot of the very beautiful country club in a canyon surrounded by trees, creeks and old orchards. The club dated to 1919 and had golfing history galore. We played with two gentlemen in a four-ball tournament and had lunch. I again embarrassed myself with a substandard performance. The golf course was not quite as difficult as Palos Verdes, but it was plenty tough. A few Sundays later, I drove Mildred and the kids up to the La Habra Heights area, which included Hacienda Country Club, the private club I had played. She loved the area and we drove around for a couple of hours scouting for sale signs. In September, Mildred was quite pregnant, but we were still looking for a building site and again Garvai called and asked if I had the next Wednesday available to play golf with a couple of customers of his who were members of the Hacienda Country Club. I replied that I would make the time!

That Wednesday changed everything! Bill's customers were Ralph Newcomer and Jack Flaherty and we were playing in a two-best-ball Wednesday men's club golf tournament, including dinner. Playing a private country club is quite different than playing public golf courses, even Palos Verdes. Our group did very well, except I truly felt like the other three hit the ball and dragged Carl! I was lucky everybody had a good time and we were invited back to play in a Saturday event a month later, as Bill had a bad time driving home after the last dinner! Nothing changed at work that next month, except that Tedford had joined my every other Sunday crack-of-dawn golf game at Lakewood with Monroe and Harris, my U.S. Steel buddies. After golfing at Palos Verdes, and even better Hacienda, Lakewood wasn't much of a golf course, but I liked all three guys. Tedford and I became even closer at work because he was experiencing the same actions from Mac that the purchasing department endured. Mac was now in his early 60s, but seemingly his batteries were recharged, which actually gave one hope for better years later in life.

The Saturday golf game came and I rode with Ralph Newcomer, who was on the board of directors and the membership chairman. Bill was with Jack Flaherty. We had a great day and were in the money and enjoyed fine food and service again. During the round of golf and lunch, Ralph was explaining to me a program that the club was starting to try and attract some new younger members. It was to be launched on the coming January 1st and last for 90 days. It was similar to the Jonathan Club's Junior Membership Plan. It started with a down payment of $500 per year, with 50% of normal dues, which would amount to $100 per month. All monies would be applied to a membership cost of $3,500 at the age of 35. Ralph said, "Carl you'd love belonging to our club, and we'd love having you. Think it over and bring your wife and kids up here and look at all our facilities. You have until March 30 to make a decision. In the meantime, Jack and I will be inviting you and Bill to play now and then, when you both are available. We make a super fun foursome!"

When I arrived home, I told Mildred about the chance to join a private club at less per month than I was spending now for green fees at public golf courses. Her only negative thought was that we were too far away to really enjoy a private club and its amenities. The next day we piled into the car and again started perusing the area close to Hacienda Country Club. The previous day I had stopped at a gas station on Highway 39 and asked where the local grammar schools were. I was directed to Macy Grammar School a short distance away at the foot of the tree covered, uninhabited hills of La Habra Heights. The next day I drove there and up the road to the last street in the housing development. At the intersection where I was forced to turn was a single lane road named Hidden Canyon. It was a private, dead-end road and there was another sign that read 'No solicitations, drive at your own risk!' In front of these signs stood a for sale sign for lots. We entered a box canyon that was approximately 3/8 of a mile long, with a few houses on it. The road then curved slightly to the northwest and we traveled a quarter of a mile to a barely-visible house, hidden by fruit trees. The canyon was gorgeous! Mildred was equally impressed and the kids were out of car instantly when I stopped. I wrote down the number and made an appointment to meet him at the property the next day. Mildred let me know that she fully agreed that this was a perfect place to raise our soon-to-be five children.

  The owner owned the total canyon, which was three acres subdivided into one-acre lots. The asking price was $20,000 for all three lots or $7,500 per site. I wanted the middle lot, because I hoped to add one other later. We dickered back and forth and settled on a price of $6,000, all cash, in 21 days for the middle acre. Mildred was ecstatic! I sold one of our last stocks which more than paid for the lot and joining Hacienda Country Club in early 1957. Scott Carl was born November 23 by Caesarian delivery and Mildred was fine.

On December 2nd, Mac called Tedford and I into his office and dropped a bombshell. Reinheimer had quit!! He gave no notice—just walked in, cleaned out his desk and removed his personal belongings and left without saying anything to anybody.

Chapter 13

New Ventures

The next two months were probably the most exciting in my life, both good and bad! About ten days into the month of December, Lee Soulé arrived unannounced in L.A. He went directly to Mac's office and approximately one hour later left without talking to anyone else. Tedford and I were very disappointed that he hadn't even said hello to us, which we both took as a bad sign going forward. We waited until mid-afternoon and Mac still had not called us in to let us know what was happening.

We finally decided that Tedford should call Mac and ask what was going on. Mac replied, "Bring Carl and come into my office." His first words to us were, "I'm not sure exactly why he was here at all unless he was letting me know that he was now 99% in charge of running Soulé and that Mr. Soulé, Sr. was totally out of the loop! There was no change in organizational structure in the last 60 days and I'm to continue managing the Southern California division, answering only to him. He assured me that I need not plan on attending any meetings in the corporate San Francisco offices. He also didn't offer me a seat on the board of directors. He did say that they were going to replace Reinheimer from outside the company. He also told me that if I knew an outstanding financial executive, to have the gentleman call him directly. He mentioned nothing about our division's present operations, other than that he was very pleased with our performance. Soulé as a whole was having a great year mostly due to our division! That was it. He could have made a 15-minute phone call and accomplished the same thing." We left Mac's office with the same impression!

In the past two to three months Bill, Dave and I became very close friends as well as golfing buddies. Dave and his wife Catherine, Mildred and I were seeing each other quite a bit while we were helping to acquaint them with Southern California. On one occasion Dave brought up the subject of why he had the laughing fit at the EPL: "Catherine and I both had very, very ugly divorces and both of our spouses owned Diamond Perforated. In our divorce agreements we had no choice but to settle for far less then we were entitled to. We were actually entitled to 50%, but, because Catherine and I fell in love and had an affair, our ex-spouses were punishing us. The only thing they offered us was this Southern California division, which on the Diamond Perforated financial statement approximated 10% of the company. We could take it or leave it. We took it and here we are! Why I was laughing so hard was because of your EPL right down the street 15 minutes away, I have an economic advantage of approximately 25% over any other perforator and expanded metal manufacturer in the U.S. I'm bidding work right now for the government and the state of California that will triple my business and increase my annual profit margin by 500%! And the funny part is that Diamond Perforated in the east can't compete with me on a competitive basis. That's what really made me laugh! Frankly Carl, I owe most of this to good timing and you."

Within 30 days of this conversation, Diamond Perforated of California received a major contract for perforated and expanded metal sheets. The specific specifications required the use of a special EPL paint line only. In addition, Dave had bid for a Department of Highways major contract for the state of California for a new product made of expanded metal requiring a special paint coating that required the use of our EPL. For approximately three to five years, Dave received every contract issued for Glare Barrier. He was the low bidder by 25-30% and his profit margin varied from 35-40%. Not too shabby!

Mildred and I had a design for a five-bedroom, three-bath house built as a ranch with three small bedrooms and bath over an enlarged garage with a closed-in storage and workroom in the rear. We had the basic floor plan and an artist's conception of the exterior. We started looking for a local contractor in the East Whittier, La Habra area. We also took the kids and toured the Hacienda Golf Club a second time, and this time more intensively. The children were far more interested this time. Even though it was midwinter, it was a beautiful day and they were encouraged and allowed to take a swim. That did it—they were eager for mom and dad to join the country club. During the Christmas season, we saw both the Halls and the Garvais socially and we played three or four rounds of golf together.

During January, the vibes coming from San Francisco were not good. One of my duties as purchasing agent was to contract with a junk collector who would buy and haul our scrap. In our L.A. division approximately 20% of our raw materials ended up in scrap. On our profit and loss statement this amounted to approximately 6% of our earnings. Our scrap dealer was Mr. Jules Dorfman. Jules had only five customers, but they were all large industrial manufacturers. Jules was about 50 years of age and built like a bull. He did all the physical work by himself and had no employees. He had been in this business for over 25 years and had never needed help, according to him. He operated only one special truck designed to specifically haul large heavy scrap metal. I investigated Jules' background and history in the scrap metal industry, as it was known to be a dishonest profession. I found Jules' background and references to be impeccable and he was a man of extremely high integrity. I really admired Jules and though we had nothing in common except for his providing Soulé with excellent service, we became close. Late in 1956 Jules confided to me that he was a golf nut and that any free time he had was golfing time. Jules lived in the West Los Angeles area in the Wilshire district, a very expensive real estate area. As I repeatedly have said, this was during my golf addiction period. We played golf together a few times over in his area on some very nice public golf courses, Riviera and Rancho, where the L.A. Open, the PGA Championship and U.S. Open were played! During these games, Jules taught me all about his business, the good and the bad. He taught me well.

    In late January I asked Mac for a little time to help me out of a dilemma I was having within myself. My question to Mac was what direction did he honestly feel Soulé, with Lee as chairman, was now headed? I received the same answer that Tedford and I received over a month before—that he didn't know. He said, "As far as you personally are concerned, I think you'll have a job for life out of loyalty for what you brought to this company in your three years employment! On the other side of the coin, Carl, both Lee and Stan have sons who will be most assuredly part of Soulé Steel in a big way within ten years. As you're aware, Soulé does not overpay their executives. In fact, just the opposite! I've heard within the last week that Reinheimer has taken over in New York as CEO of Lone Star, a company listed on the New York stock exchange, for a salary of six to eight times what Soulé paid. My guess is that he's making from the low $600,000 to the high $800,000? I have no intention of retiring until I'm 65+ years of age, which means in approximately three years. I now am paid just under $50,000 per year, and because of your age I doubt that when you take my place (as of today you are the chosen candidate), you'll be offered the position at approximately $10-$12,000 per year. That's the way the Soulés think. I wouldn't try to suggest what you should do, but I will go so far as to say that Soulé is a family company and not a large privately-traded corporation free from family ties, such as Lone Star." I thanked Mac and complimented him on giving me much to think about, and left. As I walked from Mac's office I remember thinking that someday I'd like somebody to think of me in the manner that I was thinking of Mac now! He was not only a marvelous executive, but an even better human being.

The next day I had lunch with Tedford and we discussed our opinions on Soulé and our futures. He was doing the same mental gymnastics I was, but Tedford because of his tenure and age was already making over $10,000 per year, a very good wage for a man of his age in 1957. He pretty much had made up his mind to wait until Mac retired and see what Soulé would do. In the meantime, he'd continue receiving his $900 per year raises. If he wasn't satisfied at that time, he'd start looking for a new position on the open market. I was almost sure that if I were not in the picture, Soulé would definitely pick Bill.

Since the birth of Scott on November 23, 1956, our marriage also took a turn. Neither of us wanted any more children than we already had brought into this world. During Scott's Caesarean birth, Mildred refused a small surgical operation to eliminate pregnancies. That was her prerogative, but she emphatically stated, "No more children!" I had no choice but to contact an urologist and have a vasectomy, which I had performed on the first week of December 1956. Selfishly, I was not a happy camper about this although it was a simple procedure done at his office in Beverly Hills, and I was back at work that afternoon. Mildred and the children returned from the ranch the very next day.

As January came to a close, I contacted Ralph Newcomer and mailed him my signed application and check for membership to the Hacienda Country Club. Within a week our family were members of a beautiful prestigious private club. Mildred, with five children to attend to, had her hands full and more. My world and business was spinning. I felt I must do something and if I didn't pursue other opportunities outside of Soulé now it would be a terrible mistake.

I talked first to Garvai, then to Dave, McBurney and Bill Nicolay. They asked me what I had in mind and what I would do. I replied, "There is not one Caucasian gentile in the scrap business and I think while I'm young and strong enough I'd like to become a scrap dealer! My friend Jules lives in a large home in the Wilshire District of Los Angeles and drives a truck himself and couldn't be happier. If I could acquire enough manufacturing accounts to start a business driving my own special truck, which I can afford, and do the labor myself, I think I could expand it rapidly." All four of my friends said they would give me their scrap business and none of them had formal contracts with their scrap dealer. Later, Garvai phoned and said he had two customers for me as soon as I got started, namely Nortronics, a division of Northrup Aircraft and Hughes Ground Systems division in Fullerton. I talked it over with Mildred for about a week and called my friends back and asked if they were serious about hiring me as a scrap dealer and they all emphatically replied, "Yes!" Two days later I went to the Los Angeles City Hall license department and received a junk collectors license, which was necessary to be a scrap dealer, and went home and wrote my letter of resignation.

Friday I went to Mac's office and handed him my resignation and asked him how long he would like me to stay. His reply surprised me. "As you stated Carl, I've been expecting this might happen since Reinheimer left and honestly if I were as young as you with five children I'd be doing the same! I'd appreciate you working next week and having lunch with me and Tedford and possibly a few others including Bob Moore and Gayle. I feel like I'm losing more than my right hand, I feel like I'm losing a son!" There were tears in his eyes and I've never felt prouder. I thanked him profusely from my heart and there were tears in my eyes as well.

I recommended that he look no further than Bob Moore as a replacement. With Gayle as his secretary, they were a formidable purchasing department and also recommended that he purchase a junior membership at the Jonathan Club for Bob, as he was even better suited for Soulé's good than I! The following week I had many well wishers from Soulé in L.A., but only George Ford in San Francisco phoned to congratulate me. There was no word from either Lee or Stan. Mac promoted Bob to purchasing agent as of April 1. That week I worked with Bob, bringing him up to speed on all of my duties that he was not involved in already, which were few. In the middle of the workday I shopped and ordered a truck almost identical to Jules' with a couple of newer additions. I was promised delivery in five working days and my new company, Master Metals was formed and the trademark registered.

Mac gave a nice going-away luncheon for me on Friday and there were eight people present including Tedford, his secretary, Pete, Gayle, Bob Moore and the receptionist. We ate at our favorite local delicatessen at a table for eight in the back corner where we told stories about our exploits over the past 27 months and mostly laughed our way through lunch! Mac really let his hair down and told some very funny stories about some outsiders' comments about me—his far-too-young purchasing agent. As the lunch continued, it occurred to me that I was leaving seven wonderful friends.

After lunch, we returned to Soulé where I said my last goodbyes and I advised Bob Moore that I would not be a candidate for his scrap metal business, as Jules Dorfman was my friend and mentor. I never called on Soulé for business. I did make phone calls over the next couple of years to Mac, Tedford, Gayle and Bob Moore who Mildred and I actually met socially a few times. In fact, in 1962 the Moores built a home in La Habra Heights a half mile from ours.

The next week, while waiting for my truck to be delivered, I called upon my pledged friends and customers and we drew up actual bi-lateral contracts. With Garvai's help I designed business cards and stationery. I also called upon Hughes and Nortronics who were anxious for me to begin as they had fired their scrap dealers. I was in hog heaven! My truck arrived and I started doing business the next day.

On my very first day, I called upon both Hughes and Northrup and I met Chuck Smith at Northrup and Ernie Brown at Hughes, who became more than customers as we took a instant liking to each other. This was inevitable, as Garvai was a mutual friend. The scrap I collected from both companies was totally different than what I expected. Instead of being in 55-gallon barrels, it was in heavy cardboard stackable cartons. There were cartons for aluminum, usually one carton for brass and another for copper; but the majority of cartons were filled with electronic circuit boards, which contained a little gold and the majority in silver, platinum, zirconium and a couple of other precious metals. Dollar-wise, the circuit boards were worth quite a bit of money, far more than iron and steel, but they required sorting, which meant categorizing and I didn't know how or where to begin. I wasted no time in making appointments with both Ernie and Chuck to get educated.

The next day I went to Mr. McBurney's company, National Screw. He had called and left a message that their scrap bin was full. That was a day in history. I arrived with the truck filled with 55-gallon barrels to fill by shovel from a big concrete three-sided bin filled with steel shavings. Mr. McBurney had advised me that my predecessor filled his truck and the loads average 11,000 to

11,500 pounds. My new truck's recommended capacity limit was 12,000 pounds so I had no problem, or so I thought. I shoveled these shavings into barrels for shorter and shorter periods of time and although I thought I was in great shape, I was not! Finally, approximately 4 1/2 hours later, I finished and my truck didn't look quite right. The bed of the truck was almost down on the rear tires. I then started to exit National Screw and there stood Mr. McBurney and about five men in suits and five factory workers who were applauding and cheering!

  I took my scrap three miles west on the same street to Bethlehem Steel's blast furnaces to unload, which their workers emptied into conveyor buckets. Before doing this, I first had to weigh in at their scale, which was the weight I would be paid at on a price-per-pound basis. The weight of my first load was 19,268 pounds! My predecessor was not paying National for approximately 7,000 pounds per week. As this was a Friday and I was already late, plus exhausted, I went directly home and my truck looked normal again. I was unable to park the truck within the confines of Cinderella Homes, which for good reasons was not allowed.

  The next morning I barely could move. I'd used muscles I didn't know I had, but because I had made a golf game early Saturday morning at my new club, I went. My golf game that day was much better than usual. I was so sore and restricted in my swing that I hit the ball shorter, but kept it in play, and my usual short game and putting made me the star of our foursome. We came in first and I learned not to over swing!

I called and met with McBurney and when he saw the figures he exclaimed, "Not only were we being taken advantage of weight wise, but it means that our tool and die department is doing a poor job of keeping our cutting tools in the proper condition, which is costing us almost as much as the weight issue! I'll get to work on that and I'd like you, if possible, to take out a normal load of approximately ten barrels tomorrow if you can and double back with the paperwork. If I think tomorrow's paperwork agrees, we should start having two loads a week and I'll share the extra profits gained to make it profitable for us both." I said I could and I'd see him right after lunch if that were okay? "Perfect," he replied.

The next day I arrived at approximately 9:30 a.m. and left National at 11:30 a.m. and went directly to Bethlehem, weighed in and unloaded. The weight ticket printed 10,000+ pounds. I was in Mac's office at 1:00 p.m. and so dirty from shoveling steel and dragging barrels that I preferred to stand! He said, "We've got our proof weight-wise, and from the figures and the actions of the tool and die supervisor and his people, I've got to believe that the cost savings there will be five to six cents per pound. If you agree I'd like to alter our previous agreement by minus ten cents a pound you pay for our scrap, with twice-a-week service for the balance of this month." At the end of the month Mac said, "I'm happy with our present arrangement as to price and service and if you're willing let's leave it at that." The contract was written and signed and was never changed while I owned Master Metals. This contract by itself allowed me to hire two more employees in my first 60 days in business. Years later Mac told me that in the course of that first year it both saved and made over $1 million for National Screw.

Fortunately for Master Metals, the same scenario occurred with both Cherry Rivet and Diamond Perforated who were being shorted on weight, but not as extreme. Dave Hall and Walt Wrigley, the new VP and general manager of the Townsend Corporation, Cherry Rivet Division, called and asked for a meeting. They both insisted on rewriting our agreement in Master Metals' favor! When rewritten and agreed upon, it added over $300+ per company in profit. How lucky can you get? In addition, Walt gave me a contact named Dave at Spartan Manufacturing Company in Costa Mesa, a small machine shop who did all their outside work in copper and brass. He warned me that Dave was a scratch golfer, with a 0 handicap. Walt said that Dave used the same scrap dealer as Townsend. "I'll call him right away, but you should follow up tomorrow at the latest."

Early the following morning, I called Dave at Spartan who said that Walt had advised him of Townsend's findings and he had a barrel already filled and ready to go. He further said, "We ordinarily have a pickup per week of two full barrels, but before I do anything I'd appreciate your taking this barrel and having it weighed by scales of your choice and bring the barrel back so I can be assured that I'm not accusing somebody of fraud who is innocent!" I said I'd be there early that afternoon, but warned him that he shouldn't let any of his workers see or know what we were doing. He replied, "Good idea!" I arrived at Spartan at 1:00 p.m. and Dave was the only person present. I asked Dave where the workers were. "I had a brilliant idea to improve morale," he said. "I gave them an afternoon off with pay and the reaction I received was extremely positive. I think I'll do this again in the future."

With that, we loaded the barrel onto the truck. Dave wanted to go with me, which was great as we became acquainted and of course, talked golf! And yes, he was a scratch golfer. The truck was weighed with the barrel and without, and the scrap weighed just over 1,000 pounds. On the drive back to Spartan, Dave said, "That's a significant difference than I've been seeing for the past couple of years. My man comes on Fridays and I receive the paperwork and his check on Mondays. I have your phone number and I'll call you Monday and let you know what I decide." He called on Monday afternoon and said, "You're my new scrap dealer! What day of the week do you service Townsend? If you want to coordinate it with Townsend, who is close by, I'm more than willing to have my pickups on the same day, if that would help your productivity." I said, "We've just started servicing Townsend, but it's Thursdays presently." He responded, "That's fine. Any time of day is good, but leave me three or four extra-clean barrels. You don't want to contaminate the brass and copper." We agreed on a price, which was only three cents less than he was now receiving, but it filled out my Townsend load and made Thursdays a very profitable day. Lucky, lucky and lucky!

At Diamond Perforated, to a lesser degree than National Screw, there appeared to be a 15-20% difference, according to Dave Hall. I had alerted Dave to the possibility of the weight discrepancy, so on our first pickup Dave compared it to Joe's records for the past three years. After our second pickup, and paperwork having been forwarded, I had a call from Dave asking me to meet with him and Joe as soon as possible. When I arrived at Dave's office a few days later, Dave was alone. He said, "Carl, thanks for alerting me to this situation, as we have been evidently been cheated for the past three years. My problem is that Joe, who I trust implicitly, has always liked and trusted our present scrap dealer. This news that I've uncovered from your last two pickups indicates a 15-20% weight difference per load, which is a significant amount, especially in the perforating operation where over 30% of the raw material ends up as scrap. In fact, what we make on scrap sometimes is our profit! You could help me in assuring Joe that this could happen to anybody."

Shortly thereafter Joe entered the office and I greeted him warmly as if there was nothing wrong. Dave placed on the table the records for the past three years and then the records for the past two weeks and said, "Joe, what do you conclude from these two last weeks as compared to the past three years? Is there possibly a reason why the last three years on average indicate a 15% plus underpay?" Joseph studied the paperwork for several minutes and finally said, "The last two scrap pickups should have been even less weight, because our main perforator has been down for repairs during both weeks, so these figures don't make any sense. If anything, Carl's service should have returned less money to us instead of more. I don't like the looks of this and evidently I've let a friendship interfere with good business practices. I'm really sorry and apologize, Mr. Hall." Dave looked to me and I responded, "In this industry it happens all the time because scrap dealers are forced by competition to pay higher dollar amounts for the scrap metal than is practical and are forced to make it up by fudging on the weight per load. In Diamond's case, the weight was only about a 15% difference, which hardly becomes noticeable!" Dave told Joe almost the same thing and that he personally and Diamond Perforated couldn't operate without him. After Joe withdrew from the room, Dave thanked me and mentioned that he thought we did as well as was possible to placate Joe.

The next thing Dave brought up was whether Master Metals could service their account profitably, based on our present contract and what we now knew? Before I could speak he said, "Carl, Catherine and I owe you our success here and I consider you my best friend here in California. I think you deserve a far better contract then what we now have! Go home and work on the agreement that makes you the profit margin that will help Master Metals grow in the future. Phone me in the next couple days and let me know what the new contract should include. It's up to you, within reason that is." What a friend he was for 50 years! Two days later I gave him my figures and he agreed stating, "I'll give you more." To which I replied, "Then it wouldn't be fair!" Again the Meisterlin luck of being in the right place at the right time with the right tools paid off!

Master Metals made a profit in its very first month! Within two weeks of starting, I was forced to hire two men to perform the necessary customer services. I also had to find a location that would permit a scrap dealer. Most of our business was in Orange County, except for National Screw and Diamond Perforated. The only community that allowed a scrap dealer/junk collector to locate and do business was in South Norwalk. How lucky can one get? Driving south on the main street of Norwalk, just past Imperial Avenue, I saw a real estate sign and turned left. There stood a chain link fenced-in lot with a small office structure, and to the rear an open but covered shed, with a for rent sign. The site was exactly 100 feet wide and 180 feet deep, made to order for Master Metals! The little office building could only handle one desk and a couple chairs, but it had a bathroom and a large window to the south and two smaller windows to the north. I phoned the number on the sign and a real estate agent said he'd meet me at the site in ten minutes.

On arriving we proceeded into the back lot to the shed, which also had running water and an electrical outlet. He opened the gate, which would easily accommodate our truck plus had room for three to four more trucks if needed. The shed had a concrete floor, but the balance of the site was a mixture of dirt and gravel. When I asked how much the site was being leased for, he replied that the asking price was negotiable and stated the figure. I would have paid the figure, but hearing it was negotiable I offered 20% less. We closed the site and office and drove to his agency where he placed a call to the owner who countered at 10% off of asking price to which I countered half the difference or 15%, which the owner accepted! I only mention this transaction to show how dumb some salespeople can be. The real estate agent prepared a one-year lease agreement with two one-year extensions. The next morning I drove the truck to the site, where I met the agent who gave me my signed lease and the keys to the office and padlocks. It didn't look like much, but we were within the law and the location was as good as it gets. Again, pure luck!

  As I've already mentioned, I hired two men who were quite different in age and in color. The first man I hired was Bear H. Smith, a black man eight years older than I, who worked with me for 12 years until I sold the business! Bear was one of the finest human beings I've ever known in my entire life. He came from Chicago and in 1937 was a sparring partner for the famous Joe Louis! Bear was about 6' 1" inches and weighed approximately 190 pounds. He was strong as a bull, but more important he was extremely intelligent with a great deal of common sense. He had three children—two boys and a girl. The oldest boy, named Rudy, was 20 and the other boy was

19. Eventually they both worked for Master Metals. Bear epitomized my father's statement that boys become men, but only a few become gentlemen and Bear was a supreme gentleman.

The other young man, Ken, my next-door neighbor's son, was only 18 and couldn't get a job, so I hired him. Ken was with Master Metals for two years, did 30 months in the Army Tank Corps as a mechanic and later returned and was an employee also when I sold the business. He was a valued employee, but unfortunately not 100% honest and certainly no Bear Smith, who only missed one day of work in 12 years (another story to be told.) At the end of our first six weeks, it was necessary that we purchase another truck customized to handle scrap from Hughes, Northrup and Townsend.

During the first six weeks in the scrap business I became very aware I knew very little about scrap in its entirety. The circuit boards, which were 75% of what I hauled from Northrup and Hughes, had only one purchaser in all of Southern California. It was a middleman operation that had many employees sorting the boards into five or six different containers. The man's name was Jerry, who I learned later was financed by Mr. Ray White. There was no negotiating, as Jerry was the only game in town, take it or leave it! Fortunately for me, the volume I was handling was consistent enough that I was a valuable source. His operation was very labor intensive, so much so that I never considered Master Metals performing his function. Jerry swore me to secrecy as to the prices of the boards I'd receive. The money from the boards made both Hughes and Northrup profitable and the other metals, primarily aluminum, were gravy. Jerry explained that the prices would change according to precious metals current prices, but Mr. White promised that I'd always receive over 10% of going market price.

After another couple of weeks with a second truck, we needed another employee, which was easy to procure as I always made a habit of hiring labor at minimum +15%. We now had quite an overhead, with four employees, counting me, on our books. This was 100% necessary if we were to give the service our customers deserved. Our profit margins were now reduced by over 30%. Seventy-five percent of my personal function was used to gain more accounts. This again reduced our margins, as I needed a larger expense allowance for entertaining potential customers.

On the home front, Mildred was overwhelmed with five small children to raise. Fortunately, our oldest child, Claudia, now almost seven years old, was a natural little mother and was a great help to both of us. Mildred and the children were using Hacienda's facilities as the weather became warmer. A lesson to learn: the cost of joining a private club and the dues might be very enticing, but it's the money you spend at the club for enjoyment that's the killer! It doesn't seem like much, but when four year olds can go up to the pool grill and sign "M-13" (our membership number) on their checks, at the end of the month it adds up! At this time I was giving Mildred $600 per month for her house account and Master Metals was paying the dues and expenses as a business write-off. I was definitely using the country club for business purposes, as I had resigned from the Jonathan Club upon leaving Soulé. For the first time in several years, we were watching our dollars very carefully.

For what reason I still can't fathom, Mildred's attitude toward me was rapidly worsening. It seemed that she was having a difficult time being civil. The only time she wanted to make love was after several highballs. My love for my children made my marriage tolerable, but I realized that Mildred really didn't like children. For the balance of 1957 the business expanded and the marriage just existed.

In early 1958, for the first time I needed further capitalization to purchase another type of hauling equipment. I needed $5,000 immediately to take advantage of a competitor's bad luck, who offered me a truck for less than 40% of blue book for cash that week. The equipment was exactly what I needed, but if I purchased one new, it would be around $12,500. It was less then a year old and had only 7,500 miles usage! Thinking that Big Al owed me one for the money he made off the Kaiser stock, I phoned him and presented my problem and asked if I could borrow $5,000 for 30 months, payable at $200 per month? Al answered, "No, but Emily would be happy to and she'll send you a cashier's check in the morning by special delivery." I called my competitor and told him I would meet him at whatever place of business or bank he desired with one of my drivers ready to pick up the new hauler within 48 hours. He sounded ecstatic! Two days later the deal was consummated and I now had three very different methods for recovering and hauling scrap!

In thinking back to my business relationship with Big Al, I had a strong impression that he didn't want the rest of the family to be aware in any manner, shape or form that he and I had a business relationship. I know for a fact that if he had kept the Kaiser investment to that day it had appreciated over 400%. I don't know, and I never asked. Emily, my sweetheart and favorite Gurrea, received her $200 per month for 30 months as promised on time and when the note had been paid in full I received a most wonderful thank you note.

My priorities have always been my family first and then our business! I now added a third priority, pleasing Mildred, which came before family and business. Unfortunately at the same time as my family problems, the metals and financial industries had a slight recession which further decreased profit margins and increased further borrowing costs. This economic downturn lasted for under two years, but for the first time in my life timing was poor. I truly loved Mildred and adored our children and there wasn't anything that I wouldn't do to make her life more enjoyable. I understood that raising five small children was one hell of a task! In the summer of 1958 we started planning to build our dream mini-ranch in Hidden Canyon. We had found a local custom homebuilder who we liked and thought we could work with easily. Fortunately this turned out to be true. When he presented the final building plans, which he had done at no cost to us, we were ready to start, except that now money became a problem. Again, luckily our builder needed work at the same time as in early 1959 all industries in Southern California were suffering. He gave me the name of Caldwell Banker Mortgage Brokers, the phone number and a specific contact.

For the very first time in my life, I needed a commercial lending company or bank. I phoned and made an appointment with the agent for Caldwell Banker and the next week, with our building plans in hand; we met at his office in L.A. He stated that the best loan he could offer that particular day would be 10% down on a 6% for 29-year loan, which varied from week to week based on national lending rates. Before approving any loan Caldwell Banker would have to estimate the costs of the building plans I presented and the cost and inspection of our property in East Whittier. I also needed to produce financial statements for the past two years from Master Metals and estimates of our total net worth from investments and home equity. He estimated that all of these items should be finished within four to five weeks and if approved by both parties a loan could be forthcoming in six to eight weeks. I agreed, shook hands, and the meeting was over successfully!

The next day I called the real estate agent who had handled the purchase of our Cinderella Home who was now selling real estate within the community. I made an appointment for him to give us an estimate of value towards listing for sale. This time nobody was paying for our moves and we were actually scrimping and saving in order to accomplish what we hoped would be our very last move, at least I did. The market for Cinderella Homes was still good, the agent said, but not great. There wasn't much action presently. I stated that we probably wouldn't want to move until late summer, early September at the latest. He recommended a price in excess of $20,000 that we could ask for, but unless we got one very unusual buyer, not to expect the house to bring that price! At $19,500 less commission that still brought a significant profit. Since we were not absolutely sure when we could move he suggested that we not list the house until our new home was in construction, but he knew what we wanted and when and if somebody walked in who met the time frame and price he would contact us immediately. Five weeks later Caldwell Banker gave their approval and we agreed that all monies and documents would be due and payable at the close of construction no later than September 1, 1959. Mildred seemed energized when the construction began, but there was little love or affection towards me.

Starting in mid-1958, we begin to worry about baby Scott. He wasn't talking or trying to make sounds of any kind. We were worried enough to take him to a specialist. On examination the doctor told us there was nothing wrong, but being the baby and having brothers and sisters talking and giving him everything he wanted, why should he talk? For the past two years on our trip up the canyon or to the country club with the kids, we always made a special turn off our road home to a Foster Freeze soft ice cream stand. One afternoon returning from the canyon, Mildred and I had a dinner date and we were a trifle late. We didn't make the turn for Foster Freeze, and out of the backseat in our station wagon came a cry: "No ice cream?" It was the first three words Scott uttered and we've never let him forget it!

On the business front, we were receiving large quantities of wire coils from Townsend Company, which were not heavy but potentially usable by specialized manufacturers of wire products. I called upon Mr. Orville Perkins, the general manager of Hollister Coil Spring Company. Mr. Perkins was very interested in my idea that I could furnish him wire at 50% of usual cost and I would also become his scrap metal dealer at his normal contracting price. Over the next couple of weeks I took samples of several types of wire to Mr. Perkins, some of which they could use. The quantities by weight were enough for both companies to be a profitable alliance. This arrangement allowed Hollister Coil Spring not only to be more profitable, but allowed them to increase their business by being more creative. For me, it more than doubled the amount of revenue I received from Townsend and the Hollister scrap!

In mid-May we listed our home with the broker for over $20,000. The resale market was slow, but he was encouraging as he stated that after school let out in mid-June, the serious buyers would start looking. In late July we received a decent offer and we counter offered with a move-out date on Saturday of Labor Day weekend. When we cashed out, we had more than enough money for the down payment. We also had almost six weeks to prepare for the move. With five small children, the timing was imperative! By August 1, our home was completely framed, the driveways were in, the windows were all in place and the doors were locked every night. We were down to the finishing touches inside the house like flooring, painting, wallpapering, stairway railings, plumbing fixtures, cabinetry, appliances, etc. On the Friday before Labor Day weekend I completed both real estate transactions—the selling of our Cinderella home and paying our contractor and Caldwell Banker! The last week in August, Caldwell Banker and our contractor were very cooperative. Mildred moved two loads of our household goods and in the evening I took one carload.

  The gentleman who had sold us our acre was in the furniture business and he advised Mildred that he was advertising a special three-day sale in mid-August and if she were interested he would give us an extra 20% discount. He did warn us that he didn't handle cheap goods, but all of the merchandise in his store was good value at list price, which Mildred assured me, after visiting the store in downtown Whittier, that we'd be proud to have in our home. The day I visited his store with Mildred, the last day of this sale, the place was jammed with buyers and they were not lookey-loo's—they were purchasing everything in sight! With the extra 20% discount, we were buying really good furniture, lamps, pictures, throw rugs, desks and beds, etc., at 40% off. Timing again was in our favor!

On Thursday before Labor Day the furniture store delivered all of the merchandise we purchased and even assembled certain pieces and placed them in various rooms under Mildred's supervision. On Saturday we moved all of our remaining furniture and on Saturday night the whole family had dinner at a pizza parlor down on Whittier Boulevard. The electricity, propane gas, heaters, air conditioner and telephone were all in place and working. On Tuesday morning I took Claudia, Cindy and Debbie to Macy grammar school and my promise to Mildred and the children was fulfilled.

Chapter 14

History in the Making

Everything was good. Mildred and the children were happy with their new home and new school. Master Metals continued to grow, the economy was improving and our profit margins increased accordingly. I was now firmly entrenched as a member of Hacienda Country Club. In mid-to-late October, Jack Flaherty asked me to be his campaign manager as he had decided to run for president of the club. I accepted and then asked, "What does a campaign manager do?" Jack replied, "He just talks to as many members as possible and asks them to vote for Jack Flaherty."

Later the same week I was approached by Red Brown, the captain of Hacienda's golf team, which played all of the other private clubs in Los Angeles and Orange counties. Red stated, "Your handicap is down to where you qualify to play on our team. Although you and I have never played together, several members of the team have expressed their desire for you to become a member. The matches are played on every fourth Thursday starting late March and lasting until summer or elimination. Each team consists of 14 players, 12 of whom compete and two who are substitutes. Let me know ASAP! By the way, the guys recommending you all say the same thing—you're a great guy for a partner, plus you are the best putter in the club." I accepted the following day. The matches started mid-March. For the next six years I was the anchorman, the last team to tee off and because of competitive pressure, the team most likely not to succumb! I realize this sounds very braggadocio, but it was quite an honor!

The election was held early December and Flaherty won. At dinner that evening, Jack asked me to be the social chairman for 1960. "Carl, you're the natural person to perform this particular function because you're out and around the community and business world. The main problem is finding speakers for our monthly Sunday night dinner—speakers from all walks of life that would enlighten and entertain our members! You would also chair the committee for the Scotty McGregor Member-Guest Tournament in July. Our present social chairman has already scheduled a speaker for January, so your job finding speakers starts in February and ends next January. It's very important to me and the club that you take on this responsibility!"

I was trapped, I couldn't say no! I asked what I could offer a potential speaker and Jack replied, "A round of golf earlier, dinner and $250 is our cash limit!" Even in 1960 that wasn't much! Trying to find appropriate speakers became almost a full-time job, but I got lucky as usual! The first person I called was my personal friend Mac from National Screw, who occasionally gave economic business lectures at various clubs and organizations such as the Jonathan Club. He agreed to speak, depending on the date, and I mentioned the last Sunday in February. I received an almost universal answer: 'My calendar says okay, but first I must check with my wife to make sure she doesn't have something planned for us on that particular Sunday! I'll call you tomorrow and let you know.' The next morning he called and accepted our invitation and asked for all the details about time, traffic directions, but declined the golfing. He also asked that his $250 fee be given to the United Way.

Now the pressure was off, as I had a month or two to find some possible speakers from the sports and entertainment industries where I had some connections. I had excellent connections with the L.A. Rams football organization and likewise with the L.A. Lakers basketball team. I also heard while I was recruiting Mac for February that the American Movie Guild president and General Electric Corporation spokesman gave speeches and answered questions on the subject of American leadership and statesmanship. The man's name was Ronald Reagan! Mac advised me that G.E. underwrote some of the fees so that Mr. Reagan could speak to as many people as humanly possible. Mac gave me his personal office phone number at G.E. I called the number immediately, which was answered by Mr. Reagan's personal assistant and secretary. I gave her my name, representing Hacienda Country Club in La Habra Heights and requesting Mr. Reagan to speak at our monthly social. She answered that Mr. Reagan

would not be in the office today but she expected him tomorrow and that, yes, he did like to speak to organizations such as Hacienda! She then asked about any other particulars that she should pass on with my request, such as what month, what time and how to locate the club.
I told her any month starting with March and he was invited to play golf starting around 12:30 p.m. with a light snack before and dinner starting at 5:00 p.m. I was embarrassed, but I finally bumbled that we offered a $250 fee. The lady answered that Mr. Reagan sometimes spoke for less, depending on the group, that she would relay my message and that they'd be back to me within a week's time. I received a phone call from Mr. Reagan's secretary two days later accepting our offer, but rejecting the golf, for the month of April! It couldn't be a better month, as now I could schedule either the Rams or the Lakers around Mr. Reagan's visit.

    I then placed calls to both Les Richter of the Rams and Butch van Brederkolf, the coach of the Lakers who I'd played golf with at Palos Verdes. Butch and Dave Hall had roomed together at Princeton! Neither was available and I left the same exact message inviting them and three players to join us for lunch, golf, and dinner. They were each to give a little five-minute talk explaining how they fit into the overall team concept and then take questions regarding their careers, personal lives, forecasts for next season or whatever. About a week later I received a call from Richter accepting our offer for himself, Zeke Bratkowski the quarterback, Deacon Jones the all-pro defensive end, and Charlie Wright the offensive right tackle! He had checked the last Sunday in March with them and they would all be in town and would love to play Hacienda Country Club. He further stated that he would reconfirm around March 1 and asked if we could furnish a blackboard so they could draw some X's & O's, which would help bring questions. He also mentioned that he was a 12 handicap, Zeke was a 4 handicap, and Deacon and Charlie didn't have handicaps. He classified them as beginners, but they all loved golf! When March came nothing changed and I placed Zeke in a foursome with Paul Travis (a 1 handicap), Chuck Soper (another 1 handicap) and Red Brown (a 7 handicap). I put Richter with Jack Flaherty, Ralph Newcomer and Phil Goddard all within the range of a 10 to 13 handicap. I placed Deacon and Charlie with the club's teaching pro and myself! We teed off last so we wouldn't hold everybody up with slow play.

Shortly after Richter called, I had a call from Van Brederkolf apologizing for not returning my call sooner. When I invited him now for the last Thursday in May he said he was sure he'd be in town and he'd bring along three of his players who really enjoyed golf. As basketball season was over in early April at the latest, he'd have no problem getting three players and he'd call me the day after the Laker season ended, which believe it or not, he did! When he called, he gave me the names of Jerry West, (a 6 handicap), Frank Selvy (a 10 handicap), and Jim Krebs (a 15 handicap). Van Brederkolf played to a 9.

I arranged the foursomes the same as with the Rams and I again brought up the rear with Jim Krebs—a really funny guy —who ended up that evening bringing Selvy and himself back to my house to meet Mildred and the children. The kids had never met anyone as big as Jim Krebs, who stood almost 7' tall and weighed 290 pounds! Best of all he was a big teddy bear who loved little kids. Frank Selvy was an extremely good-looking Kentuckian who spent the hour mostly talking to Mildred and sipping a soda, but I'll never forget Krebs sitting on the floor playing with my children and seemingly enjoying it as much as they did.

Luckily, in spite of all the time and effort I was giving to the club and enjoying it ever so much, my business was good. We were prospering, the future looked bright, and our children were growing like weeds and were healthy and happy. I was also making more time for Mildred and I.

McBurney's program in February was a solid success, as Mac was a polished public speaker and gave the attendees a lot to think about. The questions lasted even after the dinner was adjourned. I rarely saw Mac in person after that night, but did keep in touch by phone a couple times a year with each of us originating a call or two.

With the Rams, the night was another success with the dining room completely sold out. It was evident that the April dinner was going to tax our capacity limits and service quality, as we were already literally sold out. We were going to have to place a loudspeaker system onto the porch, veranda and bar area. We had tables for four on the porch and the veranda, which if we got lucky and the weather cooperated would handle 32 people comfortably, with easy access for the serving people. Our other two options were to tighten up the main dining room and add seating for 24 more diners. The bar area would accommodate 20 to 24 additional diners, but this was really not desirable as the bar was in another very intimate room out of sight from the main dining room. Under normal circumstances the main dining room held 180 diners, which we filled in February. For the Rams in March we increased the capacity by 16 people in the dining room. The manager that night told me we already had over 200+ reservations and he expected, based on the big awards night of the Scotty McGregor Tournament in July, at least another 20% sign-up in the last month.

On the awards night in July, they used the men's card room, which could accommodate another 80 diners. We decided to use the main dining room, which by further squeezing and placing the head table to be occupied by Mr. Reagan, Jack Flaherty, Howard Smith our golf professional and myself, would hold 200 diners. If the weather held, that would give us a total of 232. We would accept reservations up to that amount of people and anybody over that total would have to be on a waiting list. Within a week we were sold out at 232 with 10 people on the waiting list. For the rest of the month our cancellations and new reservations balanced out! This would be the first time this Sunday night dinner ever surpassed 200!

We were lucky, the last Sunday night in April turned out to be a beautiful night with no wind. The dining room manager managed to squeeze in a table each on the veranda and porch increasing our capacity to 240 with almost hundred percent being able to view Mr. Reagan. What happened that night at the Hacienda Country Club changed world history. I told this story to Mike Reagan on a cruise ship several years ago, and he had no knowledge of what transpired as he was obviously too young at the time.

At 4:30 p.m. the club was overflowing with both members and excitement. Jack and I made ourselves available in the entrance lobby to greet Mr. Reagan. While standing talking to Jack, an elderly white-haired distinguished man approached me, calling me by name. "Carl," he said, "when the dinner is over tonight, would you please introduce me to Mr. Reagan? I'll wait until the very last person leaves." I replied, "I'd be happy to." He immediately went back into the main dining room and I said to Jack, "Who was that man?" Jack replied, "That is our most famous member—Mr. Walter Knott of Knott's Berry Farm! He doesn't play golf but he and his wife do use our dining facilities for entertainment purposes a couple of times a year." Right on cue, Mr. Reagan appeared with that great smile as we approached each other. After introducing ourselves, we entered the dining room to a wave of applause! Some of our overzealous members pushed Jack and I out of the way to get close to Mr. Reagan, but he didn't seem to mind, obviously he was used to this!

Jack and I retreated to the dais and for the next 20 minutes or so we watched the most gracious man I've ever known smile, shake hands, answer questions, and even put his arm around a couple of elderly ladies.

A bell rang, everybody retreated to their assigned tables and dinner was served. The chef had prepared a very special meal for this magical occasion and it was superb! Shortly after 6:30 p.m. I introduced myself as social chairman, Howard Smith our well-known golf professional and then Jack Flaherty, our president, who said a few welcoming words. I then introduced Mr. Reagan, who rose from his chair on cue and I happily sat down. Mr. Reagan gave his speech about what it means to be a completely free human being by the Constitution and Bill of Rights given to us as American citizens. I only wish I had recorded it! The audience literally went wild and it took a few minutes before Mr. Reagan spoke again. When he gained control he then proclaimed a ten-minute break before he would answer any and all questions.

During this break, Mr. Knott approached and reminded me that he would wait patiently till the last member left, as it was very, very important to him to have this opportunity to speak in person to Mr. Reagan. Mr. Reagan answered questions for over 30 minutes and I interrupted the questions requesting only three more, as I had promised Mr. Reagan we'd release him from captivity at 8:00 p.m. He took the three questions and the evening was officially adjourned.

What happened next became history! After several

well wishers, etc., I advised Mr. Reagan that the elderly white-haired man in the rear had been promised by me that he would have the last opportunity to speak with him and he agreed. There were five people left in the dining room other than staff cleaning up. They were Mr. Reagan, his driver, Jack and I and Mr. Knott. The driver retreated to the lobby and I introduced Mr. Walter Knott to Ronald Reagan! After the usual cordialities, Mr. Reagan suggested we move to a table and sit down. Mr. Knott started asking very political questions. Jack, when given a chance, declared that he must leave and excused himself. Within five minutes I realized that this was a very private personal meeting and I certainly wasn't needed. In fact, I had the feeling I was interfering, so I also excused myself and left these two great men to talk. As I looked back, they were sitting leaning towards each other and their heads were no more than inches apart. I felt that our big night was a tremendous success, but little did I know what was forthcoming.

Two weeks later on the front page of the L.A. Times was a photograph of a check written by Walter Knott for $1 million to the committee for the election of Ronald Reagan for Governor of California! This was the seed money needed by Mr. Reagan to begin his political career. I laughingly take credit for being the person who helped start Mr. Reagan's ascendancy to Governor, to the President of the U.S.A., all because Mac gave me his phone number and I called him.

With the success in May of the L.A. Lakers night,

plus the fact that we hadn't used the $250 fee, our social committee now had an extra $500 to enable us to attain desirable speakers. With the help of other committee members, including Howard Smith and Ralph Newcomber, I only contributed one more speaker—Tommy Lasorda of the L.A. Dodgers. The Sunday night in December was changed to accommodate the Christmas holidays. The balance of the year we had capacity attendance every month, which carried on for many future years. In addition, the capacity crowds made the club so much profit that the board of directors the following year increased the speaker fee to $400 and the following year to $500, which made it much easier for the social committee to present quality entertainment.

I failed to mention that on the first weekend in March, with Mildred literally pushing me out the door, I invited Garvai, Dave Hall and Locke Barrett to join me for a weekend of golf and Bridge at The Tickle Pink in Carmel. I called the pro shop at Pebble Beach and made reservations for Friday, Saturday and asked for as early as possible for Sunday, as we planned to go directly from the golf course home to Southern California. I had been cleared to use the owners' suite at The Tickle Pink, which accommodated four people. This became an annual event until 1992!

The balance of 1960 was a blur until the national elections were held in early November. Although Bear Smith and I agreed on most everything, Bear was a leader in the African-American community of L.A. and what we now call an activist in promoting the rights of blacks! I also believed in his agenda and actions and I encouraged him! But just before the election, I changed my position as Bear disclosed to me that Joe Kennedy was paying $5 to every black to vote for his son John F. Kennedy, not only in L.A., but in all heavily-populated black communities across the country including San Francisco, Chicago, Detroit, Philadelphia, New York, Georgia, Alabama, Mississippi and Louisiana. Joe had pledged and did pay out $10 million on Election Day. That figure represents 2 million votes and over 75 electoral votes, which cost Nixon the election. The day following the election, Bear didn't show up for work. The following day he was there and I asked him what happened and he stated that he and his two sons had driven approximately 150 neighbors, who he had helped register to vote, to the polls!

With the $750+ they had held a neighborhood celebration where they had all combined their monies, which lasted until the election results were in and a couple hours more of partying. Basically, he hadn't been to bed all night. He was ecstatic with the victory, which he honestly believed would help the blacks and which I could certainly not disagree with! One thing he did say, and he believed it, "Mr. Joe Kennedy sure was a smart man and knew where and how to use his dollars!" It doesn't take Einstein to explain John F. Kennedy's victory, although the national media gave different scenarios as to why Nixon lost and to this day won't admit that Joe Kennedy bought the election for his son. One other caveat—Big Al, a staunch conservative Republican member of the ultra-right wing John Birch society, voted for Kennedy according to Emily. When I confronted him and accused him of being a hypocrite and why or how he could vote for JFK, he looked me straight in the eye and said, "Because he's a Catholic." Another reason for JFK's victory was that more Catholics than usual voted Democrat!

Things were pretty normal during this late fall. In our family life things were good, but not the way they used to be and business continued to improve. Then life threw me a curve. On November 30, 1960, one week short of his 70th birthday, my father died.

Chapter 15

Dark Days

Upon receiving the news of my father's death, we all grabbed some appropriate clothing, piled into the family station wagon and headed north! I left Mildred and the children at the ranch while I continued on to mom and dad's home in Oakland.

When mom answered the door it was very obvious to me that things were not going well. She, like myself, was totally unprepared for my dad passing on. The death certificate later stated that he died of heart failure, but in truth he was in bed with a chest cold watching a Rams and 49ers football game.

My dad and I had a very tumultuous relationship. He was a stern disciplinarian from being in the military who believed in tough love and in molding his son to become not only a man, but a gentleman like himself.

When my father died, I got very angry. I had no idea that dad had been ill. Most of all, I was angry at myself for not being close to him during that last year and not letting him know how much I loved and appreciated him. Out of this tragedy, I realized what a truly fine man my dad was. He was a man who cared for his family and who took being a father to me, instead of a pal, seriously. Nevertheless, when he died it was a very busy time in my life and I really didn't have time to grieve. I did cry, once, but that was all.

I will never forget the story my mother told of how my father passed, for in actuality if one could choose a way to die, my father found that way! My mother's story was this:

> I was in the kitchenette playing Gin Rummy with my closest and best friend Betty when I first heard your father call me and then ring his bell. I went into our bedroom and asked what he needed or wanted, he replied YOU! With that he pulled me down to him and gave me a great big kiss. When I got to my feet, he said, "Babs, I just want to thank you for making my life so wonderful. Without you my life would have been a total failure and miserable at best." I then said to him, "Oh, for gosh sakes." I then said, "Thank you!" and started back to Betty. Before I got to the kitchen I heard this awful sound of the air exhuming from one's body when they die! Somehow, your dad knew!

For the next three or four days I assisted my mother in every way possible in planning the funeral, going through all the legal papers and, lastly, her finances. Legally, everything was copacetic, but unfortunately my father hadn't left mom an estate that she could possibly live comfortably on. Dad had always taken total control of their finances and my mother had no idea what they owned other than the house and furniture. I made a mental note to myself from that day on that Mildred would keep the checkbook and know exactly where we stood financially. I didn't confide to mom at this time the problems she might be facing, but it seemed obvious by her actions that she presumed that financially things weren't good.

Mom and I followed my father's wishes and instructions for his funeral and a small wake. Mildred did not attend the funeral, but I thought that Claudia, who was now ten and dad's favorite, was just old enough to understand this side of life. I was surprised by the attendance at the funeral, as mom and dad had no immediate relatives in the San Francisco/Oakland Bay area. Over a hundred friends attended and my mom, the perfect lady that she was, hosted the gathering fabulously. I was the primary speaker at the funeral, but Bob Ramsey and his new wife Pat Smith Ramsey both spoke.

Bob Ramsey talked about all the work my father accomplished for the war effort from 1942 until late 1945. He also mentioned dad's leadership in both the Optimist Club and the Salesman's Tip Club and thanked several members of both organizations who were attending the services. His new wife, Pat, who was my old schoolmate and dad's lawyer, mentioned knowing our family for 25 years and how wonderful it was to work with my father.

In Pat's words, he was a joy and a wonderful, funny and zealous human being.

After the services, Claudia and I took mom home and she was extremely happy about how successful she thought dad's services were. We talked for approximately two hours, going over things that she needed to do and I let her know that I would be in touch every evening to monitor her progress and give her my support. Claudia and I left and went down to Gilroy where we stayed overnight and the following morning very early we left for our mini-ranch.

I did phone my mother every night for about ten days and she did her best to find and gather all the information and documents that were needed to evaluate her situation going forward. I tried my utmost to be positive about anything she chose to do. I then reduced my phone calls to two or three times in the evenings a week. After a few months she advised me she didn't want to remain in her home in Oakland, but she knew of a beautiful apartment house across the bay in San Mateo and that she would visit it over the weekend. I assured her that whatever she wanted we'd make happen. She found a one-bedroom apartment in the building for only $165 a month, including all utilities except telephone, and placed a small deposit to hold the apartment for 15 days. By coincidence, $165 a month was exactly the same that she had just started to receive from my dad's Social Security.

Before ending our conversation that night, I reminded her that she needed to put her house up for sale.

As mom already possessed a still-active California real estate license, she knew what needed to be done. I asked her to advise me of her actions so I could be of help if needed. A few days later she called to tell me she had listed the house for sale with a broker friend for just over $20,000. She also informed me that she would receive 80% of the listing agents fee and the selling agent's entire fee if she were lucky enough to sell the property herself. Her broker friend would pay for all of the advertising. Mom and dad had bought the home in 1949 for $10,000, a really good purchase price at that time for a premium location. In the 11 years they had occupied it, it had more than doubled in value.

At the time of dad's demise, mom was left with a couple of thousand dollars at the bank, 100 shares of Kaiser Steel stock purchased at $10 per share in 1951 and her home on Picardy Drive. I checked the Kaiser Steel stock price the next morning and it was selling for $160 plus per share. Unfortunately, in 1957 I presume dad must have needed money to live on for he had refinanced the house and taken $5,000 from the equity. The house didn't sell right away, but I helped mom move approximately four weeks later. For a period of two months she was making payments on her home on Picardy and her new apartment in San Mateo. But the best thing was that she was very happy and satisfied with her small apartment, where she was making friends and playing Bridge four to five days a week and indulging her addiction to crossword puzzles. She finally received an offer on the house on Picardy for just under $20,000 and it was a good clean deal cashing her out—but it was from an outside broker. Counting her remaining equity plus listing commission, she cleared $5,000.

I worked a deal with her that Master Metals would borrow $15,000 in total and pay her $200 per month for life to augment her income and I would put up our mini-ranch as security for the loan. She was very pleased with this arrangement and it gave Master Metals money for further expansion. According to federal regulations at that time, $200 per month or $2,400 per year on a $15,000 loan was the maximum amount legally. Any more would be classified as usury. When all the paperwork was signed, sealed and delivered, and mom was happy and comfortable, I felt I had taken care of my dad's responsibilities the way he would have wanted.

This period in my life passed quickly as my business and social careers were excellent. The children were fine and our son Chuck was now in kindergarten, but my relationship with Mildred was deteriorating. I had the opinion that she no longer loved me, and that she didn't even like me. This continued on for a couple of years, which in truth drove me away in other directions, some good and some bad.

In late 1963, I joined Hollister Coil Spring Company in a joint venture under the name of Master Accessories Company, which was in my new building in Santa Fe Springs, a small industrial city in East Los Angeles County directly south of Whittier. The joint venture was based on using leftover coils of scrap wire and producing reinforced concrete accessories, small wire chairs and fittings to hold reinforcing bars in place while pouring concrete. Rebar is actually engineered to be exactly in place plus or minus fractions of inches. It was a natural merger due to my background in the reinforcing steel industry and Hollister's illustrious history in producing every conceivable type of wire products for specific end uses.

The reason this merger came about dated back one year to a visit I had from my contact at Caldwell Banker. When he arrived at my shack in Norwalk, which was now even more unattractive and shoddy looking, he was not very impressed. He was dressed to the hilt—dark suit, shirt and matching tie, plus black shoes that were shined so that you could see yourself. I remember feeling ashamed asking him to be seated. He wasted no time getting to the subject for his visit. "Carl, I have a very excellent client who has been doing business with me for almost 15 years. In fact, he is now a personal friend. Over the years he has acquired strategic pieces of land, on which he builds specialized structures to suit his tenants' requirements. He leases them back at very low per square foot prices initially and then escalates their rent every three years based on economic growth. This is not always the case, as a couple times in the past 15 years he has altered the cost of living clause for what he considers to be a good honest potential company, including the people behind the company. The reason I thought of you was that last month we closed escrow on a piece of property covering 50,000 square feet that is zoned M-3 Industrial that allows scrap metal, a junkyard and recycling. It also allows all types of manufacturing, warehousing, storage and offices. I know, as I have had to investigate, that your business is growing and expanding and from what I see here I think I really have something for you and my client friend to talk and think about."

I thanked him for the complimentary statements and accepted. He reached over my desk, picked up my phone, dialed a number without looking and asked for a Mr. Flynn. He proceeded to tell Mr. Flynn that he thought they had the perfect tenant for his new property in the Springs, asking when he could be available to meet with me. We settled on a meeting two days later to see if we did indeed have common grounds. The luncheon went famously and it was obvious the elderly gentleman liked my Caldwell Banker man and seemingly me. It was mutually decided that I would sit down with Caldwell Banker and design a structure built to fulfill all my necessary requirements in order to price out the total costs and come to an estimated cost per square foot leasing agreement. Mr. Flynn stated that he would be very flexible for a young growing business such as Master Metals on the recommendations of Caldwell Banker.

This period of time and work required almost six weeks before we got it right. This was another wonderful learning opportunity. Other than my residences, I had never designed a commercial and manufacturing warehouse before. This would include offices, multiple toilet facilities, specialized storage facilities, areas built to hold monstrous manufacturing presses, loading docks, roads in and out, sump holes for drainage and parking facilities, including our own gasoline pump to service our fleet of trucks! When we finally sat down with the final architectural plans drawn up by Caldwell Banker at no cost to Master Metals, I was scared to death to hear what the figure would be. These two men had worked very hard to build Master Metals a building and environment we would be proud to work in! I was afraid that if the price were far too much for Master Metals to afford, I'd feel like a beaten dog with my tail between my legs slinking out the door.

As the price for the first three years was only 25% more than we were paying in Norwalk with the possibilities of productivity gains, including gasoline costs, it was possible that our operating costs would decrease! On top of that, the escalation clause would be 5% total or cost-of-living, whichever was least, at the end of each three-year period. My lease in Norwalk expired just over 30 days from that day and the next day I asked for a six-month lease extension, which I received. The following day, I signed the lease agreement with Caldwell Banker and the building started the very next week. With the new building in mind, my expansion and growth plans changed almost completely.

Turning back the clock slightly, there was a change in my Pebble Beach golf and Bridge group. Locke Barrett had dropped out and was replaced by one of the great Bridge players in America, Lloyd Rentsch. Lloyd was my age and president of Wyoming Construction Company. He was a neighbor of Dave Hall and lived in Palos Verdes, California. He was a training pilot instructor during World War II who had his own single-engine plane at the time, a 182. His golf game was not quite as good as mine, but he was one hell of a competitor. He and his wife Valentine became very good friends of the Garvais and we became an eightsome who traveled and played golf and Bridge together for the next two to three years. Lloyd was extremely intelligent and socially a class act.

It was during this period in time that I became a very active tournament player in golf tournaments from Pebble Beach south to Palm Springs. All of these golf tournaments were best ball of partner member's guest or invitationals and I was asked by all sorts of people to be their partner! The most fun, though, was partnering with Dave, Garvai, Rentsch and Goddard. Two or three times a year Howard Smith, Hacienda's golf pro, would ask me to join him in a pro amateur tournament, which I considered an honor! In 1962, a friend and insurance agent for Wyoming Construction and their parent company, Monolith Cement, Bob Reeves, put a team together to challenge us at Pebble Beach. Bob Reeves, Dan Compton, Bill Maxwell and Hugh Krudowski were all from Woodbridge Country Club in Lodi, California.

On Thursday morning we met in Lloyd's hangar at the Torrance Airport, where we loaded our clubs and gear into his plane. We flew mainly up the coast and then went inland above San Luis Obispo and up the Salinas Valley, very careful not to infringe on any federal lands or military airspace! We landed at the Monterey Airport around 10:45 a.m., unloaded all of our belongings into a rental car and headed straight for the pro shop at Pebble Beach. We arrived about one half hour before our starting times. The Woodbridge team was already there ready to go on the putting green. We hurriedly got dressed and met our opponents and decided that to start out the first day, the two best golfers from the north should play our two best golfers from the south, which meant Dave and Bill would be playing Maxwell and Krudowski, while Lloyd and I played Compton and Reeves. We switched partners every day thereafter until everybody played with everybody.

  We played four rounds of golf starting on Thursday and ending Sunday morning and had lunch in the Del Monte Lodge Grill with the losing team having to buy. There were a few other very small side bets. The only guy who bet everybody, including his own team members, was Krudowski. After golf on the way back to The Tickle Pink, we stopped at the old Mediterranean Market and Deli and loaded up with ham, salami, breast of chicken and sliced roast beef, plus all types of cheese, pickles, mayonnaise, mustards, horseradish and sandwich breads for a late snack supper along with our game of Bridge. None of us drank hard liquor during our cutthroat Bridge games.

  The first day as we finished after 5:00 p.m., we did have a cocktail in the grill, but we left for The Tickle Pink and the Mediterranean to load up as usual with our snack food and to play Bridge and eat. The north team headed to Carmel where they were staying at a very nice motel. There was obviously a discrepancy in handicaps, as they did not win one single bet, not even a tie. Krudowski lost every bet, including to his own teammates!

Unbelievably, this rout continued through the next three days. After the Thursday game, we changed the format so that each day the losing team had to buy the lunch and the only other bets were nominal. Krudowski won a total of one bet that week. Our south team was victorious every day! The north team then matched cards for who would pay for the entire luncheon. Compton won that honor for one day and Krudowski for two. The luncheons at the grill were expensive, as they ran close to $250 per lunch even in 1961! This group of gentlemen stayed and played together for the next 30 years, except for deaths and relocation, with the exception of Maxwell, who took the loss personally after the shellacking and chose not to return. The following year he was replaced by Tom Klinger, an absolutely superb golfer and human being—the younger brother of my friend Bob Klinger from my Soulé/Pacific States Steel days—and he played with us for the next 30 years.

With the merger with Hollister, my employee count quadrupled and I now had 28 people working in Santa Fe Springs plus a receptionist/secretary. I also had a network of distributors in all major accessory markets from San Diego to Seattle, east as far as Wyoming, and south through Arizona and Nevada. In 1965, I hired a sales manager, Doc Leonard, who did nothing else but sell our products and do most of our accessory sales traveling to visit our distributors.

In 1964 there was a massive earthquake centered near Anchorage, Alaska. That night, I had a call from Bob Klinger, the president of the Western Concrete Reinforcing Steel Institute (WCRSI), asking me if I could fly ASAP to Anchorage to investigate the damage to all types of construction, not just reinforced concrete, all at the expense of WCRSI. His request was to just find out why buildings failed to withstand the quake! There would be another man such as myself to help the total investigation, but he hadn't tried to find him yet as I was his first priority! At 7:00 a.m. the next morning, I was on the plane. A stewardess let me know that the engineering man would meet me around 12:30 p.m. in the same terminal. There must have been many people going to Anchorage for the same reason, as there wasn't an empty seat! Upon arrival, a man was standing holding a card with my name, my guide and driver. He led me a couple gates away and we awaited Mr. Murray's arrival. The driver stated that he had never lived through what he experienced yesterday and the incredible devastation that had taken place was seemingly selective. It was hard to understand why some structures completely fell to the ground and others, at least from the outside appearance, seemed untouched. I told him that I wasn't in any way an expert about those things, but that's exactly what Mr. Murray and I were there to learn.

Mr. Murray arrived and after introductions, we drove to downtown Anchorage. Just as our guide had told me, houses, barns and structures of all kinds had been totally leveled, but yet there were other structures that looked like nothing had happened. The tallest buildings in Anchorage in 1964 were only four stories high and those were mostly standing—from the outside that is! We investigated every type of construction we could find, from mud huts to structural steel, and of course reinforced concrete. Interestingly, wood construction of two stories failed almost half the time, structural steel only 20%, reinforced concrete 20% and the mud huts 10%. In the middle of Anchorage stood a two-story department store. When we entered on the ground floor, it appeared that absolutely nothing had occurred. The store covered an entire area from one street to another. Almost dead center in the building was a solid wall of dirt, gravel and pavement standing over 12 feet high, running the width of the building. We had to walk around the block to enter the building from the other street! As we walked, there was no division in the sidewalk. It was perfectly normal, except for a slight crack in the concrete that appeared to be in line with the separation in the store. Again, there was no visible damage, but in the middle of the store you were looking down a 12-foot hole. This was an isolated case.

I asked Murray if there was an explanation for this, but he didn't have a clue. He replied, "I don't understand what we're looking at. This doesn't make sense!" Murray was from San Francisco and had lived through many minor earthquakes. He was also the chief structural engineer for Murphy Pacific (the large bridge builder, structural steel building contracting firm) and the new reinforced concrete firm, Murphy Steel. It really made me wonder why Bob Klinger wanted me there!

The one thing that all the building failures had in common was that they all imploded from failure at the floor joints to the outside structural columns. The roofs would fall onto the floor below, which in turn would pancake onto the next floor. One other significant item was that whether made of wood, steel or reinforced concrete, the sleeves that covered the connecting rods adding strength to the joints flew off with such force that we found some over 1 1/2 miles from a building site. It was quite evident to Murray and I that the weakness in all multi-story structures was in the floor joints, indicating that lightweight floors would be a tremendous advantage over normal structural steel beams for flooring. The material or product to connect the floors to the outer structure would have to be improved to weather severe earthquakes.

After two days and two nights, we both flew home. On the plane, I wrote my findings for the WCRSI. A couple of weeks later, I had a call from Mr. Klinger asking me if Murray and I had collaborated on our recommendations. I told him that I had written mine independently on the flight home. Murray and I, who I told him was an excellent choice, hadn't talked since. Bob replied, "Both the reports were almost identical. Anyway, thanks for a job well done!" In truth, I was the lucky one, as I personally witnessed and learned so much that I was able to use in the future; not only for myself but for the construction industry's battle to minimize the effects of earthquakes!

In 1963, in an effort to save my marriage and the destruction of my family, Mildred and I joined the local Whittier Unitarian Church. This particular group had no minister as such, but had a core of 150 to 200 active members of which approximately 100 attended church meetings on Sunday mornings. Like Mildred and I, they all perceived themselves to be Christians. They also believed that all people should have the freedom to choose whatever religion satisfied them and their immediate families. They were very liberal in their thinking and felt that politics had no place in religion. The majority didn't believe in confessionals, but in instilling a sense of conscience, particularly in the young. I went so far as to lead a Sunday service by giving a program (not a lecture) that used music to show love, peace, serenity and bringing happiness to all souls. Happy to say, it was very well received.

For a short while this improved Mildred's and my relationship. But this didn't last very long. We tried a trial separation, which turned out for me to be a huge mistake. I was devastated without my children! For the first time, I was angry with Mildred and my love for her was gone! I couldn't believe that she could throw away our family. I then started on the downhill road trying to find love. I knew I had the love of my children, but I desired love from a woman. After a period of five to six months, I decided that if Mildred would take me back I'd do anything to reconstruct my marriage and family.

My mother, trying to help, moved from San Mateo to downtown La Habra to a small and not-so-nice apartment, which was all I could find locally. In hindsight, this didn't help, as in the 16 years of our marriage neither of these two women liked each other. Nevertheless, during this short period my mother, like myself, tried hard to save the family! Mother finally decided that the best place for her was to return to Tacoma, Washington and live with her sister Naomi, who had a large house with plenty of room. Naomi had invited her to move in and share expenses, which mom could well afford. I helped her relocate by driving her and all of her belongings in her car to Tacoma. Mom was really disappointed for all of us and her closing words were, "I love you. Please stop beating yourself to death!"

During the early 1960s I started playing in all the golf tournaments to which I was invited, particularly in the Palm Springs area. My favorite golf course by far was the La Quinta Country Club, a private club owned by the La Quinta Hotel. It was the most beautiful location in the Coachella Valley, surrounded by mountains on three sides in a cove that was simply gorgeous. The golf course was very difficult but extremely manicured and the putting surfaces were perfect. After my merger with Hollister, I had purchased a new condominium unit between Cathedral City and Rancho Mirage just off Highway 111. This was only the second condominium project built in California. The management of Hollister and I shared the ownership. In late 1964, I received an invitation to join the La Quinta Country Club as a junior member. To qualify, one had to be less than 37 years of age. The terms were $500 down and $500 per year towards a membership, to cost $3000, with all the yearly payments to be applied against the total membership cost. The dues during this time were $100 per month for junior members. I felt that this was too good to be true and a wonderful opportunity to escape the city. With Hollister's encouragement, I joined La Quinta Country Club.

After the trial separation with Mildred and moving back in and trying everything in my power to bring love and happiness back to our family, in a heated exchange between Mildred and I she ordered me out of the house! I refused to leave and Mildred retreated to our bedroom. Shortly thereafter she reappeared, suitcase in hand, climbed into our new family station wagon and drove off. Self incrimination struck me like a ton of bricks. Was I really that rotten that the woman I loved who shared five wonderful children with me would leave her children? I thought I knew where she went and when I saw our car in the parking lot I returned home and called the motel. I simply said that if she would come back to the children I would move out instantly and that if she wanted a divorce I would be agreeable.

That's pretty much the way our marriage ended. In the divorce settlement Mildred gave me legal custody of the boys, even though at that moment there was no way that was possible. She asked for no alimony and only equitable child support. The day after our divorce was final, she remarried a man from the Unitarian church who had recently divorced his wife. I had a telephone call from Big Al, offering me money for my half share in the Gurrea trust. It was a very fair and sizable amount, but I told him that I didn't want money, but would like it to be divided equally between my five children. He agreed. This ended the darkest days in my life.

MEISTERLIN FAMILY PHOTOS

1957
Cinderella Homes in Anaheim, California
(L-R) Carl Meisterlin, Cynthia, Debbie, Chuck,
Claudia and Baby Scott on floor

1958
Cinderella Homes in Anaheim, California
Chuck, Carl, Scott, Mildred, Debbie,
Cynthia, Claudia

Seal Beach, California 1967
(L-R) Claudia, Edith Rose Palmer Meisterlin,
Cynthia, Debbie, Chuck and Scott

Disneyland, Anaheim, California 1978
On Stairway:
Tim, Becky, Claudia, Timmy, Scott, Julie, Irene,
Carl, Debbie, Catherine Hamblin, Roy Hamblin,
Chuck, Annie
Front Row: Shane, Dick, R. Scott, Cynthia

1977
On the Queen Mary in the Winston Churchill Suite
Top Row: Carl Meisterlin and Irene, Roy Hamblin
Bottom Row: Irene's Mother Julia Carlson
and Catherine Paprocki Hamblin

1989
Del Mar Race Track
Irene's Brother, J. Vernon Carlson
(Note the cane now used by Carl
and Irene's racing handbag!)

The Meisterlin Family
Carly, Julie and Scott, Max

1969
La Quinta Country Club
Scott Meisterlin's First Hole in One, Age 13
With Jack Renner
Pro Golfer now playing the Senior Tour

The Mezenski Family
Shane, Dick, R. Scott, Cynthia

The Wills Family
Julie, Kathryn, Jamie, Michael

The Meisterlin Family
Mindy, Chuck, Suzi, Leah

The Keller Family
Debbie and Scott

Chapter 16

Tragedies and Tribulations

The next few years of my life were not pretty but did serve to prepare me for success! I had lost a great portion of my self-confidence, particularly with the opposite sex. Fortunately my business continued to grow and prosper, which became critical as paying child support and living like a chief executive, plus having accommodations to house five children ate up all surplus cash flow! During this period Master Accessories began doing a large amount of business in Las Vegas, which was in the midst of a building boom.

As mentioned, Mildred married her boyfriend Roger the day after our divorce became final. She sold our home in Hidden Canyon, which caused another legal problem as Master Metals had secured my mother's loan by using the home as security. I had no choice but to attach the escrow for the amount of mom's loan. This money went directly into a joint account of Master Metals and Accessories and these two firms were the collateral for her loan. The children were with me when she and Roger were honeymooning. I was now residing in an apartment on Ocean Avenue in Seal Beach, a stone's throw from the Belmont Shore district of Long Beach, and had an ocean view and a swimming pool. I remember that on the night of Mildred's marriage, Claudia and I were walking on the beach and I felt not only hysteria, but suicidal for the first and only time in my life!

    I saw the children whenever I was permitted, which for me was never enough. I had been given legal custody of Chuck and Scott, but I still wasn't in a position, nor did I desire, to break up our family. Doc Leonard was proving to be an excellent sales manager for Master Accessories and expanding our profits. Sam Peters, who worked for the American Brass Company, approached me one day and suggested that he could join with me to grow Master Metal's profits enough to more than pay his salary and expenses. He asked if I would consider him and an opportunity for ownership? Sam was about my age and had a very nice wife and two children between eight and twelve years old. I told Sam to make up a document stating exactly what he wanted or needed for a salary, plus all expenses required of a sales manager and that I'd make it a priority. The following week Sam stopped by the office and left his document. There were no legal problems to consider according to my lawyer—it all came down to business economics. Brass and copper scrap metal at the time were very profitable items. I liked Sam and his family, plus I thought he was a gentleman of honesty and integrity. I offered him a salary with full expenses including a company car, approximately 15% less than Doc's plus 10% of Master Metals as well as the first option to purchase if I decided to sell. I included a 5% additional ownership clause per year for two years! When we next met and I presented this offer, I could tell he was disappointed. I told him to take it home, to talk to his wife and get back to me. I also told him how much I liked him and his idea to join our talents together. The next morning, Sam was waiting for me at the office and requested 5% of the annual profits of Master Metals. We agreed and shook hands and I had my secretary send it to our lawyer. Two weeks later, Sam came to work and again I got lucky as he accomplished exactly what I envisioned but far more!

A year later, the Master Accessory factory payroll had increased to 34 full-time workers. The metals division increased to five drivers and seven workers, including Bear. We called Bear the plant manager as everybody knew he was the glue that held both divisions together and set the example for others to follow. Shortly thereafter we had another hiccup in the metals industry economy. We hadn't over expanded, but we were all in agreement that we needed to tighten up our operations—not cost-cutting—but giving even better service and working with our customers to enable both of us to weather the storm ahead. For the balance of the year we weren't losing money, but we did have cash flow problems and for the first time I was forced to lay off employees. This is the low point in any entrepreneur's life!

As far as my personal life was concerned, after the move to Seal Beach I had many lady friends. Some came from business, some were friends of friends, and others from hangouts of mine where maître d's and bartenders would introduce me. I had a couple of girlfriends during this period, one of which was Sherry Nelson, an owner of a local employment agency that was used by the L.A. Rams organization. In the middle of 1967, I dated her after she called upon me at my office. At that time we were in the negative transition and I spent most of that first interview trying to find if she could solve the problem I had for having to let really good, fine and loyal employees go! She said that she would be pleased if I sent these people to her agency and in fact she did find work for two of them. After this, I asked her for a date and as the year was coming to a close she was the only female I was dating, but it was not a love affair. Sherry was approximately ten years younger than I, not beautiful but attractive, and a very good businesswoman.

Doc, Sam and I were working countless extra hours trying to drum up new business and hanging onto what we had. But hard work does pay, as both divisions were holding their own and improving in late September to early November. We weren't yet ready to hire people back, but the workers had plenty of work to do.

My mother had called from Tacoma and asked if she could come and stay with me for a couple days and if she could use the Palm Springs condo for a few weeks if it was available. She was sick and tired of all the rain in her area, stating that it had been raining for over 40 straight days. I said, "Sure, you can come in time for Thanksgiving Day if you'd like. You can stay through New Year's if that's agreeable, and I'll join you for the week between Christmas and New Year's Day." She thought that was wonderful! The next day I received a call giving me her travel information and a few days later I confirmed that both Chuck and Scott were going to be with us for Thanksgiving weekend! The condo would accommodate four, so I wasn't concerned about space.

    She arrived on Tuesday afternoon looking great, but obviously paler than usual due to no sunshine. We spent the night at my flat in Seal Beach and I went to work as usual on Wednesday morning. I had a lunch appointment with a prospective customer which I kept, went back to the office where Chuck and Scott were waiting and then back to Seal Beach for mom. Off we went on our Thanksgiving holiday as well as to celebrate Scott's 11th birthday on Thanksgiving Day! The traffic on the 15 Freeway was quite heavy heading east as expected. We reached Riverside and the traffic was moving slower than usual, about 45 m.p.h., when all of a sudden, out of nowhere, a car came hurtling over the center divider and hit us head-on! We were seated with Scott sitting between mom and I in the front seat, and Chuck sleeping in the back. The center divider at that time was a strip of gravel about 12-feet wide and the freeway was on a curve where the accident took place. I didn't see the car coming until the last instant but I did get my right arm up and deflected Scott over to the right, otherwise I'm sure he would've been killed! He did have some lacerations and a small scar, which lasted for years. Chuck had nothing more than a couple of bruises. Even though I had a seatbelt on I was pinned behind the steering wheel and mom sitting in the right-hand passenger seat was badly hurt. Luckily, we were driving my Buick Riviera, which was very solidly built. The other car was a Ford.

I remember very little on impact except for the windshield crystallizing and smoke coming from under the hood of the car! Our Buick had moved to the right one lane, but again luckily no other cars were involved. Help came almost immediately and I remember somebody prying the driver's side door open and a man carefully trying to pull me out from behind the wheel. After a few minutes, which seemed like forever, another man joined and they were able to remove me. I don't remember anything after that until I awoke in the emergency room of the Riverside Hospital.

When I awakened, there was a doctor there. I asked him what he was doing. He replied, "I'm giving you a new nose. I'm taking skin from your left ear and grafting it to the nose you lost!" I asked, "How's my mother?" He replied, "I understand she's okay but has some broken bones!" I asked him about my sons. "Only one son was admitted to the hospital. He's right over there and will be released as soon as somebody picks him up." He told me that unfortunately the one person in the other car had died about an hour ago. A few hours later Claudia, Cynthia and Debbie arrived and were allowed to see me. I'm not sure they spoke to their grandmother. I do know that Scott went home. Thursday and Friday I don't remember at all.

On Saturday morning, my regular doctor appeared and told me that I was being moved after breakfast to a private room on Sunday. He wanted me to make some plans, as I was now out of danger and would be better off at home with around-the-clock care until the Christmas holidays. We discussed my mother's problems. She had a fractured kneecap and a broken hip. These would take time and she was not out of danger yet, but there was a good chance they could move her to a private room within a week. He thought she would recover but it would take a hip replacement and a couple months for the knee to heal normally.

He also asked if my condo in Palm Springs had a heated swimming pool? I told him there was and guessed it was around 81 to 82 degrees. He asked if I could get my homeowners association to increase the heat to 86 degrees? I told him I would try to find out. He stated, "If you can have the pool like that, it would be perfect body temperature and swimming three times a day would be the greatest therapy you can find!" He also told me off the record that the car that hit me was a company car of a large corporation and that the accident was 100% caused by their unfortunate driver! He advised me that when I was moved to a private room, one of the first people to call on me would be their insurance claim representative, which happened the next day. He reported that Scott was seeing a doctor in Long Beach and his problems were easily taken care of and not to worry, that he wouldn't be scarred for life and there were no signs of head trauma. Again he said off the record, "I don't think all your medical care, your mother's care and Scott's will be a problem, as your insurance will pay for every bit of it. Money should not be a part of the equation."

I called the homeowner's association and agreed to pay the difference between the normal pool heating bill and what it would cost to raise the heat for 30 days starting the following Wednesday. I phoned Sherry Nelson and told her I was in the emergency room at the Riverside Hospital and what had occurred. I asked her if she could visit me and that I needed some help to find a 24-hour caregiver. She said she could make it that night about 8:00 p.m. That evening directly after dinner they rolled my mother's bed into my cubicle for us to talk. Mom was not feeling well, but we talked anyway. The conversation had mostly to do with her wishes for what was to come next. The doctors had told her that morning the news that they had shared with me. She was not very happy!

We were discussing all of her options, none of which seemed to please her, when Sherry Nelson arrived. I introduced them and explained to my mom that I'd requested her to join us in our conversation. Sherry told mom that she could get her around-the-clock nursing care in a place of residence so she would not have to go to a nursing home or hospital, and I assured mom that it would be at no cost to her as my insurance would take care of it all. Mom said she'd think about it and excused herself and was rolled back to her cubicle. Sherry told me she would have somebody pick me up on Tuesday and take me to the condo, as I no longer had an automobile. The Riviera was totaled! We talked for a short time thereafter and she left.

On Sunday morning, my doctor was standing at the foot of my bed in my private room explaining to me how close I had come to death. My chest had literally been crushed within fractions of an inch, which easily could have been fatal. He said that I must be in great physical condition, as my recuperative powers were outstanding. He then said mom was also doing better this morning, looking and sounding great. A short time after finishing breakfast and reading the Sunday paper, I looked up to see my doctor standing at the foot of the bed again. "Carl, I don't know how to tell you or explain, but your mother has passed on."

I knew that my mom had chosen to die! She had been a lost soul ever since my dad passed away in 1960. I was fortunate in that I was prepared for this terrible outcome. Although I was sad, we had time to say goodbye the night before and by all accounts hers was a peaceful death. Her passing was a completely different experience for me than the loss of my birth mother. Edith was the greatest mother a son could ever have! I truly loved her.

On Tuesday, I was released to my home-care lady, who arrived right on time and checked me out and signed documents along with me. The lady was Sherry herself. Surprise, surprise! She explained that her business was doing well and she needed a working vacation. A month in the desert taking care of me was perfect. She drove us to the condo, unloaded the car, doing all the physical work herself, put me to bed and left for the market with money I had given her. She returned home a couple of hours later with bags of food and we were in business. I was in the large bed in the bedroom and she set up her sleeping quarters in the den. The doctor had given me instructions that I absolutely should not have any alcohol until he saw me in ten days! That afternoon we walked out to the pool and tested the temperature of the water. It felt warmer then usual, but not quite body temperature. The next morning it was exactly what the doctor ordered! I enjoyed my three swims a day for which Sherry was always there, and sometimes even entered the pool.

Before going on, there were two things that I accomplished on Monday before being released. First, both Doc and Sam arrived and we had a very short meeting where they assured me that I wouldn't be missed at the company. Secondly, in keeping with mother's wishes, I had her cremated and the ashes sent to Chapel of the Chimes in Oakland to be placed in a book matching my father's to stand next to his.

On the Thursday of the following week, we left the condo early for an appointment with the doctor in Riverside, which went very well. I could resume my normal life slowly was the way the doctor put it—absolutely no excessive drinking or exercise and to see him in another ten days. From Riverside, we drove to my plant in Santa Fe Springs where Sherry left me and proceeded to her office.

In the early afternoon, we drove back to the condo. That night, much to my surprise, Sherry climbed into my bed. She stayed with me and took care of me until the Christmas holidays.

Sherry had a son the same age as my Scott and I began thinking of uniting our families. In January, I continued living in Seal Beach but occasionally I would stay overnight at Sherry's. This continued on for several months and when her son, Gary, would be visiting his father, Sherry stayed with me in Seal Beach. We were married on July 4th and took a week's honeymoon in Hawaii. In June, the month before the wedding, I'd leased a home in Huntington Harbor for one year starting on June 15th and we both moved all of our belongings that month. We started cohabitation with Gary, Chuck and Scott on returning from the honeymoon. From the very start the boys didn't get along well! All three boys had completely different personalities! Sherry's business was not doing well do to her negligence and was experiencing cash flow problems and she made no secret that she expected me to help her financially, which was the best solution. As a family, we were strapped for cash.

At the same time, Doc Leonard came to me and said he'd had an offer from my largest competitor at a salary much greater than he was now receiving. As cash had been tight for many months prior, I knew exactly how much Master Accessories could afford. I offered Doc a 10% raise to which he responded, "Carl, I wish I could accept that because you've changed my life for the better and I love working with you, but the offer is much, much larger! Would you like me to stay for a short period of time?" I said, "No, Doc, as you're going to work for our competitor it would be better if you left today." I had no hard feelings as I had enjoyed our relationship, both in business and as friends.

I had been paying Doc and Sam over 80% of the combined salary that I received from both divisions. There was no way with my personal income crunch that I could afford to replace Doc, which meant many more hours traveling and entertaining. The cost to the accessory division for travel and expenses did not increase and we were saving Doc's salary, but after two months I was totally exhausted. I put out a feeler to Superior Concrete Accessories (SCA), the largest concrete accessory company based in Chicago, who had a small production and sales division in L.A. They made me a decent offer for our total accessory business including machinery, production inventory, and raw material and predicated on my personally becoming their west coast general sales manager! In talking the offer over with Sam (who was operating the scrap metal division), I explained that if I accepted SCA's proposal, the metals division would have to carry the complete overhead for the plant and offices minus my salary. Sam, who now already owned a 20% interest in Master Metals, agreed that this was our only solution. I accepted SCA's proposal and was now working full time for them. My employment actually started approximately a week later as my contract had to be signed in Chicago at their corporate headquarters.

On my flight to Chicago, they had sent me a first-class ticket where I found myself setting on the aisle in the row directly behind Zsa Zsa Gabor! During the flight, Zsa Zsa's little girl moved back into my seat and I sat next to her famous mother. Zsa Zsa was very pretty, but wore extremely heavy make up. What really excited me was her accent. Just listening to her talk and believe me, she was a talker, was a sexual experience! Before we disembarked at the airport, she told me she'd be at the famous Pump Room that night.

I was met on arrival and taken directly to SCA's corporate offices in the heart of Chicago. After meeting all the top brass and signing my formal contract, I was escorted to a hotel close by. There was no invitation for dinner or meetings for the next day, just hello and goodbye. I had brought with me the working drawings on two new products, the first to be used in the National Highway Program, which called for reinforced concrete highways across the U.S.A. and the other on the new highway bridges' specifications using lightweight reinforced concrete. I had asked to be allowed to speak with their top engineering people, but was ignored. I left their offices prior to dinnertime very disheartened. On arriving at my hotel, I immediately called my airline for which I had an open first-class ticket and requested reservations back to L.A. ASAP. I phoned Sherry and advised her I'd be home for dinner tomorrow.

After shaving and bathing and making myself look

as good as possible, I started for the Pump Room. Before I left the hotel lobby, the doorman stopped me and said, "Sir, I must accompany you out to your cab as here in Chicago it's too dangerous for a person alone to be standing waiting for a cab. Where are you headed tonight?" I replied, "The Pump Room." He called a cab, didn't accept a tip, and I was on my way to meet Zsa Zsa for dinner—or so I hoped. I arrived early and I advised the maître d' that I was waiting for my party. She arrived with four people, two men and two women, and I jumped to my feet to greet her. Without acknowledging me in the slightest, she walked right on by without the blink of an eye. I took a cab back to my hotel and had dinner in the coffee shop. In the morning nobody appeared to take me to O'Hare and again I took a cab. I arrived at LAX at noon and proceeded to my new place of employment. They weren't expecting me until the next day, but I was shown to a small office without any windows. This whole trip was a farce! I thought back to the previous 36 hours and I thought then and I know now that they purchased Master Accessories only to eliminate a competitor.

    I didn't give up easily, and to prove my worth with the State of Oregon Highway Department, I used the first of my new products on a five-mile stretch of highway outside of Pendleton, Oregon running beside the Columbia River. Previously using other clips and ties, the workers would accomplish a mile a day. With my product, they finished six miles in less than two days! We were a big success and the State of Washington Division of Highways ordered product to be used on Interstate 5 north of the Columbia River.

The following month, we used a newer lightweight assembly on the crucial top section of the Coronado Bridge in San Diego, which also was successful. It was during the inspection of the very first section being installed that I experienced the most terrifying—yes, terrifying—hour of my life. I'm afraid of heights, with more than a slight case of vertigo. That day the Coronado Bridge was available from either side by a chain-link catwalk, which is rather unstable. We were able to walk on solid concrete about one third of the way up the bridge and I could see that the distance from there to the very top was a catwalk, which at its peak was approximately 1,750 feet high. When we finished our inspection of the new product, the State of California inspector and chief engineer for the contractor said, "Let's go over to the other side and see how the conventional construction appears?" I agreed, thinking that we would walk down and take a car around to the other side. This was stupid on my part, as it would have taken hours, as you would have to use ferryboat services! There were four of us in all that stepped onto the catwalk. I was the third person in line, and I started out with my eyes open clinging on to the tubular rails that were 42" to 45" high. As we continued heading up what felt like a steep incline, the catwalk began swaying. I could no longer keep my eyes open and I walked the balance of the distance to the other side by feeling my way! On arriving on the other side all three men complimented me on not upchucking. One of them said, "Nine out of ten people we walk the bridge with actually throw up!" I told them that I was far too scared to get sick!

There was no word from Chicago about our progress and it was obvious in my phone conversations with my two superiors that they could care less. In the L.A. factory itself, most of the machinery from Master Accessories wasn't being used. I had nine months to go on my contract with SCA and I started making plans for a move in some other direction.

On the home front, the three boys had become a major problem! In Long Beach there was a very highly accredited military boys school with boarding if needed. As we had three prospective students, there was bus service right to a corner in Huntington Harbor only a couple of blocks away. It was actually more than we could afford at the time but we agreed it would to be the best decision to give them two semesters there, and hope for some success as well as growth towards becoming young men. Chuck seemed to like military school, Scott hated it and Larry spent far too much time in the principal's office! Sherry wanted to start a second office closer to home and have her father run the Downey office as he was available. I liked and trusted her mom and dad and I thought that this was a good idea, as it would help both her folks and Sherry. Unfortunately, this put a larger strain on our finances. To complicate matters in November, Sam came to me and wanted to buy me out. We had a buy-sell arrangement and he bid more per share then I did. In mid-December I no longer was a part of Master Metals and receiving no income!

Luckily, just before Thanksgiving in 1968, I had a call from Philip Murphy, Rich Murphy's older brother and the sole owner of Murphy Pacific Corporation in San Francisco, whose chief engineer I'd worked with in Alaska. I acknowledged that I had seen him once, but unfortunately was not introduced. He stated, "Carl, both Rich and my chief engineer have said you're the solution to a problem I have, a really good problem! I would like you to fly to San Francisco ASAP for a personal meeting and lunch. I'll make myself available to fit your schedule."
I replied I could be there tomorrow morning if I could get a seat on a plane. He gave me his private phone number to call so he would have someone at the airport to meet me. I hung up and was able to get a round-trip ticket.
I had no idea what Phil had in mind and I'd heard nothing from Rich Murphy, but I was in Phil's office shortly after 11:00 a.m. Phil did most of the talking and started by saying he'd seen me for the first time at Del Monte Lodge on the day Kennedy was assassinated and that I was the carrier of the bad news to the podium! He also said his vice president in charge of engineering had great respect for my work ethic and more important, my astute judgment! 'Wow!' I thought to myself, and I was really wondering what was coming. He said, "Carl, I want to start a new company using a different method for building high-rise buildings and parking garages that are significantly more

earthquake proof then what we now construct. My first question to you is if I were to make you an offer to run this new company would you be interested?" I replied, "Yes sir, I would!" With that, he started asking questions about my personal background and people within the industry that he could call for references and/or opinions. We then took the elevator to the top of the building where there was a lounge and restaurant. We talked about the industry as a whole, where we were headed and about my ideas for starting a new company in a brand new industry. I stressed how important it was going to be to promote a totally different approach to constructing high-rise structures. My suggestion was to buy some work so that the structural engineers and architects would begin designing all high-rise buildings using post-tensioned concrete floors. We knew these would cost less both in material and labor and be 90% percent safer. "Exactly!" he replied.

    After lunch, we returned to his office. He said, "Carl, there is no need for me to talk to anybody else. The people I know who know you vouch for you 100% and you obviously think the way I do! Here's the deal, I'll put up unlimited lines of credit at three banks: Bank of America, Crocker Bank and Security Pacific. I'll own 75% of the company and the remaining 25% will go to you. When we start making money a few years hence, we'll work out a very lucrative bonus plan for both of us! Go home, think about it, call me next Monday and tell me how much money you want for a salary and how many internal people you'll need to get started. I'll put cash directly into the bank the day we start, which I would like to do on January 2, 1969!"

The following day I came up with a figure of $21,750 per year, plus car and all expenses pertaining to my duties. I also submitted a name that was appropriate, Tenscon, Inc., a private corporation per Phil's orders. I received a message from Phil approving the salary and the new name—which he complimented me on as it was simple and told the world what we were all about! The papers of incorporation and my salary contract all would be delivered special delivery as soon as his law firm finished them and he approved for my signature and approval. He suggested that I hire a lawyer to make sure that everything was the way I desired. He also authorized my being paid from Tenscon's new bank account all my expenses incurred from my visit there, all lawyer fees and any other appropriate personal costs! He advised me to start looking at automobiles, but reminded me of something he'd learned a long time ago—that I shouldn't drive a car that's better than my customers, just a good solid car that could be used for business and pleasure. That had always worked for him as he climbed the ladder. The paperwork arrived. I had my lawyer study it and when he approved it as written, I signed all documents with the notary there to witness it. I had the biggest opportunity in my life—a new industry, a new company I was president of, and if anything, over capitalized. I should also add that Phil Murphy gave me his word that he would never interfere or question my decisions as long as any mistakes were honest. "It's your company, Carl!" he told me. "Call me if you have a problem, but frankly I'll be happy if I don't hear from you as I'll know everything's okay. I'll be depositing $25,000 on January 2nd with Bank of America and Tenscon's checkbook should be available for you to pick up at your local branch on January 3rd. For the balance of the year I will forward $10,000 per month until you receive some contracts, at which time I will increase these amounts to cover what we hope will be a large increase in labor costs." I was overwhelmed. The documents, when they arrived for my lawyer's approval, were already signed and notarized by Phil.

On the day before the Christmas holidays, I went to my little office at SCA and removed all my personal items. Oddly I had made no friends at SCA, even there in L.A. During the week I sent a registered letter, which had been prepared by my lawyer, resigning effective January 1, 1969. I never received a reply or phone call, but I did have the satisfaction of doing what I could for SCA and that in the short time I was there I improved their balance sheet.

The day after my last conversation with Phil, I received a call from Rich Murphy welcoming me to the Murphy clan! He stated that Phil had made a point of the two of us working together and he was supposed to give me two key employees, a trained field superintendent and a professional estimator who in his words was a drawing board genius! I said that would be fine except before I hired anyone I would like the opportunity to interview them. He agreed and then we chatted about things in general. Rich and I had known each other for several years and more importantly we liked and respected each other professionally and socially, which is a great help in the business world!

From the time Phil and I shook hands, I began searching for a location for Tenscon. I found the ideal situation in a small industrial strip center in Fountain Valley which backed up to the 405 freeway and adjacent to a on and off ramp. It was 1,500 square feet, comprised of 300 square feel of office space and 1,200 square feet of warehouse, and toilets. I asked the leasing agent if he could hold the space for me for a week and he agreed. I then started looking at cars. Taking Phil's advice, I settled on an Oldsmobile 98 Sedan, loaded with extras, and ordered one for delivery after January 2nd. It was a very special color that Oldsmobile created that year—a brownish gold metallic that was very fashionable, but not gaudy, almost one-of-a-kind.

When all the legal work had been signed, sealed and delivered, I called the leasing agent and said that I wanted the space on a five-year lease with two five-year extensions on the terms he had offered. I promised him the down payment on January 3rd. On the morning of January 2nd, I went to the local Bank of America branch and asked for the manager who had just hung up his phone from talking to corporate headquarters in San Francisco. When I told him my name he laughed and said, "I've heard of the importance of timing before, but I was given your name just two to three minutes ago with the instructions that anything you wanted or needed I should take care of personally!" I asked if the $25,000 had been deposited and when I would have Tenscon's checkbook in order to start our new company? He told me that the money was already deposited and the checks were ordered on December 30 and we were promised delivery after noon today, but definitely before closing time. I picked up the checkbook mid-afternoon and proceeded to the leasing office, signed the lease and wrote my very first check with somebody else's money!

The leasing agent gave me a list of phone numbers to use to have all of the utilities including phone service turned on. He handed me his phone and I called and made arrangements for the very next day. The next day I called Rich and asked him to set up an appointment with the estimator in my office in Fountain Valley ASAP. He called me back the next morning and the man he liked so much with his wife arrived on Friday. Both the gentleman and his wife really desired to move to Southern California. I recommended a section in older Garden Grove less than ten minutes away, which was beautiful but not overpriced, or possibly older sections of Santa Ana. He said he would return on Monday morning to give me their decision and that Rich was paying their complete expenses. On Monday morning he returned saying they'd found a fantastic house in Garden Grove and they would like to join Tenscon! I asked what type of salary he made now in Oakland? Knowing fully well that the cost of living and housing was cheaper, I still offered him 10% more, as I wanted this particular position filled by a very happy cohort! He was more than thrilled, as the home they found was twice as nice as the present dwelling in the Oakland area and over 20% less rent! We set the date for his arrival for two weeks to the day. He left, I called Rich and told him I liked Greg very much and everything we agreed upon and Rich sounded pleased. The two of us would be Tenscon's only employees for the next four months!

The next ten days until Greg arrived were spent mostly making phone calls to various large steel building contractors and creating a common concept as to what our new method of lightweight reinforced concrete would accomplish. In addition, I was able to procure the names of the architectural engineering companies that were designing projects that should be using our services! I started methodically through the list, and after a week or two found that we only had three major participants in southern California. There were two more in the San Francisco area, but the majority of them were based in New York and Chicago, as well as one located in Honolulu. All in all, 15 firms controlled the high-rise building design industry in the United States. For the next 18 months our largest office expense was our telephone bill.

As soon as Greg settled in we were fortunate to find there were two projects already designed for reinforced concrete and Greg and I both called upon the two firms immediately. Bids were to be taken in late April on one and the first week of May on the other, with expected construction starts the first week in June. We picked up all the plans and specifications and Greg had weeks of work ahead of him. I in turn made one visit to the local iron-workers' union hall to introduce myself to its head man. He knew all about our company and had been expecting us to be in touch and welcomed Tenscon to Los Angeles. He was surprised by my visit rather than by a union labor superintendent. I explained that I hadn't hired one, as I hadn't found the right man. I felt the meeting went very well—I usually don't get along with union chiefs.

Chapter 17

Bogies and Birdies

After Greg arrived, I had quite a bit of free time. The Bob Hope Desert Classic Golf Tournament was scheduled during the first week in February, the week before the 1969 Classic. The field for amateurs had not filled. Our PGA resident golf professional at La Quinta Country Club called me and asked me to enter. The entry fee was $500 for four days of golf at Indian Wells Country Club, Tamarisk Country Club, Bermuda Dunes Country Club and our club, La Quinta! Four hundred dollars would go to our local desert charities, including the Eisenhower Medical Center. We would also receive all types of entry prizes, from clothing to gift bottles of premium liquors as well as special new-styled Johnston and Murphy golf shoes designed for The Classic. All of that added up to a retail value of over $250. Four hundred dollars would be tax deductible from our personal taxes. As I had nothing planned for that week, and Greg would be in the office on Wednesday through Friday, I accepted and told them I'd bring a check that coming weekend and sign the entry form.

On Saturday, I entered the tournament. Dick, our

pro, explained that the drawings of team members would be done the coming Friday and that the pairings of who I would be playing with as a team and the four different golf professionals we would be paired with would be in the tournament program the following day. Each team consisted of a player with a handicap of +1 to a 6, another player from 7 to 11, and the last player from 12 to 15, the maximum allowed. I was a 13 handicap for the tournament. I went to the desert that weekend not to play golf but to receive the program for the week! I was paired with Dean Beman on Wednesday at Indian Wells. I played with a young pro I'd never heard of at Tamarisk on Thursday and another young pro who was in his second year on the tour but hadn't done much yet on Friday at Bermuda Dunes. Finally, I played with a very ancient old pro from upper New York State who only played a few celebrity tournaments such as the Bob Hope at La Quinta.

We were not in the celebrity field that you see on TV on Saturday or Sunday when the golf professionals played by themselves. I was still excited to be there, but the professionals I drew except for Beman were disappointing, at least on paper. My low handicap golfer was Mike Barr, a 5 handicap from Oakland, California who owned Barr Industries and 25% of the Oakland Raiders professional football team. Our second player was a man from the east coast who had paid The Classic $5,000 to play and he was a 9 handicap. Of course I was the high handicap at 13!

Upon arriving at the first tee on Wednesday at

Indian Wells, the announcer/starter introduced me to my two partners and then to Dean Beman. As we started on the first tee that day, Dean drove it right down the middle. Mike, playing from the amateur tees, hit a fair drive to the left about the same distance as Dean's. Our next player whiffed the ball completely and we found out that he really didn't possess any handicap at all. When our non-golfing partner finally escaped the tee box, Dean told him to pick up his ball. I then hit my tee shot down the fairway, but far short of Dean's. Nobody in our foursome parred the first hole, except Dean who had a two-foot putt for a Birdie! This round of golf was totally weird. How Dean kept his poise and temper under control was beyond belief! The man in the middle for three days was an obstacle rather than an ally. He not only couldn't play golf, he was a total distraction to Dean, Mike and I. He was from New York and he was a jerk! He threw clubs, used profanity and even insulted the fans following Dean.

    At the end of Wednesday, our team playing Indian Wells was in third place. The only two teams ahead of us were also from the Indian Wells field. We shot a 58! Mike helped two strokes and I helped another two strokes. With everything that happened that morning, Dean tied the course record by scoring a 10 under the par 62! Indian Wells Country Club sat in a cove like La Quinta, protected from the winds, and played 5 to 6 strokes per day easier than La Quinta. Both Tamarisk and Bermuda Dunes sat in the middle of the desert where the wind always blows; the only difference being how hard the wind blew! Because of length and condition, Bermuda Dunes ordinarily played two strokes higher than Tamarisk.

The next day our group teed off a little later and off the 10th tee. The winds were blowing in excess of 20 m.p.h. and our man in the middle was just as abominable! Our young pro, after three or four holes, started losing control of his golf game as well as his temper. Both Mike and I gutted it out and our young pro had an Eagle on our second hole, Number 11, and did manage two more Birdies to help the team. Unfortunately, he didn't help himself as he shot an even 80. I really felt sorry for the kid. Somehow Mike and I managed to, in golf terminology, ham-and-egg it. The team posted a 67 score—in the middle of the field for Tamarisk.

On Friday, we drew Bermuda Dunes with our pro. Again we luckily had our earliest starting time of the tournament, as the winds were really up that day. The winds were blowing 20 m.p.h.+ as we teed off on Number 1. By the time we finished, they were gusting from 30 to 40 m.p.h. As usual, our middleman was a total embarrassment, but the young pro had evidently been warned of his lack of any type of golf ability and ungentlemanly etiquette, which frankly would have any member of a private club removed from membership. Of course for the third day in a row he didn't help our team a stroke. On that particular day, on the windiest of the four courses and the windiest day of the tournament, our young man had a 77—which doesn't sound very good, but it was the sixth lowest score of the 32 professionals. In addition he had three Birdies! Mike played very well considering the elements. I chipped in on the 18th hole for a net Birdie and we scored an even 70. The lowest team score at Bermuda Dunes that day was a 68 and only three teams shot less than 70, but on the big scoreboard for all four courses we fell back over 30 places!

On our last day playing my home course of La Quinta, we were again on the 10th tee and had a mid-morning starting time. It was a perfect day at La Quinta, no appreciable wind; the temperature at 9:30 a.m. was in the high 60s and climbing. It was a day I liked to call "another lousy day in paradise." We were introduced to our professional and a new man who was going to play with us to fill out our foursome, but his score and game would not count. Our middleman had had enough and withdrawn! Our pro was a typical private country club golf pro now in his 60s. He had played the tour for 20 years, and was a fine gentleman and a credit to the game.

On our second hole, Number 11, a 5 par, I received a handicap stroke. I had a long putt, which I sunk for a net Eagle and I was off and running. On Number 13 I also received a handicap stroke and I parred the hole for a Birdie. I continued playing very well, much better than usual. When we finished the first 9 holes, I was only one over par gross, the best back 9 score I'd ever shot at La Quinta! Unfortunately, our pro was not playing well at all. I truly think that playing four days in a row under the conditions we'd incurred was a little too much! Mike was playing better and putting better as I was reading the greens, which I knew like the back of my hand. On the front side I continued to strike the ball and chip and putt beautifully. On 5th hole, a par 5, I got lucky and holed a shot from the sand! I had another handicap stroke and it was another Birdie. I was only 1 over par on each 9 holes, giving me a 74 for the day. With my 13 handicap that netted out 61 by myself and Mike helped our team by 4 more shots and we posted a 57 by ourselves—the lowest round of the day at any course. It was the lowest score in golf that I've ever shot to this day! With Dean Beman's great round the first day, Mike and I by ourselves came in sixth place overall. For coming in 6th, we received a beautiful Bob Hope professional-style golf bag, all white leather trimmed with Bob Hope colors! I enjoyed myself in spite of the jerk who bragged about buying himself into the tournament, but I never played in the Bob Hope Classic again.

Another story that football fans might appreciate came from Mike Barr during the four days we spent together on the golf course—a wonderful place to find out about people, both good and bad! Mike and I had plenty of time together on the golf course because as a contestant you must go out of your way not to bother your professional who is trying to make his living. As our other partner was so rotten and ridiculous, we only had each other to talk to before, during and after our rounds of golf. Mike confided in me that the managing partner of the Raiders wasn't an honest man and was trying to remove them from the organization without returning their percentage share of the present market value or even their original investments. He said it was very frustrating just talking to the guy, as he was a total liar who used a gullible media and fabricated un-truths. This, Mike stated, was after having been pursued by the man to invest money with two other friends Mike had brought into the group to help the man buy the Raiders! All three were now facing an ugly court trial and according to Mike the legal costs were going to be greater than what they had invested in the beginning. Years later I read in the paper that the case was settled out of court and their general partner became the good guy; at least the media portrayed it so!

I returned home Sunday and didn't even watch the conclusion. Everything at work was status quo and Greg and I went back to trying to make inroads with our local potential customers, mostly making phone calls and typing letters to Chicago, New York City and Honolulu where there appeared to be a high-rise building boom hitting Waikiki Beach. We finally bid our first job, a four-story parking garage on Wilshire Boulevard in the heart of Beverly Hills. We added only a 7 1/2% profit margin and received the contract. I called Rich and asked him if he still had a man worthy of my interviewing. Rich replied he would have him in my office the day after tomorrow morning. I interviewed Bob and we talked all morning about Southern California and the growth potential. We spent a long time talking about the ironworkers union here as compared to San Francisco and there was no doubt that he was a union man! The other impression I had was that he presumed he was being transferred from Murphy Steel to Tenscon, not being hired as a new employee. We parted for a few hours, during which I phoned Rich and told him my uneasy feelings about Bob. Rich assured me that I was wrong and that Bob was an outstanding man who put the company first and the union second, but more importantly was honest and would work well with Greg. That afternoon I hired Bob strictly on Rich's recommendation. I became even more concerned when he told me he had brought all his clothing, personal belongings and equipment with him and that he was ready to begin work tomorrow.

    The next morning Greg, Bob and I studied the results of all the bids on the parking garage that I had been able to procure. Our winning bid was 25% lower than the next bid and 35% lower than the only other bidder. I suggested that we change our bid on the 11-story high-rise office building in Long Beach which had two stories of underground parking and add a somewhat higher profit percentage to cover any potential mistakes in our estimating and possible unforeseen weather and union problems. Greg and Bob agreed. I suggested an extra 5%, making our profit margin 12 1/2%, which Greg thought was great. Bob immediately started being a contrarian and actually started arguing that that wasn't near enough and we should raise the bid by 25%! It was two against one. We raised the bid by 12 1/2% and we were the low bidder by less than 6%. When the bids were disclosed, this only made Bob even more aloof from Greg and I, and created tension that we really didn't need. I called Rich a couple weeks later and discussed my feelings about Bob and asked if he would he take him back. Rich tried to calm my concerns by saying he would have a long talk with Bob and get our problems resolved.

During the school year at the military academy, Sherry and I had promised the boys that if they did well in school both scholastically and behavior-wise, we would spend four weeks in Maui, Hawaii from mid-June to mid-July. As the school year was coming to a close, both of my boys Chuck and Scott were doing great scholastically and had no disciplinary problems whatsoever. Unfortunately, Sherry's son, Gary, was failing one course, had a "D" in another and three "C's" and even worse he had six disciplinary infractions on his record. Because we had made an issue of the scholastic and disciplinary bribes to make the boys better students and citizens, we both agreed that Gary did not qualify for the Hawaii vacation. We located a military academy summer school in Carlsbad, California where we entered Gary for a six-week semester, which started in the second week of June and ended in late July. This was tough on all of us, including Chuck and Scott, who didn't understand how we could not take Gary.

I received a phone call from Phil saying first that I was doing a superb job. He said he understood this from various people in our industry, not just Rich and my local cohorts. He had recently won a 28-day corporate management educational training program at a great business school and asked if I'd like to attend. It was completely paid for, including airfare, plus a rental car, food expense account and first class lodging. "Carl," he said, "Don't misunderstand me—this is not something I think you need, but I think with Tenscon progressing the way it is, the timing is perfect and I'd like you to have this opportunity!" I told him I would talk to my wife and call him back tomorrow. Sherry was happy to see me go, but I needed to work out the boys' summer schedules. The next day I called Phil's office and accepted and asked him to send me all the literature, paperwork and everything else I needed to return to school, which I gave to his secretary. That was the last time I ever spoke to Phil Murphy!

Almost instantly our little company changed when the work started in Beverly Hills and Ocean Boulevard in downtown Long Beach. Bob was out of the office and Greg was busy with work from various sources from out of nowhere. It seems that the word that our bids for the parking garage and office building were not only less expensive, but contained major safety factors. Every structural engineer recognized the significant improvement in resistance to earthquakes. On Ocean Avenue in Long Beach, the Holiday Inns had just finished their new signature round hotel and were planning their second round hotel to be located in downtown Hollywood. They also had plans for these round Holiday Inns to be placed in all the major cities in the western United States! They had already started on a trial program for redesigning the structures to use post-tension reinforcement concrete and when our bid surfaced they went into a crash program, keeping their signature round structure but using our system. Within a month's time we had a finished set of plans to bid the construction of the Hollywood Holiday Inn. In addition, we received a set of plans from Huber, Hunt and Nichols, a company in New Orleans, for a Sheraton Hotel in San Diego! Greg was now flooded with work. He suggested that we hire a receptionist to handle calls so he wouldn't have any interruptions, and a secretary so that he could devote 100% of his time to estimating and bidding. He mentioned that we really needed a woman around the office. I called Sherry and by afternoon we had a very qualified young lady by the name of Sue who turned out to be a jewel!

  We received the contract to build the Hollywood Holiday Inn and one week later we received the contract for the Sheraton in San Diego, our largest contract to date! Just before leaving for our vacation in Hawaii, I received a phone call from the corporate offices in L.A. for a meeting with the executive VP for all Holiday Inns. He stated that they had eight more signature round hotels to build within the next 30 months and based on our bid for the Hollywood Holiday Inn and the safety factors we included, that they would like us to consider building all eight of these hotels! I assured him that if they were happy with our performance in Hollywood we'd be more than happy to consider an alliance with Holiday Inn.

  That coming weekend, Sherry, Chuck, and Scott and I headed for Maui. The location of our condo was ideal. We could see the island of Molokai off to the right and the island of Lanai equidistant to the left and on two very clear evenings we actually saw lights from the east side of Oahu. Our four weeks on Maui were wonderful, at least for the boys and I, but I could tell that Sherry did not share our enthusiasm. We rented a car and most mornings Sherry would drive us down to Kanapali, which had two wonderful golf courses—one of which was considered world class. We were able to find games with all sorts of personages, including three famous Football Hall of Famers! On one day we played with Elroy "Crazy Legs" Hirsch of the L.A. Rams. Another day we played with Bob Devaney, the coach of Nebraska University, and we also were lucky enough to play with one of the funniest men I've ever met in my whole life, Duffy Daugherty of Michigan State University. On these three days all three of these men took their time to have lunch with the boys and I. Duffy even went so far as to take our name and address and promised if Michigan State made it to the Rose Bowl this coming year, they would be invited to sit on the Michigan State bench!

Early during our stay on Maui a world event happened. The condo we were enjoying was wired for reception, but didn't possess a TV set. Sherry and I drove into Lahaina and rented a RCA 21-inch black-and-white TV, and the next day we all watched the greatest show on earth. To me it was truly a spectacular moment in world history to see Neil Armstrong walk on the moon! To our delight he took out of his spacesuit a rod, which unfolded making a golf club, placed a golf ball on the surface of the moon, and hit it! Even Sherry was ecstatic! Every time I've visited Maui I think of that great day!

The boys were responsible enough for Sherry and I to enjoy a few sunset dinners at the finest restaurants in Lahaina and Kanapali alone. One night we were sitting in the beautiful, romantic open-air dining room in Lahaina's number one restaurant, the Coconut Grove. Crash, bang! Glassware and broken china began flying in all directions! A large ripe coconut had fallen directly between us making a direct hit and almost everything sitting on our table was obliterated! Luckily, our dinner had not been served and we were enjoying a glass of wine. Neither of us had a scratch or a cut to show, although we did have a few glasses of water spill onto our clothes. We returned home on the 28th day relaxed and tired from a vacation that was near perfection for the boys and myself. Unfortunately, as the days sped by, Sherry increasingly (and understandably) had a guilt complex over Gary's absence.

On arriving home, both Sherry and I immediately went straight to work. Scott and Chuck were scheduled to leave in a few days to spend a month with their mother and sisters. Sherry was now working close to Huntington Harbor, but she spent equal time for the first week at both of her offices. I, in turn, only had to go to Fountain Valley, where I found Greg and Sue in great spirits. Sue immediately said she really enjoyed her new job and Greg was wonderful and easy to work with and kept her busy doing all sorts of new things. Greg, on the other hand, was equally complimentary about Sue and her attitude plus aptitude: "Thanks to her we won't ever need another estimator, unless I screw up!" He laughingly mentioned that with me gone, Bob came around quite a bit. The first thing I asked Greg was if had he heard from the head man at Holiday Inn and the answer was no.

    I phoned Rich, who informed me that all was well and he'd heard rumors that Tenscon was making great strides in the Los Angeles market. He also mentioned that he'd had a conversation with Bob, explaining to him that I was not only the chief executive of the company but I was also an owner along with Phil. He then said about a week later Bob called me and wanted to fully understand his and my workplace relationship. Rich stated that he'd told Bob in very explicit words that he worked for me (the owner of Tenscon) directly, and that he was totally an outsider. I thanked Rich for his efforts.

    The work in Beverly Hills, Long Beach and Hollywood just starting was occupying our workforce. We had approximately 40 ironworkers on the payroll and Phil increased our monthly allowance to $50,000 per month. One of the calls I made was to the head man at the union headquarters and chatted with him about the supply of really good ironworkers going forward as we were looking at a few more jobs and needing qualified people. He assured me that the labor supply was no problem. Without me asking he made a statement to the effect that Bob was a hard guy to like. That was it, nothing more. I thanked him and said I'd stay in touch and if there was a problem to let me know. I was going to be gone again starting in less than a week to go to school for 28 days, but I told him to call Sue in my absence and ask for Greg if any decisions had to be made. He laughed about my going to school and thanked me.

The last call I made before leaving for school was to the head man at Holiday Inn, who was surprised to hear from me as he thought I was still in Hawaii. I told him that I was leaving again the very next morning to go back to school and he also laughed. When I explained the type of school and what it entailed for 28 days, plus the fact that it was all paid for in advance, he offered to purchase the scholarship. Then I laughed and we started the real conversation, which was about an alliance in the future. I was hoping by the time I returned that we both would be in a position to really analyze effectively our companies relationships to each other. He replied that he would expect to hear from me in about five weeks and that if something came up he would call Greg.

The 28 days in school was well worth all the money! The headmaster of the graduate school started by saying we were there as educators. He said he knew that most of us were far more intelligent and successful businessman than the instructors, who could not compete with us in the real world of business! What they were there to teach us was that the wrong decision at the right time was far better than the right decision at the wrong time—and that either one was far better than procrastination! In addition to that they would endeavor to prove that in corporate management an intelligent but lazy top executive was far better than an aggressive executive! Another way to look at the problem was that a dumb and lazy executive wasn't going to get anything accomplished, but a dumb, aggressive executive could destroy a company! The last item to go along with our curriculum was how to stay out of our own way! He told us that we would discuss everything openly and all our classes would be dedicated to proving those facts.

 He then introduced a group of a half dozen professors who gave us their personal backgrounds and credentials and what types of specialized business classes they would be holding. None of these professors ever used the word teaching; it was always a word similar to open discussion! For 28 days we enjoyed all kinds of business discussions, which were very provocative because 95% of the reasons for the discussions came from us. I never felt like a student! When I left, in my mind the most important business lesson—as well as life in general—was to be in the right place at the right time with the knowledge and equipment to make the correct decision. Simply put, TIMING in life is everything!

 I returned home to Sherry and Gary and the following day Chuck and Scott returned from their mother's home and a vacation in Gilroy. Scott informed me that he wanted to move back to live with his mother and sisters. I was extremely disappointed as because I had legal custody I could have said no, but because he was no longer a small child and the environment in our home was poor, I couldn't and didn't say no. At least my son Chuck stayed on. This really was another low point in my life.

Also around the time Sherry and I blended families, we added another important member to our home, a purebred 13-week-old miniature schnauzer who was perfect in every way and became one of my closest friends for many years! We named this new member Bourbon von Meisterlin. Bourbon was the smartest animal I've ever known. If there were a dog on our TV screen, Bourbon would sit down directly in front of the TV and watch the show. No dog, no Bourbon! In retrospect, I believe Bourbon had the intellect of a four to five-year-old child. He had a very strong male personality in that you did it his way or no way! Regardless, the addition of Bourbon was in every way a positive influence on my personal life.

After Scott moved out, both Chuck and Gary attended the local public school within walking distance from our home. One day I had forgotten something and returned to the house and encountered Gary and two other kids running around acting very strangely. When I drove in our driveway, the other two boys took off leaving Gary and I to confront each other. He and his two friends had cut school and on entering the house I found both the liquor cabinet and two medicine cabinets, including Sherry's and mine in the master bathroom, open. I accused him of drinking and possibly taking some pills. He was very unstable and immediately became hostile and started screaming at me, "You're not my father and I don't give a f---! Just leave me alone!" I then took the worst possible action. I hit him! Gary was now well over

5' and perfectly built and my blow did not knock him over, but it did stop the yelling. I took him by the arm. He came willingly to the car and we drove to school where I left him after a few words with the principal.

After this encounter, Sherry and I became noticeably distanced and again I blamed myself. Shades of my father! I should have never lost my temper! The next week the principal's office called and asked me to come in. I asked if should I bring Sherry and the principal said, "No, I just want to talk to you about Gary." The principal said that he thought that on the day I brought Gary in that he was indeed drugged. He also said that Gary was a troublemaker and had been reported as such by all of his teachers, but that wasn't why he asked me here. "Gary is your stepson, Mr. Meisterlin, which is a very delicate position for both you and I. By rights I should advise the authorities of your striking the boy, but under the circumstances I witnessed and his track record, I have not. But if you strike or cause physical harm to Gary I will have to report it and you will be incarcerated."

That night Sherry and I had a long conversation about what we should do. Sherry told me something that the principal had not revealed. She had talked with the principal a few days earlier and pretty much heard the exact story with the exception of my possible potential incarceration. This was now a problem that was bigger than both of us and I suggested seeing a professional children's psychiatrist. This never happened as Sherry, without consulting me, shipped Gary off to his father in Kansas.

Things changed very rapidly as now there was just Sherry, Chuck, Bourbon and I, and we had no need for the large home. That week I was a guest at a PGA golf tournament held in Costa Mesa at the Mesa Verde Country Club, a club I'd never visited before. On the way in and out of the clubhouse, I noticed an enclave of townhomes within 250 yards from the clubhouse entrance, which had a for lease sign. I was impressed with the location, as it was close to two new freeways and made both Sherry's and my drives half the distance we were now traveling to work. Before leaving the clubhouse, I stopped by the club's business office and picked up all the information necessary to join, as I thought both our businesses could use a country club for business entertainment—a tax deduction in those days! I mentioned this to Sherry that evening and the next day we went to Mesa Verde for lunch. On the way to the clubhouse, we wrote down the phone number on the real estate sign and proceeded to lunch. We phoned the number and we made an appointment for two hours later. The lady in the business office recognized me from the previous day and asked if she could show us the clubhouse and pro shop facilities. She was extremely proud to show Sherry the ladies' locker room, dressing room and mini-bar! Mesa Verde was no Hacienda Country Club, but it had everything we needed.

After lunch, a man was waiting for us at the townhomes. He had two units for lease, which were identical in floor plan; the only difference was location within the property. He asked if he could show us his favorite of the two? We agreed and entered. I immediately thought the place fitted our needs perfectly. It had a living room, dining room, kitchen, half-bath off the kitchen and a large TV room. Upstairs were two bedrooms, a master bedroom suite and another bedroom with a small bath. He quoted a figure for a year's lease that was just over 50% of what we were paying in Huntington Harbor. The homeowner association fees were only $50 per month. All in all the savings were almost 40%. Sherry said that she thought that this would be a better location for us and she really liked the place. I gave the realtor my card and made an appointment with him for the following day to officially lease the condo. We then returned to the country club, where I signed documents for a membership. Ten days later we were living in Costa Mesa and belonged to Mesa Verde Country Club.

    This proved to be an extremely smart move, not only from a monetary standpoint, as the townhouse plus the golf membership saved us over 20% of our housing budget. On top of that, we were much closer to work and also had the use of a country club and better-than-average golf course. In addition we were now very close to two new freeways, which made the whole Southern California basin easier and more efficient to navigate!

    After the move, everything went fine socially, economically and within the family. The months flew by, Sherry's business was improving and she seemed happy, Tenscon added more work, Sue and Greg were working as a team fantastically, as Sue was learning different ways to help Greg with his estimating, and loving it! Bob, with all the work we now had, rarely came to the office, which was fine with the three of us. I had no complaints from any of our customers about our work and service in the field. I did call the union chief about once a month just to stay in touch.

We were making money, barely, but we were in the black for now. Our payroll had now increased to the point that Murphy had now increased our monthly allowance to $80,000 per month. We had new work, and that would soon increase this amount to over $100,000 per month. Everything couldn't be better—it was as good as it gets! I started playing in even more golf tournaments with friends and customers.

The more successful we became, the more both Sherry and I realized that our relationship was more convenience than love. I know I did! We spent more and more time on our own—Chuck and I playing golf and basketball in the early evenings at Chuck's high school and Sherry spending more time socially with her women employees. We seemingly had less and less time together even on weekends. One weekend she told me she was going to spend time with her mom and dad. When I called there to ask a routine question about our attending an event, her dad said that she wasn't there and didn't expect her, but to try the Downey office. I was unable to locate her all weekend and when she returned that Sunday evening and I asked her where she had been, she became very angry and evasive. I knew I had not been a very loving husband for a long time and somewhat blamed myself for her actions.

On November 6 and 7th, La Quinta Country Club had its fall Member-Guest Tournament. Our Mesa Verde Country Club golf champion was a young man named Jack O'Neill, who was a 2 handicap at the time. In turn, my handicap that November was 12, and the rules for the tournament allowed a 10-stroke handicap difference between partners. I asked Jack whether he'd like to play with me at La Quinta Country Club as my partner in this event. He replied, "I've never been to the Palm Springs area and I've only heard great things about La Quinta Country Club, particularly the golf course, which everybody raves about! I'm accepting your invite now as I'd love to play with you, but I must check with my wife first to make sure I've not forgotten some obligation. I'll call you first thing tomorrow morning. We'll make a great team!"

Jack did indeed accept the invitation and we made plans to meet and leave Mesa Verde Country Club after work on Thursday, November 5th. When the time came, I could see that Jack was excited about the weekend. I drove us to La Quinta, where I had booked reservations for three nights as the condo in Rancho Mirage was booked that weekend. On Friday morning we signed in for the tournament in the pro shop and were given our tee time and pairing. We had a quick breakfast at the club and proceeded to the practice range. There was a full field of 72 teams and it was what I called "another lousy day in paradise!" This meant perfect weather—and we took advantage of that to shoot a 61, which put us in third place entering the final day. That night, November 7, 1970 became a special night in the history of Carl Meisterlin.

That night we drove to Palm Springs to the famous Jilly's Restaurant and Bar, which was owned in partnership by Jilly, a restaurateur from New York City, and his close friend and business partner, Frank Sinatra. We arrived at the restaurant at 5:30 p.m., which was early for dining in downtown Palm Springs, but Jilly's did not take reservations, so we sat in the bar lounge for an hour or so waiting for our booth, sipping our drinks. All of a sudden Jack exclaimed, "Look, there's Harry White from Mesa Verde." Harry had a very attractive lady at his side and had just entered the lounge. I recognized Harry from a poker game I'd played in at the club previously. Jack evidently had played golf with Harry many times. Jack called Harry over to our table and we had a brief conversation about why we were in the desert and Harry explaining that he was visiting the lady with him, whom he had known for 15+ years and who was at least 15 years younger. Just then the loudspeaker in the lounge said, "Mr. Meisterlin, your table is ready." We excused ourselves and went to the dining room to be seated.

When taken to our booth, one that would hold six or more diners comfortably, I suggested to Jack that with the crowd now waiting to be seated it would be a long, long wait for Harry and his lady friend and if Jack thought it would be a good idea, we should invite them to join us. Jack agreed and a minute later he reappeared with Harry's lady and Harry! The pretty lady who appeared to be my age was named Irene. She lived up in the Caliente Indian Canyon on the eighth fairway of the Canyon Country Club year round. We ordered cocktails and Irene ordered a Beefeater Gin straight up. I interrupted and asked her if she had ever tried Bombay Gin, to which she said, "Oh yes, I drank a whole case of that once!" and changed her order to Bombay Gin straight up. I thought to myself, 'Now that's my type of woman!'

    I didn't realize that Harry was a heavy drinker and after our first round of drinks arrived he immediately ordered a second round. Before dinner arrived Harry had a third drink. Our dinner was delicious and before we left Harry ordered after dinner drinks. Harry decided that we should go back to Irene's house. He wanted Jack and I to see what a beautiful desert home she lived in with her teenage daughter, Julie. On arriving at Irene's home with Irene in my car and Jack in Harry's, we were given a tour of the house, which was extremely beautiful and custom designed for desert living. It included a bar and lounge where Harry immediately started making more drinks. It was decided that we should all go down the hill to the Ocottillo Lodge, where the Guadalajara Boys were playing music for dancing and entertainment and, as it turned out, more drinking.

    Jack, who was in his early 30s, was an excellent dancer, especially Latin dancing. Irene was a superb dancer and she enjoyed Latin dancing particularly. Because there weren't many men who knew how to dance to Latin music, consequently Irene and Jack spent most of the time dancing together while Harry continued drinking. I'd had enough drinking so I found a couple of young ladies at the bar to dance with and counteract the alcohol. Unbelievably, we closed the lounge at the Ocotillo at 2:00 a.m. and returned again to Irene's. Again, Harry poured more drinks. He sat down in a chair after doing so and it was scary. Harry was more than drunk—he was stoned! His face was that of a statute, his eyes were wide open like he was dead and there was no expression in his face! The three of us escorted Harry to his car where he absolutely wouldn't let us drive him home to the Ocotillo where he was staying. Before we could stop him he was weaving down the street leaving us standing in the driveway. We hastily said goodnight and thanks to Irene and hurried to follow Harry's car, and arrived at La Quinta at 4:00 a.m.

During the time spent dancing, I did get one dance with Irene—swing dancing, which I enjoyed. During the dance I told Irene I would be back in the desert between Christmas and New Year's and would she like to have dinner and she replied yes! I then asked for her phone number, which she said was 327-2065 and I replied, "I can remember that. I don't even have to write it down." She asked how that was possible and I replied, "The only first three numbers in Palm Springs are 327 and 2065 is easy in that 20 is your age and 65 is Harry's." She laughed!

When I returned to Mesa Verde, Sherry announced she was moving out and divorcing me the next weekend. This came as no surprise, as there had been no intimacy between us for well over a month. From previous experience, I knew that Sherry was having an affair, but with whom I had no idea. The following weekend she moved back to a motel bordering Huntington Harbor. She took all of the living room furniture as well as a TV room couch and chairs, but removed no furniture from the upstairs bedrooms, not even sheets, blankets or towels from the bathrooms. Less than a week later, I received papers suing me for divorce and asking for 50% of my personal estate! Instead of being devastated, I actually was elated as I honestly felt that the marriage was my fault. I was too stupid to recognize that I was being used on her ladder to financial success! Ten days later I heard that she'd moved in with Dick Lang, a friend of mine originally from Hacienda Country Club years ago, who now lived in Huntington Harbor. Dick had a home at the end of our street in Huntington Harbor that had a 50-foot Chris-Craft tied up at his private slip in the harbor, plus a swimming pool in his living room! The Los Angeles Times Sunday home section had featured Dick's home on the front page a couple of years earlier. As soon as Sherry's and my divorce decree was given, Sherry and Dick married. She took me all the way to court and the case was decided 100% in my favor and I was my own attorney. Again, what a farce!

    We were down now to just Chuck, Bourbon and I living in the condo. I purchased the most inexpensive furniture I could find for the living room, dining room and beanbags for chairs in the TV room. Chuck went to his mother's for the Christmas holidays and Bourbon and I headed for the desert. A few months previously, my close friend Orv Perkins had retired to Bullhead City, Arizona, across the river from Laughlin, Nevada and subsequently became Mayor of Bullhead! On Perk's retirement, the new CEO of Hollister called in my note for one half of the condo, which I paid willingly.

    As I now had no place to live, I took a room in a small motel with a great restaurant called The Nest. We arrived Christmas night and the next day before leaving for a round of golf at the club I placed a call to 327-2065 and Irene answered. I said, "This is Carl Meisterlin and are we still on for tomorrow night?" Irene stammered and asked again what my name was and I replied, "Carl Meisterlin. We made a date for tomorrow night at the Ocotillo Lodge on November 7th when you were with Harry." She remembered and asked what time was she expected to be ready? I answered, "We have dinner reservations at Lord Fletcher's at 6:30 p.m. and I think that 6:00 p.m. would be perfect timing?" Irene agreed and we spoke shortly about Christmas, then hung up and I left for La Quinta. Bourbon was not too happy with our room and when I arrived home after golf he had messed up the furnishings royally and somehow had found some gum, which was deposited everywhere. When I entered the room he was on the top of the bed looking straight at me with the guilty look he always had when he'd been naughty! It took me an hour to clean the room and then another hour to walk a very lovable, but guilty dog. The next morning, I played golf very early and returned to The Nest shortly after lunch to a guilty dog again. After tidying up the room and taking Bourbon for a silent walk, he could tell that I was angry. I returned home and took a short nap, something I'd never done!

When I awoke, I groomed myself for a very important date. I arrived at Irene's house right on time and when I rang the doorbell she was ready to leave and did not invite me in. When she walked out the door I had remembered her being a very pretty woman, but the lady I was looking at now was beautiful! 'Wow,' was all I remember thinking. We arrived at Fletcher's a little early and our booth was not quite ready, so we went into the bar and Mike the bartender brought us two "Meisterlins"— Bombay Gin on the rocks with an orange slice hanging on the side of the glass.

I was fortunate to have been present four years prior on their opening night and Michael knew me well as did Lord Ron and Lady Shirley who were present 90% of the time. I started off talking too much and it wasn't long before Irene interrupted me and asked the question, "Are you an Aquarius? I answered, "Yes, but how did you know?" And she really got me, because she said, "You're so gabby!" I was not offended as I had seen this particular response in a Charles Schultz's "Peanuts" cartoon and I knew right then that Irene had an extraordinary sense of humor! With her 'you're so gabby' response, the battle of the nitwits began! In my lifetime I have never enjoyed a dinner and evening any more than I did on this, our first date!

Very honestly, we should have had a movie camera and recorded that evening. It was hilarious and everything about it was first class—the food, service, atmosphere and each of us answering each other's statements before we finished. I got even for the 'gabby' comment later by asking Irene what her golf handicap was as she lived on a golf course. I had said there were only three things important to me in a relationship with the golf handicap being the first and she replied, "I don't play golf, I knit and make clothes." I replied, "Well, you flunked the first one! The second thing is how many Bridge master points do you have, being you were a sorority girl?" I then received her answer, "I don't play Bridge or cards, I knit!" My last statement was, "You flunked that requirement also, you better be damn good at the third or I'm out of here!" And we both understood and thought it was funny! When we drove home and I escorted her to the front door she opened the door, turned and I gave her a big kiss, which she responded to wonderfully. I said good night and turned and went home. Oh yes, on the way home from Fletcher's, she invited me to a New Year's Eve party at her house, which I accepted.

Chapter 18

Ready for Love

The next day, after what was the most enjoyable dinner date in my whole life, I couldn't get Irene out of my mind! That evening I phoned her again and invited her for dinner the next night, which was Wednesday, telling her that I needed to introduce her to a very important family member. I played golf and walked Bourbon both days and he was getting used to his new routine, somewhat.

On Wednesday night I called for Irene at 6:00 p.m. again and we headed south to The Nest, where I had a 6:30 p.m. reservation. We arrived on time and again partook of a marvelous meal and received special attention from the owner. In fact, he gave Irene most of the attention, with his wife who was the greeter and hostess standing right there! After dinner, I took Irene back to my room. I don't know what she thought I was going to do next, but I entered and woke Bourbon who was sleeping on a pillow on the bed. I introduced Bourbon, my closest pal, to Irene and attached his leash and the three of us drove back to Irene's. She did invite us in but I declined, gave her another kiss, which again was well received, and Bourbon and I headed back.

Each workday I had made a call to the office and Sue and Greg, who had decided they would work alternate days that week, answered the phone. Fortunately for the company these two people were a wonderful working team who enjoyed what they were doing (I should say accomplishing) and left to their own they were nothing less then super professionals. From what they said I gathered that Bob worked all five days, but a half-day at the most. This just made my week easier with no stress.

On New Year's Eve, Bourbon and I arrived shortly after 8:00 p.m. and I noticed there were no other cars in the driveway or in front of the house. Irene introduced Bourbon and I to a little lady who lived directly across the street by the name of Jean Carter who was approximately 20 years older than Irene. Jeannie was Scottish and still spoke with a delightful accent. She made a big fuss over Bourbon and we all went into Irene's game room/bar. I volunteered to be the bartender, which I'd been doing since the age of nine, so it came naturally. I made drinks for the three of us and Jeannie put a bowl of water down for Bourbon. At 9:00 p.m. nobody else had arrived. Irene finally admitted that her party was just for the four of us, including Bourbon. We sipped another drink or two, which I made much weaker than the original drink! Irene, in the course of conversation, said that her daughter Julie was at a New Year's party at her high school baseball coach's home and was spending the night with two of her high school buddies. At 11:00 p.m. Irene took out a bottle of champagne to celebrate the New Year. Irene, Bourbon and Jeannie sat on bar stools and I behind the bar. We all toasted the New Year with a sterling silver champagne glass. Yes, even Bourbon stood with his paws on the bar sipping champagne and we took pictures of that! The whole evening we told funny stories about our lives and ourselves and the evening flew by. There was no need for any more guests.

Jeannie was hilarious in telling how she managed to get from Scotland to New York City and end up in Palm Springs. Her life story would've been one of the great comedic books ever written. She was a wonderful friend to Irene and it worked both ways. About 11:15 p.m., Jeannie attached Bourbon to his leash and said she'd had enough and that it was time to leave. She took Bourbon and went home. I looked at Irene and we embraced and we had a very memorable kiss and I allowed myself to be seduced. Irene insists that it was the other way around! All I know is that it was the most satisfying night of my life in all ways!

I was madly in love with a beautiful, bright, educated lady with a sense of humor much like mine! My biggest problem at that moment turned out to be that I had competition—two very worthy gentlemen! One disappeared back to Long Island, New York and the other was a wonderful veteran who lived in San Diego, a retired naval captain with four daughters ages 8 to 15. Kent was a first-class gentleman; luckily for me, the four girls were too much for Irene at that time! My household at that time was only Chuck and Bourbon. By the end of January, I had Irene all to myself and my life was great! I called Irene every night when I was in Costa Mesa and even read romantic poetry, which came from my heart. In addition, on a couple of weekdays I flew to Palm Springs just to have lunch with Irene and flew back on a 3:00 p.m. flight. That spring Irene and I were walking through the grounds of the gorgeous La Quinta Hotel and I blurted out a proposal of marriage. I received a laugh with this statement: "Are you crazy?" "Yes, I'm crazy in love with you," I said, which drew another laugh!

In late spring, a new young developer, Bill Bone, started a new development a mile north of Irene's home called Sunrise Homes. It was an entirely new concept of four attached homes with four different floor plans on each of the four sides of a park-like common area containing a swimming pool. Irene and I toured the model complex at the pre-opening sale that weekend, which was drawing hundreds of potential buyers. I liked one particular plan and Irene agreed that it would be perfect for Chuck, Bourbon and I. The rear of the plan I preferred was almost completely glass, with sliding glass doors opening onto the common area from both the living room and master bedroom. It was one of the two smaller, less expensive homes. In Phase Two there was a unit that looked over an area to the southwest, which had the most desirable view. I made a cash deposit!

On the day after the New Year's party, I returned to work. That week all hell broke loose. We received contracts for three Holiday Inns plus two huge developments, one of which we wanted and one we were forced to accept. In addition, we received plans on five other projects to bid on. I should explain that we actually had a partner we were tied to in 100% of our work who supplied us with all our raw material, the steel cables. When bids were circulated, Bethlehem Steel would bid the steel portion and we bid the labor as a team and for a year now we controlled the western post-tensioning industry. We were now starting to see competition from other steel cable producers and placing firms. To me the major problem was that the labor employees all came from one source, the Union Hall! Most ironworkers were not qualified and/or capable of our type of construction. Both Phil and I had underestimated how quickly the architects and structural engineers would desert the traditional construction methods! I told Sue and Greg that week that we were going to have to increase our labor costs due to poor labor productivity.

The job we really wanted was in West Los Angeles off Sunset Boulevard at a new yacht harbor basin. It consisted of 196 condominiums averaging 1,600 square feet and stood 12 stories high. Unfortunately, we had bid this job two months prior, but they changed the plans slightly which actually helped our bid and we rebid the job the week prior to Christmas. The second job was an almost exact duplicate of the Sheraton Hotel in San Diego, which was 98% complete! Both Bethlehem Steel and the same contractor, Hubert, Hunt and Nichols, wanted this work and had put pressure on me to join them in their bidding.

The job was in Honolulu, Hawaii! I did not want to go into the Hawaiian marketplace. The Sheraton Waikiki was exactly twice the size of the San Diego Sheraton. The main difference was it stood 18 floors high, but the rooms were identical except for the quantity, which was double. Some of the ground floor and mezzanine were larger, but all in all it was 95% the same as San Diego. When we bid the job, Greg assured me that the price we bid per pound of steel in San Diego +10% would be very profitable. At the time we made our bid I took Greg's bid plus the 10% and doubled it! I didn't want the job! Unfortunately when they opened the bids we were the low bidder.

    Both the condominium building and the Honolulu project were due to begin the last week in January. We already were using close to a thousand ironworkers and both Greg and I were worrying about the quality of the ironworkers who were being sent to our projects. There was no word from Bob, our field superintendent. I had Greg call him twice a week to find out what was happening at all our projects, and it was always the same answer, "Everything's fine." At the same time I started calling the union chief more often and he admitted he had the same concerns as Greg and I.

    In late January, I left for Honolulu with Ted, a bachelor who was more than happy to be a superintendent in Honolulu! Ted was forty-ish and had movie star looks. He had also been Bob's assistant on the San Diego Sheraton. On arriving in Honolulu we drove to the new job site. A few hundred yards away was a very good businessman's hotel, where I took a room for myself for two nights and bargained with the hotel manager for a four-month lease with a four-month extension for Ted at company expense. It pays to think ahead, as the manager first offered a discount of 15% for one month, 30% for two months, 40% for three months and 50% for four months. When we requested the four-month extension he then gave us an additional 10% making a total of 60% off nightly rates! The next morning Ted and I walked down the street to the jobsite and met with the general contractor and later visited the ironworkers' union chief at their offices approximately five miles west of the jobsite on the south shore. Everything went well and Ted was extremely pleased.

On the way back to our hotel I asked Ted about what he needed for transportation. He replied, "I don't need a car and from what I just learned about cab fare, I'm satisfied with the way things stand." The next day Ted went shopping on his own for all the things he needed to set up shop in the hotel room which did have a small mini-kitchen. Food and drink were not on his approved expense list, but cab fare Monday through Friday was. That day I traveled by cab on a tour of Honolulu proper to see what had happened since 1968, my last visit to Honolulu, and already the city's landscape had changed. This was going to be one of the biggest markets in the world for post-tensioned concrete! Ted and I had dinner that night and I left the next morning and Ted had already ordered workers from the Union Hall and they started work on the Sheraton the next day. I left one happy guy that morning!

Returning home, Greg and I visited the condominium site with Bob, the first time I'd seen him in a couple of months. The work had begun the previous morning and we started with 30 ironworkers. Bob expected we would need well over 100 within 60 days. In Honolulu, Ted had predicted almost the same numbers, but approximately 10% more. If they were correct that meant we would need over 1,200 workers per day! On the first of February all three banks that were now being used to forwarding cash would be extending us a total dollar figure that would add up to $125,000 per month. As I've previously mentioned, we were now slightly profitable, but our cash flow was still negative and not slightly!

The first week in February arrived and I chose not to play, but became a Bob Hope volunteer and became the assistant starter and announcer on the celebrity tee! My mentor, who had been the starter on the celebrity tee for the past five years, said to me, "Carl, this is the Bob Hope Tournament and we're here to provide fun and entertainment. We don't follow normal golf etiquette for announcers and starters except for introducing the amateurs and professionals to each other before they tee off. Unless you know the professional personally, don't get too sarcastic and/or say anything that would be out of line!"

I enjoyed this position in the Bob Hope Classic at the La Quinta Country Club for the following 13 years, as the chief starter and announcer retired. During the first year, Irene would come out and watch me perform my duties. She thoroughly enjoyed herself and critiqued my actions good and bad! I kid you not, her critiques were well given and used by me! From the very start, the ladies of La Quinta Country Club welcomed Irene and from then on we attended most important social functions.

In Los Angeles, we continued to add more projects in our adjoining areas and we also added more ironworkers. In our fourth week of work in Honolulu, I received a phone call from the job superintendent saying that Ted hadn't appeared for work in four days and his room at the hotel appeared unused. I asked what I could do and he told me that there was a man from our company filling his vacancy well, but that he was concerned about Ted's welfare. I thanked him and told him I'd get onto it immediately. I hung up, called Sue and asked her to get me the manager of Ted's hotel right away. A minute later the manager was on the line and he explained that they had been in the room yesterday at the request of the Sheraton superintendent and everything was in order. The maid service had told him that the bed hadn't been slept in for the past four nights and nothing in the room had moved including things in the closet and the bathroom. The little food that was stored in the tiny fridge was still there. He said he had no authority to call in the police. I would have to make a personal appearance at the police station and file a missing person report to get things moving. I called both the union chiefs in Los Angeles and Honolulu and told them of Ted's disappearance and asked if they had anybody in their files that I could contact who might possibly know of his whereabouts. I received a negative answer from both.

I called Hawaiian Airlines and they had a flight leaving at 7:00 p.m. I ordered a ticket; called home and told Chuck that I had to fly to Honolulu on an emergency that night, and he assured me that he and Bourbon would be fine. With only my wallet, some money and a comb, I left for LAX. I was on a speakerphone so Sue and Greg had heard everything. I arrived at about midnight and left a wake-up call for 7:00 a.m. The first thing I did the following morning was go to the site and speak to the young Hawaiian who was acting as our superintendent. He was very nice and educated but he had no idea where Ted was! He did say that a mainland (or as Hawaiian's say Haole) company was not well received in Hawaii. I filed a missing person report There was nothing else I could accomplish in Honolulu, and so I caught the first plane home.

I waited a week, talked to Murphy about our Hawaii situation, and passed along some ideas. I asked Rich after a week, hoping that Ted somehow would reappear, but if he didn't, if Murphy had any connections with the company that could take our place and possibly would Murphy Steel be interested? A couple days later Rich called back and said Murphy Steel was not interested, but he gave me a name of a company in Honolulu, plus the man to talk to. I called the gentleman and mentioned that Rich Murphy had given me his name and explained our situation. Beggars can't be choosers! The gentleman was very cordial and mentioned that he had performed work in conjunction with the Murphys for a couple of decades. He said he'd look into it personally as a courtesy to Phil Murphy and he'd be back to me within five working days. I asked Sue to make a copy of our contract and all current work documents showing our progress and to take them to the post office and mail them express to his company. While she was getting all the papers together, I wrote a cover letter for her to type. After mailing the documents, I told her she could take whatever the balance of the day was left for her pleasure. Incredibly, Sue accomplished it all in about 20 minutes.

  The gentleman contacted me in less than the five days and verbally gave me a buyout amount. He said it was important that we come to an agreement within 72 hours for reasons he could not disclose. The offer would leave us losing almost $50,000 up to the 72-hour limit. We had far more than that figure in our banks, but as our payrolls were increasing rapidly this was a definite negative to our cash flow requirements. I called Rich the next day and all he said was that it was my decision to sell the contract. He doubted whether we could get a better offer in Honolulu or for that matter here on the mainland. I called the gentleman the next day and the legal paperwork accepting the deal was signed and sealed. When all expenses, including the hotel and my plane trips were added up we lost $49,000. Worse than that, Ted was never to be seen again. In retrospect, the complete Hawaiian disaster began with our outlandish bid! Ted's disappearance obviously was foul play pointing directly to organized labor! There is no other possibility . . .

Looking back, the mess in Hawaii was unavoidable. No matter what we bid, we would have received that contract! There was no possible way to refuse Bethlehem Steel and Huber, Hunt and Nichols, our valuable partners on this project, by not bidding. This was one time that timing was against me! Our business was hectic, but that was good. It was so good in fact, that I was seriously considering adding another estimator to help Greg.

The loss on the Hawaiian disaster more than wiped out the profits that we were now generating. Almost immediately the amount of work out for bid decreased significantly. Greg advised me that some of the work he was estimating wouldn't be good for us. This was the first time Greg had ever come close to saying this. In just two months we'd come full circle from everything being great to falling behind in our projections and game plan for the future! All thoughts for expansion were put on hold and we prudently tightened our operation.

On the home front, everything was good. I was madly in love with Irene and I moved heaven and earth to be with her as much as possible. In fact, I moved Bourbon into her house. I made another decision at this time to let Chuck move to his best friend's home for the final weeks of the school year, as I was back and forth from Fountain Valley to Palm Springs continually. In addition, I was taking over some of Bob's duties due to our cost cutting. I was working 12-hour days. Whatever time I could spare, I spent with Irene.

Six weeks later I had a phone call on a Friday mid-morning from Rich Murphy that was devastating! "Carl," he said, "Early this morning my brother Phil had a severe stroke and died!" Phil was only 58 years old and I thought he was in superb physical condition. I was stunned to the point that I don't remember my reply. "I thought you should know right away," Rich commented, "As I believe we're liable to have some severe business repercussions." I do remember not thinking about business, but about Phil the man! Honest, reliable, understanding, empathetic, extremely intelligent, Phil was always a gentleman! He ranks in my memory with all the finest men I've been privileged to know.

On Tuesday of the following week, Greg said he'd just received a phone call from Oakland from Bob and that he'd quit! There was no letter, nothing but a phone call. My first thought was 'good riddance!' From the reaction by both Greg and Sue, I knew they thought the same. He had left a forwarding address and phone number. Three days later on Friday, one week from Phil's death, at exactly 9:00 a.m. I received a phone call from Crocker Bank in San Francisco informing me that my line of credit with their bank had been reduced by 60%! At 9:30 a.m. I received another phone call, this from Bank of America stating the same exact words, that my line of credit had been reduced by 60%! Finally, at 10:00 a.m., I received the third call, this from Security Pacific Bank, with exactly the same terminology, a 60% cut in our line of credit! Don't ever try to tell me there is no collusion between banks!

I placed a call to Rich Murphy, who was out, and left a request for him to call me back. That afternoon Rich said, "I suppose you heard from our banks? They have just cut our lines of credit by 60%, but we're lucky as our cash position is at an all-time high! After your Hawaiian problem I hope you can survive!" He then added, "Bob was in here earlier this week looking for work and I politely told him to look elsewhere!" I thanked Rich for the info and said I'd stay in touch. I told Greg and Sue what Rich said and they both agreed that Bob got what he deserved!

Word travels quickly in most industries and it seemed like overnight Tenscon was not a part of the reinforcing steel business. The phone wasn't ringing, salesman weren't visiting us, and requests for bids were almost nonexistent. Greg said he could take over Bob's duties also, which helped significantly. We had a sufficient cash position at that time which gave me hope we could survive. Our employee numbers were down from a peak of 1,400 to about 1,000, and falling.

I received no visits or phone calls from Bethlehem's sales manager for a couple of months, which was very unusual. Even worse, they were not returning my calls! One morning, without calling, a salesman from Bethlehem arrived in my office. Tenscon's casket had just arrived! The salesman advised me that the credit department of Bethlehem had removed our company from the bid list and they could no longer furnish our raw material or do business with us! Without any further explanation, he left. Because of no new business and our dwindling cash in the bank, the only action I could take was to declare bankruptcy! About three weeks prior, Sue had graciously resigned to take an even better position, for which I was very happy to write her a letter of recommendation. We were now working on only two jobs and down to 100 ironworkers.

  From my experience in Hawaii, I was able to call a friend of mine to take over these two jobs at no loss for Tenscon, but no gain either! After the bankruptcy hearing, we had no cash whatsoever. A few years prior, I personally had set aside $10,000 in a special bank account for the college educations of Chuck and Scott and a few hundred dollars in my own personal checking account. I also owned the condo in Palm Springs where my equity had increased to approximately $6,000. I had a car completely paid for, my clothes and a few personal belongings. I gave up the condo at Mesa Verde immediately and Chuck and I moved to Palm Springs where I decided to start over! The main reason for this was to be with the lady I loved in an atmosphere that I also loved! Having Bourbon, Chuck and Irene's daughter Julie also figured in the equation. Chuck and Julie bonded better than I could ever dream. They were two great kids! I immediately started studying to attain a California real estate license. The first appointment to take a license test would be in San Diego in just under two months.

During this time I had quite a lot of time on my hands but I was ashamed to attend my country club. I was also eligible for unemployment benefits. Because of my previous salary, I was in the top benefit bracket, which at that time was over $200 per month, not much, but something. This was another humiliating experience. You really don't realize until you stand in an unemployment line what the real world is all about. I did this only two times and it was even more humiliating the second time. It's really a strange experience to stand with people who are so different seemingly from yourself, but who are people the same as you! I found the majority to be men. Ninety-five percent looked as if they needed a bath, and the room where we gathered stank! Also after talking twice with the employee personnel, I realized that 80% were just happy to receive unemployment and really didn't want a job. I was by far the best-dressed applicant and I received terrible stares and glances from most everybody in the room!

The evening before, I mentioned to Irene stopping by La Quinta Country Club and possibly playing golf. Irene's reply surprised me, as I was planning on finding out how much my membership was worth. Irene instead said, "It's about time you got out there and started using your membership! You need to spend more time with movers and shakers than ordinary people!" After what was to become my last time in an unemployment line, I proceeded to La Quinta. I had $40 on me, two $20 bills. When I stopped in the pro shop and asked our pro, Davey Evans, if there was anybody looking for a golf game companion and that I was available. Davey responded that the last group teed off 20 minutes before and there was nobody else around. I also asked if he had any idea what a membership was worth today. He said the last one sold for $10,000 two weeks ago. I then entered the men's private card room and was immediately hailed by three men I knew well, who begged me to join them for a game of Bridge. I had never played Bridge at the club before, only Gin Rummy. As I had no other plans and nobody to play golf with, I sat down with a glass of water and said, "Deal!"

What happened next was a total surprise. The three men were immensely wealthy, the oldest being Tom Spiegel, the founder and owner of the famous Spiegel Catalog from Chicago. The next gentleman was Sy Frank, the owner of the only two department stores in the state of Utah. The last man, who was by far the youngest and only two to three years older than I, was named George Collins, who inherited at a very early age the Collins Ranch, a strip of land along the I-10 freeway that extended from just east of the I-15 freeway in San Bernardino, west through Fontana, and covered over 3,400 acres, all zoned commercial. At that time, the ranch was worth mostly potential as it was largely barren property with questionable water availability and soil conditions for farmland. I mention this because starting about 25 years ago George's property sold not by the acre, but by the square foot!

We played for approximately two hours and we

changed partners after every four deals, a game now called "Chicago." It was one of those days where I couldn't do anything wrong no matter who became my partner. I was the player who won the bid and played the hand! That day I found out that it was Tom Spiegel who actually ran the game and had played Bridge forever from the seat of his pants. He was strictly an over-aggressive bidder and was an awful player of the cards. He loved the game so much and he was such a bad Bridge player, it actually hurt. He was the nicest man alive, certainly one of the nicest at La Quinta Country Club. Sy Frank, on the other hand, was a very quiet individual who was conventional and conservative player and if he bid I'd know that his cards were better than the bid! He also was a gentleman and he and I over the years did some real estate business together. George Collins knew every new bidding contract and took the time to try to instruct us all on how to play and bid. The problem with George was that he had no card sense and though his bidding was impeccable, his playing of the cards was much like Tom's.

The game ended in just over two hours, and because I held the best cards and successfully played most of the hands dealt, I was the only winner. They all lost, with Tom being the biggest loser and Sy and George losing about the same. I was up 5,200 points. As I stood up to leave, I noticed that all three were taking money out of their billfolds. I had no idea that we had been playing for money, nor the amount of money, which was now being placed, on the table! When I picked up the money, I was embarrassed and I didn't bother to count it. Tom, the leader, said, "Carl, we need you to play every weekday as our usual partner won't be here until after New Year's. And if you'd like to join us regularly thereafter you'd be very welcome. In the meantime, we'll be here tomorrow after lunch and we all hope you'll join us." I went to my car and there were several members standing near. I decided that wasn't the time and place to be counting my winnings. On arriving home, I had $560 in my pocket. I had won $520 playing Bridge that day—the same amount I made per week at Tenscon! I started playing golf in the mornings and meeting my three Bridge partners every weekday for the next five weeks. The worst day I had during that time was losing $50. On the average I won $150 to $200 per day and they still wanted me to play and enjoyed my company. Only George and I didn't see eye-to-eye, as there was a jealousy factor, which worked both ways. George actually became a much better man as he aged!

  On August 23, Chuck became 16 years of age and I matched his savings and helped him find and purchase a used classic Ford Mustang! This was a banner day for both of us. Chuck was an excellent driver and I never had to worry about his actions. He was a young gentleman and because of that, when I introduced him to Ron Fletcher of Lord Fletcher's, Ron immediately hired him as a busboy. I'm proud to say that Ron hired Chuck based on Chuck's personality and interview, not because Ron and I were close friends! Chuck was now a very busy young man during that school year.

In November, I took my real estate exam and passed and went to work for the largest residential real estate firm in California, Walker and Lee. I could no longer play Bridge in the afternoon, which cost me a lot of income, but again it gave me back some of my self-respect. I really wasn't comfortable winning money as a card shark gambler, especially with good friends such as Tom, Sy and George! They honestly acted sorry to see me leave their game, but wished me well in my new profession. They also in time sent me customers, leads and when they left La Quinta I sold their houses to their satisfaction! The first week working at Walker and Lee office in Palm Desert I sold my first house. The buyer was the chief of the Caliente Indian tribe's ex-wife, who bought it for cash and closed the escrow in ten days! My commission was $432 and Irene, Julie, Bourbon, Chuck and I celebrated!

Chapter 19

Life Gets Better

I enjoyed my new profession and from the beginning I was lucky as the real estate business in the desert region was good and became even stronger for the next several years. Irene became the center of my social life. I weathered the storm and our financial well being became stronger as the months flew by. Irene and I were on the same philosophical wavelength, which made life much easier and less stressful.

Due to many past tragedies in my life, such as my mother's death, Lloyd Rentsch's plane crash at the age of 43, Ted's disappearance, my own flirts with death in 1946, my car crash in 1967, and Phil Murphy's death at the age of 58, I had changed my outlook on life itself. I became somewhat fatalistic in my thinking. With my beloved Irene at my side we made the decision to live one day at a time and use every opportunity to enjoy our lives. This might sound very selfish, but we also worked hard to help those around us to enjoy better lives.

During this period I had the opportunity of assisting Irene and Julie, who had become caregivers to the elderly lady next door. "Stormy" was her nickname and she was battling brain cancer. She had no family and all of her old friends were miles away or gone. Julie and Irene literally took care of her around the clock. I helped as much as possible as she slowly died. When this occurred, the vultures struck. There appeared lawyers, one legitimate old friend now living in San Diego, and a couple of so-called financial advisors. I was able to help by advising Irene on several matters, but it was Irene's decisions that counted, some good and some bad.

Janet "Stormy" Olson was, in the late 1930s until her death in 1971, one of the great benefactors to the Ladies Professional Golf Tour. She had been a friend to such famous Hall of Fame lady professionals such as "Babe" Didricksen-Zaharias, Patty Berg, Mickey Wright, Carol Mann and countless others. For over three decades she gave a $1,000 bonus to any player having a hole-in-one. Back in this era this was a huge amount of money to a lady professional golfer! Over the bed in her master bedroom hung the famous picture of "The Babe" sitting on a rail fence—a large oil painting of "Babe" Didrikson-Zaharias, which Stormy bequeathed to Irene.

In March of 1971 I drove Stormy, Irene and myself to Mission Hills Country Club in Rancho Mirage for the Dinah Shore LPGA Golf Tournament. When Stormy appeared, she was surrounded by all the pros who knew her and others that had heard of her. She was truly a legend in women's golf and on that particular day she was treated as such. It brought tears to both Irene's and my eyes to see little Janet, who was now less than 90 pounds, having so much fun! Stormy didn't live much longer before she passed on, but she fought valiantly to the very end.

When the Will was read, both Stormy's attorney and Irene's choice for an attorney did not represent Stormy's dying wishes honestly. Stormy's attorney went so far as to have his adult sons enter the house and steal valuables. The other attorney just didn't have Irene's best interests at heart. After the first raid on the house, Irene and I went over and took the items that had been bequeathed to Irene and one Japanese paneled screen that Janet had promised me. Among the things we removed was "The Babe" portrait, for which I was physically present when Janet bequeathed it to Irene. A year later, Babe's husband, George Zahariasa, came to Irene's house and asked for the painting. Irene, believing in her heart that this was what Janet would have liked, gave the portrait to George.

Another interesting development occurred in the first summer of being a real estate salesman. The manager, Bert, had always closed the Palm Desert office from June 15 until Labor Day, stating there wasn't enough business during these hot blistering months to warrant the office being open. At the time we had, including myself, six salespeople and Bert. That spring real estate became busier and then much busier. I was already an infamous member at La Quinta Country Club because of my success both in the card room and shooting the best golf round of my life in the Hope Classic. The President and CEO of Walker and Lee, William Stagger, was a member and I occasionally played golf with him. On the golf course with Bill shortly thereafter, I told Bill that I didn't think that with business being so excellent at the moment that the Palm Desert office should close for the summer. Bill said he'd look into it.

  The next day at the office I had a furious manager. Bert had made his plans for the summer and they did not include selling real estate! He had been ordered by his boss in Anaheim to stay open for the summer on the orders of the CEO and largest stockholder! He finally cooled down enough to ask the other five people what they would like to do? All five wanted to stay open! With that knowledge, Bert called his superior and said that the office staff wished to stay open, but he was still taking the summer off. On the next Monday he was given the word that I was to be promoted to assistant manager for the summer months. He didn't like that at all, nor did the senior sales person, a lady who was an excellent real estate professional. She almost quit right then and there, but luckily I was able to take her aside and explain the relationship between William Stagger and myself and how staying open evolved. As she, like all of us, had wanted to stay open badly, she agreed to stay.

  I was not aware that by being assistant manager I was entitled to 40% of an override that office managers make on all sales within their office. Bert was receiving 6% of the commissions on all of our sales in addition to whatever commissions he received from his own listings and/or sales or if lucky, both. When June 15 arrived, Bert left and our close-knit six some became even more of an efficient, happier and more profitable group. I was extremely lucky to be in the right place at the right time again!

The balance of June was excellent and the weather was still tolerable, but our office was busier than ever with people looking to buy. In July, our business was over 50% greater in dollars earned than in May. The weather by the end of July was very hot, up to 108 degrees. August is usually the warmest month in the desert, as it is also the most humid. This August was no exception, but all the lookey-loo traffic we had seen in June and early July reappeared and we sold the largest amount of real estate and sales commissions in the history of the Palm Desert office!

On September 6th, the day Bert returned, the final sales figures plus commissions for the month of August arrived. Bert also received a call from his superior to compliment Bert for his office's outstanding performance for August and advised Bert that Palm Desert had sold more profitable real estate then any other office in Walker and Lee. Bert did a very stupid thing. He quit the next day! In the early afternoon I received a phone call from Bert's superior promoting me to manager if I wanted the position. Before I could answer, he invited Irene and I to dinner that evening and to make reservations at a nice restaurant in Palm Desert. We had never met, but he obviously was well advised by someone, perhaps because of knowing Irene. This became quite complicated as in mid-August I'd had a phone conversation with Stagger, who had asked me to call personally on the famous Jacqueline Cochran and her husband at their mega-estate in Indio. He told me that they were planning to make the estate into two or three golf courses eventually, with condominiums on all sides of the fairways and greens. It covered one square mile or 640 acres. The Walker and Lee architectural department had been working with Mrs. Cochran and her husband, who owned RKO Studios, for over six months and before anything was announced they wished to purchase a smaller mini-sized dwelling on about five acres of land. Stagger also said that Walker and Lee would be the marketing and sales agents when the development started, presumably within six weeks!

I contacted Mrs. Cochran and discussed over the phone exactly what she desired and it became evident to me that the land was far more important to her than the dwelling and buildings. I went searching the following day and found three beautiful parcels of properties that fitted Jacqueline's requirements—one in particular that was exactly four acres on Monroe Street directly across the street from their present home. I called Jacqueline the following day to make an appointment. She replied, "I'm ready right now. If you can—let's go!" Twenty minutes later I was at her front door. The main house was truly magnificent, but before I exited my car, there came a woman towards me dressed handsomely in very mannish attire. I remember having to literally run to the passenger side door to meet her and introduce myself. She was very pleasant, had a big smile on her face and said, "Let's go, I can't wait to see what you found!"

It could have been a huge error on my part, but because it was so close, I took her to the property on Monroe Street. We first looked at the main house, then a garage with a fully-equipped machine shop. From there we walked to a barn that would accommodate eight to ten horses or animals of all kinds, with a hayloft that appeared quite a few years newer than the other buildings. For at least one hour Jacqueline, leading the way, walked us over the complete four acres. We then reentered the main house where she was jotting down sizes of all nine rooms, which included two opulent bedroom suites and baths that even Irene would have loved. As we started to leave, Jacqueline asked the price, which I quoted as $585,000. She answered, "That's a steal, but what do you think the owners would accept on an all-cash, ten-day transaction?" Being as penurious as I am, I suggested $475,000 with a one-week escrow. She agreed and told me to write up a contract for her to sign. She had her husband's legal authority to do so, as the home would be part of their family trust, and she would sign it first thing in the morning so I could present it. We returned to her mansion and she told me not to wait around, to get to work and that she would see me first thing in the morning. I called her at 8:30 a.m. hoping that it wasn't too early, only to have her say to me, "Get your ass over here!" I have never met a woman who swore, used profane language and insulted people like Jacqueline! I loved her for what she was and portrayed, as she was also totally honest.

I took the offer to the listing brokerage located in Indio, where the broker and his clients were waiting, as I had alerted him to the pending offer. I submitted my offer and the other broker asked me to wait in the lobby while he talked to his clients in private. About 30 minutes later, I was asked back into his office and the sellers had countered at a price of $515,000 with everything else being acceptable. I called Jacqueline. She asked me what I would do and I advised that if she really wanted the property, that I would split the difference offering $495,000 and have me tell them to take it or leave it. She agreed, but cautioned me that she really wanted the property. I assured her that I wouldn't leave there until we made a deal. I presented them with Jacqueline's new counter offer. This time I was not asked to leave and the sellers, an elderly couple and their realtor, started debating the new offer. It was interesting, as the realtor, because of the take-it or leave-it option, wanted them to accept it, while the husband wanted to split the difference again. But the deciding vote and strongest person in the room was the wife, who said, "That's an offer for almost a half a million in cash that we'll receive in one week's time. Quit playing games, we accept the offer!" The husband picked up a pen and signed the contract as soon as I changed the final sales figure to $495,000. All four of us then initialed the change and I left without calling Jacqueline and went to the gate where the guard had to call the main house to receive approval for my entry.

This time no one came to greet me and I climbed

the stairs to the elegant entry doors, where I rang the bell. A formally-dressed man opened the door and led me into a private office that contained two massive gorgeous executive desks, shades of Downton Abbey! Jacqueline was not alone and introduced me to the gentleman with her as the local attorney for their trust. I handed the signed contract to the man to study and politely said to Jacqueline, "I hope this has been a good experience. It sure has been for me, as I'm not used to these types of dealings, except that I'd love to have more!" Jacqueline replied, "Carl you're a wonder. I would've paid a lot more and my husband is going to be so surprised and proud of what I've accomplished in the last 24 hours, you'll never know!" She didn't say one profane word! The attorney looked over our standard California real estate contract form and had Jacqueline sign. He then directed me to a local Indio escrow and title firm to open the escrow. He phoned Kelli Lee saying that I'd be there directly and that he expected special service for this escrow, which must close seven days from now! The escrow closed as ordered and I received a phone call from Jacqueline thanking me for being such a professional.

    The next weekend Stagger came to the desert and requested that I come to Anaheim and meet with the architectural design team and involve myself with the new golf course development for Indio, which I was happy to do as it was another great learning experience! I'd made a second trip to the architectural team before, the night I met my new superior, whom I felt was unqualified for his position in the company. Irene and I arrived at the restaurant and a few minutes later Larry entered with a 6' 4" tall Las Vegas showgirl. She certainly was beautiful facially and with an equally beautiful body, but exposing far too much flesh. We went to the bar while we waited for our booth to be ready. The young lady spoke very broken English and Irene said later that she doubted if she understood two words of what we were talking about. Irene actually felt very sorry for the young girl.

Then something happened totally out of the ordinary. Irene excused herself and went to the ladies room. During this time Larry complimented me on being the new manager and how well our desert office was performing. We were sipping our drinks and making trivial conversation when the maître d' came and led us to our booth. On the walk to the booth as we entered the dining room, the noise stopped completely and everybody was staring at this statuesque French beauty. The young lady, I presume, was used to this, as she started walking slightly slower to give her audience a better opportunity to look her over. We arrived at the booth and sat down and ordered another drink for the three of us, as Irene's drink was still almost full. I finally asked our young lady if she would enter the ladies room to make sure that Irene was all right. The two reappeared a couple minutes later and Irene had completely changed her hairdo trying to make herself look taller! We enjoyed our dinner, but we really were sorry for Larry's date. To quote Jacqueline Cochran, "What an ass he was!" On the way home I teased Irene about her hairdo and nicknamed her "Woodstock," the little yellow bird in Charlie Brown! I still call her "My little Woodstock" on occasion.

Business was continuing to be excellent, not quite as good as August, but very profitable for all six people in the office. My trips to Anaheim were a wonderful learning experience because it entailed the creation of a huge golf course development containing approximately 800 condominiums, with each one having a golf course view. I was able to help the design somewhat, taking the plans from the very successful Sunrise Villas in Palm Springs as an example of what buyers in the desert were looking for in a condo atmosphere. The most intriguing thing about the Indio project was using and changing the mansion into a clubhouse. The architects knew very little about what new clubhouses consisted of, particularly in the desert. I hosted the two men assigned to redesigning the mansion. We first visited the mansion and then the three clubhouses just built at Mission Hills, La Quinta and Ironwood. Listening to them discussing how they would do this and that and all of the ramifications of each little change was fascinating! After ten hours of what was truly mental strain, they departed. After that day, it was decided that the exterior of the mansion had to be kept the way it was. The insides were changed about 50% of what they first envisioned, but in the end it was as beautiful and functional as any clubhouse in the desert.

My family life had changed during my beginning in real estate and Chuck was planning to leave Palm Springs upon graduation in June to live and work in Costa Mesa. Debbie was playing on the girls' golf team at Cal State Fullerton College and was making plans to move to the desert with me temporarily, which I wanted. That summer Debbie won the Los Angeles County Ladies Amateur Championship and was on her way to a career in golf.

A surprising thing happened one day—the man next door approached me and asked if I would consider selling him my unit, as he loved his location and wanted to expand his unit. As the condominium bylaws prohibited any additions to the unit, the only method of expansion had to be within the units themselves. He said he'd pay me $40,000 cash for my unit in 30 days, no escrow, no title search, no other costs, just a cash contract of sale notarized and no additional expenses for either of us! This would give me an $11,000 net profit—a large amount of money then. I moved to a small apartment complex in the heart of Palm Desert, a two-minute drive from my office, where I lived until early 1974! With money given to her by her mother, and Irene and I coming up with the balance, we purchased a little home high on the hill overlooking the valley in Cathedral City and started living together, as Irene had been forced to leave her home at Canyon Estates.

Shortly after my work with the architects, Stagger visited me in my office and stated that Walker and Lee could have the marketing and sales for the Indio project except there was one minor problem, Jacqueline wouldn't sign the contract unless she was assured that I would be the manager overall representing Walker and Lee. I asked if that meant that I'd have to be on site or if could I appoint a sales manager and sales force as necessary and be involved from our office here? Bill said, "You can be an absentee manager, but her husband requires that you be available when necessary, as he trusts your judgment and marketing skills." I remember laughing and saying, "Bill, that's laying it on kind of strong isn't it?" Bill laughed also and then said, "Carl, as you know we separate the new home sales from the resale division, but for you I would like to make an exception to the rule. I would like you to be the desert region sales manager handling both new home sales as well as your current resale position. This is to be an isolated position within the company. You'll have no superior but will govern the desert regions, answering only to me! As far as your management monetary overrides are concerned, you'll receive 4% of the commissions on all desert income. This figure is strictly between you and I, and except for our chief accountant nobody in the organization will know. There will be no contract except for a handshake and my promise that this is law. Do you accept?" I agreed and we shook hands.

  I spoke to my number one salesgirl, Sylvia, and clued her on this turn of events and gave her the first opportunity to be the sales manager for the new project opening in Indio. This carried a commission of 50% of Walker and Lee's sales commission of 10%, which would pay her based on our projected sales prices per condo of $30,000, or $1,500 per home. Sylvia, much to my delight, accepted instantly!

I received a phone call from Jacqueline asking me to be present for the first management meeting that coming Saturday. That day I arrived and was ushered into the boardroom and there were several people I had not met before and one unexpected member, the head of our architectural design department. Jacqueline introduced me first to her husband, the equally famous Floyd Odlum, the owner of RKO Studios, which he had purchased from Howard Hughes. He had a big smile on his face and he said, "So you're the man that taught Jackie how to do business! Thank you and I'm glad that you're on our team!" Floyd turned and introduced me to his son Bruce Odlum, a man slightly older than myself. We shook hands, but Bruce never uttered a word, just nodded his head. Floyd introduced me to another gentleman who represented a major architectural firm from Las Vegas. The architectural work was being taken over by the Las Vegas firm and Walker and Lee Design was now on a consulting contract and had turned over all of their work! Two other men appeared: a golf course designer and Mr. Odlum's personal trust attorney from Beverly Hills.

Mr. Odlum called the meeting to order and politely reintroduced everybody at the table. There was no doubt in my mind at that moment that he was the man in charge, but Jackie and Bruce would be the top management on site! He also stated that I would furnish on-site sales people with a sales manager available at all times. He further said that any marketing and sales top management decisions were to be made by me only. Toward the end of the meeting he stated that all serious occurrences and questions would be handled by both Jackie and Bruce and that I would get my information from both, as he must himself devote full time to RKO! Either Jackie or Bruce would chair the meetings in the future. At the end of the meeting I shook hands with Floyd and thanked him for his kind words and told him how much I appreciated and looked forward to this opportunity. As before in my life, this was the last time I ever spoke to Mr. Odlum, Sr.

    The on-site sales office was to be placed in the garage of the first model home complex closest to the remodeled mansion clubhouse, but in the meantime we rented a sales trailer adjacent to a new hastily prepared grass parking area. The trailer and the new model office space would each hold a manager and two sales agents. I attended monthly meetings and spoke occasionally to Jackie, but I realized quickly that Bruce was totally a fish out of water and why I had become so important to his father.

    When our local desert newspapers, plus an article in the real estate section of the Los Angeles Times appeared, not only did the project draw heavy traffic, but our Palm Desert office was far too small to handle the potential customers. We immediately had two veteran local real estate sales people interview for our open positions. Only because my other agents knew the man and woman and gave their blessing did I hire them. We now had my large cubicle in the back corner of the room with two chairs and a lamp, seven salesman cubicles (which barely held two chairs) and no lobby, only a small space near the entrance for two chairs.

In the past year, I had become reacquainted with Ray White, the retired scrap dealer from Cleveland, Ohio. He owned the Los Angeles scrap dealership where I sold all my copper scrap prior to bringing in my partner. Ray, under my tutelage and recommendations, had bought three excellent pieces of property through Walker and Lee, with me as the sales agent. Two of these prime pieces of commercial sites were located in Rancho Mirage on the main corner of Bob Hope Drive and Highway 111. The other, less expensive property was a 42,000 square foot empty lot across the street and one block east of our present location. The major property on the corner of Bob Hope Drive cost Ray exactly $1 million! The property was originally for sale for $1,400,000. This is how I learned to bargain like a professional Jewish businessman, which describes Ray White perfectly!

Ray offered $700,000, all cash, with a 30-day escrow. The seller countered at $1,300,000. Ray countered at $800,000, with a 21-day escrow. The seller re-countered at $1,200,000. Ray re-countered at $875,000 with a 14-day escrow. The seller, waiting a couple of days, re-countered at $1,125,000. After several days, Ray raised his offer to $950,000 with a 10-day escrow, and after a week, when I honestly thought we'd lost the seller, he lowered the price to $1,100,000. Now it was Ray's turn to play chicken! Ray asked me to find out from the best escrow title company in the area how quickly could they promise they could give title and close escrow? I called a friend at the local escrow title insurance with whom I had a personal relationship with a really nice guy named James. He told me if I placed an all-cash transaction by 4:00 p.m. on a Tuesday, I could close escrow on Friday at 11:00 a.m.! I relayed this information to Ray. He said, "On Monday morning I'll be in and sign a new offer for $1 million with the closing date of Friday. Tell the broker I said it is take it or leave it, as I've used up six weeks of my time."

I prepared the offer and alerted the other broker that my client was making his last and final offer for me to present to him Monday morning, but I did not tell him the price or terms. I delivered the offer and told the real estate agent that Mr. White wouldn't budge a dollar more, but the title company assured me that he would receive a cashier's check for $1 million on Friday before noon. Late Monday afternoon, the real estate agent appeared at our office and gave me the signed acceptance, which I took to the escrow company at opening time on Tuesday. The escrow and title documents plus the check were all received before noon on Friday. Ray had also purchased across the street from this famous corner a building in a small strip center of approximately 7,500 square feet at a bargain price of $375,000, again all cash. The small empty lot in Palm Desert was for sale for $50,000 but again Ray bargained like it was life or death and ended up buying the property for $37,500, all cash.

Right after making the deal with Stagger I went to a

couple of my fellow club members at La Quinta Country Club who were pestering me for a good business deal if one became available. I contacted both of these gentlemen, Mike Kaiser and James Walker, and told them of a proposition that included all three of us to build a new office building on the empty lot on Highway 111 to be occupied by Walker and Lee, and possibly by PaineWebber Brokerage and a 31 Flavors ice cream store on both corners, with my offices in between. Without any thought they gave me their promise to participate!

Timing is everything. The morning before meeting with James and Mike, Ray White appeared in my office and said, "Carl, I want to roll the Palm Desert lot ASAP as I'm a little short on cash." I took out a listing form, filled it out and asked Ray what price. He signed a listing for $87,500 and left. After talking with Mike and James, I was confident if I could get Ray down in price close to a reasonable market value, I could build what we named briefly the JMR building (later changed to RMJ). I left phone messages with both Lou Sandor, a wonderful local architect, and Dave Hall, who was now working for the Japanese conglomerate Matsui in the banking division in Los Angeles, and asked them to give me a call tomorrow if possible.

Lou said his business was slow momentarily, but the last couple of years had been the best in his life and asked when could we get together. I replied that I only had an idea of what we needed in my head, nothing on paper. He said that was no problem. We agreed to meet that week. Dave called the next morning also and we renewed our old relationship. We still saw each other every first weekend in March for golf and Bridge at Pebble Beach, but not like the old days when the four of us were together as much as possible. I told Dave that I was hoping to build a new commercial office building in Palm Desert. I asked him if Mitsui would like to be my lender and if so, what I needed to do to get the ball rolling. Dave answered, "You bet they will. I'll handle it myself and the only thing that will be required is that nobody but you and your partners know how low the rate will be. Let me know when you're ready to talk and have some drawings and I'll get the appraisal process moving. Say hi to Irene and tell her we miss her." I replied, "Ditto to Catherine!" I met with Lou for lunch and after about two hours of talking he said, "Carl, I can give you a set of plans, plus I will be your job superintendent and your building will be a landmark in Palm Desert. If we can start construction within 30 days with all my costs added in, we can build the structure for $30 per square foot which is $10 per square foot under market for the quality of building I envision, which should help your borrowing cost."

I contacted both PaineWebber and 31 Flavors and told them I had a superb location on Highway 111, which was indeed location, location, location! They both said they would be at my office within the week. My only problem now was Ray White, because I knew how he negotiated, but that was to be to my advantage. I gambled that nobody would be interested in the lot for $87,500 knowing Ray had bought it seven to eight months prior for $50,000 less. So I did nothing until the representatives from PaineWebber and 31 Flavors came by. I took both separately to see this site and showed them a very rough drawing of the site with a building site almost in the middle showing them the square footage available and the potential parking areas. There were 24 parking places in front, 18 on the side, and 24 more in back with a possible 12 more in the rear if we squeezed a little. There was also frontage road parking and on the cross street side of the building, parking for at least 10 cars.

Paine-Webber decided the corner suite on the east end with the extra 18 spaces was more ideal. This was perfect as I envisioned that 31 Flavors should be on the other corner! They both said they wanted the first right of refusal on leasing those spaces. Because the building was new, and during construction they could customize their spaces at their own cost, they would pay 50 cents a square foot plus agree to a 5% per square foot annual increase for ten years for 31 Flavors and five years for PaineWebber! Now I was ready to tackle Mr. White!

I called Ray and said I had a prospective serious buyer for his Palm Desert lot. Ray replied he would be at his new building in Rancho Mirage after lunch and to stop by. The first thing he asked was whether I had an offer to which I replied, "No, but I have a serious buyer, The RMJ partnership of which I am the "M." Thanks to you, Ray, I have enough cash available along with my two friends from La Quinta Country Club to build a small office building to house Walker and Lee. I'd like your cooperation in doing so, but frankly your asking price is way above market and what we can afford." In typical fashion, he said, "Carl, because of you, I'll take $75,000." I replied, "Ray, I just had two local appraisers price your property and because you only paid $37,500, it appraised by one at that exact price and the other at $40,000. The price my partners and I will offer will be an all-cash offer with a 30-day escrow. Sharpen your pencil and let me know."

Ray and his wife, who were both individually extremely wealthy, had become friends with Irene and I. The gals had a lot in common and enjoyed each other's company. A couple of days went by and I'd heard nothing from Ray, so I called him and asked it if he was trying to make me sweat. He more or less grunted, "No." I replied. "Well, are you going to give me a new figure, or do I go find another piece of property?" There was a pause and then he said, "I'll give you one hell of a deal, Carl, $67,500 all cash in two weeks." I replied that I'd talk to my partners and see what they thought.

Thanks to Irene, I received the most important help in my bargaining, as Ray's wife, Ruth, called Irene and asked if I was really serious about their Palm Desert property, which was in her name also. She wondered if it would be helpful to us personally. Irene told me that she told Ruth that we wanted the property badly, but that Ray was asking far too much for a cash deal. She didn't tell Irene that she couldn't speak to me of their conversation, but I was definitely not to advise Ray that they had spoken. I then wrote an offer to Ray White for the price of $47,500 with a 14-day escrow, which I presented the following day. Much to my surprise, I had a phone call a couple hours later saying $62,500, all cash, 14 days. I waited until the following day and countered $51,000 with a 10-day escrow and Ray playing his game called back in an hour and dropped the price to $59,500. I waited two days and called Ray and told him that our final offer and all we could afford to pay was $55,000 to which Ray said, "I can't sell it to you for that price." I then heard a voice in the background yell, "For God sakes, Ray, they're friends of ours. Take the offer if they can close the escrow by next Friday and quit playing games!" Ray stammered, "Bring me the offer at $55,000 with an escrow to close next Friday before noon." On that Sunday we met Ruth and Ray and had lunch together, signed the documents and we all had fun, including Ray. With the money we saved and being we were working on a $450,000 gross budget for land, building, paving and loan costs, Lou Sandor estimated we had enough extra money to add an elevator to the second floor removing one stairwell at the elevator end of the building while adding only $2,500 to our total cost.

  I met with both James and Mike on Tuesday and showed them the purchase agreement on the property and the budget plus a rough draft of a two-story building with 6,500 square feet of store and office on the ground floor and 6,000 square feet of office space on the second floor. We had not yet signed a partnership agreement and I outlined my proposal. I asked for 25% of the partnership and they would take 37 1/2% each. We would only have to buy the property free and clear and Mitsui would give us a 100% building loan, which in turn would become a mortgage for 25 years on the property. Irene's and my total cash investment would be $13,750 and both Mike and James would have to come up with $20,625 but we needed to have all $55,000 deposited in 48 hours to make it work. Thank God they were both in good cash positions. I had their checks the next day and we closed the escrow Friday morning.

We were fortunate that Lou Sandor that next month could devote full time to designing our building! He loved the site of the building and it was a great challenge as the property itself was a great advertisement for him as an architect. Lou, for the next four to five weeks, worked 10 to 12 hour days, six days a week, and we were ready to solicit bids for the construction five weeks later. Again we got lucky, as the State of California Water Control Department heard of our new building and came to us asking for 4,000 square feet of space, customized at their expense, on the second floor, preferably in the middle of the structure. They offered to pay 50 cents a square foot per month with an annual escalation of 3 1/4% for 15 years with an option for 15 more. I drew up a contract immediately and two days later their head man from Sacramento arrived with all documents and plans for the customizing. We now had over 80% of the building leased! When I called Dave Hall in Los Angeles, he said, "Based on what you've just told me of the amount of space pre-leased and the quality of the lessees, I'll be able to get you a better loan of only 4% for 29 years with no closing costs. Based on an appraisal, we will order and pay if the amount is high enough. We will probably add whatever is needed to your original loan to give you some wiggle room."

For the very first time since my divorce from Mildred, my monthly income was exceeding my cost of living comfortably, and I had a bank account, savings account and I invested some money with PaineWebber. I also found a prime office space for lease in Palm Springs across the street from Alan Ladd's beautiful building, which housed a hardware store but was far more diversified. The building had the most important requirement in the real estate business, which was excellent location. I began a long pursuit for an office in the building that we really could afford. I called monthly on the leasing agent for the building, but he wouldn't budge on his asking price. Again I got lucky, as the building stayed vacant and I received many phone calls from sales agents saying that if Walker and Lee moved to Palm Springs that they'd like to interview for a position! From the time we started clearing the Palm Desert site and beginning the foundation, thanks to Lou we finished five months later to the day, with no cost overruns and under budget! Even more important, the building was extremely impressive from all directions. The view from Highway 111 was magnificent! Lou Sandor was one great architect!

Two weeks prior to finishing the building, Lou asked me about the sign that had been designed to stand on top of the building and to be dimly lit but very identifiable from Highway 111 after dark. Stagger was in town that weekend and I drove him to the building for his perusal. I showed him our space, which would hold 14 salespeople, with room for four more if needed. On the way out of the building I pointed to the sign area, which was very close to being over our entrance, and asked Bill what he would pay to have the Walker and Lee signage on top of the building?

I could tell from his reaction that he was surprised and wanted to think about it for a few minutes. On the way back to La Quinta, Bill said, "I just assumed that you would be putting your name on the building; which by the way is magnificent, easily the finest office in outside appearance in the county. I personally would approve a monthly charge of $200 per month, plus a small electricity charge, which if it's too great we'd split!" I answered, "I think that would be very fair and I believe it would bring Walker and Lee a lot of business plus prestige." He said he'd get back to me on Monday or Tuesday.

Funny, but in all the work and conversations Walker and Lee and I had, it was never mentioned how much we were charging and/or paying for the office space. Bill asked the question, to which I replied that everybody else on the ground floor was paying 50 cents per square foot as were the other offices upstairs, with the exception of the water department, who were paying 40 cents. I told him I was preparing the lease for Walker and Lee charging 50 cents per square foot. I asked, "Who signs as the lessee, because I sign for the lessor?" I remember we both kind of chuckled. I honestly had never thought about that little item before. Bill answered, "I guess I do and in certain parts of southern and northern California we pay far more than fifty cents per square foot for offices that look like dumps compared to Palm Desert." I told him of the five-year lease with a 5% annual increase until the first five years were completed, at which time the lease would be re-evaluated by both parties with a five-year additional option to the lessee. He agreed and said on Tuesday he would complete the lease agreement, including the $200+ plus monthly sign agreement, and mail it to me ASAP. I reminded him that he should have his design department send me an exact drawing of the sign that I could take to our local sign company, which I was sure would save us some money as compared to Anaheim and Los Angeles. I mailed the lease agreement special delivery the next day and before the end of the week I received the drawing of the new sign saying 'Walker and Lee Building' handsomely drawn in keeping with the building.

Within ten days on a Friday night we had a grand opening party, not only for the building but for Walker and Lee and for all of Palm Desert, Indian Wells, La Quinta, Rancho Mirage and all surrounding communities! We had 11 sales people and myself totaling an even dozen, and we all worked as greeters, tour guides, bartenders, waiters and waitresses. We served all types of beverages including every alcoholic drink imaginable, including beer and wine. We also had catered hors d'oeuvres delivered. Stagger and a few top executives from Anaheim appeared, and the party, which started at 5:00 p.m., lasted past the 8:00 p.m. closing time. We counted over 325 people, of which I probably knew 25 people in all. It was a fabulous success and our local Desert Sun newspaper had pictures and an article in Saturday's paper, which was very complimentary. Both Stagger and myself were shown shaking hands in one of the pictures!

On Saturday from 3:00 p.m. until 6:00 p.m., 31 Flavors had their grand opening, giving all attendees a free ice cream cone. The owners told me the following week they gave away over 500 cones. In Monday's Desert Sun there appeared pictures of the 31 Flavors new store and an article, again complimentary, to go with it. Finally, on Monday Paine-Webber had their grand opening, which again the Desert Sun covered with pictures and an article, but this time there was a picture of the building taken midafternoon and another picture taken with the building somewhat lit up at night, with an article about Lou Sandor the architect and a couple of the local subcontractors and tradesmen.

The building had only one suite not leased at the party Friday night and on Monday a doctor appeared and leased it. The completion date for the State Water Control Board finished the following week and was occupied within 10 days and had 15 employees, which increased monthly from then on. The first weeks after the opening,

I received requests for interviews from other licensed real estate agents, plus even more from women wanting to pursue a career in real estate. I also received more inquiries pertaining to working in Palm Springs.

I had previously interviewed a young man with a real estate license who lived in Palm Springs who had graduated from the University of California Berkeley where he also played three years on the baseball team and was captain in his senior year. He had gone on to play three years of professional baseball in the minor leagues before giving up the game and entering the real estate profession. He, his wife and two small children had moved to Palm Springs only about a year before I met him and was looking to settle in with a large real estate company. He was well acquainted with Walker and Lee from its offices in Oakland, Berkeley, and Sacramento, his hometown. He was now in his mid-30s and had eight years experience in real estate and had supplied me with solid references as to his character, honesty and professionalism. I had been extremely impressed and I had even offered him a position in Palm Desert, but the drive took too long from where he lived on the northeast side of Palm Springs so he thanked me but declined.

Shortly after our opening of the new building, I received a phone call from the leasing agent of the building across from Alan Ladd's in downtown Palm Springs asking me if I would meet him at the building at my convenience. He thought that there was a possibility because we were Walker and Lee that we just might be able to work something mutually beneficial to the owner and ourselves. He asked if there was any specific time I could meet him at the building and using a quote from Jackie Cochran I said, "How about right now!" Thirty minutes later, I entered the building in Palm Springs. He asked me what we could afford to pay to which I answered; "I'm now paying 50 a square foot for my new office in Palm Desert." He said that's a little low for a Class A freestanding office building on Canyon Boulevard in Palm Springs. Four months ago when we first talked we were asking 85 cents per square foot for a minimum three-year lease and two months ago we reduced our asking price to 75 cents per square foot. Two days ago the owner contacted me and asked me if I knew anybody in your company, as they appeared to be the new number one real estate operation in the desert. He'd also read somewhere that they were the largest residential real estate firm in California. I replied that he was accurate. He said, "Frankly, Carl, and this is my idea trying to do the best I can for my client, I think I would recommend that an offer for 60 cents a square foot plus a five-year lease with a five-year option might sell. I can't promise you that and this particular gentleman doesn't play games, but seeing that he initiated my call to you, this might work and give me hope that I can sell the deal. I've done business with this man for over 15 years and he walks away from chiselers. If you're interested, I'll talk to him tonight and suggest that I can get you to pay the 60 cents per square foot with the two five-year lease periods and I'll call you tomorrow hopefully with an affirmative reply. Remember this is my idea because I think it's good for both parties, but I feel that the property is worth at least 70 cents per square foot. I've been leasing property in downtown Palm Springs for over 20 years, so cross your fingers."

As soon as I returned to my office, I placed a call to the young man in Palm Springs at his home number and a very young little girl who I presumed was trying to talk like an adult answered the phone. She sounded as cute as a four- or five-year-old child can be. Her mother finally got to the phone and when I announced who I was and asked for her husband she told me he'd call me back. Ten minutes later the phone rang. I asked the young man if I were to open an office in Palm Springs if he would be interested in managing the office. If it were possible that he had connections and could bring along veteran successful real estate agents, it would be ideal. The overhead would be large and cash flow would be a big negative if we didn't start making sales almost immediately. He responded that he would love to have the opportunity to manage my Palm Springs office and that he knew at least five agents who would join him immediately if the location was good. I mentioned I was thinking of leasing the freestanding building across from Alan Ladd's on Canyon. He responded, "Wow! It doesn't get any better than that! How many agents do you think the office can accommodate?" I told him approximately 16 but if we were to do this, we would have to plan accordingly for now and the future and we didn't do anything that wasn't first class!

The following morning I received a phone call with an affirmative response and I got the location for less than expected. I called and we met at the building that day, signed the lease and we spent time planning how we could use the space effectively until we turned profitable. I promised Merle we would make whatever alterations he deemed necessary at that time. Merle joined Walker and Lee officially that day in my office. Within the week, he opened the office in Palm Springs with five other agents and in the next two weeks added three more. Merle was extremely intelligent, and after the first month he told me that he didn't need any more agents until he could make the alterations that were necessary to accommodate customers better and that the quantity of agents was not as important as the quality! The young man understood real estate!

Within a short period of time from the opening of the Palm Springs office, I opened another office on Highway 62 in the heart of Yucca Valley. It was a small office space that would accommodate approximately six people, but again it had location, location, location! I had already interviewed three agents from Yucca Valley and one from Twenty-nine Palms. I leased this office space for 25 cents a square foot and I might have left some money on the table.

At the same time I was looking at Yucca Valley, Juan Chavez, a young Hispanic agent in my Palm Desert office, told me of a store space of 900 square feet that had just become available in a corner building in Indio located at Monroe and Highway 111. We went to the site, which again was totally location, plus the size I had been searching for. I told Juan to get in touch with the leasing agent, find out all their particulars and to set up a meeting ASAP. We met the next day and the asking price was 35 cents a square foot. I offered 30 cents a square foot with a five-year lease and another five-year option tied to the cost of living index. The following day I signed the lease and one week later we opened the office in Indio with Juan as the manager. He already had three other veteran agents signed on.

In less than one month we had added 12 new agents to our resale division and from the very beginning all three new offices were bringing in money. They were not profitable as yet, but they were adding to their cash flow. Something very unexpected happened, a lady dropped in at the Palm Desert office and asked for Mr. Meisterlin. She handed the agent a business card with the name Laura Williams, CEO, Lewis Homes of California and told the agent that she had come a long way to see me personally; that she was staying at the Indian Wells Hotel and that she hoped I'd call her. I received the message about 4:00 p.m. and recognized the name Lewis Homes, as they were the largest homebuilders in the state of California at that time. When I called, she asked if she could see me right away. I hung up and told our agent I would be at the Indian Wells Hotel in case of an emergency or if Irene called. I arrived on time and as I entered the hotel a very nicely-dressed lady approached me with her hand outstretched, saying, "You must be Carl." She then led me to the lounge and we ordered a drink.

"Carl," she said, "Lewis Homes believes that the Coachella Valley, particularly from Rancho Mirage to Indio, is going to be a major new home market for the next five years. We just paid several thousand dollars to a national home research company to identify markets that will be strong for the next five years and there were three: the suburbs of Sacramento, South Orange County and the Coachella Valley east of Palm Springs. We're interested in building, in less expensive areas, regular homes for first-time buyers and, in upper middle class areas, houses that fit the desert and have some pizzazz and all possible amenities for the comfort of retirees and snow bunnies. Lastly, we're interested in building step-up housing for second- and third-time buyers. While driving around today waiting for us to meet I had the distinct impression that Indian Wells and Palm Desert were markets for our highest-class products. I also got the impression in Indian Wells that almost all of the housing was golf course oriented. Is there any good land still available for a merchant homebuilder like Lewis?"

I replied, "First, Laura, you did your work well today. You basically hit the nail right on the head! As you're aware, business timing is everything and there is one parcel of land up on the hill that I believe can be bought particularly because you're Lewis Homes. There are many parcels of land directly northeast of Indian Wells and Palm Desert towards the I-10 freeway that can be purchased for start-up housing. I'm sure the research firm identified these multi-thousand acres, which are in the center of the valley. The parcel on the hill is 60 acres, rectangular in shape, and is zoned presently three residences per acre. It's a natural for a development of 200+ homes, with the extra homes being allowed by adding a few amenities such as swimming pools, a couple of small one-acre parks, and some recreational facilities. I'm sure the seller, who has powerful political strength in Palm Desert, can and will sell you the property based on the quantity of home sites." We met the next morning and I drove to the best property on the hill. When Laura looked at the views, the land that needed very little grading, no flood problems, the availability of water and electricity as well as sewers in development on two sides, it didn't take five minutes before she said, "If you can deliver this property at a decent price, Lewis Homes will buy it today." I told her I thought the property would probably cost a shade over $1 million. Laura said, "I'll pay $1 million right now for just the right to build 180 homes." I responded that I was 80% sure that could be worked out.

  We then headed directly northeast on Highway 74, past the College of the Desert through the wash used for flood waters on occasion and had sand dunes after sand dunes for a mile and a half, stretching a full mile to our left and four to five miles to the right. All this property was in a wind belt, which wasn't that bad except there was no protection from sand storms. Once the sand was covered with streets, housing, and landscaping, particularly grass, there would be no problem. Someday the whole barren landscape would be completely covered and there would be no more sand storms. The cost of development there was almost prohibitive, except for the fact that the land could be purchased very cheaply and the county of Riverside would give a developer any type of zoning they required. The people who lived there wouldn't object because they wanted to see the sand covered up!

We continued driving the perimeter of the sand dunes and Laura asked, "What is cheap?" I told her that the smaller properties were almost worthless because you couldn't cover up enough sand. I thought you could probably buy a ten-acre parcel for $4,000 or less. The 160-acre parcel along Country Club Drive would cost $2,500 per acre and the 320-acre parcel would cost $4-5,000 per acre because that was what was needed to build a first-class golf course development. We went back to the office and Laura freshened up, made one phone call from my personal conference room and thanked me profusely and then crossed her fingers and said, "Let's get lucky!" and she left. Laura and her husband James became close personal friends of Irene and I until we left the desert in 1993.

I met with my friend who was retired as the land acquisition and sales of land and properties for Home Savings and Loan. I explained that I had one of the major developers in the state of California who would like to build about 200 elegant homes on his last remaining property up on the hill and asked him the current price.

I should have stated that this elderly retired gentleman was still working and receiving a commission for the sales of homes. He was now down to the parcel we were talking about plus two commercial corners in Rancho Mirage and Palm Desert. He had let me know a year ago that it was still his responsibility to set the price to be paid on all properties, whether he was buying or selling. He said, "I really don't want to go through the work of zoning, I'm getting too old for that type of thing! Do you think they'd pay $1 million as is, cash in 15 days?" I replied I thought that would be an excellent asking price and that I'd try and have an offer for him in 72 hours. I mentioned that my client was Lewis Homes of California and watched his face light up! He agreed to the deal. Escrow was opened the next day and closed within 15 days. Lewis Homes became a customer of mine and Walker and Lee from that day forward.

The following day Merv Johnson called, stating he was a builder who wanted to talk with me about the do's and don'ts for a developer here in the desert. We met and here again was another close friend in the making! Merv was a very easy-going individual with a big smile, accompanied by a wonderful sense of humor. We went to La Quinta Country Club and had lunch and Merv asked if this was the club Stagger was always talking about. I told him yes. He talked about the desert and where he might purchase a 40-acre parcel, zoned, preferably three to five units per acre, on which he could construct a gated planned residential development (PRD), preferably in the center of the desert and close to Highway 111. He changed the subject and asked the cost of a membership at La Quinta Country Club. I really didn't know, but I walked to the front desk and found our manager and I introduced them.

I think I was almost as interested in what a membership now cost as he was as it was four years since I'd last asked. There were memberships available for $10,000. The dues were now $285 per month and the club had 380 members. The memberships would close upon reaching 400 members and then you would have to buy a member's membership. The manager told Merv that he fully expected a membership to increase no less than 50% when we reached the 400-member mark. Marv asked the manager to bring him a membership form and asked if sponsors were needed? The manager told him only two sponsors were needed. He was sure that Carl could go to the card room and get any number of members to sign. Right then and there Merv pulled out a checkbook, wrote one to the La Quinta Country Club for $10,000, and filled out the form. I signed and Merv and I walked back through the men's locker room to the private men's card room where I found my good friend Bud Nagler playing Gin Rummy. I introduced Merv to Bud and Bud signed under my signature. We went back to the manager's office and 48 hours later Merv was a member of La Quinta! On the way back to the office, I showed Merv a small 32-acre parcel. It was long and narrow but certainly buildable, that backed up to a date palm orchard on Highway 111 with approximately 400-foot frontage. On returning to my office a short half-mile from the parcel I pulled out the listing form. They were asking just under $50,000 per acre. I made a copy of the listing and gave it to Merv, who said he'd see me next week for lunch and a round of golf and that hopefully we'd do business the same day. As he was leaving he looked at me and said, "I haven't been this excited in years!'

The following week Merv appeared, presented me with an offer which he and I took to the other realtor on the way to the golf course for our golf game, and returned to the other realtor's office later where the seller had rejected Merv's offer, but did make a counter offer. Merv took the counter offer, studied it for a few minutes, sat down at a table and started crossing things out and adding things. I couldn't see the counteroffer and what Merv was writing, but I had the feeling he was excluding me. He finished writing, initialing and dating the changes, handed it back to the realtor and said, "This is my final offer, I don't play games." He turned around and walked out and I followed. When we arrived at the office, Merv left me in the parking lot telling me he was staying tonight at the La Quinta Hotel and playing golf first thing in the morning, having lunch and then heading back to Whittier, but if I heard anything in the morning, to leave a message at the club. He would call me to let me know his plans.

The next morning I received a phone call from the other realtor saying the seller had accepted Merv's counter offer! I picked up the signed counter offer and returned to my office, called Merv and told him of his success and that I had the papers. Merv arrived and we went to First American Title and Escrow Company, and opened escrow! Merv left for Whittier and I made another healthy commission and a friend for life!

The wonderful thing about the sales to Laura and Merv was that Walker and Lee received the marketing and sales through our new home sales division for years to come! I was in hog heaven again and making money that I would never in my lifetime have dreamed of and I had the most wonderful woman in the world to share our good fortune! Like a lot of things in life, Irene's personal problems during the two-year period were extremely painful. She lost her beautiful house before I became successful enough to save it. Her daughter Julie left for college at San Diego State, and Chuck had gone back to Orange County, so Irene only had Bourbon and I. My daughter Cynthia also married during these years and had two sons, Shane and R. Scott. Debbie was now a touring golf professional whom I rarely heard from. My son Scott received a scholarship at Utah State and I did hear from him now and then. We cohabitated in the little home in Cathedral City until 1976 when we sold it for a nice little profit and moved to a small two-bedroom two-bath superb desert home on the grounds of La Quinta Country Club.

At the end of 1975, we were married in Santa Barbara with Irene's sister, Larla, and her husband Roy Coursey standing up for us. We didn't invite any of our children because of petty jealousies and we wanted a private ceremony. Somehow Julie got word and showed up with Bourbon for the wedding, which was fine and we loved having her there, but when she left she didn't take Bourbon with her, so Irene and I and Bourbon honeymooned together! I have been supremely happy many times in my life but none surpassed this moment!

Chapter 20

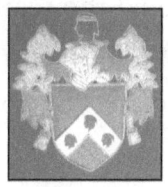

Life is Wonderful

I was making more money than I ever dreamed possible! With Irene's help, we were working with many desert charities and I became involved with the United Way, the largest charity organization in our desert, even greater than the Bob Hope Classic. We were elected to the Committee of Ninety-Nine, the governing body of all the charitable and social functions of the Bob Hope Classic, and because of all these activities we were in the local newspaper plus the popular Palm Springs Life magazine all the time!

Irene was a tremendous hostess and made it great for company morale when we would entertain all of our agents and their spouses or guests at what eventually became pool parties, which grew to well over 100 people. Originally these were house parties, but as we grew so quickly from late 1973-1977 our only logical choice for parties was our homeowner's association pool in La Quinta. Social life in the Palm Springs–Indio area almost always slows down in late May and picks up again in late October. It became a twice-a-year party, which Irene hosted completely on her own! These events were held on the last Saturday in May and October from 1976 to 1978. Irene's enthusiasm instilled the teamwork and morale in the desert division. I always had the impression that all my people loved and appreciated Irene, and that I was simply tolerated.

**January 1979
Irene and Carl Meisterlin
La Quinta Country Club / Bob Hope Desert Classic**

In 1975, I made as much money as Stagger and in 1976 more money than Bill. In 1977 it was no contest! Towards the end of 1977, I began having corporate VPs from Anaheim representing both new home sales and re-sale divisions calling on me regularly. Obviously Stagger had changed his game plan. Irene and I were working around the clock with all the various requirements that go with success. Our immediate family was also growing and we had four wonderful grandchildren in addition to our six children who were now reaching marriageable age (two of whom were obviously married)! During 1976 and 1977

I had no problem finding new business or agents as organizations such as the Chicago Teamsters and St. Louis Teamsters had decided to invest and build sizable developments in the area. In addition, Bill Bone of Sunrise Corporation, the best builder who understood the desert, was spreading out. He came to me personally and asked me to find him some sizable parcels of land, preferably in 2,000-3,000-acre contiguous parcels, but he didn't want his own organization or mine to know! We didn't become close friends but we certainly respected each other and years later we did the biggest land deal ever in our desert!

In late 1975 there was a large developer in Palm Springs whose 72-unit condominium project we had sold out. He had started a similar one overlooking the golf course at the La Costa Country Club and he had hired our desert new home sales division to market and sell these condos located in Carlsbad in north San Diego County. That fall Stagger opened the first Walker and Lee resale office in San Diego County with a really good charismatic manager, Paul Calhoun. Paul was a graduate in marketing from the business school at USC. He was a typical USC alumnus and had connections everywhere due to his involvement with the famous USC Trojan Club. Paul also had another great asset in his wife Nina, who was slightly younger, very attractive and had far more common sense than Paul. They made a great team! It was an excellent choice and move for them as San Diego County, similar to the desert communities, was a rapidly expanding housing market. By the middle of 1976, Paul had 12 resale agents and oversaw four major housing developments and joined me as the only two individuals who had both resale and new-home sales under their command. At the end of 1976, Paul and my divisions accounted for less than 3% of the corporate overhead but we represented 20% of Walker and Lee's net profit. By the end of 1977 that figure rose to 28% net profit on an overhead cost of 3 1/2%. The desert represented 19 1/2% and San Diego 9 1/2%! In 1976, I made just a little more than Stagger, but in 1977 I made 75% more than he did. In the first half of 1978 I had already made the same amount of money as in 1977! You must remember though that every dollar I made accounted for three dollars for Walker and Lee. At the end of 1977 I was named "Man of the Year!"

    In mid-1977, a man entered my office in Palm Desert and introduced himself as Dave Thomas, the acquisition manager of the Thomas Brothers Cadillac Trust. He said, "My brother and I want to buy your building. I've researched all the information that's available and we both agree that it is excellently located and designed. I've walked through the state offices upstairs, used the elevator, bought an ice cream cone next door and now witnessed your operation. We will offer you a clean cash deal." I responded that the building wasn't for sale! He replied, "If you'll make me a copy of all the leases I will bring you an offer you can't refuse!" I then went to my files and pulled out all the leases and made copies for his perusal. I handed the copy to Mr. Thomas with the statement that I was only a 25% partner and I had two other partners who equally owned the balance, so any offer would have to be approved by them. He understood and said he'd be back to see me within the week. I called James and Mike and told them of Mr. Thomas' visit and I received the same almost exact answer from both, which was to let him bid and then we would decide. However, I had the final decision.

Mr. Thomas returned with an all-cash offer of $670,000 with a 30-day escrow. I stated that I needed to take this up with my partners and asked him to give me four days to chase my partners down. He told me to call him next week. I called Matsui to see what our month-ending balance would be on our mortgage, calculated our escrow and closing costs, and placed calls to James and Mike. They both thought that the offer was in the ballpark, but they had no hurry to sell, so it depended on Irene and I. On Monday I called Mr. Thomas and told him their offer was insufficient to interest us. He asked if we had any figure in mind, to which I said we all thought the building was worth in excess of $700,000. He replied that it was too much even though it was a magnificent building, however his brother had instructed him to go as high as $690,000. I thought that was a very fair price but again told him that I must talk to my partners. On the last day of the month we would owe $427,000 on the loan and our closing costs would be $6,000, netting us $251,000. My brokerage commission would be $3,000. I apprised Mike and James of the new offer and they said great! I called Mr. Thomas the next day and he said he'd be in my office tomorrow and we could open escrow and he would take me to lunch. The escrow closed and I gave Irene a check for over $51,000, which she deposited in our savings account.

      In January 1978 we took our first cruise from Miami to St. Martin and back, a seven-day trip where I attended real estate courses for a broker's license four mornings for 2 1/2 hours each, 10 hours in all. We enjoyed the cruise but decided that cruising and going to school wasn't a good idea. On the last Saturday in January we traveled to San Diego and took a room in the lodge where the California Brokers Real Estate Exam was being given. While I was taking the brokers exam, Paul Calhoun had a saleslady direct Irene to houses or condos that were for sale in our price range that were on the water. The test started at 11:00 a.m. and I exited before 2:00 p.m. I went to the room and relaxed. Irene arrived shortly after 3:00 p.m. and said that she had looked at five different homes and condos, but only one was worth my viewing. I suggested that we take a drive in the area she found the most interesting and I'd look at the one place she possibly liked.

      We drove over to an area on the east side of Point Loma with a view of San Diego across the bay. It was a beautiful day and the sun was beginning to set and the view of the city was spectacular! We drove to the home that Irene had found and she gave me all of the particulars. I took one look and decided that it was too old and run down and far too large for what I had in mind—which was a getaway from the desert. It was also far too much money than I wanted to spend at that time. As we were driving north on Rosecrans, I saw the infamous Le Rondelet round building which was now a 6-story condominium. This beautiful building was approved by the city of San Diego as a 12-story building and after they were in construction and had structurally completed four floors, the newly formed coastal commission stopped the construction and it was in the courts for three years. The original developer went broke and it was finally approved as a 6-story structure and auctioned off! I turned because I was curious and wanted to see the building close-up.

Driving by the entrance I saw a leasing sign plus a smaller for sale sign. The signs for both indicated there was a leasing agent on site seven days a week and the for sale sign gave the leasing agent's phone number and hours. I called and made an appointment for Sunday at 10:00 a.m. The agent was also the building manager. In the building they actually had four different floor plans. One plan was for the penthouses on the sixth floor and the other five floors had three different plans—a 1,400 square foot two-bedroom, two-bath unit; a 1,500 square foot three-bedroom, two-bath unit; and a 1,650 square foot three-bedroom, two and a half bath unit with a den. He had three or four of the three-bedroom plans for lease and one for sale. The other two-bedroom two-bath condo for sale was on the fifth floor and from the balcony you had a view of the planes landing at San Diego Airport all the way to the south of North Island and the Coronado Bridge. The asking price was $140,000. I thanked the manager and said we were interested but really didn't expect to find something today and that it was little bit out of our price range. I asked the manager if he thought the owner might consider a low offer to which he replied that he might! On our drive back to the desert, Irene started talking about how much she liked that floor plan, location and everything good she could think of. Finally she started yelling at me, "I want that house, I want that condo!" and this went on until she lost her voice!

  The next morning I called the manager and told him we would offer $125,000 cash with an escrow period of three to six weeks, dependent upon receiving a $75,000 loan. Before lunchtime I received a call back and the manager had a counter offer of $135,000 with all other conditions acceptable. I waited three or four days and before I could call the manager, he called me and said the owner was having second thoughts. He suggested that we counter as much as we could afford and that he would present our offer and recommend acceptance. I sat there silently until he asked, "Are you there, Carl?" I responded, "I shouldn't do this, but I'll raise my price to $130,000 with all other conditions staying the same except for obtaining an $80,000 loan." I then asked him to call me at my home where Irene could be part of the conversation. That evening we received a phone call accepting our offer for $130,000. Irene was ecstatic! We closed the escrow on March 1, 1978 and began going to San Diego every weekend until we finished furnishing and making it livable.

  The money used to purchase the new condo came

from the sale of the building, which came entirely from being lucky enough to be in the right place at the right time! My situation at Walker and Lee started changing in April after the year-end 1977 earnings were published, which included the top 50 monies earned by all employees and agents! I was on top of the list and Paul Calhoun was second. Stagger was third and then numerous agents from all over the state. My earnings were more than double Stagger's salary! I was visited by Stagger's right hand man, who began the conversation by first congratulating me for the wonderful resale figures for 1977 and then started talking about a readjustment in my commissions. I politely acted surprised as I reiterated that I thought that Bill Stagger and I had a private agreement. He looked around my office and saw our last expansion for the resale department, which now contained over 20 agents. Only the resale office in Anaheim had more agents than Palm Desert. Approximately ten days later, Stagger's left hand man, who was in charge of the new home sales division, arrived and went through almost exactly the same dog-and-pony show. After he departed, I wondered what would happen next. The resale VP was young and was a poor choice, not very smart. Rick, the new home sales VP, was a charming gentleman who had attended high school with Stagger and was strictly a yes man! Another bad executive choice!

In 1975, Stagger and his wife invited Irene and I to be a part of their Mulligans Club, which met at La Quinta Country Club once a year for a weekend of golf, Gin Rummy, eating, drinking and having fun! In '75 and '76 I won the Gin Rummy Tournament, which had the men playing against the men and the women playing against the women and then the champions of each playing against each other.

In 1977, on our way to Rosarito Beach in Mexico, we stopped at a liquor store before crossing the border and I bought a bottle of our Bombay Gin. When I went to pay, Irene joined me at the counter with a new deck of playing cards, which we purchased. Surprised, I asked her why the cards? She responded, "Because you're going to teach me how to play Gin Rummy so next weekend at the Mulligans Club party I can join in. I thought, 'Great!' All day Saturday and Sunday we did only two things other than eating and drinking—that being playing Gin Rummy with the cards facing up and collecting Pet Rocks, a craze at that time. The Gin Rummy game started with my teaching Irene how to shuffle the cards and on her first try we played 52 Pickup! Almost all 52 cards were all over the floor. What a way to get started! But I must admit I enjoyed every minute of teaching Irene to play. We left Mexico late Sunday afternoon with a trunk filled with Pet Rocks and Irene able to shuffle the cards perfectly. I was sure she wouldn't embarrass herself at Gin Rummy.

There were eight couples in the Mulligans Club, so to win a division title you had to win three games against your own sex and then play for the individual championship. I kept a close eye on Irene and I was not surprised when she won her first match, as she was playing against a lady I considered the weakest player among the women.

I got lucky as I drew the best player among the men and got all the cards. It wasn't skill and I won. Irene's next opponent was one of the two best lady players, Lida Ric's wife. The match was very close and lasted longer than usual, but Irene prevailed and everyone but me was stunned!

I had drawn possibly the weakest player in the room and I wondered how he had won his first match. This time I didn't receive all the best cards, but my opponent was so bad that he literally handed me the match. Irene's opponent in her last match for the women's championship was another good player, but not nearly the best. In Gin Rummy there's definitely a skill factor over a long pull, but in one game luck matters most! I remember in 1964 while on business in Las Vegas that to kill time I played in a tournament and kept winning and winning and made it as one of the final two players. In the last game I made what I thought was a huge mistake considering the cards that were dealt me, and discarded the wrong card. I was punishing myself mentally while waiting for my opponent to play when in fact he then discarded the same card in another suit which gave me a four card run and Gin Rummy in only two plays! I made over 100 points on that hand and won one more hand to win the championship. There was no skill involved, it was just plain good luck!

In the finals, Irene started badly but it was not because of skill—she wasn't getting the necessary cards. When it looked like she was going to lose suddenly, every card she drew fell into place and she won four straight large hands, game over! Irene the champion! Nobody in the room believed it, except me. In my championship game, I again received much better cards than my opponent and I easily won the men's championship. In the finals I won the first hand and then Irene went through me like Grant through Richmond! It was no contest and I was accused of throwing the match. I am setting the record straight here and now—Irene won fair and square. She beat me honestly and with skill and a little luck! On the way home in our golf cart she announced, "I've done that and I don't need to prove myself anymore!" and retired from Gin Rummy for life.

The following weekend I had a call from Rick asking if he and the resale VP could call on Irene and I at our home during a late afternoon. We agreed on a day and they both arrived. The resale VP did most of the talking and it became apparent they were not taking questions! He let me know that the company was changing the commission structure for all division managers, office managers and sales managers. This new commission and salary monetary structure would be in the mail next week, take it or leave it! When I asked if Staggers was going to talk to me, they both answered that they didn't know. When I received the new commission schedule it affected my income by over 20%. It was a large sum of money, but I was making a large amount!

The following week I called Stagger and for the first time he did not return my call. I called a second time the next week and again my call went unanswered. The following weekend, he and his wife Jeannie were at the club and when I made eye contact he immediately went the other way and disappeared. It was then that I lost most of my respect for Mr. Stagger! One of the many management principles I believe in is always train a person to replace yourself so that you can move up the executive ladder and I had one who I felt could do a better job than I. I had lost all desire to work for Walker and Lee.

During the following months, I was looking around for a new place to land and actually planning to start my own real estate firm in Palm Desert or Indian Wells, which were now the busiest real estate communities in the Coachella Valley. I received a phone call from a George Jones, the CEO of HMS Real Estate, a local Palm Desert firm that owned several office buildings on El Paseo, who asked if he could meet with me. I knew George, not well, but I always had a great deal of respect for his firm and the people he surrounded himself with. George was a class act! We met in his office and George said, "Carl, HMS is at a crossroads and we need to revitalize and restructure our corporation. I'd like your input. In our four buildings we have 16 tenants, the largest of which is our real estate division, which represents 15% of our rental income. As you're aware, the real estate office is the prime office space on El Paseo and very honestly it is totally stagnant and without a rudder! What action would you recommend?"

"First of all," I told him, " If I were you, I'd pursue

the best real estate broker available who would, I'm sure, bring several excellent professional agents with him if the commission schedule was liberal for both the broker and his agents. George, the right broker and three or four good agents would solve your income problem in less then 120 days the way the real estate market is today! Your main problem will be obtaining the outstanding individual that's needed to represent the extremely high profile of the HMS Corporation. My guess is that in your reorganizing and restructuring of HMS, you're probably going to have to give this individual a large piece of the action." George then asked if there were any people available to meet the challenge successfully and worthy, as I had put it, of being a major part of HMS. I replied that I could think of a couple, but it all depended on family and timing. We talked for a little while about where I thought the desert was moving in all respects and what was important in business management today as the world seemed to be changing, particularly human beings. His last words as I left were, "You've given me a lot to think about as well as pass on to my partners and board of directors, thanks." Shortly after, I received another call from George asking if he could come to my office. He asked if I would give him a tour of our operation and I did. He thought that the atmosphere, enthusiasm, quantity of agents and layout was totally different then HMS Real Estate! "No wonder we're doing so poorly!" he remarked. I surprised him by stating that HMS was a prestige real estate firm located on the most prestigious street in the whole Coachella Valley, whereas we were located on Highway 111 next to 31 Flavors. We would always have some clients in common, but it stood to reason that they would draw more high-end customers than the middle class that we attracted. His last statement before leaving was, "I've learned an awful lot about real estate just being in your office today and I can't thank you enough for being so gracious!" That weekend George invited Irene and I to dinner at the finest restaurant on El Paseo with he and his wife.

We met and had a wonderful evening together. Irene and George's wife had a lot in common—mainly they were gracious ladies! The dinner and service were excellent and the four of us obviously enjoyed just being together. There wasn't one word of business spoken! We left with Irene and I stating that we would like to reciprocate and their answering, "Anytime, we'd love to!" I received a phone call on Friday asking me if I could meet for lunch on Monday. We met at Johnny Bash's—walking distance from HMS Real Estate—only George was not alone, he had brought along two other board members. Before ordering lunch George said, "Carl, after being with you and picking your brain, plus seeing your operation and spending an evening with Irene, I've recommended to my partners that you're the man that HMS Corporation needs! What's it going to take for you to leave Walker and Lee?" I remember being surprised at that moment, although I probably shouldn't have been. I thanked them for the opportunity to join a wonderful organization such as HMS Corporation, but I stated that it would take an extremely attractive contract with ownership to make me change companies. George, who was dominating the conversation and speaking for HMS said, "Carl give us whatever it takes for you to join HMS!" He had a briefcase with him and he handed me a rather thick file and stated, "This is everything that HMS owns and or operates here in the Coachella Valley, with all the financial information that we have. We've held nothing back! After reading all this I ask you to not reprint or talk about anything you've read here—this is all very private information! We trust you will be very discreet in your use of this file and return it ASAP." We had our lunch and I locked the file in my car and took it home that evening to study.

I was surprised at how many orchards, restaurant/gas stations on Highway 10 and Highway 86, land that was being farmed and other commercial properties HMS owned in Indio, Coachella, Thermal and Valley Center. Most of their holdings definitely were in the path of progress—the only question was when. Their main problems were two things—cash flow, which was very poor from their commercial properties other than those on El Paseo, and a negative cash flow from the real estate division. The raw land was a loser and there was no income but they owed property taxes annually. The orchards showed a decent profit some years and not so good others probably due to weather conditions. This left the restaurant/gas stations and the balance of the commercial properties on El Paseo to pay all the taxes. There were also increasing maintenance costs on all the properties, which were now 15 years old except for the restaurant/gas stations, which had been built in 1946. Their annual repair and maintenance costs were increasing faster than the leasing revenue. As most of their properties were in the path of progress, but what I guessed to be 15 to 20 years away, they needed the real estate company to make a large sum of money. I also wondered if the two other gentlemen needed income in their retirement now.

From talking to George, I realized that the immediate income was not a factor in his present lifestyle. It would be a challenge to take this seemingly successful real estate company and turn it around. Irene and I were not worried about dollars. I accompanied them back to the real estate offices, which really needed very little restructuring. The style of the offices was popular more than a decade or more prior and mostly needed painting, flooring and more lighting. There was also a need for new professional office furniture. One of the partners finally spoke up and said, "I don't think we have the money now to do that!" I caught George out of the corner of my eye giving the gentleman a disgusted look!

Before George said anything, I mentioned that I knew of several furniture companies located in Southern California who made a business of leasing furniture for a period of seven years on a quarterly basis where the lease payments would pay off the furniture at the end of the lease and you'd own it outright. The furniture was quality and would last a minimum of 10 to 12 years. They seemed to agree with this idea. I left and studied all the material, which was all 15 years old, and some documents and accounting sheets that were current. After studying them, I really wasn't interested in ownership as the real value was so many years down the road, but I did like the challenge and I had confidence in my ability. Of course, I'd always been lucky! I decided that if they would give me complete control and authority to run the real estate company without any interference and a better commission override then I had previously, then that's what I desired!

Their offer was excellent! They would repaint, re-carpet and tile the entries to my specifications and put in a whole new modern lighting system at no cost to the new real estate company. In addition, they would give me a 10% ownership in the HMS Corporation. Also, they had found a complete board room ensemble and an executive suite with some beautiful desert oil paintings—all at no cost to the real estate company. I responded that their offer was excellent but that I would pass on the 10% ownership. However, I did ask for an executive override on all commissions of 6%. I also requested that we lease all the necessary furniture as previously suggested, with the condition that we pay no rent on the offices for the first three months until we could initiate our own cash flow. Lastly, we would need $5,000 in the bank to start, non-repayable! I think my offer and rejection of the 10% surprised them and George said they would consider it and asked to meet in the morning.

Our desert real estate market for new homes was

generally an upscale condominium second family market. These condominiums were 95% built-in gated private enclaves with homeowner associations' governance. In the past four years, over 80% of new home sales were homeowner association units. The only thing I could think of that could go wrong was that we were headed into country-wide inflation due to the idiots in Washington, D.C. where the Congress was now controlled by the Democrats and possibly a peanut farmer President who might go down in history as the dumbest of all time! I was now 50 years old and in my lifetime I'd seen our economy rise and fall, the Republicans taking all the blame but planting the seeds for economic recovery and then the Democrats taking all the credit and the political northeastern Beltway media spreading the untruths!

The next morning we met and HMS accepted my offer entirely. We decided to start the new subsidiary of HMS on the first day of November 1978. I waited until the last week of October to write my letter of resignation along with a personal letter to Stagger in which I thanked him for everything he had done for Irene and I, both in business and as friends. At the same time I advised all the managers and agents, thanking them for being such good friends and associates and making real estate so much fun! When I was asked, I admitted I was moving to HMS Real Estate and several agents asked if they could join me. I replied that I could only talk to them about that subject after my employment at HMS began. I never received a reply from Stagger or his right hand man and when we crossed paths at La Quinta he never spoke to me. Worse than that, his wife Jeannie never again spoke to Irene. It's hard to say anything bad about a man who has done so much and put you in a position for success, but Irene and I missed their presence and friendship!

On November 1st, I opened the door to my new company and found three employees, actually two real estate agents and a secretary whom I had agreed to take on. HMS had kept their part of the contract 110%! The offices were totally restored and everything was first class. The secretary/bookkeeper office furniture had also been upgraded and the young lady said the only thing original was her typewriter and telephone. My office looked very familiar, as George had moved all of his almost-new furniture into my office. That morning I had five of my previous agents appear and I hired all five. The furniture from the leasing company had arrived only the day before and the agents and myself moved the desks to make an efficient office. In the afternoon two more agents appeared and I hired them also. I now had nine agents and a secretary, but there were three individuals that I desired badly all for mid-management positions. With the help of my secretary and two of the sales agents, within the next 48 hours all three were in my office. I hired Tom as resale department manager and Tony as the new home sales manager and the third, the young manager of the Palm Springs office, declined as the timing for he and his family wasn't right, but as soon as his family finished relocating he wanted to join HMS. Late that summer he began working with us managing one major condominium development.

On the third day in business, Merv Johnson appeared and asked me if he and his sales agent from Walker and Lee were to cancel their contracts, would HMS and I take over the sales and marketing? Of course I was interested. Later that day Merv and Peggy appeared and HMS had their first new home sales contract and more importantly a profitable developer with whom I worked with very well! Within 30 days we closed our first escrow and had some cash flow by the end of 90 days. We were closing escrows that included sales and/or listings sold for every agent in the office. Things were good!

During our first 90 days, I received a lengthy letter from Asjerd in Norway that Trygve's younger brother in Pennsylvania had passed on and wanted me to invest in America the $30,000 bequeathed to Trygve for Christian. Tom had a previous listing at Walker and Lee from a young man for the past six months. When the listing expired, he called on Tom and listed a city of Coachella property. It was zoned commercial with just over 70,000 square feet, with frontage on Highway 86 of just under 700 feet. The square block adjacent to the northeast was completely built out! The property had been for sale for $115,000 and Tony listed it for $99,999. Within a month my bank called and advised me they had received an electronic cash deposit to my account from Norway. Three or four days later I received a letter stating to use my best judgment and invest the money for Christian however I wished. Slightly over a month later, Tom had a visit from

his client again and this time the client expressed a desire to sell the property immediately as his family was in the need of money. Tom's contract called for a 10% commission, as it was raw land. I asked Tom what he thought the property could be bought for? He replied $75,000 and I then asked Tom if he would want to buy a one third interest in this property for $25,000 or less? "If we could get it for under $25,000 and make a full 10% commission I would," he replied. The next day I asked Tom when he could come up with his share. "I will have the money in ten days," he responded. I said, "My Norwegian cousin and I, along with you, will sign a partnership agreement. Offer your client $69,000, all cash in ten days and each of us will put $23,000 into the partnership. The closing and escrow costs you and I will pay from our share of the commission. We will each have less than a $23,000 investment and HMS will make a tidy amount of cash."
I told Nina, our secretary, to draw up a partnership agreement and Tom called his client to say he had an all-cash offer of $69,000 within ten days. He told him that's as far as his boss and cousin would go. I told him to be sure and let him know that he was an equal partner with the two of us! Two days later we opened escrow and closed nine days later! Tom said his client was ecstatic and we might've left some money on the table.

    I had been working for several months with a young U.S. citizen originally from Iran who represented himself as a business manager for a relative of the Shah of Iran. I had spent a great deal of time with Mike who had been educated in Paris, France, Harvard University and received his MBA from USC. Everything we looked at for the business manager (mostly raw land in the path of progress) had to be high-density residential. Industrial or commercial properties must be cleared through a Beverly Hills attorney, Larry Petrovich. At the main intersection of Interstate 10 and Washington Avenue was the entrance to La Quinta, but it was 90% vacant land from the interstate until you reached La Quinta.

The famous La Quinta Hotel and Resort was now being considered as viable for development sooner than had been expected, as it was not as susceptible to sandstorms. Tony garnered a listing for a 1,480-acre piece of raw land contiguous to the northeast corner of this interchange at a price of $3,500 per acre, with a 10% commission. That weekend Mike arrived with Larry and we drove over to the property in question. After looking at the property Mike explained that Larry was not only his lawyer but also his real estate broker. Larry would receive 50% of the commission! I wasn't very happy about this after all the months I had personally devoted to Mike and Mike could tell I was unhappy. He quickly said, "Carl, this is the first of five pieces of land we expect to purchase and you will have the listing on all of them." The following week we received an offer from a man named Klar Zafar with a $100,000 cashiers check drawn on Columbia Savings and Loan of Beverly Hills. The offer was for $10 million cash with a 30-day escrow. Tony took the offer to the seller and it was rejected as Tony expected, but he did receive a counter offer and after Mike re-countered, the seller again countered and the seller's offer of $12,500,000 was accepted! From that moment forward my personal real estate sales more than tripled thanks to Mike and Klar. Sun City Palm Springs occupies this property today!

I received a phone call from Mr. Tom Siegel, the CEO president of Columbia Savings and Loan, who would be in the desert this coming weekend and asked if could we meet at his home in the Springs Country Club on Saturday at 11:00 a.m. Tom, who was younger than I, had recently taken the reins from his father who had founded Columbia Savings and Loan. He stated that he did a lot of business with the Shah's family and they had recommended me highly! He was interested in expansion of Columbia in the desert and wondered if there were any great corner locations left. I knew of two corners that would be ideal, but I wasn't sure if they were for sale at any price. He asked to see them. After looking at both corners, Tom said they were perfect and he'd purchase either and pay better than market price. I knew both owners very well personally and I told him if I could talk either one into selling, he'd have his corner.

Ray White owned one of the corners, as I had brokered his purchase. Knowing Ray so well, he wasn't ready to sell. I turned my attention to the last piece of commercial property owned by Home Savings and Loan. I called the old gentleman who represented the bank and asked if his commercial corner in Palm Desert was for sale. He replied it could be if I brought him another buyer as good as Lewis homes. "Suppose the buyer is a rival savings and loan?" I queried. "Carl," he said, "you've hit my hot button! I'll have to talk to Mr. Ahmundson and I'm sure the price will have to be over market." The following day I received his call stating they would accept an offer of $100 per square foot for the 30,000-square-foot site, but it would have to be all-cash, a 30-day escrow and pay me a 5% commission. In addition, the buyer and seller would split all escrow fees and closing costs. "In case you haven't figured it out," he said, "that's $3 million." I stated that Mr. Ahmundson struck a hard bargain, and that the price was far higher than market. "Mr. Ahmundson doesn't like Columbia," he said, "and especially since the son became their CEO. That's it, Carl, take it or leave it!"

    I phoned Tom in Beverly Hills on Monday morning with the purchase price and terms, omitting Mr. Ahmundson's personal remarks. We discussed the merits of the two corners. I told him if I if were up to me and immediate money wasn't an issue, in the long run the Palm Desert Corner was the better of the two for a savings and loan. When I stated this to Tom, I wasn't being a salesman, I was telling the honest truth! Tom's reply was, "I agree with you. Sunday I took my wife and we drove to both sites three times. She's very knowledgeable about location and she was adamant that the Palm Desert corner was far better! We have a big management meeting this week and I'll be back in the desert next Saturday. If we have something to talk about, I'll call you." Late Thursday I received his call and we met on Saturday at his home in the Springs. He handed me a real estate offer obviously from a legal counsel with every requirement that Mr. Ahmundson demanded. I went back to my office and phoned my man who immediately came to HMS. I presented Tom's offer accompanied by a check from Columbia for a $50,000 down payment and he signed for Home Savings and Loan. I called Kelli at the escrow company and asked her if I could open an escrow in 15-20 minutes, made copies of the initial contract and the check for all three parties, shook hands again and said goodbye and headed to open the escrow. The escrow closed 30 days later without a single problem and HMS Real Estate was doing fine!

Two things happened that had a large influence on my business and personal life. My son Scott, who was now a real estate agent, came to the desert and finally settled in my resale division at HMS. The timing was not good as some of the resale agents were jealous if I tried to help him by giving him leads and/or having him help me with some of my personal clients, something I'd done with Mike, who required a great deal of attention! Although HMS Real Estate was doing fine, unfortunately my personal sales were now 50% of our gross income. One of the reasons was the political mess in Washington, D.C. where our incompetent President was encouraging inflation in most every decision. People stopped purchasing second homes. Our new home sales were now down 80% and the little builders were going bankrupt and only the major builders with deep pockets could weather the economic storm. Inflation got so bad that you could go to the bank and purchase a six-month CD that would pay 13-14%. People with money were not buying second homes when they could safely invest in CDs paying these enormous returns! This caused the resale market to be so bad that the desert went from a seller's market to a buyer's market in a few month's time!

My son Scott and I took advantage of the situation and we bought an excellent condo on the fairway at the Indian Wells Country Club. Scott lived in it and decorated only the master bedroom and used the kitchen. In six months the market improved a little and we were able to sell it and we both made $10,000. Fortunately for the desert, the election of Ronald Reagan as our new President, along with changes in Congress by the end of 1981, meant that both of our real estate divisions were doing better. We sold a couple of more pieces of land to Mike and Klar and one major piece to Merv, who bought the major corner next to the La Quinta Country Club on the corner of Eisenhower and Washington Street. There was one contingency—removing a 500-foot strip of Avenue 48, which dissected the 60-acre parcel. That piece of Avenue 48 only existed on a Riverside County zoning map, and except for people across the street at La Quinta Country Club and a Catholic church 1,500+ feet to the north from Merv's property line, there were no other developed properties, just sand dunes!

Irene came to the rescue. Irene took a petition for eliminating the 500-foot easement road and received signatures from all 12 closest landowners, including the church, to the county planning commission in Indio and they immediately removed the easement from the map! This was Merv's last and most successful project before he retired. He didn't start this project for well over a year and the timing was perfect! The challenged desert economy was particularly hard on almost all of my agents and there was bad blood between some of them. My personally being active for my own account became a very unhealthy situation. It occurred to me that I might be better off financially by being a salesman rather than a CEO.

When it rains it pours. I received two phone calls on the same day—the first from Klar—that Mike had been diagnosed with leukemia! He also said that Mike did not and would not work with my son Scott and the only person he would work with was myself! The second call came from Tom Siegel asking me to meet them at his residence in the Springs, as it was extremely important. I arrived and the first thing Tom said was, "This is to be a secret meeting. Anything that is said or takes place didn't occur! I need to look at any residences that could be leased for the Shah's mother to reside for a year. Absolutely nobody, including Mike and Klar, would be aware of this and it's my job to make sure of that!" Before the day ended, I found a very excellent furnished unit on the fairway and only 10-12 houses from Tom's. It was actually a much nicer and better located home. We visited the unit and Tom told me to draw up a standard one-year lease and he would sign it in his name for Columbia. We hadn't even mentioned the cost. Obviously it didn't matter! Later I found out that the Shah, who was in exile in Acapulco, was planning on either leasing or buying the Annenberg Estate one half mile to the north. Unfortunately for the Shah, our government would not give him a visa to live in the U.S.A. As Tom was handling this transaction strictly on his own except for my little part, I don't know if the mother ever lived at the Springs.

    Scott, who had moved into a nice little condo in Palm Desert, never understood or learned that the large and major potential customers usually visited the desert only on weekends. He started taking more and more weekends off and I began getting calls from the office from large customers such as Howard Keck, Jr. and a young gentleman by the name of Ridgeway, who were both interested in buying or selling good properties. I did everything I could to cover for Scott. I had two young agents who had been doing poorly and just scraping by. Each came into my office and complained. They said that I wasn't treating them properly by giving my son preference and one threatened to report me to the Real Estate Commissioner. The second agent (and I believe they were not in collusion), entered and accused me of favoring Scott, but politely did mention Mr. Keck and Mr. Ridgeway, as he was the person who took their phone calls and relayed them on. He worked the desk on Saturdays and Sundays and took his time off in the middle of the week when business was good. This young man I liked and respected very much. He didn't threaten me like the other, but he was very unhappy. I don't quite remember the outcome of both deals, but I believe Scott was successful and the day Scott informed me that he was leaving the desert to return to San Diego and attend law school was a happy one. I've always felt that Scott was a natural born lawyer and much better suited for that profession than real estate. After finishing law school as number one in his class, he passed the California Bar Exam on his first try, which rarely happens in California, and immediately received a position in a very prominent law firm in La Jolla!

In the summer of 1980, I ran across an article pertaining to using computers for bookkeeping and accounting for small companies. It advertised a special training school in L.A. I asked Nina if this could help her in any way? She responded yes, if she could learn how to use it. I asked if attending the school for a week in L.A. for a week at company expense would be worth it? She replied, "Absolutely and I'd love the opportunity!" Nina was very special and I knew if anybody could learn to use a computer, she could. Upon finishing school, HMS Real Estate put into service the second computer ever used in real estate! Nina was happy and it more than paid for itself and her schooling in less than six months!

I invited George to lunch as I hadn't talked business with him in almost a year, and we discussed my thoughts about being a salesman rather than an executive. George understood my situation exactly and even went so far as to state that he was in the same position about 20 years ago. He mentioned that there was nothing in our contract between HMS Corporation and HMS Real Estate that prevented me from stepping down and letting someone else run the company. He mentioned something I'd never thought about. Under our contract I had the right to sell the company to an outside party with our board of directors approval. George and I still saw each other along with our wives socially, usually for dinner about once every three months and I looked upon him now more than ever as a friend and a mentor!

The new rising company in the desert was the large golf resort developer, Landmark Land Company, which was in the process of purchasing Mission Hills Country Club from David Foster of Colgate-Palmolive Corporation. They had purchased The La Quinta Hotel property and built two golf courses—the mountain course for private members of the club and the dunes course on which members could play. Hotel guests were welcomed to play on the Dunes course as well as any golfer who could pay the extremely high greens fees. The hotel guests played for free as it was included in their room rates, which were also exorbitant. When the two golf courses had opened for play, I went to the head man at Landmark, Ernie Blosser, and asked if I could buy a private membership at the La Quinta Hotel Country Club at the full price of $20,000 with $5,000 down and $5,000 every six months until fully paid. He accepted. I delivered my check the following day and received my charter membership 48 hours later. This not only gave me three golf courses to enjoy but certain privileges at the hotel, especially for dining, which Irene and I then started using in place of Lord Fletcher's.

With the idea that George gave me, I called Ernie and made an appointment to meet with him at the hotel clubhouse. I had Nina gather all our financial records from the time we started HMS Real Estate, make three copies of all documents and place one set in a nice file for my briefcase. When I called upon Ernie and showed him the file, I pointed out that he really didn't have a professional real estate company at Mission Hills Country Club and nothing yet at the hotel. I felt that a professional company was needed. I ran into Ernie occasionally, but I knew him to be very quick on the trigger and didn't think things through. He responded, "What you're saying is you'd like to sell HMS Real Estate to Landmark?" I replied, "Absolutely. I think it would make a great fit for Landmark and my firm." Ernie mentioned that he would be with the majority owner and CEO of Landmark next week in Carmel where their corporate headquarters resided and attending the U.S. Open at Pebble Beach Country Club. He would forward my file to Felix overnight and if the boss agreed maybe we could set up a meeting while we were there. He also said if I wanted to play the new private golf course in Carmel Valley called Carmel Valley Ranch Country Club, he'd treat me and my guests, one foursome for golf and lunch on Landmark! I had a call at home that evening from Ernie saying that Felix would very much like to meet with me, and he had taken the liberty of making the appointment for me on Tuesday at

2:30 p.m. with a starting time that morning at 8:30 a.m. for a foursome. I told him I'd be there for both starting times!

I arrived at the clubhouse at 8:00 a.m. with Irene who was going to ride around the golf course while I played and met Reeves and Compton my buddies from the north team every March. It was another gorgeous day and the golf course was beautiful, except it was very tricky as it had too many blind holes. In golf terms this means that you cannot see where you're going and need to be while hitting your next shot. We reached the 12th tee box and I was the first one to hit. This was the signature hole on the golf course. It looked west down the Carmel Valley to the Pacific Ocean! It was a spectacular view; in fact in the lobby of the clubhouse was an oil painting by a well-known Carmel artist of this scene for sale at only $65,000. Irene was out of the cart watching me and admiring the view when I hit my tee shot, a 6-iron, which landed a foot from the hole bounced forward and spun back into the hole! My first hole-in-one and Irene was there to witness it! What fun! The rest of the golf was a blur. I registered my hole-in-one in the pro shop and Reeves and Compton signed as witnesses.

The four of us then had lunch and Reeves took Irene back to our motel in Carmel while I cleaned up and headed for Landmark's offices. I arrived and was directed into a large, impressive executive office. Ernie and the owner Felix were waiting for me, fortunately I was on time. After introductions and my not being able to control myself, I had to tell the story of my hole-in-one on the 12th hole! Ernie immediately said, "Where was the pin placement?" I said, "Up on top, short about eight to ten feet from going down to the second level!" He said, "That's amazing! I don't believe from what Johnny Pott, our pro, tells me that anyone has had a hole-in-one with the pin up there. I'll call him today and I'll let you know."

From there on that conversation was strictly between Felix and I. I definitely had the feeling that he and Ernie had more than casually assessed my offer to sell. Felix finally said and leaned forward to make sure I would understand every word, "Carl, Ernie wants you in our organization badly. He thinks that you bring the missing piece to our golf resort organization and I agree 100%! My problem is we need you, not your organization. Whatever agents you deem worthy will follow you to Landmark eventually. I'm willing to make you the second highest salaried employee in Landmark and will set up a completely new real estate division where you will be in charge of not just selling real estate but you will also be entirely in charge of purchasing all of our lands for future development west of the Mississippi. You'll receive all the ordinary executive perks such as automobile, expense account and privileges to play all our golf courses free of charge and perks for your key employees here and at Mission Hills. The reason we need you the most is not only because Ernie recommends you, but in the last week I placed calls to three men who are active and know the desert better than anybody except you. You understand land

and how to use it to its best advantage, plus there is nobody that comes close to you in bargaining! I thought to myself, 'Thank you, Ray White!' I was not prepared to make a decision on this new challenge and although I was sure that I wouldn't make as much money, I loved golf and to be a part of Landmark was tempting. I asked how long this offer would be on the table and Felix replied, "Anytime in the next 90 days, you're one-of-a-kind." I told them I'd be in touch within two weeks! The Open was a tremendous success as on the 17th green on Sunday, the last day, Tom Watson chipped in for a Birdie to steal the title from Jack Nicklaus.

On Monday morning I received a phone call from President Reagan's secretary inviting Irene and I to visit the White House and Congress plus join Mr. and Mrs. Reagan for a special cocktail party in the East Room on Friday evening. She said she would handle our hotel reservations for whatever nights we wished and to let her know by tomorrow. I asked her what protocol was for men and women's apparel? She told me business suits only for the men and cocktail dresses for the ladies. The party and tour of the White House would take approximately three hours and after hors d'oeuvres would be a dinner. I accepted and told her I'd call her as I could acquire plane tickets and buy a suit, as here in Palm Springs we didn't wear suits! She laughed and said, "You mean business suits!" I was able to book our flights and called our close friends Dave and Catherine Hall. They had received the same call from the White House and were planning a similar itinerary. They were booked at the Benjamin Franklin Hotel within walking distance from the White House. They had already inquired as to our attending and were happy to hear that we'd be staying at the Benjamin Franklin also. Being at the White House as the guests of Ronald Reagan and spending a couple of days with Catherine and Dave made it even more special. I called George at HMS and made sure that he would be available next week, as I needed his counseling. I then called Ernie and advised him that Irene and I had been invited to the White House by Mr. Reagan and would be gone all week and asked him to pass along our good fortune to Felix. The next and last item on my agenda was to have Irene join me to travel to Palm Springs to find a business suit.

    We went to one store and the one suit that slightly came close to fitting me was an ugly brown. The second store carried Hart Schaffner and Marx men's suits. One was a beauty—a medium gray suit that fitted me like a glove. Irene approved and when we asked about the pants, which fit but needed alteration for length, they said that they wouldn't be ready until tomorrow. Irene told them to mark them and she would hem them herself! As usual in my life, Irene came to the rescue! The next morning I called and gave the lady in the White House our schedule and was told we had reservations at the Benjamin Franklin.

    We arrived early at Dulles Airport in time to meet Catherine and Dave for an hour or two. The next day all four of us went to the Capital and watched a session of

Congress, which was very uninspiring as the floor of Congress was mostly empty and the speakers one after another were talking to an empty room. The one time they called for a vote, people came actually running, cast their vote and ran out—and this was with a Republican President and Congress. Later we went to the Jefferson, Lincoln and Washington Memorials. They were all magnificent. I noticed that Irene had tears in her eyes a couple of times and I know that I choked up several times.

The next day we visited our local Riverside County representative to Congress, a fine gentleman named Jerry Lewis who invited us into his office and was more impressed by our being invited by Mr. Reagan personally to the White House than we were. We visited the Library of Congress and the U.S. Mint. Back to the hotel, we freshened up and met the Halls in the lobby and we four walked to the east entrance of the White House. We were escorted to the East Room and given a tour of the downstairs and the second floor where the East Room is located. After the tour, we returned to the East Room where the cocktail party was now in full swing and we arrived no more than five minutes before Nancy and Ron entered.

The one thing I remember most is that after a couple of cocktails I stood up on the podium from where Ron had welcomed us and looked over the crowd and imagined myself as President of the U.S.A. While standing on top of the podium I noticed Irene and President Reagan in deep conversation, although they were both smiling and laughing. I also noticed Nancy standing to the side watching Ronald very closely and she moved in and separated Irene from her husband. The evening was one of the highlights in our lives! It was made even better because that night and the following day, Catherine and Dave and Irene and I were able to sit and discuss our joint recollections together. Catherine and Dave left early the next day and Irene and I walked around and had a nice fresh lobster lunch at the restaurant of presidents! We flew home that evening pinching ourselves to make sure that this experience was truly real!

    We didn't arrive until midnight, but that was all right and the next day I called George and told him I needed to talk with him ASAP. I explained my conversation with Landmark and their offer to me. George was very understanding and was not surprised. He also knew that I had an unhappy sales group until the last two months when all of us realized that our local economy was recovering. He also said something that helped me to a decision. "Carl, if it wasn't for your personal contribution to the bottom line of the real estate company, all of HMS might not have survived to see another day. We most certainly would have been on the verge of failure or even bankruptcy. Today, we have a chance and the real estate division with you is perfect, but without you we still have a strong chance of survival. You do what's best for Irene and yourself going forward and whatever that may be you'll have our support and friendship forever." I was not only appreciative, I was humbled! There was nothing else to say and for the first time in our relationship we hugged each other, and then shook hands and I left for home to discuss our plans with Irene.

After George's remarks and Irene's words of advice, I came to the conclusion that a three-year contract with Landmark and being in the land and golf business primarily was something I couldn't resist. I visited Ernie's office on Friday and asked him if it were possible that we could set up a conference call in Carmel between ourselves and Felix. He dialed and Ernie switched on a speaker box and I asked Felix if the offer he made was still available. He replied, "Absolutely!" I said, "You have a new employee starting a week from Monday if that's agreeable." Again he responded, "Absolutely, and Ernie will have your new contract Monday morning for your attorney to approve. Welcome to Landmark—Ernie and I might be more excited than you!" I said simply, "Thank you for the opportunity that fulfills a dream . . ."

Chapter 21

The La Quinta Years

The La Quinta Hotel was built in 1926 as a resort deep in a cove surrounded by beautiful reddish-brown mountains on three sides. It was actually the most protected cove from the wind in the Palm Springs area. During World War II, it served General Patton's Africa Corps in training as its home base. General Patton lived at The Desert Club, a small tennis facility a mile away. All of his immediate staff and commanding officers were quartered at the hotel. This included the tank corps, the air corps, artillery, Calvary and the massive infantry corps, which trained south of Indio! Every morning at 6:00 a.m. they all met for breakfast, then in the meeting room for their daily assignments. (Note: training in the summer caused a complete redesign of our tanks for desert warfare, as we actually had corpsman suffocate in our standard tanks!)

In approximately 1976 or 1977, a Chicago bank foreclosed on this small, but precious gem of history! Prince Philip, accompanied by the famous entertainer Anthony Newly, twice stayed on site, and by records kept by the hotel; over 100 major Hollywood stars had vacationed in the cottages surrounding the beautiful gardens, tennis courts and pool areas. The hotel also had extensive horse-oriented activities, such as riding trails, a riding academy and nightly hayrides back into the canyons for campfires and Bar-B-Q dinners. These were extremely popular, as year-round weather permitted very light casual clothing—jeans and cowboy shirts for both men and women were perfect!

Leonard Edelson, who operated a large law firm in Chicago, had visited several times prior with his wife who loved the hotel and it was her favorite vacation destination. On more than one occurrence, she stated, "Why don't we buy the hotel in La Quinta? Leonard, you could put a group together no problem. I'll help you and we can do it!" Leonard's law firm's bank owned the hotel and was extremely anxious to sell. According to Leonard, his wife began calling all of her Chicago society friends and within days he had more husbands wanting in on the action than he could believe! The total property went west from Washington Avenue and ran to the peaks of the surrounding mountains. Subtracting for the unusable and unbuildable mountain slopes, there were a good 1,000 acres of usable land including the hotel and its amenities. In addition, on three different locations on the property were three fabulous natural spring water wells, which were the La Quinta Water Company. Two of these wells pumped water just enough to keep them operating and the other was used by the hotel for the existing property and was selling water to residences adjacent in the upper cove. This little water company became extremely important and looking back, may have been worth a lot more than the hotel itself. With his wife's insistence, Leonard's group grabbed the opportunity and bought all of the La Quinta Hotel property including the water company! Mr. Edelson never did disclose to anybody what was paid.

In 1959, the hotel broke ground for the first nine holes of their new golf course. There was no clubhouse, but commercial house trailers to accommodate all customers—anybody who would pay a greens fee! In 1960, they opened the second nine holes and the golf course was the best I had ever played anywhere, plus the weather was seemingly always perfect! In 1961, CBS filmed a four-day PGA golf tournament nationwide. This was repeated in '62 and '63 when their contract with the hotel expired and it was moved to the Firestone Country Club in Ohio. It is still being played in 2014. I've already recounted how I joined as a junior member and was fortunate enough to play and work in the Bob Hope Desert Classic.

In 1973, I was awakened by my telephone at 6:00 a.m. by Peder, the general manager of the hotel as well as the country club. He seldom visited the club as he had a manager to handle all club matters, but the manager answered to Peder. He asked—it was almost an order—for me to be in his office at 9:00 a.m. for a special phone call from Mr. Edelson! There had been some rumors at the club that Mr. Edelson was having some legal problems. Our membership was now 300 members. The membership committee had appointed two wealthy bankers, John

Popkiss and Lauren Lewis, to negotiate a deal for the country club, including all club facilities and amenities and our new gorgeous clubhouse. It was my understanding that they had met with Peder twice and that Mr. Edelson had countered to their original offer and things were looking good. I really had no idea why I was being summoned!

I arrived. Peder was not alone. There was another man about my age with him. (I always mention the age because in the desert I was always one of the young people!) Peder introduced me to Ernie Blosser, the desert VP of Landmark Land Company! Peder then dialed a number and switched on a speaker box placed between us. I recognized Mr. Edelson's voice as he started by thanking Ernie and myself for attending. He spoke first to Ernie and said, "Are you sure you can buy and take legal ownership of the hotel, country club and surrounding properties including the water company in dispute by Thursday if the members can't get it done by then?" Ernie replied, "Absolutely, all the documents were handed personally to Felix in Carmel at 8:00 a.m., including the documents for the country club properties. It is our intention to purchase the country club properties only if the members can't accomplish purchasing by Thursday, but if we buy the club we have no intention on selling it to the membership. You're aware of that Mr. Edelson?" Leonard said, "Yes, but I really desire the members to have the club."

He then said, "Carl, you've heard what Landmark is prepared to do and my wishes are that your membership purchase the club by Thursday with the terms and condi-

tions we've already agreed on. If there are any changes, then Landmark will buy the club. That's all I have to say, good luck and thanks for being here for me when I need you the most." Before any of us could respond he hung up! I asked Peder why I was chosen to be the club's representative? He responded, "Because in his words, you're the only one who he trusted to get things done!"
I shook hands with Mr. Blosser and left. I went to the club and even though it was early on a Monday morning our resident manager was available. I asked him if he could locate Mr. Popkiss and Mr. Lewis for an emergency meeting in the dining room! He called and received an affirmative answer for 11:00 a.m. from both. Then I had a brilliant idea. I asked him to call Mr. Spiegel and see if he'd attend and to tell him I'm on my hands and knees begging for his presence—it was critical to the club! Again he received a yes and at 11:00 a.m. the four of us sat around a table on the far end of the dining room by ourselves and with orders to the manager to not allow anyone in the dining room.

While I was waiting I thought back to my Hawaiian adventure wondering 'why me?' All three of these wealthy learned gentlemen, who were at least a generation older than I, probably wondered what I had to do with the club's business. As carefully as I could, I tried to use Mr. Edelson's exact words to the group. When I finished I could see by the expressions on Lauren and John's faces they weren't too impressed, but La Quinta Country Club got lucky, as Tom Spiegel started talking. He admitted that he and his wife were one of the couples that Mrs. Edelson had recruited and to this point it was a great decision! He then made a statement that changed everything. He had received a phone call early that morning from Chicago from a close friend who had also invested with Edelson who said that Leonard was to be indicted on Friday in federal court for selling the water company over the past three years to three different buyers, totaling millions of dollars. All four of us looked at each other in shock!

    John Popkiss stated that he could put up the money from his banks in Kansas City on a temporary basis until we could get permanent financing, and Lauren said his banks in South Dakota would also step forward and work with John's institutions and they would have the money in place in less than 48 hours. Their legal counsel would make 100% sure that nothing could go wrong. I was again out of the loop and the country club on Thursday belonged to the membership thanks to Tom Spiegel being in the right place at the right time with the important information, luck and timing! It was not shocking to learn that Leonard died that Thursday night.

    In 1982, when I started working with Landmark, they indeed needed me and from day one I was swamped with unexpected duties to perform. I had been lucky enough for Tom, Tony and Merle to join me at Landmark. I became a full-time land buyer. My challenge was to not pay over-the-market prices for the land and properties we needed to assemble contiguous to one another from various owners. Word got out that Landmark was expanding in several directions, primarily in conjunction with the properties adjacent to La Quinta Hotel and Mission Hills Country Club. These were assembled with many parcels needed from various wealthy owners, who were the toughest to deal with, as it was a game with them and money was no object! For example: on adding to Mission Hills, the least difficult of the three, we only had to deal with five owners who each owned 40 acres or more totaling the 320 adjoining acres to our present holdings to create two golf courses and 640 homes. Adjacent to La Quinta Hotel, we needed 240 acres and we had 19 owners, some of which owned ten-acre parcels and we had to deal with the estate of Vons Market's deceased owner dealing entirely with a law firm!

We also dealt with Burt Lancaster and Richard Widmark's attorneys for their trusts. In this case, we attempted to buy the five largest pieces all within 48 hours before word got out. Fortunately, Burt Lancaster's was one of the five. The first offer we made, which was just slightly over market, was accepted. We were lucky to purchase the other four right at market, which for that area was now $10,000 per acre. There was an old house on five acres. The land was worth considerably more than the rundown dwelling, but it had a water line to 50th Street, which was worth something. We paid $100,000 for that piece of property. The owner was overjoyed and we would've paid a lot more if necessary. When we were finished, we had spent an average cost of $17,000+ per acre and our budget was $20,000 per acre. Felix was delighted.

Across the south boundary of this property, which was Avenue 52, a Mr. Ridgeway owned a 60-acre parcel, which had a beautiful home, swimming pool, tennis court and stables for a small string of riding horses. Ernie decided he wanted that ranch for Landmark's new offices and after traveling south Felix told me to see if I could get the Ridgeways to sell, regardless of price. I had the phone number for Mr. Ridgeway, who lived at the Biltmore Hotel in downtown Los Angeles and when I phoned he remembered me from my son Scott and our previous successful dealings. He was not surprised at all when I asked if the ranch was possibly for sale to a first-class owner on a cash and short escrow basis. He called me back and offered me the ranch at $1,600,000 on a 30-day escrow, all cash! I didn't call anybody after telling him I'd be back to him within 72 hours. I waited the three days and called and said my buyer would pay $1,200,000. My son Scott had sold Mr. Ridgeway not only the ranch property, but the 40-acre parcel directly east that ran along Avenue 52 to the corner of Jefferson Street 2 1/2 years prior for approximately the same exact amount of money. I explained that the offer was for the 20-acre parcel with the ranch house on it and did not include the 40-acre parcel to the east. My buyer did not want the 40-acre piece, at least not presently. He asked what I thought the 40-acre piece would bring on today's market and I told him $12-15,000 per acre on a cash basis, but frankly because of the corner and the possibility of the county changing five to ten acres to commercial on the corner of Jefferson and Washington, I'd wait a couple years and that he might receive close to $2 million. He then said, "How about splitting the difference on the 20-acre ranch and paying $1,400,000?" I told him that was a fair counter and I'd talk to the buyer. The next day I called him back and said we had a deal and asked where he wanted me to open escrow? He must have liked Kelli as he remembered her. We bought the property and closed escrow within two weeks. When Felix visited the property, he thought that the property was worth around $2 1/2 million dollars. I reminded him that housing and comparable acreage between Carmel and Pebble Beach was worth 30% to 40% more than property in the Coachella Valley. Everybody was pleased and happy, even Ernie. All this occurred within my first 120 days!

From June 15 to July 15, Irene and I spent our time at Landmark's new golf course resort Carmel Valley Ranch where I'd had my first hole-in-one. There were several reasons for my stay at the ranch, the first being that the housing development was a disaster and wasn't selling. Secondly, I was there to work with our in-house architectural department on the design of the new housing to be built at La Quinta and Mission Hills Country Club. Unfortunately, the housing at Carmel Valley Ranch had been built on two different parcels of land that really required two different types of housing. Landmark had built only one set of homes and had missed the market completely. They had totally underbuilt the best location on the property and the floor plans were so bad that the poor location made it an even worse disaster! In spite of the improving economy, thanks to Mr. Reagan, I decided the only solution was to not finish construction on each parcel at this time and lower the price to where we'd break even. This did not sit well with Ernie, who I found out was the culprit who designed and planned the housing with the help of the architectural department.

The summer of '83 was a year of La Nina, a warmer than usual ocean temperature that also effects the atmospheric temperature. Monterey Bay was overcome by an invasion of swordfish. Never in history had swordfish been this far north and they were literally jumping into amateur fishing boats. These amateur anglers were catching the swordfish and had no idea what to do with them and were selling them to the local markets for next to nothing. We loved swordfish and were buying it for as little as twenty-five cents a pound. Needless to say, I had so much that month that I started looking like one!

Things were never quite the same between Ernie and I after we returned from Carmel. I found out that Ernie was never wrong, but he actually was almost always wrong in his business decisions. Luckily for Landmark, Ernie had two wonderful people working for him that hid or corrected his mistakes, namely Joe Walser and Leota his personal secretary/assistant. I found out that if I wanted to get anything done with Ernie, my only chance was working with Leota. Ernie had become an adversary! That summer as usual I worked Monday, Tuesday and left the desert for Del Mar on Wednesday at 11:00 a.m. and arrived at the racetrack for lunch and a day at the races!

Irene had always stayed at our condo on Shelter Island full-time through Labor Day. We had sold the condo on Shelter Island the previous year for an unbelievable figure, pure luck! We had rented a small two-bedroom two-bath condo at Lake San Marcos for the racing season. Thanks to La Nina, for three straight days San Marcos was the hottest place in the U.S.A. averaging 108 degrees! We decided that we should start exploring the possibilities of again buying a vacation home, but this time in the Carlsbad area near Interstate 5 close to the ocean.

When the summer season ended and I returned to the desert, everything was going well and we were now building our new floor plans at both the new golf courses at Mission Hills and La Quinta Hotel. We had over 25 reservations each at both locations! On opening night in November at Mission Hills, we had a grand opening party at which we converted 21 reservations and had seven members purchase units that night. La Quinta didn't have its fairway grand opening until late December, as the priority that autumn was the building of the Tennis Club Villas, which opened November 1 and sold out before the end of the year! The right product, at the right price, at the right time! This did not improve my relationship with Ernie. The La Quinta Hotel's fairway units' grand opening did not go as well, but it was good for that time of year.

The Landmark Real Estate Company had a wonderful year and all the agents were making money and were busier than usual. The desert economy was excellent, thanks in part to Washington balancing the budget and correcting inflation. I had a call from Ernie asking me to come to his new office. When I arrived Ernie was outside and climbed into my car and said he wanted to show me something. He directed me east to Jefferson Boulevard and then south to the end of the road and then we proceeded on dirt roads driving a circle of no less than eight miles. He said, "I want to buy all this land to build the biggest golf complex in the United States. Now let's see what you can do." We returned to his office and he stated, "Get to work!" This was to be my biggest challenge of all, except maybe getting Irene to marry me!

    I called a meeting of the resale agents associated with the real estate office for the next morning with the order that they must attend! Counting myself, we had nine agents present, and I remember opening the meeting by saying, "This will possibly be the biggest event in your real estate life. We've been given the opportunity to build the greatest golf course resort in the United States! Like the Dunes and Citrus courses, we'll need to identify the parameters and ownership of the total acreage from Avenue 54 to the mountains south to the reservoir and quarry and then east two miles and back north as far as we can purchase vacant land and then west back to Jefferson. Our goal is to purchase 3,000+ acres. If you remember when we purchased the Citrus land with all the various owners, we couldn't talk about our objective and when we leave this office today this becomes our secret!" Eight of us left the office in two cars and I retraced our route, with the exception that we followed the mountains east for another couple of miles, as it was totally vacant sandy land, but not dunes. I gave Tom the job to go discreetly to the County of Riverside offices located in Indio to procure the maps and ownership registers within the boundaries we identified. Taking into consideration the extra two miles, we identified 3,200+ acres. Fortunately, there was only one 60-acre parcel that was sand dunes and had obviously never been used!

     Approximately 2,300 acres were owned by one landowner, a former county commissioner who was very politically active in Indio and East Riverside County. He lived on the north side of the end of Avenue 54 on a 40-acre parcel adjacent to the mountains, which was not within our parameters. Over 90% of his land had been farmed in the past 20+ years with mostly cotton fields and row crops. He still had one little parcel of table grapes. As Mr. Kennedy had a notorious reputation for being a crafty politician and a very tough man to deal with, I advised our team that Tom and I would be responsible for dealing with Mr. Kennedy. The balance of owners was divided and each agent ended up with two prospective clients. I repeated to them: "Give your perspective seller your business card and let them know that you're interested in listing their property but until we make our formal offer and they accept don't disclose the plans for PGA West. Make sure you're absolutely honest and get the best price that they'd be satisfied with. You are their representative and you can fight with me to get them the best price. We fully expect to pay in all cases better than market price and it's your responsibility to do the best job for that client that's possible!"

I phoned George at HMS and asked him if he knew Ed Kennedy and if he'd ever done any business with him? "Of course I do, who doesn't!" he replied. I said, "Well, I don't. I hate to admit it but I've never met him, what's he like?" "He's a large man around 75 years old who bought his properties in 1944 during the war and after General Patton finished training the Africa Corps. He's never done much with the land except grow cotton and I don't think making money early in his lifetime was a problem, as he supposedly received a large inheritance from his grandfather while still in his 20s. He's not a favorite of mine, but that doesn't mean he's a bad guy, but he likes to muddy the water politically. I've only had one business dealing with him and it went satisfactorily, but I have heard lately that he's been financially strapped, as he has little or no income from the ranch and he and his wife have lived lavishly for over 40 years in the desert. It's funny you asked today, as a workman doing some work at home for my wife had just finished a job for Ed and his check bounced!" I said, "Thanks. I'll let you know my impression after I have my meeting with him next week."

You win some and you lose some. With Mr. Kennedy, that's what happened. After Tom and I put all the maps together with all the parcels, I called Mr. Kennedy and asked if I could visit him. He recognized my name and stated, "Carl I've heard about you—good and bad." He chuckled and invited me to his home. On Monday I was met on the porch of a very old home that at one time I'm sure was spectacular, but obviously wasn't being taken care of properly. We sat down outside on the porch into nice old rocking chairs and started talking. He never introduced me to his wife and then in our subsequent conversation I began to wonder if he was a widower. He did not seem like he was a tough guy at all, but he didn't look healthy. I finally asked Ed, which was how he wanted me to address him, if he would be interested in selling his property? "As a matter of fact, Carl, I was just thinking about that yesterday! What do you think it's worth?" I responded, "At least $10 million dollars." He looked at me very quizzically and I hurriedly explained that I was talking about all of his property—the complete Kennedy ranch of 2,300 acres. Ed had put a pitcher of ice water out and he had just taken a sip of water. When I said $10 million, he started choking badly enough to scare me. I started pounding on his back and finally after a short time he was all right. He then inquired, "Well, $10 million for the property, the ranch, but how much for the house and the 40 acres?" I replied, "That's included in the $10 million!" "No," he said, "It's a matter of principle. I want the house sold separately." I replied, "All right! $9 3/4 million and $250,000 for the home and 40 acres." He was adamant. "No, I want $10 million and $400,000 for the home." I told him I would talk to the buyer tonight and see what he said and call him tomorrow. I asked Ed if I could bring him an all-cash offer how long would it take him to vacate the house, acknowledging how after all these years that moving was going to be tough.

I phoned him the next morning and stated I had an excellent counter offer to present. He told me he'd be waiting for me on the porch. When I approached, he was much better groomed than the day prior and looked like a different man. Without taking any time or talking, I handed him an official legal offer with a deposit check from Wells Fargo Bank for $250,000 to open escrow. I let him study the contract, which said $10 million plus $250,000 for his home. Before he could say yes or no, I said, "How soon could you vacate and when can we close the escrow?" He responded, "Thirty days would be fine." I said, "If you would accept this offer, my buyer has said he would close the escrow and you'd have your $10 million in ten days." This statement stopped him in his tracks and he finally got the words out saying, "Carl, with me it's a principle of receiving $400,000 for the house, I can't explain it or why." To which I replied again, "Well, we can lower the $10 million accordingly to $9,850,000 and we'll both be happy, plus the sales commission is only one percent." He then replied, "I'll tell you what, Carl, you tell your buyer that I'll agree to sell you the property for $10,000,000 and the house for $400,000 and pay a commission of 1 1/2%." I said I'd be more than happy to take that back to my buyer and I thought I could get him to pay that price if I had his signature on the contract with the changes made and initialed by both he and I. "Is there another person in the house who could witness the changes?" I asked. He called the maid, a young Caucasian

421

girl who definitely understood what she was participating in. Before leaving, I asked one more question which was, "You really didn't advise me of the escrow period when you'd receive your $10,400,000?" and he picked a Friday 12 days away. I took the signed offer to the Wells Fargo appointed escrow company for Connie to work on. We might have left some money on the table, but it was critical that we purchased the Kennedy properties first. We had budgeted $18,500,000 for the property without the house and 40 acres, which was restored and sold a couple years later for $750,000. Mr. Kennedy appeared by himself at the bank on the Friday and then evidently left the desert.

  The next morning the team met again and we had made contact with all owners. We analyzed as a team each property and the circumstances surrounding each seller and if it became necessary we were in a position to be very generous, so I told my people to cut their commissions and literally have the seller dictate whatever price they desired. That didn't mean we gave outlandish offers to some greedy people, but we did our homework and bought the balance of their properties with only one exception for above-market prices that pleased both parties. The only problem we had was a little old lady whom we paid $432,000 for her five-acre home, which was actually a shack with running water. She had a little vegetable garden and kept pigs, which were not pets. Her property was on the only other paved street—that being 56th almost dead center in the middle of the 3,000 acres. When given the price of $432,000, we established a cost for the land of $350,000 or $70,000 per acre on land that we had just purchased for $5,000 per acre surrounding her house and put a price of $82,000 on a 1,100 square foot dwelling that was anything but a home. Because of her age and the fact that she was living there by herself, no husband, children or relatives, we closed the escrow within 30 days but gave her a full year of free rent to remain. About 60 days later we received a letter from a local lawyer suing us for taking advantage of his client. Unfortunately, this was another of my many duties and after a year's time when it went to court, the case was thrown out because our evidence conclusively proved that her total property was worth less than $60,000. What a waste of time!

We closed every escrow within six weeks of beginning the assemblage of PGA West for a total cost of $15 million against $27,606,000, the approved budgeted amount. My agents split $406,000 and were a part of something very special in real estate. Work began immediately on certain parts of the property and both Arnold Palmer and Jack Nicklaus were hired to design golf courses and at that time the most famous golf course designer Pete Dye was on our annual payroll. These three great designers separately planned the first three unique but different courses that would challenge golfers worldwide! Landmark actually built the golf courses under the supervision of the aforementioned professionals. One of the funnier things about the announcement for all golf enthusiasts that went nationwide was that our PR firm chose to have the opening shovel of sand pictures taken on the worst piece of land on the property, the sand dunes, and put into the local newspapers plus many golf magazines. Irene and I also had our picture taken, which appeared in the Desert Sun and Palm Springs Life.

As our projects were being completed at Mission Hills, Duna La Quinta and the Citrus courses, we were creating gated communities, which were considered planned unit developments. During construction and immediately after being purchased, these units were governed by homeowner associations and the builder always had two seats on what would be a five-member board of directors until such time as the project had 60% of the owners occupying, at which time the builder would turn the reins over to the homeowners association and they would elect two more owners to the board. This unenviable job also fell on my shoulders, along with the sales manager at each project. Early in 1985, I had eight HOAs at Mission Hills, five at La Quinta, six at the Citrus and already three at PGA. There was no way I could handle everything I was needed to do, plus I was no longer in the land business. I told Ernie that I didn't have enough time! We turned that responsibility over to the building contractor on each project along with the project sales manager.

In 1984 I had a call from Carmel from the boss Felix Barton who said that he wanted to sell the old La Quinta Hotel, which had been enlarged from 72 cottages to a total of 240 rooms with 120 one-bedroom cottages. He asked if I could find a buyer—not any buyer, but a first-class hotel chain if possible. I placed a phone call to Barron Hilton, whom I had met at a charitable golf tournament. Mr. Hilton sponsored the Guide Dogs of America. I had won the tournament and he had presented me with a beautiful trophy of a guide dog. He took my call and remembered me from the tournament, which was very special to him. When I mentioned why I was calling and would he have any interest in buying the famous La Quinta Hotel, he said, "I'll have my man in charge of all our acquisitions call you and I assure you he will come to the hotel to meet with you. Thanks for thinking of Hilton!"

The following week a gentleman arrived and spent almost a full day only to inform me that although our hotel was beautiful and potentially profitable, it just didn't fit Hilton's agenda at this time. He then added, "If you ever want to sell the two adjoining golf courses, the mountain and the dunes courses along with the hotel, give me a call and if the timing is right I believe Mr. Hilton would be very interested." I reported back to Mr. Barton and told him of the final conversation. That weekend I was playing in a foursome at my club across the street with somebody from the Chicago area and I mentioned the hotel might be looking for a major hotel chain to operate the La Quinta Hotel. I didn't want to tell anybody that the hotel might be for sale. Keller said, "Is Hyatt good enough for you?" and when I laughed and said, "You bet!" he stated he'd get the phone number for Nick Pritzker, one of the sons of the owner, when we finished. On Monday morn-

425

ing I called Chicago and asked for Nick Pritzker, who surprised me by saying he'd been expecting my call and we made an appointment for the following day. I answered that I really didn't want anybody at the club knowing that we're not looking for an operator but actually our owner wishes to sell. "That's even better Carl, I'll see you at the hotel before noon on Thursday. Book me a room for the night!"

Nick arrived and he was much younger than I expected, but again after touring the hotel and grounds he said that without the golf courses it really wasn't a viable operation. We treated him to a free night in one of the cottages and he left for San Diego. While we were walking the property he had asked me if there was anything special in the San Diego area as Hyatt felt that San Diego could use two to three more elegant first-class hotels. Primarily that was the reason for his visit. I mentioned that I was looking at some choice properties for a golf course resort, which the area needed. He let me know that if I ever found the right property, he would like the first opportunity to join Landmark in creating a five-star golf resort in San Diego. The last thing he asked was if I knew of a special place either in or near San Francisco for a second honeymoon Friday with his wife. I said, "If you would drive a little over two hours from San Francisco airport, I know the most beautiful honeymoon spot on the West Coast just south of Monterey called The Tickle Pink. It's a small 35-room motor inn located in Carmel Highlands.

The next week I received a call from Nick stating

that The Tickle Pink was even better than I had made it out to be and his wife absolutely loved their stay and the area, which neither had visited before. He said, "I just wanted you to know how wonderful you made our second honeymoon!" Before hanging up he added, "My trip to San Diego was really eye-opening. I'm going to be spending some time there in the near future trying to put some deals together and I would be very interested if you and Landmark could be involved. Let me know if anything happens and I'll see you again, I hope."

I had recently been working for the United Way, reviewing a couple of the charities in respect to their use of the funds provided. My partner was a man named Lon Varnedor. He was semi-retired from Weyerhaeuser Corporation and had been in charge of land acquisition for 30 years. We had much in common, except Lon's experience was far greater! One day while we were traveling to a charity, he mentioned that he'd bought several thousand acres of land in San Diego's north county over ten years ago that should be ready for development in the next few years and that it might eventually prove to be the very best acquisition in his career for Weyerhaeuser. I said, "If Landmark, along with a major hotel, were to build a five-star golf resort, wouldn't that increase the price per acre of your holdings going forward?" After doing our review at the charity on the way home he said, "Carl, that's a great idea! We should do exactly what you suggested. I can envision the total property increasing in value by 50%."

I asked for the maps and that I would visit the property on my own and see if I could find a parcel of 360 contiguous acres that would hold a five-star hotel with two golf courses and a tennis club. The next morning I phoned Nick in Chicago and asked if he would be in San Diego in the near future. He responded, "I'd like an excuse to be there right now, but none of the opportunities have blossomed as yet. Give me an excuse!" I outlined what I had in mind and he said, "If I fly to San Diego I can bring my wife and kids for a long weekend and we could meet and view the property on Friday next week." We met as planned and spent most of the day traveling on dirt roads from Interstate 5 all the way to Interstate 15 on what is today the 56 Freeway corridor. We found a gorgeous piece of land approximately a mile inland from Interstate 5 high on a hill that would have 360-degree views! The surrounding property was a natural for golf courses as it had topography. The maps indicated the availability of water and that we were in an area governed by the city of Del Mar. We hurried immediately to the planning commission offices where we met the Del Mar planning commissioner. Upon glancing at our business cards, he became very agreeable. When we discussed the potential possibilities for a major hotel golf and tennis complex on the location we identified, he stated unequivocally that it was viable! He did add one negative—that it fell into needing coastal commission approval, which would take probably an additional six-months. When we asked what the chances would be that they wouldn't approve, he stated that as there were no dwellings we'd be interfering with, that he was 99% sure we'd receive approval. It was just a question of how long of a delay? Before we parted, Nick said, "I need 40 acres, which will include the tennis club for my hotel, and I'll pay $10 million."

I met Lon the next day while working for the United Way and we talked about the land I identified as the perfect parcel for Landmark and he agreed. "In fact," he said, "that's the exact parcel I would've chosen." I said, "Tell me the price and terms, including when the sale closes and when the governing agencies approve the final development plans. I call my superiors, but think it's a slam-dunk!" He later called me saying that they would accept $5 million and our conditions, but they wanted a $1 million deposit upon opening escrow applicable to the sales price when approved.

The following week, Ernie, Lon and I visited the site. I thought everything had gone well but the next day I couldn't believe it when Ernie said, "No, we don't want it!" I asked why not and Ernie replied, "Because I don't want it!" I tried arguing, reminding him that it would have the most valuable 320 acres, not only in San Diego, but the entire U.S. for a golf course. I received the same answer. I had to call both Lon and Nick and advise them that Landmark refused and I apologized for using their valuable time to no avail. It might interest you to know that on the Highway 56 corridor today sits a five-star hotel called the Grand Del Mar with a golf course operated by Hyatt. In addition, Hyatt operates three other hotels in

San Diego. Nick really liked San Diego! In addition, a couple years later after Bob Ramsey's death, Nick bought the Highlands Inn, which adjoins The Tickle Pink, for his own family trust!

Approximately a month later, Ernie hired Charles Fairwood, an ex-football coach from the University of Oklahoma and the New York Jets, who was lovingly known in Oklahoma City as 'Dumb Chuck'—and he was! He was a handsome man that didn't have any business sense or logic. He honestly couldn't understand a balance sheet. What really bothered me was that Ernie had him looking over my shoulder as his full-time employment position. A month later Ernie called and asked to see me and told me that Landmark was not renewing my contract. "We'll pay you for the next 2 1/2 months of your present contract and at that time hand in your automobile and any other possible items that belong to Landmark." And with that, my fabulous opportunity, which I enjoyed doing and I thought to the best of my ability, ended!

I contacted the Iranian son-in-law of the Shah and asked if he would lease me a 50' x 150' parcel of land on the property I sold him in Indian Wells on the corner of Highway 111 and El Dorado Boulevard. Without pausing he said, "Of course, as long as you pay me a market price." I agreed. Tom, Tony and I traveled to San Bernardino and leased a special sales trailer that was large enough for four people delivered to the site the following week and CWM Properties and Investments began business! The four of us, including Ted Enoch, had no problem making money, but in early 1991 I semi-retired. I started drawing Social Security and we closed the business.

In the fall I had a very unusual business occurrence. In one day starting at 1:00 p.m. three close friends of mine at La Quinta Country Club asked me to sell their homes. Unbelievably, by 5:00 p.m., I sold all three, making $65,000! A few months later, in helping my long-time friend Ed Stamp, I found an apartment site in Palm Springs proper. He purchased it on the spot and I made another $20,000. In 1992, I didn't receive any Social Security. On my 65th birthday in 1993 I then resumed taking social security and retired completely. Irene and I started searching for a new place to live and we traveled all over the western United States looking for the perfect place that fit our lifestyle and that we could afford. We finally found it in southern Arizona, but it was very hard for me to leave my special life and friends at La Quinta Country Club! Irene was totally shocked when I said I'd leave, but she had been ready to move on for several years, so in the summer of 1993 we sold our home and moved to Green Valley, Arizona.

Chapter 22

Green Valley

Months before we moved to Green Valley, we had purchased a lot on the golf course at the famous Ventana Resort. This included a clause that before an escrow could close we would have a membership in the club, which had a course for private members and a public course for hotel guests and the public.

In late spring we drove to Tucson, which we really liked, and stayed at the hotel located on the private course. When we checked in the day before, I visited the pro shop and announced that I was a prospective new member and that I'd like to play the private course Friday morning. The pro fixed me up with a foursome starting at 8:00 a.m. the next day, which was perfect. The next morning I retrieved my golf clubs from the car, checked in with the starter at the first tee and was directed to the driving range. I hit a couple of balls loosening up and it was about 7:50 a.m., so I drove the golf cart they gave me to the first tee, but nobody was there. About 8:10 a.m. five people arrived at the tee—three with golf clubs and two extra men who were obviously gallery. One man put his golf bag on my cart and another waved for me to start! I only had two problems: the first being they were not members and should not have been allowed on the members-only course; and secondly, they were all Japanese and could not speak one word of English! It was miserable, not only for me but I'm sure for the Japanese entourage! I quit after nine holes and went to the room, collected Irene and we went looking at housing near a couple of other Tucson courses. Someone told Irene that because of our age we should be looking at Green Valley, a community 30 minutes away with four golf courses and where the homes were still inexpensive. The Meisterlin luck never leaves us! We arrived two minutes before the model complex closed and one saleslady was kind enough to say that she would stay with us and show us the models and answer all our questions. As we left the office, I noticed behind us that the other salesman was leaving and locking up and I remember asking the lady if she had a key so we could get back in the office as I wasn't very good at climbing eight-foot fences.

There were two sets of very different housing. The first homes were larger than our home in La Quinta and the second homes were in the area of 1,600 square feet, and attached by a common outside brick wall. It was very cleverly done and all the homes entered from the side. We looked at the large homes, which were approximately 2,400 square feet and were priced just under $200,000, but it wasn't the money—none of the floor plans suited us. In fact, as we walked the distance of approximately 100 yards Irene said, "I don't think they have a very good architect, you design housing better than this." When we looked at the four models in this category, there were two throw outs, one maybe, and the last a very strong possibility if we could make a few changes at an acceptable cost! The price on the one we liked was $148,000 the way it was. It was now almost 7:00 p.m. and our gracious agent was being very patient. I asked her if she would be working tomorrow and we agreed to meet at 10:00 a.m. on Saturday.

Our lady was waiting for us and we immediately went to the model in question. I started asking particular questions about specific customizing of certain parts of the structure, but all under the existing structural roof. First, I asked if we could restructure the master bedroom by extending the back wall all the way out to the roofline, which covered a back porch area across the back of the house. We wanted to move the sliding glass door from the rear to the side opening onto the porch and put in a picture window in the rear that would enable a gorgeous view of the valley and mountains. I then asked for an extension of the small kitchenette eliminating a small atrium area and placing additional cabinets on the far wall. In addition, we wanted to move the laundry equipment from the laundry room to the other side of the wall in the back of the garage, thereby creating a small office space for me. We would retain the existing cabinets, plus add the same cabinetry over the washer and dryer now in the garage. And lastly we wanted to eliminate the golf cart storage area in the garage, which would add three feet to the guest room and a large walk-in closet. Irene chimed in saying, "This would make our home perfect for our lifestyle!"

One of the main features we liked was the 12-foot ceilings in all rooms. The peak of the open ceilings was 15 feet high, which gave a wonderful spacious feeling!

Our saleslady liked our ideas and questions and said she would run them past the builders. Late that afternoon she called and asked if we all could meet with the construction superintendent in the morning who was willing, although it was Sunday, to meet at the model at 10:00 a.m. We went over each item carefully as we stood in each room so there would be no mistakes on what we were requesting. The superintendent had brought a small hand calculator and a pad and pencil and was using it after each request. When finished he said he could do 100% of what we wanted and the cost of the house instead of $148,000 would be $151,500. The square footage of the original model was 1,545 square feet. The restructured home would now be 1,875 square feet and he suggested that the home would fit better in the development on the end site on Anastasia Court, which was still available at no extra cost. The kitchen side there overlooked a small patch of natural desert that could never be built on. We placed a deposit and signed all the documents that day. We then canceled everything at Ventana!

On the way home we both laughed about how if it hadn't been for the stupid golf pro we probably would have built that house in Ventana and would have been miserable! Also, if our saleslady hadn't stayed behind and showed us everything, this probably would never have happened. The one thing we kept repeating was how lucky we were! Irene couldn't remember where she heard of Green Valley, but without her mentioning it we would never have gone there. All of this was pure luck and meant to be! For the very first time I was 100% sure our decision to leave La Quinta was correct!

We heard from Julie at Fairfield Homes a month later saying that our new home was now in construction. Approximately seven weeks later we had a call saying that house was totally framed, with the roof on and the windows and doors in place. The superintendent asked us to visit ASAP to make sure everything was correct. When we arrived on a beautiful Green Valley day, the home looked fabulous on the outside. We entered through the front door on the side of the house where Julie and the superintendent greeted us. They guided us into the master bedroom and it was far nicer than we imagined. We passed through the kitchen to the new extended casual dining area and it did have one little problem—the sliding glass door which had been moved to the side of the house looking out over the natural desert to the first green on the San Ignacio golf course was only seven feet high and looked very out of place with a 12-foot ceiling! When I pointed this out to the superintendent, he fully agreed. He said they'd substitute a new 10-foot slider that was standard and in stock and get it done immediately at no extra charge, as he felt that it was his mistake. We then ventured into the new office space and out to the garage and everything was correct. Finally we entered the guest room. The huge walk-in closet and extra area made it a suite!

They both wanted us to see the model again for good reason. The master bedroom had been changed to our specifications, except the picture window was enclosed by bookcases on top of a bench, which had storage space and ran across from a wall-to-wall sliding door! It was beautiful and I said to both, "We would like to add the bookcases exactly as you have done here to our master bedroom!"

When we entered the kitchen area, on an easel stood architectural drawings of two possible changes or additions to this plan. The first was in the kitchen identical to our home and the second was in the guest room, including using the golf cart storage to create a guest suite. The cost for the kitchen dining area was $1,950 and the guest suite was $1,500. The new sales price for the home was now $152,000. I asked our girl what the price was for the new bookcases? Before she could answer, the superintendent said, "They're a gift from Fairfield! We've already sold six of your model since finishing the master bedroom suite, five have changed the kitchen dining area and all six have adapted the guest suite! Unfortunately the other three models are not moving as well and we only sold one of two plans and two of the other. We'd be very pleased if you would critique the other three plans." I told them I'd be happy to but not to expect much as I didn't have much hope for two of the plans, although the third could be saved. The ride home was again very joyful and we patted each other on the back saying how lucky we were!

My real estate license was still active and I put the

house up for sale. A close neighbor who lived between Andy Williams' home and ours knocked on the door and said he had a doctor friend in Alabama who had said if a house such as his, which was identical to ours, came on the market, to phone him! He said, "Don't do anything for 48 hours until I track him down and I'll let you know right away." The next evening he told us his doctor friend was very interested in our asking price and terms. I gave my price and my neighbor said, "Is that a trifle high?" I replied, "I don't think so. Have him make me an offer, there is no real estate commission involved, so he might consider that!" An hour later he reappeared and said the doctor would pay $5,000 less than my asking price, which Irene and I accepted! I told my neighbor to have the doctor mail a $10,000 check to open escrow, to close when our new home in Arizona was completed about one month away.

Fairfield Homes had an in-house designer and Irene upgraded the carpeting and ordered blinds for all the windows including the sliding glass doors. She also asked for all the bathroom walls to be readied for wallpaper and the showers for tiling when we arrived. The walling in the showers and doors were to be a special clouded glass to give privacy and have a bench in the back away from the original showerhead, plus a second European style showerhead over the bench. Anything Irene desired she received.

On the last day there on our way out of town we stopped by the Green Valley Country Club. The club was almost empty. It was approximately 2:00 p.m. on a Sunday afternoon, but in what was the private men's card room there were three tables of card players, two of which I recognized to be playing Gin Rummy and the other Bridge, my favorite card games. One of the gentlemen facing Irene and I asked if he could be of help and I said, "We're possibly interested in joining the club, are there any open memberships?" He told us he would send us the particulars. Before leaving I asked him if on weekdays the card room was occupied? He laughed and stated, "You better have an early starting time on the golf course because by noon we're so full you can't find a seat!" I knew I'd found the right place unless the membership fee was outlandish! Irene was slightly impressed but upon entering the pro shop there were some excellent lines of women's attire to choose from, which raised the quality of the club in her eyes! Again I felt blessed! The following week I received an application for membership with a membership price of $2,500. I was in the process of selling my La Quinta membership for $40,000. How lucky can a person be? The monthly dues at La Quinta were $425 per month and the HOA dues were the same. The dues in Green Valley were only $175 per month and the HOA fees were $100 per year.

  We moved into our new home on October 20, 1993, and lived in the guest room for the first week while we moved in and workers finished the bathrooms and kitchen. That week we also had cabinetry, including a place for a 27-inch television to fill. The rest of the cabinetry was a chest of drawers and it stood facing the king-size bed in the master bedroom. The only other item we needed was a table and chairs for the new kitchen dining room, which required shopping in Tucson. In ten days we were settled in and from that day until we sold our house we never lived happier. It was by far the most comfortable home we've ever owned! Shortly after moving in I visited the pro shop up the street at San Ignacio Golf Club, which was strictly public and had open play except for a Thursday morning men's club which cost $100 a year annually and discounted rates on all days for members. I joined on the spot. From there I went to the Country Club of Green Valley and inquired about my application and was told by the manager that everything was in order but I must first meet with two members of the membership committee; namely a retired colonel, Dave Howe, and another retired military officer, Richard Henry.

The manager stated that they would call me within the next 24 hours to make an appointment for me to join them for lunch at the club. That evening Colonel Howe called and we met the following day and my application was approved. I now had two golf courses to play regularly. Green Valley itself was designed for extremely active seniors in retirement. There were activities and things to do for both men and women separately or together—sports, art, religion, writing, dancing, computers, hiking, horseback riding club—you name it. There were five senior centers scattered from one end of Green Valley to the other, almost within walking distance for everyone. The population was then 19,000 people, with 18,000 being seniors.

Irene was especially pleased because she had upgraded all of her kitchen appliances and added a second microwave oven! Always a superb chef, she now started experimenting with all her new toys and serving all sorts of new dishes, spoiling me royally and my waistline showed it. We loved everything about our new home and Green Valley. Soon after being accepted at the country club, Dave Howe, who was the VP of the club, asked me to play golf with him. Dave had his own golf cart which he kept at the club and during our game he began talking about the failure financially of the most important annual tournament, the Member-Guest Tournament held in October just two weeks ago! He then started asking me questions pertaining to items in my membership application having to do with the Bob Hope Classic, the Roadrunner Member-Guest held at the La Quinta Country Club and the Scotty McGregor at Hacienda Country Club. At lunch after our game, a member, Fred Schudel, joined us, who was a member of the tournament committee and I then became aware that Dave was the directors' appointee to the committee. They requested that I study the past Member-Guest Tournament and recommend what could be done to make it a first-class event. He suggested that the three of us should meet again and handed me all the data pertaining to the past tournament, including the financial statements!

We met again the following week and I gave them

my report, which wasn't good! It was so negative that I asked that it not be reported! Fred asked what I thought the main problems were? I think I laughed and then stated, "Just a few things—such as name, tournament format, cocktails and dinner parties, etc., etc." A week later the tournament committee unanimously voted me to be tournament chairman for 1994. He further said that the board would give me complete authority to run all the tournaments I wished, plus any committee appointees. Schudel would stay on the committee to help me implement all changes. "Carl," he said, "The club really needs your help, as you can see from the financial statements." I accepted this new challenge!

I had Fred call a meeting as usual for the new committee. I was introduced to three members I had never met, two holdovers and one new committee member. The first question I asked was: what was the percentage of women members using the golf course compared to men? Nobody, including Fred, had the slightest idea. Fred stood up and stated, "That's interesting," and headed for the pro shop. Gordy said, "I'll check with the manager and dining room maître d'." We received three unofficial results, which by coincidence were almost exactly the same—50/50! I then stated from my information that the ladies had only 25% of the tournaments. They all agreed. I told them that I thought one of our problems was not giving the ladies club their fair share of golf course activities, including more couples tournaments on Sunday, which we could organize with the social committee to make a Sunday tournament with lunch included. Three of the committee had wives who played regularly and they immediately were very open to this suggestion!

From that moment on our full committee bonded and with help from the social committee within a period of two months, use of the golf course and dining room facilities grew almost 15% and continued to grow for years. We had no less than 50 couples play golf, have lunch and with the help of the social committee, have an outside speaker one Sunday every month. We also increased ladies-only privileges from 8:30 to 11:00 a.m. on Thursdays and designated afternoons after 1:00 p.m. as a special men's gambling group who had been playing on Thursdays already. Interestingly, the week this was published in the club newsletter, that group grew from 25 to 50 and our bar business on Thursday evenings doubled.

All of these little things had a positive effect on the club's profit and loss statement! Dave Howe's background was as the chief finance officer for his last 12 years in the service in Honolulu, Hawaii and his main job on the club's board was finance. Dave attended all our committee meetings as well as the social committee. He had a presence and voiced his opinions often, but had no vote! During the next several months in 1994, Dave, Fred and I became even closer as friends and cohorts. In August while Irene and I were vacationing at our summer place in Carlsbad, I received a call from Dave saying the board had taken the Billy Roy Member-Guest Tournament away from our golf pro, Billy Roy, and that it was our tournament now! He asked what they could do immediately to prepare and wondered when in the hell I was coming back? I told him I'd talk to Irene and cut our stay short this summer and if Irene agreed we'd be back during the week after Labor Day.

The first thing I proposed was to get a new name for the tournament, something Arizonian like an Indian God. Dave, Fred and I met and played golf together that Saturday morning. Fred had called a special meeting of our committee for that afternoon as he had found what he thought was the perfect name for the tournament. When the meeting started Fred brought out a picture of Kokopelli, the God of fertility and life of the Hopi Indians! There was no doubt that this was exactly what we needed and the committee approved unanimously. We knew we had something special! The next thing on the agenda was how we could earn extra dollars to enable us to have the best golf tournament in southern Arizona? Even the wealthy private clubs that I'd been associated with sold advertising on each golf tee being used for the tournament. I asked which of us would take on this job and that I thought that this is where Dave could help a lot. I suggested that the suppliers could have personal business signs no larger than 18" x 24" and no more than three on each tee box. They were to furnish their own signs or we would charge $100 in addition to the $25 per tee box fee, the total cost being $75 per tee or $175 if we furnished the three signs. The reason I asked Dave to handle this was that we had many, many suppliers for our food and services in the kitchen area as well as suppliers for the clubhouse and pro shop. I had a hunch if he twisted their arms a little they'd be happy to contribute to making our Kokopelli a success! As an added incentive, if they were ardent golfers, we would put them on a waiting list to be called in order to be partners for members who needed guest players.

We asked Billy Roy, our excellent golf professional to join us, which he did. Billy wasn't too happy about the Billy Roy Member-Guest Tournament no longer carrying his name, but by the end of this meeting I honestly believe he changed his opinion. My first question to Billy after the committee had approved of Kokopelli had to do with the entry gift for each player. I wondered whether having a Foot Joy shoe representative fit them personally would be an appropriate entry prize? The committee, turning to Billy for his reaction (who nodded yes), agreed unanimously. I asked Billy what type of discount Foot Joy gave for 250 or more shoes if we ordered the same special top-of-the-line shoes I had in mind? He answered, "I've never ordered over 200 pairs of one kind, but I expect I would receive a pretty good discount." He also said, "I'm not sure that the representative will come in the evening to fit shoes . . ." I replied, "I don't know everything, but in Southern California our Foot Joy representatives appeared any time of day or evening for an order like this. I'm guessing if the price is right you'll probably be buying an additional 100. They're the top-of-the-line shoe, white trimmed in brown and black, which match 90% of golf clothing."

Billy now was extremely interested and said, "I'm almost sure I can find our representative and ask your questions. I'll be right back!" We then went onto the subject of format for the tournament and I gave my recommendations, with the women's permission, a practice round on Wednesday starting at 10:00 a.m. using both front and back nines, with a men's-only cocktail party starting at 6:00 p.m. where we would hand out the entry prizes to all participants. This would include drinks and heavy hors d'oeuvres tailored to men's appetites which would last until 8:00 p.m. One of the committee questioned if we could legitimately afford this? I replied, "I hope so!" I surprised them by adding that on Thursday, Friday and Saturday at 7:00 a.m. we would put out a continental buffet breakfast with a side of hot scrambled eggs until 9:00 a.m. It would be up to the kitchen to make sure the buffet table was always full, but the golfers served themselves, keeping the labor to a minimum. If by chance you had an afternoon starting time, you could still come to the continental breakfast. On the golf course during the rounds starting at 11:00 a.m. and lasting to 3:00 p.m. we would have a golf cart bar and bartender driving the course and serving all types of beverages, even water!

By now Billy was back and said, "I've contacted my man and he has confirmed your opinions and knows the exact shoe you're talking about, which is his new best seller, and he'll give me 25%, 15%, 10% and another 10% and will be here whenever you say. There might even be a further discount because if I bought all the other types of shoes that I purchase once a year I might receive a lower list price to start with. He needs to talk to the factory in Mississippi and promised to call me no later than Tuesday afternoon." Billy laughed and said, "This would be the largest order our Foot Joy man has ever received!"

We went back to the format conversation and Friday night was open but we suggested that we have a special evening menu for couples such as a fish fry or Mexican night and advertise it in the newsletter at a price that would not only attract contestants and their wives but all club members! On the last night starting at 6:00 p.m. we would have free cocktails for all the contestants and people who worked in running the tournament and their spouses. Dinner would be served at 7:00 p.m. sharp and presentations between 8:30-9:00 p.m. and dancing and partying until 11:00 p.m. All the costs pertaining to partying after 9:00 p.m. would not be part of the Kokopelli budget! The consensus of my committee was that this was possible and I agreed. I stated that with help from the social committee, for $20 per team and only $10 more per contestant we could do all the things I'd outlined and with Billy's help on the shoes, we could do that, too. That meant the cost would be only $170 per team!

The board of directors, the social committee and members of our committee began an in-depth search of all suppliers and people who were financially involved with the club. We were able to identify several and by the time the tournament began we had raised another $3,000.

We also sold raffle tickets for donated prizes mostly from the pro shop for another $1,000. We then added a pari-mutuel horse track type betting on the teams for the three days, where the tournament took 20% off the top and distributed 80% to the bettors, a better return for the bettors then you receive at any racetrack. Betting began at the contestants' cocktail party on Wednesday night, plus on Thursday morning before teeing off you could purchase all four bets. On Friday and Saturday you could bet that day individually. Gayle Cooper had done this previously and she volunteered to shoulder this large responsibility. By the close of betting on Saturday morning, Gayle had collected $25,000 with $5,000 going to the tournament budget!

On the Monday prior to the tournament, we had over 90 teams entered. This compared to 72 teams for any year previously. We could handle 90 teams with no problem and by Wednesday morning this had grown to 96 teams. As usual on Wednesday night we lost two teams and four teams were very disappointed! Everything we planned on doing, including all the free drinking, breakfasts, golf cart bar and the prizes were in the budget. One of the main surprises was that Billy Roy only charged us $39 per player for the $100 special Foot Joy's! All the parties and food and the golf were great! The weather was perfect, the pari-mutuel was a tremendous success thanks to Gayle, and even Billy Roy exclaimed this is by far the best tournament ever held at this club!

The committee had copied the La Quinta Country

Club Roadrunner Tournament completely. There were no new additions or changes, it was just a great, fun, successful format and when we met to analyze and improve the tournament for next year we were still celebrating our success! I suggested one change only—that we have the tournament two weeks earlier in October, which would give us 30 minutes more daylight and start the morning round 15 minutes earlier. We could then accommodate 108 teams and hopefully everybody would get to play. That was agreed upon instantly. Billy Roy informed us that three of our benefactor guests who had been asked to play by members and were asked back for next year, had accepted and off-the-cuff mentioned they would contribute more next year. Dave Howe then gave his financial report and the tournament had a $5,800 surplus that the tournament committee could now use to improve our weekly and monthly tournaments for members only. Then, the best news yet, the dining room and bar had the biggest gross dollars earned in one week since the club started keeping records. Also, the month of October was the most profitable for the club overall in history! During the week of the Kokopelli, the club made over $14,000 and for the month of October almost $25,000. There's nothing quite like being the head of a successful venture. I loved my new country club and they liked me!

Irene and I were popular at all the social events and made many new friends at the club and always had cocktails and dinner with a specific group of members on what was called "Special Tuesday" night. We usually had Saturday night dinner, which included dancing at least three times a month. We never missed a special club function and our group of friends kept growing. I also played Bridge one day a week with Dave Howe and two members who were terrible Bridge players but great guys, Dick Freeman and Frank Martin. They were so bad that Dave and I took turns having each one for a partner, but it wasn't fair if we were partners! Three days of the week I played Gin Rummy. I gave up playing golf at San Ignacio where I lived and didn't renew my annual membership.

In the spring of 1995 I saw an article on the sports page of the Tucson newspaper mentioning the annual Tucson Best Ball of Partners Tournament on the Tucson City Golf Course, which was a really tough test of golf. It cost $150 per team to enter, but you received a free practice round plus another tournament round free. This continued on until you lost and were eliminated. Lunches were included as long as you stayed unbeaten! I asked my friend Dean Robinson if he'd like to be my partner and he agreed. The practice round and the qualifying round for flights of 16 teams were played on the next Wednesday with tee times starting at 7:30 a.m. Because we lived in Green Valley, they accommodated us and we received a nice comfortable 9:30 a.m. starting time. When we arrived at the course on Wednesday to qualify, the wind was blowing in excess of 20 m.p.h., with gusts as high as 35 m.p.h. Dean was a 15 handicap and I was a 13. It was a brutal day, but we hung in there and managed a 66, six under par. It was lousy day to play golf and we had no idea whether 66 was a good score or not, so we decided to have lunch and hang around a little longer to see where we qualified, and depending on that what time we would play our match the next day.

At 3:30 p.m. we went to the big scoreboard where there were six flights of 16 teams listed. There were only eight teams still on the golf course and the weather was still awful! We were standing looking for our names on the board as they had been listing teams by their scores into the various flights. I was looking at one end and Dean at the other. Dean yelled, "Hey, we made the championship flight!" The championship flight teed off the next day at 10:00 a.m. We won our first match and before leaving we checked with the man in charge who congratulated us on our round and said we were the oldest team in the tournament and that our combined handicaps were within the five highest! I couldn't have cared less and I was not looking forward to playing in these windy conditions again.

On Friday morning our opponents were two young 20 year olds who played on the University of Arizona golf team and they were playing to zero handicaps. I began like my infamous round of golf in the Bob Hope Classic shooting two over par on the front nine holes and we were two up going to a number 10, which I parred. On number 11 and again on 12, I parred for a Birdie! The two young men were playing superbly and we were only two up going to number 13. Starting on number 13, I became a spastic and lost my swing and golf game altogether.

I completely fell apart and my partner was on his own. I Double Bogeyed the four holes starting on 13 and as we stood on the 17th tee, we were still one up, thanks to Dean who was playing beautifully. Dean hit his best drive of the day on the par 5 number 17, the toughest five par on the course. I then hit my drive into the trees to the right. The young men hit their usual long drives right down the middle. Because Dean had hit his drive so well, they were only 20 yards longer. From the trees on the right I hit my second shot, which hit a tree branch and careened out of bounds. I then hit my fourth shot, which hit the same tree with the same results! I picked up and I was out of the hole and poor Dean was again all on his own.

When we reached Dean's drive he had 225 yards to the hole and approximately a second shot of 200 yards to carry a lake directly in front of the green. Dean wanted to go for the green, but I talked him into laying up in front of the lake where he would have approximately an 80-yard shot to the green. He stroked on the hole. He pulled a seven iron from his golf bag and I suggested an eight iron was safer. He changed to an eight iron and hit the best eight iron of his life! There was an approximately 30 foot slightly downhill slope in front of the lake and the ball disappeared from our view. Both the young men hit their tee shots on to the green and they had putts for Eagles although they were 50 feet away from the pin. Unbelievably, in a little patch of rough three feet short of the lake sat Dean's second shot. He now hit his wedge and the ball barely cleared the lake and bounced forward and rolled directly at the pin and stopped for a Tap-in Birdie for a Net Eagle. They missed their long putts and we won the match two and one and advanced to the semi-finals! Our super young gentlemen were very gracious in defeat and the University of Arizona could be proud to have two young men of such character representing it. But I'll never forget how Dean rose to the occasion when the chips were down! The following day we ran into a buzz saw and though we played well we weren't good enough and we were eliminated. I loved telling Mary Alice, Dean's wife about what a great competitor her husband was and if I remember correctly Mary Alice replied, "Tell me something new, Carl!"

Life in Green Valley was truly a joy for both Irene and I. Not only were there multiple activities to choose from to keep us busy and active, but the city of Tucson was also special. We made so many friends and had the best neighbors in the world who we had so much in common with, that life was not only good but flew by!

While we were purchasing our home in 1993, we met Wilma and Dick Stempel, who built one of the large model homes directly behind our home. Dick was not a golfer nor did he possess any athletic skills, but he was something far more special, a great friend and confidante. He was an actual rocket scientist. For over 25 years, Dick worked for Rocketdyne, and finally for North American Aviation Rocket Division where he was the lead scientist for North American on the Challenger Rocket Program. Quoting Dick, he was adamant about not blasting off on the ill-fated Challenger attempt! He told me on several private occasions that he had informed both NASA and the Senate Appropriation Committee that the O-rings wouldn't perform correctly if frozen. After it blew up, the final blame was on the frozen the O-rings! He put the disaster strictly on the backs of the Senate Appropriations Committee, whom he claimed didn't have a brain in their collective heads. More than once he stated that it was the usual Washington cover-up, in which the Beltway media misinformed the nation.

Dick became very ill with cancer and at the very end, the hospital and doctors sent him home to die. Wilma called on a Sunday morning to tell us Dick was home and we were welcome to visit him. In fact, she encouraged us to do so. We walked down the street to their house and found Dick lying in bed. We tried to bring good cheer and he responded wonderfully, except he spoke barely above a whisper. We reminisced about some things the four of us had enjoyed, plus a few things that were common to only Dick and I. After a short time I looked at Wilma and she nodded and we said what Irene and I thought were our last goodbyes. We left the house and had walked over 30 yards when Wilma came out the front door yelling, "Carl, Dick has to tell you something!" I went back to the bedside and Dick, dying, had a big grin on his face. These were his exact words: "It's the opening game of the baseball season at Fenway Park in Boston and two old gals with a bottle of brandy are huddled together in their seats. Now, tell me what's happening in the ballgame?" I thought but I couldn't think of anything and I said, "I don't know." Dick then said in a whisper, "It's the bottom of the fifth and the bags are loaded!" He actually smiled and a little tiny laugh rattled! A fine honest man and friend died that night!

Another great friend was Pete Cole, a very successful retired industrialist who belonged to our little club. It was rumored not only at the country club, but at the library, that Pete was the wealthiest man in Green Valley. You'd never think it if you knew Pete as Irene and I did. He was just a down-to-earth, fun-loving and giving person who went out of his way to make life better for anybody he encountered, including Irene and I. He did numerous things at the club that nobody knew about and never ever took credit for anything. I mention the library because Irene and I visited the library once a week and little Green Valley had the most up-to-date books, computers, records, maps, globes and atlases. One day while waiting for Irene, who was picking out some books, I found myself standing next to the man who ran the library. I complimented him on how great our library was and he replied, "It's easy when you have benefactors in the community who bestow $50,000 grants like Mr. Cole does when we need something!"

On one of our usual Tuesday night gatherings, we were seated with Dick and Fanny Freeman, Pete and Betty his significant other, Dean and Mary Alice, and Irene and I. Dick started talking about his daughter who lived in Santa Barbara, California, who was in charge of the Make-

A-Wish Foundation and what great work she was accomplishing. Dick continued telling stories about his daughter and at the end of the evening Pete asked Dick for his daughter's address. The next Tuesday Pete and Betty had other plans but we joined Fanny and Dick as usual. Dick stated that his daughter received a $10,000 donation from the Pete Cole Foundation yesterday. One of our most enjoyable cruises was 15 days with Pete and Betty to Hawaii! Pete died in an auto crash the next year.

    Why am I the luckiest man in the world? The last gentlemen from our Green Valley days, James Cluff, came into our lives in 1994. I played with Jim on a Saturday morning golf game at the club but we didn't share a golf cart and it wasn't until having lunch that I asked Jim what he did to make a living? He replied, "I am a semi-retired financial advisor or simply put, I'm a stockbroker!" Everybody in Green Valley has migrated there from elsewhere and my next question was where he was from? "I started in Chicago for a decade and I've spent my last 20 in San Francisco at a large brokerage firm named Sutro's," he replied. I mentioned my fortunate dealings with the man in charge at Sutro's in the 1950s. Jim responded he was a legend at Sutro's and probably still was, but unfortunately by the time he had arrived he had passed away. We talked investments all through lunch and when we parted I made an appointment to see him on Monday.

    I had a fair amount of cash investments, mostly CDs, savings account and bonds. That day as Jim and I talked, I realized that he was the most knowledgeable financial advisor, including the legend at Sutro's, that I'd ever met. (That might be because we agreed 95% of the time.) I opened an account with Jim's firm, Piper Jeffray, and transferred approximately $100,000 in assets to the account. For the next 6 1/2 years, thanks to the Republican regime in Washington for 12 years and Newt Gingrich in 1996, any idiot made money in the stock market, which I did, and then some! I gave Jim full authority to buy and sell on a moment's notice and for all those years he made Irene and I more money by far than the sales commissions he earned. In the year 2000, Jim had quadrupled our investment minus the monies that Irene and I were using to travel the world. In retrospect, when we left Green Valley in 2005 our net worth had increased by 50%!

    Distressingly, the media during these years gave all the credit to the liberals in the government and the pervert in the presidency! In my lifetime, with the exception of Ronald Reagan, I've never met a president, senator or congressman who could be successful in business and most certainly not a CEO of a large corporation! Looking forward, if we're to have a black president and a lady president I'd suggest Condoleezza Rice, the former Secretary of State, professor at Stanford, a member of Augusta Golf Club in Georgia and addicted to golf just like me! She's an economic disciple of Arthur Laffer from Stanford who served our country under Reagan and not those idiots from Harvard, Princeton and Yale who keep trying to socialize and destroy our Constitution!

There were so many people that I should mention from Green Valley who truly made our 12 years there the happiest and luckiest years of our lives, but that doesn't make good reading—you know who you are and Irene and I love and thank you all for being one of the best parts of our lives!

Chapter 23

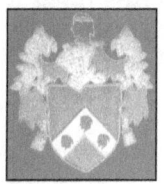

Trips and Travels

During our life together, Irene and I made many interesting trips, both in the U.S. and abroad. In early January 1978, Irene came into my office all excited and handed me a letter from Sokna, Norway that came from an Asjerd Meisterlin. The letter stated that their son had been at Disneyland in Anaheim and had found my son Chuck's phone number in the phone book and brought it home. She wondered if could I possibly be related to the Carl Meisterlin who once lived near San Francisco? We responded to the letter that yes we were and that was my father. From there on we were in constant communication and Irene and I planned a trip that summer to coincide with Debbie playing in the Ladies Professional Golf World Championship in Sunningdale, England. This became our first big journey together and began our many world travels.

We flew directly from LAX, after a three-hour delay for a bomb scare, to Heathrow in London. We spent four days in London sightseeing and then caught a train from Waterloo station to Ascot where we rented a car and proceeded to a small hotel located near Sunningdale. There were several noteworthy features about this beautiful old estate located in a very heavily wooded forest. On entering the hotel, the front desk was directly in front of me and I was greeted by a huge but friendly dog who put its paws on the counter and stared at me until I rang a little bell for the innkeeper. Every day during our five-day stay, whenever we crossed the lobby, the dog was behind the counter. I presume he was the official greeter! The estate dated back to the 1870s and was originally built and owned by Lady Churchill, Winston's mother. Our room was on the second floor with a fabulous view and was unusual in its floor plan, but it had an adequate bathroom. The room obviously was not a bedroom before becoming a hotel, but it was comfortable and charismatic.

We watched Debbie play for all four days and walked all 18 holes each day, attempting to be as inconspicuous as possible. Debbie played mediocre golf for the first three days. That evening we invited Debbie, Betsy King and her parents to our hotel for dinner, which was interesting and enjoyable. The next day Debbie played slightly better and on the last hole, the 18th, Debbie's second shot hit the grandstand and bounced back into the high rough directly in front of where Irene and I had found a place to sit momentarily. She had, what golfers would say, short sided herself and had an impossible shot to the pin. And then she did what only Debbie was capable of—she holed the shot for a Birdie! She finished the tournament in 18th Place. The following day I had made reservations at St. Andrews, Scotland for three days and nights for all three of us at the Old Course Hotel and had starting times for two days for Debbie and I to play golf on the very course where golf originated! This was my dream, to play golf at St. Andrews. Having Debbie there made it even more special. Unfortunately, Debbie had other plans, and Irene and I journeyed to St. Andrews on our own. We cut our stay one day and flew from Glascow to Oslo, Norway the following day and were greeted at the airport by Asjerd and Trygve Meisterlin.

After a two-hour drive from Oslo to Sokna, we arrived at a quaint house on a hill overlooking a gorgeous valley with two flags flying—a Norwegian flag and a United States flag—in honor of our visit. On our way to Sokna, we passed the Sonya Heine Museum and the city of Oslo, the capitol of Norway. Oslo, the largest city in Norway, was surprisingly small but was beautifully planned. It had a large park square, with the Capital on one end and the Royal Palace on the other, and the finest hotels, stores, restaurants and office buildings on the sides. When we were changing planes in Copenhagen, there was a duty-free store where I decided to purchase a bottle of gin for Irene and I to drink plus a bottle of Martell Cognac for our hosts. At customs in Oslo we were told to declare any alcohol we were bringing in or it would be confiscated. I had no idea that Irene had put the bottles in my carry-on suitcase and when the customs official asked me did I have any alcohol I responded no and walked through. Irene had her carry-on toiletry case and handbag and she followed. Our major suitcase was then placed on the table, opened and searched and, to my surprise, no alcohol was there.

The first thing we did on arriving at their home was to ask if we could freshen up. They showed us to a very nice room on the end of the house, but the only entrance was from the outside. There was a big pot sitting in a large bowl in a special piece of furniture, but there were no water or bathroom facilities. When we reentered the main house, they were very proud of the fact that they had a modern bathroom with both a tub and shower! Asjerd advised us that they were one of very few families to have an indoor bathroom in Sokna. It was late afternoon and in Norway that meant snack time. She had put out some delicious pastries, plus a few local delicacies. Trygve did not speak a word of English, but Asjerd spoke perfect English with a melodic Norwegian accent. When she asked, "Do the American Meisterlins by chance have an evening martini? We would be happy to welcome you by drinking together." I looked to Irene and asked what happened to the two bottles we bought in Copenhagen? "Oh, they're in your carry-on!" she said. I could not help wondering what would have happened if the customs official had opened my bag! I went directly back to our room and retrieved the two bottles for our welcoming party. I presented both the premium bottle of gin and cognac to the man of the house, who was now beaming with appreciation, and we all had a martini, just like at home as we presented them with our Meisterlin martini card and Asjerd appeared with an orange. The snacks were delicious, but we stopped at only one martini.

Less than three hours passed before we sat down at the dining room table, which was set with every conceivable sterling silver dinner piece including goblets, gorgeous ancient candlesticks and two knives, three different size forks and three different spoons! Irene said later that evening that it was the most elegant table setting she had ever seen, and I agreed. The dinner that night was either six or seven courses and the main entrée was reindeer, an entrée in Norway that was very, very special and not served in restaurants. I liked it, but unfortunately by the time it appeared on the table I had already had five excellent courses and I was stuffed! We retired to the living room where Trygve opened the bottle of cognac and we all had a sip. It was now time for us to retire, as it had been an extremely long but wonderful day, when much to our surprise we were served desserts. Again, the desserts were presented beautifully and Irene and I didn't want to offend our hosts, so we took the smallest slices possible. Once a break in the conversation presented itself, we asked if we could retire for the night and went to our room.

The next three days were spent sightseeing in the valley surrounding Sokna and meeting a couple of Meisterlins and Arbos, Asjerd's relatives. The area was all heavily wooded, with the exception of the base of the valley, and we learned that Trygve was the minister of forestry for Norway. This was the reason they lived in this particular area, as there were heavy forests of three types of trees necessary to be preserved as well as cut! He was on the road five days a week and had a car with a chauffeur and an assistant and he truly loved the responsibility of serving his beloved Norway. Another day we traveled to Hannefoss, a very small community bordering a beautiful lake and we visited a small home hidden in the trees where Asjerd explained that in World War II was home to the underground movement after Germany had taken control of Norway. Trygve had been active in the movement. We were also the honored guests of a neighborhood party for approximately 30 people where I discovered both of our hosts disappearing down into a basement and reappearing carrying clear liquids. When the door to the cellar was opened, the smell of alcohol was unmistakable. I told Irene that night, "I think they have a still down there!"

The next morning we left extremely early and drove to the Oslo train station where we took a train for Trondheim, our ancestors' hometown. We spent the next one and three-quarter days and one night on this train with Irene sleeping with five ladies in one cabin and I with five men in another cabin. I was fortunate, as a foreigner to be given one of the two lower bunks! During the day we had regular coach train cars with ordinary windows, which opened up and down for fresh air. We could purchase bags of food, but there was no kitchen on board. The train traveled straight north through the center of Norway and made four stops in all. Other than the little train station and platform, there was no sign of any community in the next three stops. The scenery was extraordinary, but this was summertime and I'd hate to be there in the winter! There were no signs of any roads, not even dirt roads other than at the four stops! We arrived in Trondheim in mid-afternoon on the second day. It, like Oslo, was a beautiful but small city sitting on the south side of a major fjord, which contained an island with a prison. I mentioned to Irene that this looked the same as San Francisco Bay without the bridges and she replied, "I was thinking the same thing."

We checked into Norway's most famous hotel, the Britannia, which was over 100 years old, but still a magnificent structure. The manager welcomed Irene and I personally and told the clerk at the desk that we were to be given the King's Suite on the corner of the second floor overlooking the plaza and the fjord. The suite also had a balcony with the same view and looked directly at Norway's largest and most beautiful cathedral where every king was crowned for over 200 years. The cathedral dated back to the mid-18th century. For a decade in 1870, Trondheim was the capital of a country called Scandinavia, comprised of Sweden, Denmark and Norway. We retired to our suite and caught a little shut-eye, changed clothes and then invited our hosts to our suite for our evening martini. We stood on the balcony like a king and queen and admired the gorgeous views. In the far north at that time of year, daylight lasted until almost 11:00 p.m. and became daylight again in approximately 2 1/2 hours. We enjoyed our dinner in a spectacular dining room, which reminded us of the one at the Del Coronado Hotel in San Diego. After dinner we found comfortable seating in a beautiful dimly-lit lounge and again sipped our cognac. Except for the night on the train, our martini before dinner and a cognac after became standard procedure!

  The next morning we had a light breakfast in our suite and met Asjerd and Trygve and walked to the beautiful cathedral. The interior was as impressive as the exterior. We were free to wander within the cathedral by ourselves. We looked at all the rooms on the ground floor and there was not one person other than ourselves present. On returning to the main hall, Asjerd sat down in one of the pews and started crying. In all the years they'd been married, she had never visited Trondheim and this beautiful cathedral. Her words were, "I never knew that Norway had anything as beautiful as this!" We exited the building and went to the south side where there were headstones by the hundreds in a cemetery. At the very front, no more than 15 feet from the south wall, was a small plot apart from the masses, which held approximately 12 headstones, all of which said Meisterlin. Trygve walked over to what appeared to be a very new marble headstone that had been ordered from Italy for his first cousin who had died in Bethlehem, Pennsylvania and whose body had been transported back to Norway to be placed in the family plot. We followed him to the grave and none of us noticed except Irene that the name Meisterlin was misspelled. Trygve was furious and lost his temper, completely out of character for the man we'd been with for a week. We left the cathedral and spent the balance of the day walking and being tourists. We found a small train station different from the one we had disembarked from and while we were there a little old train arrived, which look like trains that were used in California during the gold rush. Irene, who is crazy about riding on trains, asked the clerk where the train went. The train traveled 12 km to the resort city of Hell, which is located on the very east end of Trondheim fjord. It contained several vacation resorts and was very beautiful! My curiosity and sense of humor got the best of me and I asked the man what it would cost for a round-trip ticket? The cost was less than $10 American, so I bought one. We still have this ticket in a scrapbook to prove that we've been to HELL and made it back.

The next day we visited two sets of Irene's Carlson families that lived in the valley approximately 15 miles south of Hell. In the morning we visited one family who took a book off the shelf, opened it and showed us a picture of Irene's uncle who had left for the U.S. years ago. In Irene's family were men of the cloth, both in Norway and the U.S. In the afternoon we visited a family of farmers about 5 km north of Irene's relatives and had lunch at a small but nice restaurant on the shore of Lake Selbu, which is the name given to the valley. To say we were treated royally is an understatement. All these people were the salt of the earth and we were both so proud of our heritage, and even more so today!

The last morning before going to the train station, we visited the Meisterlin home above the city of Trondheim looking over the fjord, the island prison, the city square and the beautiful cathedral in the background. We took a picture of ourselves standing under a street sign with the old family estate in the background with the sign reading 'Meisterlin vei' in one direction and 'Amundsen vei' in the other. We left that afternoon on what appeared to be the same train with better accommodations and arrived in Oslo the following evening.

**August 1978
Trondheim, Norway
Carl and Irene Meisterlin
Corner of Amundsen Vei and Meisterlin Vei**

The following day we visited their mountain retreat consisting of a main house and three log cabins which were relocated from some other area but had been taken apart log by log, marked and transported to this site and reconstructed exactly as the original cabins. These log cabins had been originally built in 1575 and our relatives saved them from extinction! The doors were so low that even Irene had to bend from the waist to enter. I mentioned to Asjerd that evening that their Norwegian predecessors must be terribly short in height and she responded, "Not at all. This was a precaution to keep people out! If somebody tried to enter they must bend over and you would defend yourself by hitting them on the head or even worse, decapitating them." Oh yes, there was no indoor plumbing nor outhouse, so if you needed to relieve yourself you walked up a trail about 30 yards and sat on two branches nailed to two trees! We stayed one night and returned to Sokna and that afternoon we visited a couple of fjords that had magnificent waterfalls. The following day our hosts deposited us at the Grand Hotel on the square in Oslo explaining that their son Christian would be returning from Beirut where he was serving with the United Nation forces and he would be calling for us in the morning at our hotel. We thanked them as much as possible, but words sometimes just don't get the job done. On checking in, the manager met us in the lobby, took us to the clerk and said we were to have the King's Suite, the same as in Trondheim!

The following day Christian arrived and gave us a tour of Oslo and as luck will have it, the parade of tall ships arrived in the harbor. Those big old sailing ships in full sail were truly something to see! Christian, who resembled his father, had been a military officer from the age of 21 and now held the rank of captain. He spoke of the war in which he was serving on behalf of the United Nations with mixed emotions. His opinion at that time was that the Lebanese were in the right and that the Israelites were wrong. The U.S. media at that time was telling us it was the other way around. The following morning Christian escorted us to the airport and we started our direct journey home. Christian is still a very active member of our family and reaches the age of 70 on February 6, 2014.

  On our long flight home we discussed many of our wonderful experiences and all the wonderful people we enjoyed, especially members of each of our families. The one memory that stood out in both our minds was of a tall statuesque beautiful and intelligent Norwegian goddess named Asjerd! Even today our memories of this Norwegian queen have never changed. She was a graduate in education and had degrees that allowed her to teach at any grade level from first grade to the university level. She chose to teach the younger children. The Norwegian educational system at that time was that a teacher would start with approximately 25 students in first grade and stay with those same students through fifth grade. She strongly believed that this system was far better for both the students and the teacher. Our days with Asjerd as our tour guide, friend and confidant were priceless. Irene and I often speak of her and agree that she was physically beautiful, but more than that, the most remarkable lady we've ever been lucky enough to be with. She made our first major world excursion so special that we've traveled extensively ever since.

In 1982, we embarked on a tour beginning in China and ending in Hong Kong. This trip lasted 21 days and was not a vacation but one of the great experiences in our lives. We were given numbers as identification and our tour guides treated us as such! China was 200 years behind Western civilization in 1982. The main transportation in China was by bicycle or walking. Nobody made eye contact, everybody's heads were bowed and you never saw a smile or heard a laugh! Our trip ended in Hong Kong, which was totally modern and thriving economically under British rule, quite a contrast to China proper! Our four days in Hong Kong we went broke saving money on custom-tailored clothes, which were fitted and made overnight and tried on the following day. They were then tailored again if they didn't fit perfectly that day! The materials used were finer then we had available in the U.S.A. and cost about 40% of what we paid at home.

We were walking by a furrier store and in the window was the most beautiful fur coat I'd ever seen. Somehow that coat flew out the window and onto Irene's body and was a perfect fit! The price of the coat in the window was $1,750 American dollars. On entering the store, we asked the lady about the coat and she replied that it really wasn't for sale. It had only arrived that week and it was in the window only to attract attention. I asked if they would consider selling it for $1,400 and showed my American

Express Card, to which the lady said, "No, it's not for sale." I asked to see the manager and she said, "I'm the owner and it's not for sale!" I carefully turned my back and started for the door, taking my wallet out and removed 14 $100 bills. I turned and walked back to the counter and counted out one at a time the $1,400 in cold hard American cash! She turned and went through a curtain and Irene and I could hear her talking to someone and she returned immediately carrying a box, went to the window, removed the coat, came back to the counter, placed the coat in the box and scribbled some type of a receipt I didn't understand. Irene then had the most beautiful fur coat I've ever seen. I did see an identical coat in 1986 when Mrs. Gorbachev came with her husband to see President Reagan. She was wearing an identical coat as she departed the plane!

In 1986, we were joined by our good friends Ed and Ruth Stamp for a trip to Hong Kong and then on to Singapore and back to Hong Kong for a trip that lasted 12 days. Heading west as usual, our plane arrived in Hong Kong a couple of hours late and when we arrived at the Regent Hotel, the rooms that we had reserved were filled and they had supposedly only two rooms available—one being a room one category higher and the other a suite on the top floor—which we could have that night at the cost on our reservation. We gave Ruth and Ed the suite and we took the other room, which was great, and we never moved. Ruth and Ed were so enamored with their suite that they also remained!

The following day we went to our Princeton custom tailors and started ordering all types of clothing. Irene and I were into formal attire and quickly Ruth followed. Ed sarcastically exclaimed, "This is not a shopping contest!" He soon discovered how little the clothing was costing and he ordered a beautiful all-white suit! Our next stop was a camera store close by that Ed spied and he went in and found a motion picture camera that he had admired at home which was selling in Hong Kong for 60% less! In size and weight it was only 1/10 the size of his present camera. He of course bought it and we had ten days of constant picture taking.

The next store we stumbled on was a shop that sold only women's skirts and sweaters made of the most expensive fabrics at unbelievably inexpensive prices and Ruthie started pulling cashmere sweaters of all types and colors off the shelf. Again Ed stated, "This is not a shopping contest!" Irene joined in and bought a few cashmeres, actually only one style in three colors. I bought two cashmeres just because they were so cheap. Finally Ed gave in and purchased a couple.

On our third day in Hong Kong, we went back to our tailors and were refitted and made an appointment for the final fitting after we returned from Singapore. We left the following morning on China Airlines for Singapore, commonly called "the finest city in the world." The reason for the name is that if you litter the street you automatically are fined! If you steal something, the fine is having a hand cut off and if you murder somebody you are hung in the city square on a gallows that is a permanent fixture!

On arriving in Singapore, we entered what was then the most beautiful airport building I've ever visited. Our hotel was first-class and walking distance to most everything. The first thing I wanted to see in Singapore was the famous Raffles Bar, made famous in the movies by Humphrey Bogart, and to have a Singapore Sling cocktail! The bar was not disappointing, as it had a typical, half-open, half-closed island-style architecture. The Singapore Sling was terrible, which all four of us agreed upon. The city of Singapore was beautiful and was also famous for its zoo. We took a cab to the zoo, which contained several species of animals none of us had ever seen, but it was the orangutans that made Singapore so special! We were standing on a landing approximately 30-40 feet above the large enclosure and watching, talking and then laughing. Rapidly, a family of 15 apes congregated in front of us. They started jumping up and down, jabbering, pointing at us and laughing! They were making fun of us! I still wonder today which species is the most intelligent.

After three full days in Singapore, we flew back to Hong Kong to relax, pick up our new wardrobes and fly home. We were circling the airport in Hong Kong to land when the captain announced we would be delayed while the Queen's plane landed. The Queen was arriving in Hong Kong to announce that Hong Kong was to be given back to China in exactly ten years! There was a huge celebration for the next three days while we were there.

The concierge at our Regent Hotel stated this was to be the largest firework celebration of all time. This was held on our last night in Hong Kong as we were dining at a window table in the main dining room of the Regent. The fireworks lasted almost as long as we dined and we had the best view in all of Hong Kong!

We left for home the next morning on China Airlines and as we were at the end of the runway to take off, the captain came on the speaker and announced again that we must wait until the Queen's plane took off. I love exaggerating the truth in adding that Irene and I spent three days in Hong Kong with the Queen of England! (Oh yes, Ed easily won the shopping contest!)

In the first week of January 1995 I noticed an advertisement in our local paper for Bon Voyage Travel Agency having an annual sale for Holland America Cruise Line. The ad stated that on any cruise for over ten days you would receive a two-tier upgrade free. That day I stopped by the agency and picked up a brochure and talked to a travel agent who I recognized as being a hostess at the club occasionally. She had very excitedly told me of this special cruise from London through the Baltic nations to St. Petersburg and there were still excellent staterooms available. She gave me all the information and Irene and I studied it that evening and this became one of the signature cruises in our lifetime.

This trip started by flying from San Diego to New York and on to London where we stayed for five days, which were spent touring the British Museum, Piccadilly,

Soho, London Bridge and the Tower of London. One evening we went to a live theater production of the American classic *Sunset Boulevard*, starring Britain's most famous stage actress. It was fabulous! Of all the museums Irene and I have toured, none compared to the British Museum. You could spend weeks and not see everything. We boarded our ship near London and our first stop was Oslo, Norway. We sailed in the late evening for Denmark where we visited the home of Hans Christian Andersen the following day. That evening we sailed again for Stockholm, Sweden and arrived early in the morning, stayed overnight and remained until late that evening before sailing for Rostov, Germany. The next morning we left Rostov on the original train that carried Kaiser Wilhelm of Prussia from and to Berlin at the turn of the 20th century! That afternoon in East Berlin we visited the Pergamon Museum, which appeared to be the only building not bombed in World War II. We stayed in Berlin overnight and were raw tourists. We went to the infamous Berlin Wall and touched it. The contrast between East and West Berlin was unbelievable, not only in the bombed out East Berlin, which still hadn't been rebuilt, but in the actions of the human beings who occupied each side. West Berlin was a bustling Western city that reminded us of San Francisco on any given day—noisy and filled with cars, buses and trolleys and people everywhere; whereas East Berlin was old, in ruins and the people were very few with their heads bowed and no noise or conversation, just like Bejing, China!

Returning to our ship, we left for St. Petersburg, Russia where we were to visit The Hermitage, more commonly named The Winter Palace. The main reason for our cruise was to view all the famous artwork the Germans had taken from Russia during World War II, which Russia had finally been able to recover and were now restored. We arrived at The Hermitage after a tour of St. Petersburg shortly after noon. Our escorted tour was to be from 1:00 to 4:00 p.m. The Winter Palace itself was unbelievably magnificent. The opulence was beyond description! Room after room of the most magnificent paintings by Rembrandt, da Vinci, Raphael and hundreds of equally famous artists were there to view from a few feet away. At approximately 2:30 p.m., I lost my group as I was in a room with paintings by Rafael and Rembrandt and forgot the time. There was an announcement in English that the palace was to be evacuated immediately and I hurried to catch up with my guide and group only to have a Russian army guard physically stop me. I tried to explain that I was with a tour group that was over there a couple of rooms ahead with my wife. He just kept saying "No! Go!" and pointed in the opposite direction. I tried to explain that my wife needed me and then he became very annoyed and pulled a gun from its holster and actually pushed it into my belly and repeated, "Go!" When I turned he raised his gun and escorted me out of The Winter Palace to the parking lot where I sat on a curb waiting for our group and Irene to return, which was only 15 minutes later. I continue to laugh, as I'm probably one of very few human beings ever escorted out of The Winter Palace at gunpoint!

We left late that evening for Helsinki, Finland where we were met at our ship by a beautiful Finnish lady who was a girlfriend of cousin Christian and who gave us a wonderful walking tour of Helsinki as well as joining us for a delightful meal aboard ship. After Helsinki we returned to Copenhagen where we saw The Little Mermaid statue in the harbor and went to the famous Tivoli Gardens Amusement Park, which was the same as any American amusement park. That evening we flew nonstop over the North Pole in daylight to New York where somebody had opened our suitcase and stolen our new camera with all of our pictures from the trip. Welcome back to the U.S.A.! We then flew to Chicago, changed planes and returned to San Diego and then drove back to Green Valley. Our trip was wonderful, the ship and the veranda cabin were equally great, and we started cruising Holland America every year.

There were many other trips throughout the world that were very special. The two most memorable were the London to St. Petersburg cruise and the cruise from Athens, Greece through the Mediterranean Sea and across the Atlantic Ocean ending in Miami. The longest cruise was round trip from San Diego to Hawaii and then French Polynesia, Bora Bora, Moorea, Tahiti and back home. Don't waste your time going to the South Seas! The Hawaiian Islands, especially the little island of Kauai, are far more beautiful and everybody speaks English!

In our lifetime we have cruised a total of 520 days —506 of those on Holland America. The more we cruised, the better the service and rewards were, including discounts. We also learned from experience that in rough seas the lower decks and cabins in the middle of the ship were far better for sailing then the expensive suites on the higher decks! Irene and I both enjoyed being spoiled on a cruise ship and, as we aged, sailing to and from San Diego became important. Consequently we took several of the same cruises—to Mexico, the Panama Canal and Hawaii. While we were still young enough, we took cruises to and from Alaska while Holland America was repositioning their ships, adding four or five days to a cruise. In our 39 cruises, we've gone to Mexico seven times, the Panama Canal twice, Hawaii eight times and Alaska six times. When we first started cruising, we took three Caribbean cruises and three cruises in the Gulf of Mexico, all of which were for a week. We found these to be way too short, as you spend two days getting there and leaving, with only five days to enjoy. Over the years we found we both enjoyed a 14-18-day cruise much better.

Our most memorable sights were the Winter Palace in St. Petersburg, the British Museum in London, the Acropolis in Athens, the ruins in Ephesus, the Pyramids and Sphinx near Cairo, the Alhambra in Spain, the monkey sitting on Irene's head at Gibraltar and too many more to mention here! Most important was our good health, which allowed us the freedom to enjoy these wonderful years, thank you Lord!

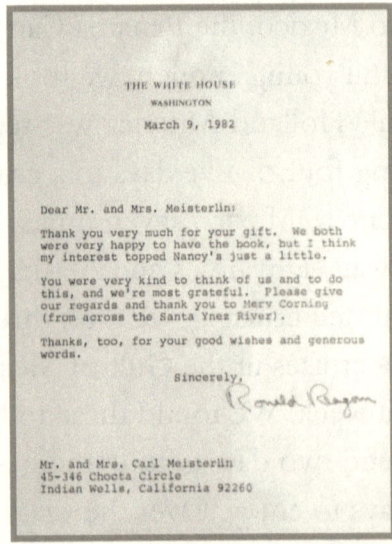

**Photo by Irene:
"The Best Picture I Ever Took of Carl!"**

Chapter 24

All the Celebrities

On a night in the mid-1960s, I made a date for dinner with Chuck Smith, my contact at Northrup, at Perina's on Wilshire Boulevard. Both of us were alone at the time and neither had ever eaten at what was then the number one restaurant in Los Angeles. Northrup was one of my biggest customers at the time and Chuck was a favorite of mine as he had a great sense of humor! As I was entertaining Chuck, I arrived early and found a bar stool in the lounge. The lounge was beautiful, dimly lit and lived up to the restaurant's reputation. When the bartender asked for my order, I answered, "Bombay on the rocks with an onion, my usual martini." At the same time the bartender served my Bombay, the gentleman sitting to my right rose and departed. The lounge was filled but a man standing behind me quickly sat down. The bartender obviously knew this customer as he asked: "Your usual Bombay, sir?" The man didn't answer but did nod his head. At hearing Bombay being ordered I became interested, but said nothing until he was served a beautiful stem glass martini, which the bartender made a big show of shaking over ice and then placing an orange slice on the lip. I couldn't help myself and I turned and said, "I'm a

Bombay drinker also, but I've never seen it served quite like yours." The gentleman turned to me and very politely exclaimed, "The orange slice gives the Bombay an aroma like a fine wine, which I personally enjoy! You should try it, it's different and wonderful!"

    The voice was very familiar and I was only inches away from looking into the eyes of an idol, Cary Grant! I asked the bartender for an orange slice and removed the onion and as Cary Grant suggested, it was seemingly much smoother with a slightly different flavor due to the aroma from the orange slice. Mr. Grant and I talked for about ten minutes and Chuck appeared and I introduced him to Mr. Cary Grant! We talked for another five minutes or so (I don't remember about what), but Mr. Grant was as gracious and ordinary as any man I've ever met, including Ronald Reagan. A maître d' assistant came to the bar and said our booth was ready and I asked Cary to join us. He thanked me for the invitation but had other plans. I had the bill sent to the table and because of Mr. Grant I left an unusually large tip for the bartender. This was the last time I had a Bombay martini without an orange slice. Both Chuck and I were awestruck and the rest of the evening wasn't as memorable. There are not many moments in life when you meet a legend that turns out to be a really good guy!

    In the next ten days I probably told everybody I talked to about meeting Cary Grant and how I viewed him, even physically. This is one story I've never embellished! A couple of months later, I received a small box containing 1,000 business cards with 'Meisterlin' on the front and 'Bombay Gin on the rocks in an 8 oz. glass snifter garnished with an orange slice' on the other! Dave Hall had started a printing business on the side to help his son-in-law in Pennsylvania. Because all of our joint friends were now using my Cary Grant experience and were drinking their Bombay Gin with an orange slice, he had made cards for about six of us with the recipe on the back. Over the balance of my life, I've gotten a ton of mileage telling my story. My close friends did also, but after receiving the cards they could no longer repeat the story in the first person, which was exactly what happened for the first couple of months! The story became famous, and I, infamous. I had Meisterlin martinis brought to me at famous restaurants such as Canlis in Seattle and Honolulu, Michel's in Honolulu, The Blue Fox and Ernie's in San Francisco, 21 Club in New York, the Del Coronado in San Diego and our favorite two restaurants in the desert—Lord Fletcher's and the La Quinta Hotel—by just asking for a Meisterlin! Unfortunately, neither Irene nor I are allowed to drink hard liquor now and in fact I haven't had a Meisterlin in over 20 years, but it was sure a lot of fun!

Another of my favorite, totally unexpected stories has to do with a fun trip to Las Vegas with Ernie Brown, my customer from Hughes aircraft in Fullerton. We had a weekend of fun and games while his family was out of town. I had reserved a mini-suite at the Desert Inn on this trip. When we checked in, everything was fine and as we had very little luggage we went directly by ourselves to our suite. We had driven about seven hours including a short stop in Barstow for a bite to eat and when we reached our room we both decided to shower and clean up somewhat for the evening. We had separate small bedrooms and baths and were in no rush, so it was a little over an hour when we met in the main room and kitchen area. The phone rang and my first thought was that it must be from the front desk as nobody knew that Ernie and I were in Las Vegas—Ernie had made it clear to me that I was to not to mention him to anybody. The voice on the phone said, "Can I speak to Ernie, please? I handed the phone to Ernie, who had a strange look on his face. He replied, "Ernie Brown," and then I could hear but couldn't understand what the voice on the other end of the line was saying. Ernie was saying, "Yes sir, yes sir, yes sir," and continued on saying 'yes sir' until the call ended three or four minutes later! I knew from the tone and Ernie's voice and the look on his face that something must be terribly wrong. I waited but obviously Ernie was deep in thought and I finally asked him what was going on. Ernie, who was upper middle management in the Hughes Fullerton Ground Systems division and middle management in the Hughes Aircraft Company, could hardly speak. When he did, he said, "That was Howard Hughes, who requests our presence in his offices upstairs in 15 minutes!" I asked, "You mean he wants to see me also?" He replied, "Yes, he specifically said to bring you along."

    How he knew we were even there, we both didn't

have a clue! He did say he would have two men escort us up to his office. We were both dressed as well as possible already, so we waited for the knock on the door. When the knock came, I was almost certain that it was exactly 15 minutes to the second! The two men took us to a private elevator which only went to Mr. Hughes' office and residence, which we learned from the men were the complete top two floors. As the one man was unlocking the private elevator, I asked, "How did Mr. Hughes know I was here? I hadn't told anybody, including my immediate family." "Mr. Hughes has eyes and ears everywhere at all times!" he answered.

When we arrived in Mr. Hughes' office, he was alone standing by a window with the light at his back and it was hard to see his face, but he did move forward and shake both of our hands. He was taller than both of us and I thought very thin. He didn't appear very muscular, but he certainly was anything but weak when it came to the handshake. I remember thinking he was almost 6' 1" and weighed 175 pounds. He offered us drinks from a mini-bar. Ernie asked for water and I had a soft drink. He had a half-full glass of clear liquid, which could have been water but was not in a water glass. I could tell that Ernie was not his usual exuberant self, but I became even more alert to my surroundings and the man we were facing! Frankly, I was frightened for Ernie; except for wondering why was I included. Mr. Hughes, at that moment, possibly having the same exact thoughts, said to Ernie, "Please relax, you've done nothing wrong, your job is not in danger, the opposite in fact, and I just need to talk to you about a personal problem that I'm trying to prevent within the Hughes Corporation. I think there is a possibility that you can help me make a very critical management decision either now or in the future. I don't think Carl being here is a problem. In fact I asked him so that you would be more comfortable as we talk!"

Ernie did seem to visibly relax. Mr. Hughes was looking at Ernie mostly, but watching my reaction also. He then questioned Ernie about all the media attention being given to his ex-top management executives Ramos and Woolridge, who had recently resigned and started a new electronic corporation called TRW. He then asked Ernie, "Have you heard of any other of our associates that might be thinking of doing the same? Ernie, it's extremely important to me that I don't lose men of this caliber from our team. Have you heard any rumors about Brubaker at Fullerton, who is irreplaceable? Anything at all? I'm not asking you to rat or squeal on anybody, I just need to know so I can do a better job of holding this company together in the future. If you know nothing at all, fine, but if anything comes to your ears in the future, both at Fullerton or any other division, I'd like you to call me on my private line immediately. Again, anything that has to do with management!" He then took a pen and a small piece of paper and I assumed he wrote his private number and folded it and handed it to Ernie who placed it carefully in his billfold. Mr. Hughes then said to me that our weekend was on Hughes Aircraft, including food, drinks, our suite, all tips and the shows in the showroom.

With that he stood up and walked us to the door, shook our hands, opened the door and told the two men to return us to our suite and be sure to give us first-class attention and anything we wanted during our stay. The men did just that except now they were very talkative and on the way down to our room explained that Ernie was seen on camera entering the hotel and as a management employee was recognized. Somehow they also found a picture of me in the files entering Hughes Fullerton and put the connection between my being the scrap collector and Ernie being responsible for such together and Mr. Hughes took it from there! He really did want to talk to Ernie and I believe the subject matter was weighing heavily on his mind. The balance of the weekend went super for me, but Ernie never quite recovered! This didn't end here for both Ernie and I. Corporate called Master Metals to bid for the scrap contract at two other divisions within four months and we actually won one of the two. The following month Ernie had a change in title to general manager and moved up a notch on the corporate chart and an increase in wages. He didn't say how much, but I had the impression it was sizable!

Having met Mr. Hughes and read all about his health problems in the later years and then with the coming of AIDS and/or HIV in the 1980s, I've always thought that he might have been one of the first victims of this horrible disease! This is pure speculation on my part, but from what I've read before and after his demise it sure sounds like AIDS to me. The man that Ernie met that afternoon was a considerate, empathetic corporate gentleman—not what the media generally portrayed.

Thanks to my being an announcer and starter on the celebrity tee box at La Quinta Country Club for 14+ years and our involvement with the Bob Hope Sponsorship Committee (and at times the second largest employer in the Valley), I met all types of celebrities from sports figures, movie stars, musicians and lots of politicians—both Democrats, Republicans and Independents. The one thing these people had in common was they liked the game of golf! Bob Hope gave participation in the Classic to anybody that would draw people. He also had about 50 people a year who still bought their way into the Classic. By 1994, for a $20,000 entry fee anyone could play.

President Eisenhower, who lived at El Dorado Country Club, was very close to Arnold Palmer and another wonderful desert rat and close friend of Arnie's, namely Ernie Dunlevie, who owned Bermuda Dunes Country Club, which had a small airport. In the early years of the Classic you could land an Air Force One, a 707 there. President Eisenhower and many other prominent members of Congress used this airport regularly. Bob Hope lent his name to the tournament in the early 1960s and donated 40 acres of his 640 acres of land bordering Bob Hope Drive to build the famous Eisenhower Medical Center, which attracted the finest medical professionals in the world! But the glue that made the classic so successful was actually President Eisenhower to begin with, and then

Arnie and Ernie, who attracted the leading people in the desert and primarily Arnie, who attracted golf professionals and fans from all over! In the 30 years I lived in the desert, Ernie was the behind the scenes and unpaid general manager of the Classic!

President Ford, a very avid golfer who was better than the TV showed, preferred to play La Quinta Country Club over any other golf course in the Valley! The club always allowed President Ford to play when requested. There was a major problem with this, as La Quinta Country Club was a private club owned by 400 members. When the president would play, he had a group of eight Secret Service men carrying guns who would be escorting and guarding him—in front, to the side and back—knocking on windows and doors and even entering your home if the door happened to be unlocked! If you had a home on the fairway, and La Quinta had approximately 150, it was no fun to have the Secret Service performing their duties!

There was a vacant 3 1/2 acre parcel of land between the second and eighth fairways near the first and eighth greens directly in front of our home. I found out that President Ford was dealing with the contractor/owner of the property and had made an application for membership to the club. I went to the presidents of five HOAs, which were greatly affected by the Secret Service, and to a few famous members such as Andy Williams, Ed Crowley and Bill Pettibone, and called an emergency meeting. I explained what I had just learned and asked for their opinion on the matter. The vote was 8 to 1 to blackball President Ford! We wrote on a normal piece of writing paper that we, the members of the five HOAs, did not approve the membership application of President Gerald Ford! I then carried this letter and presented it to the manager of the club to be handed to the La Quinta Country Club president and his board. The very next day I received a call from the manager asking if I were available to meet with the board of directors at a special meeting that evening at 5:00 p.m. The meeting didn't take very long as the first question was how many residences do your five HOAs include? I stated 130. There was one member of the board who had a private residence on the 10th hole. The president asked his fellow board members for comments and the gentleman living on the 10th hole stated emphatically he was against President Ford and the Secret Service in our gated community! One member spoke in favor of having the President being a member but wasn't sure that having the Secret Service on the property 24 hours a day was tolerable. The president then asked for a show of votes about the application and the vote was 3 to 1 and he added his vote making the final vote 4 to 1! It was immediately decided that we should visit President Ford and ask him to withdraw his application and the reasons why. The manager of the club then placed the call to President Ford asking for an appointment. The President graciously invited our president to his home late afternoon on a Monday after his golf game. While waiting for the manager to return, a couple of the board members asked me what the president should do about the Secret

Service, as all country clubs would have the same problem? I suggested that the President might buy a parcel of land outside the gated community where they could live and not be visible except when President Ford played golf!

When the manager returned with a message, the board president asked me to join him in speaking with President Ford! We drove to the residence in Thunderbird Heights where President Ford and Betty were residing. We gave the President the club's decision and he understood entirely and was very gracious! He asked me, as he knew me from many years on the celebrity tee, if there was a solution to his problem? I said, "You don't have the same problem right here at Thunderbird, as there aren't over 20 houses fronting the fairways, which is an old but unique design—the golf course came first and then the homes! If you can find a piece of land close by, it would be ideal for a small compound!"

This story had a happy ending as President Ford did find a parcel of land big enough to build his home and compound outside the perimeter of the course, but was allowed an entrance gate for golf carts! From then on when I saw President Ford he greeted me calling me Carl. Betty Ford is another story. When sober she was the greatest asset the President had. She was so strong—she overcame her alcoholism and founded the Betty Ford Clinic for alcoholism on the grounds of the Eisenhower Medical Center, which over the years due to its celebrity status has saved millions of alcoholics from self-destruction. They were a wonderful couple!

The list of politicians who participated in the Classic were many from both political parties but one worth mentioning was Tip O'Neill, a Democrat and adversary to President Reagan. He was a typical, funny, handshaking, and holding babies for the camera type of politician and was particularly a pal of the media. He made it a point to always be on camera. In truth, if he had been in private business, it would've crashed and burned immediately!
I found this to be true about most politicians during my lifetime and not just Democrats!

The celebrities I was lucky to meet who were special gentleman were many: Jack Lemmon, Walter Matthau, John Wayne, Ward Bond, Frank Sinatra (when sober), Leo Durocher, Jimmy Van Husen, Desi Arnaz, Neil Armstrong, Lawrence Welk, Jackie Gleason, Frank Capra and coach Colonel Red Blaik, to name a few. On the other side of the coin were guys who weren't the public image as reported. Frank Sinatra was the most generous man I ever met, but if he had one drink too many he physically wanted to fight. He had a mean streak. His last wife Barbara wouldn't marry him unless he gave up drinking, which he did on their wedding day! The night before at his bachelor party he had too much and got in trouble with the law, which was reported in the local paper the following day, and the wedding was almost terminated!

Contrary to everything reported, the most dishonest man I ever met and did business with was Bob Hope. I had a business dealing where I brought him a buyer for

40 acres of commercial property adjoining the Eisenhower Medical Center. We all agreed to the purchase agreement 100%, shook hands and turned the paperwork over to our legal counsels to approve. After 10 days, the buyer called and asked why we hadn't received any documents. I called our legal counsel and he responded that Mr. Hope's lawyers had just informed him that Mr. Hope had sold the property to another party! When I called Hope's business office and asked for an explanation, I was told, "tough luck!" I personally was on the hook for my lawyer's bill. Approximately two years later, representing Lewis homes, again with Laura Williams at my side, I had a luncheon meeting with Mr. Hope and his business manager in Los Angeles. Lewis Homes wished to purchase the 160-acre parcel on the north side of Eisenhower Medical Center to build a small golf course, with middle-class homes all having golf-course views. We again agreed on price and terms and of course I bought lunch. The business manager, Laura, and myself all signed a piece of paper and Hope initialed. Ten days later again with no word from Bob Hope, I called the business manager and received the same answer as before, Mr. Hope has sold the property to another buyer and again I paid a fee to my lawyer. How stupid can one be?

    Hope hired a wonderful retired general by the name of Bill Yancy to work on a year around basis for the Classic organization and tournament around 1980—a wonderful choice and a true honest gentleman! In 1984, when Irene and I were helping host the Classic Ball, I worked with General Yancy for several weeks. During this time, I let General Yancy know my true feelings about Hope! The Classic Ball was its usual success and Bob Hope filmed the performers and then used the clips on his Bob Hope TV specials. A week after the Classic Tournament, General Yancy called me and said that he had talked with Hope and persuaded him to play golf with us and whoever I invited for a game at La Quinta on a mutually agreed-upon day and time. Bill and I worked out a day and time that agreed with Hope, and I invited my close friend Dave Hall down from Palos Verdes.

The day before, I was stricken with an Asian muscle virus and if I'd had any brains I would've stayed in bed. Because the General had put this game together and Dave was already making his three-hour drive, and it was with Bob Hope, I dragged myself to the golf course. When I arrived at the club, General Yancy and Dave were there and eager to start. We waited for over an hour and then the General called Hope and got no answer. He then called Hope's business office in Los Angeles and received a negative response. He called his own desert office, and then his own home number and there was no message from Hope. After waiting nearly two hours, I found a member to complete our foursome and bad back and all I teed up and foolishly played 18 holes! At 3:30 a.m. that night I was rushed to Eisenhower Medical Center to the emergency room where I was admitted and spent four days. For the next three weeks I could do nothing but lie there until I got better. For the rest of my life I've had a bad lower back, which comes and goes, and is a major painful problem for me today. General Yancy never explained to me why Hope didn't keep our date. I like telling anybody that wants to listen that Bob Hope not only welched on two business deals that cost me money, but even caused me bodily harm!

There were four men who traveled the world together having fun and playing games of all kinds who spent at least four months a year in the desert. As they aged and retired, their time in the desert increased. The four men I'm speaking of were Bing Crosby, Phil Harris, Father Len Scannell and Ted Enoch. I knew all four personally and I heard by phone from Phil's wife, Alice Faye, at least once a week. Ted Enoch, who was not an avid golfer or card player, was bored and had a real estate salesman's license and worked with and for me for eight years until I retired. Whenever Alice couldn't find Phil, she would call our office asking for Ted and if Ted was unavailable, the calls would be forwarded to me, as Alice knew wherever Ted was, Phil was sure to be there! The ringleader of this group was not Bing Crosby. The brains, the humor and the business acumen were all Phil Harris! He was a hell of a guy. Alice and Phil belonged and resided at Thunderbird Country Club. In the card room there was a small private game room for poker. Over the entrance Phil had a gorgeous plaque made that stated, "God's Waiting Room!" Hanging on the golf course at the halfway house men's bathroom on the inside above the entry door, another plaque was placed much like the card room. It stated: "Never pass a Pisser, Never trust a Fart, Never waste a Hard On!" These plaques were strictly for men's eyes only!

Father Scannell was by far the best golfer of the four, a 2 handicap. The Father, a Catholic priest who was a wartime chaplain who was right there on the border of WWII combat, was a large physical man. He traveled with Crosby at least six months a year and was never asked to pay for anything. Crosby, I was told, footed the bill entirely. If Len needed or wanted anything, it was taken care of. He was not just a religious priest—he was a real gentleman. Ted told me on several occasions that Father Scannell was able to extricate the three wild men companions from all sorts of trouble all over the world. By being a man of the cloth, the group escaped many serious situations!

Ted Enoch was a little man who was a very successful Chevrolet dealer in Southgate, California. Adjoining the dealership on Long Beach Boulevard, Ted also owned Enoch's Supper Club, a large excellent bar and grill. He also owned and leased commercial properties on both sides of the boulevard. What he really enjoyed was yachting and he had a 62-foot yacht anchored in Newport Harbor, which the group used once or twice a year for their fun and games. He just loved being a part of this group and he was the sweetest, most easy-going gentleman you'll ever meet! I think of Ted as the "go for" of the group. They were infamous for their card games held in a special party house at Crosby's compound high up in the cove in Palm Desert.

Another celebrity who was a close neighbor at the La Quinta Country Club was Andy Williams, whom I played golf with quite often! Most of the membership at the club thought that Andy was aloof or stuck up, as he didn't communicate unless forced to do so. He also drank Becks beer and we could always tell when Andy was in town because of the empty bottles of Becks in the waste containers on the tee boxes. Andy admitted one day that he had become an alcoholic, drinking no hard liquor but only beer, and he had quit his beer drinking just last week. I had no idea. I was there when he married Claudine and I was there when their first child was born. Even after their ugly divorce, Andy financially took care of Claudine for the rest of his life. I played golf with him on his last game at the club before moving to Branson, Missouri. What the membership didn't realize about Andy was that he was extraordinarily shy. They don't make many men as down-to-earth and genuine as Andy Williams, particularly celebrities!

The finest celebrity I've ever known was President Ronald Reagan and the second finest was golfer Arnold Palmer! They had two qualities in common—the first was graciousness and the second was that they were both leaders. They touched the lives of everyone they met or who took the time to listen to what they said! They were supreme gentlemen!

Chapter 25

Timing
and Dumb Luck

Today I believe in genetics and timing. These next two stories have to do with luck associated with timing. In December 1963, my buddy Orv Perkins of Hollister Coil Spring arranged a luncheon meeting for me with the President of Mattel Toy Company at Mattel's corporate headquarters in Los Angeles. There were no freeways available, so I was forced to drive from Santa Fe Springs via Imperial Highway to Mattel. This took over an hour and with no available communications, I arrived barely on time.

When I announced myself to the girl at the entrance she said, "Mr. Meisterlin, I don't think Mr. Miramontes is here, but let me get you his special assistant." A very nice looking lady appeared immediately and said that he'd had an emergency at home and had to leave, but he would like to reschedule this luncheon early next week if possible? I had $50 exactly in cash to buy lunch. I arrived back at the corner of Imperial Boulevard and Prairie just before noon and I was staring directly at the Hollywood Park Racetrack. I had no plans and I was not due back in the office until approximately 3:30 p.m. 'Why not take in a couple of races,' I thought, so I continued into the racetrack parking lot, which cost nothing in those days. I paid a dollar and a half grandstand entry fee and $.75 for a racing form—the daily racing program came free with the entry.

I went in and found a seat on a bench in the sun and began handicapping the first two races. I settled on a horse in the first race that was approximately 6 to 1 and as I had over $40 to bet and buy a hot dog and a soft drink, I decided to bet $10 to win—after all I was only staying two races. The horse I bet won and paid $75 even! I now had time to go get my hot dog and drink, as I already knew who I'd bet on in the second race. My horse in the second race was 9 to 2 and I bet $10 to win and $10 to place. While waiting for the second race to start, I looked at the third race and one horse jumped out of the form. It would be in my estimation one of the three favorites in the race, but it looked darn good in the form! The second race was run and my horse won! When I cashed this ticket it paid close to $65. The third race was due to start at 1:50 p.m. and figuring an hour to the office I still had plenty of time to stay for one more race. For a change I didn't change my mind at the last minute, an occasionally bad habit of mine. My horse was 5 to 2, the second choice, and place money wouldn't be great enough to bother betting, so I bet $30 to win. While I was waiting, I began looking at the fourth race. My horse won and paid $7.60 to win and I received $114. The next race was to start at 2:24 p.m. and figuring time for the race leaving the parking lot, and driving home, I'd be only about ten minutes late, but I was on Hollywood Park's money so I decided to stay one more race. The horse I liked in the fourth race at race time was 4 to 1 and I bet $50 to win which it did and paid $10.40 to win and I collected $260 Wow! Now I was really in the money. I couldn't go back to work now!

So I looked at race number five and again there was a standout horse that was going to be a big favorite, so I bet $100 to win. Winning makes one hungry, so I had another hot dog and soft drink. I started looking at race number six and again found a horse that looked pretty solid and might pay a good price. My horse in the fifth won and paid $5.80 to win and I collected another $290. No way was I going to leave now! In the sixth race, the horse I liked wasn't even 5 to 1 on the board, so as a fourth choice I decided to bet $100 to win and $100 to place and started handicapping the seventh and feature race of the day. My horse in the sixth won and I collected $760! The horse in the feature race that I liked started at 4 to 1 on the board, but the betting public didn't agree and by race time the odds were up to 6 to 1. When they were 5 to 1, I still had confidence and I bet $200 to win and $200 to place. About 30 seconds before the race started, my odds increased to 6 to 1 and I began doubting myself. My horse won again and I collected $1,750.

It was now the time of day that driving across Los Angeles would be the worst, so I decided to wait one more race. The horse I liked was a favorite so I bet $200 to win, which it did, and I left Hollywood Park with almost exactly $4,150. I had won eight straight races—

thank you Willie Shoemaker, my racetrack mentor! I gave Irene $150 that night to buy a new outfit or whatever, and bought a new fork truck for Master Metals, which cost in excess of $3,500!

Before I start my very last story, which has everything to do with the Del Mar Racetrack and then the Del Mar Thoroughbred Club, I would like to thank all the people who for over 38 years have been friends, particularly: Barbara Miller, Peter Caruso and Nancy, Sue, Kathy, Jimmy, Joe, Mike, Juan and a few others who've provided me with fun and good luck!

In early September 1951 on a Thursday before Labor Day weekend, Mildred took Claudia (then almost two) home to visit her parents for a long weekend. On Friday at work a couple of my cohorts who knew I was a racetrack addict mentioned San Diego and its wonderful racetrack, Del Mar, which was a 2 1/2 hour drive. On Saturday, with nothing better to do, I walked down the street and purchased a racing form and started handicapping the races for Sunday. There were eight races beginning at 2:00 p.m. I only found one horse that appeared to be a long shot and that fit a race perfectly. The horse's name was Two Ton Tony and was entered in the second race, which would start approximately at 2:28 p.m. There were seven horses entered and all six of the others were front-runners who had to take the lead to win. The fastest of all out of the starting gate appeared to be number seven, which would be a tremendous advantage for my number six horse, Two Ton Tony. I had actually seen this horse being worked at Golden Gate Fields as a two-year-old. I knew he had some talent, but the racing form showed that he was a one-time closer and usually came up short and had mostly third, fourth and fifth finishes, all making the stable money, but not the betting public.

    I left on Sunday at 10:30 a.m. and drove to San Diego on the Pacific Coast Highway. There were no freeways at the time, leaving myself an extra hour before the first race to be on time. Mistake! It was a Sunday morning on Labor Day weekend and I was driving strictly through the beach cities and it was very crowded. I arrived in Oceanside only 12 miles from the racetrack at 1:30 p.m. The weather was much nicer in San Diego and the beaches were all packed with people and cars and by the time I made it to the racetrack parking lot it was 2:00 p.m. and the parking place I found was barely in the lot.

    As I left my car, I heard the roar of the crowd of the start of the first race! There was only one entrance gate and I was as far away as possible. When I made the gate, I could see that the general admission entrance was on the far end of the grandstand and as it was 2:15 p.m. I started running as fast as I was able, to buy my ticket. Luckily, there wasn't any line at the entry gate, but on entering the grandstand where the pari-mutuel windows were, the betting lines were long and I didn't see any screens posting the odds for the second race. I chose the shortest line I could find and waited and waited and finally got to the window and bet $20 to win on number six, which was one half the money I came with! I then pushed my way out to the racetrack and found the best place I could to watch the race just as the track announcer said, "They're at the gate!" I finally found an odds board and almost had a heart attack. Two Ton Tony was 50 to 1! I never had bet a horse over 25 to 1 in my life and still haven't except win, place and show. I turned and started running back to the window and the track announcer said, "And they're off!"

By the time I got back to where I could see the race, they were entering the far turn and my horse was dead last and appeared to be falling back. And then, all of a sudden, the first, then the second and then the third began falling back rapidly and number six was fourth. At the top of the stretch Two Ton Tony had moved into third and was gaining and number seven started slowing and with over a 16th of a mile to go we were second and still gaining. With 25 yards left, we took first and won by over one length! The horse had a masterful ride from George Tanaguchi and I won $1,020, the largest amount I've ever won on a single bet. The reason this story is so important is, if everything hadn't gone wrong that day, there is no way I would've bet $20 to win when I saw the odds at 50 to 1. It was just plain dumb stupid luck!

I learned a couple things that day. First, San Diego was far nicer then L.A., which is still true. The second thing was: when you do a good job handicapping, stay with your choice! In my lifetime, in addition to the two stories mentioned, in the early days of pick six wagers, I won $5,700 on a $24 ticket and $7,200 on a $32 ticket.

I quit playing pick sixes in the mid-1970s when they started having betting seminars before the races and started pooling money from 50 to 100 bettors. Instead of picking winners, they eliminated losers and the winning ticket could cost as much as $10,000. It's a bad bet for an average horseplayer! I'm still lucky today, although I don't come close to making my expenses. I bet very little and I'm there purely for enjoyment. Irene fares better than I do by betting gray horses with cute names!

Chapter 26

The Natural, The Inspirational, The Adhesive, The Challenge, The Mother and The Sons

Our next-to-youngest daughter was born on January 28, 1953, a beautiful baby girl we named Deborah Susan, who became "Debbie" forever. From the beginning, she was "The Natural."

When you have several children you remember many little trivial things and one of my first memories of Debbie as a baby was when holding her in my arms, she was like a feather, whereas all of my other children had weight! When she was just out of diapers, I came home to find her walking around the room on her hands. When she was five years old, without lessons, she sat at our piano and played melodies. She also drew comic stick figures with a pencil or pen, not crayons, before reaching kindergarten. By the age of four she was very much a tomboy and resented being dressed as a very cute little girl, which she was!

In the early spring of 1958, when Debbie had just turned five, she was small for her age and not yet in kindergarten. I would take the girls to the swimming pool at Hacienda Country Club regularly. The swimming pool had a five-meter diving platform, which was allowed back then. Chuck Soper's son was an Olympic Team diver from USC who practiced regularly using the diving platform. He practiced all types of exotic athletic dives and everybody at the pool watched and admired.

One day I was standing talking to my friend Syd Hayes when I noticed Debbie starting to climb the ladder to the platform. She was barely big enough to reach the next rung on the ladder and I was afraid she might fall. I didn't want to frighten her, so without uttering a sound I ran to the bottom of the ladder in case she lost her grasp. She made it to the platform and I still said nothing. The Soper boy had been practicing a dive where he stood with his back to the pool, shoved off backwards and then touched his toes and entered the water perfectly. I had no idea what Debbie was going to do and I was scared to death! She went to the edge of the platform, looked down, turned around, poised on the end on her toes and duplicated his dive—not perfectly but it was damn good! I then asked her to get out of the pool and told her that the platform was not to be used by anyone under the age of six. I fibbed! I really wasn't worried about her diving, she had no fear, but I was concerned with the difficulty of the ladder reaching the platform. I remember Syd remarking, "That's one hell of a little girl you've got there!"

When Debbie was nine, she decided she wanted a bike to ride to school and back, but she didn't want any old bike, she wanted a unicycle. So, on her birthday Debbie received her unicycle and proceeded to ride to school and back daily. The neighbor next door during the trampoline craze bought a full-size trampoline and had it installed in their backyard. When I arrived home that evening my kids all wanted me to go next door and see the new trampoline that our neighbors had invited them to use. They forced me onto the trampoline and I took one bounce and a second where I ended flat on my face, half on and half off! Debbie proceeded to get on the trampoline and started bouncing and then doing front flips and backflips perfectly and within minutes was doing the flips with twists! No problem, she had perfect balance.

When we purchased our second horse, a gorgeous black-and-white half-quarter horse and half-Welsh pony, it was intended for Debbie more or less. The horse, which we named "Princess," was almost 12 hands high and weighed less than 1,000 pounds. She was truly a beautiful little horse. The only trouble was that she didn't want anybody on her back, and so we sent Princess to Knotts Berry Farm to be re-broken. The following week after she returned and was cured of bucking, there was a big horse show in East Whittier, which the girls entered. In the gala entrance parade, Debbie was riding Princess towards the rear of the string of horses. She looked magnificent and honestly the crowd was loud with applause! All of a sudden, Princess took off and started running around the ring and then started bucking. Everybody started yelling and finally Debbie was thrown into the air where she did a complete flip and landed on her two feet without a problem. The crowd exploded! Debbie walked to the rail, getting out of the way of all of the horses. Princess continued running faster and faster around the ring and nobody could catch her. As she approached where I was standing, I yelled, "Princess!" and she stopped dead in her tracks, walked over to me and started nuzzling me. We tried one more time to have her broken and it didn't work, so we were forced to sell her. We did see her one more time, by accident. We went to a Barnum and Bailey Circus at The Forum in L.A. and when the program began, there was Princess pulling the cart with the Queen of the show! It was definitely Princess!

When Debbie was in the fifth grade, the school had a softball team on the playground and there was only one fifth grader on the team, the catcher, which was Debbie. The PTA at the grammar school didn't think it was appropriate and the principal had some complaints, but after the next summer when football season started and Debbie was now an upperclassman and playing quarterback, the school district cracked down on the after school playground program by originating a girls program to go along with the boys' program. They banned Debbie from playing with the boys!

Another funny story about Debbie indirectly has to do with Chuck and Scott starting in T-Ball. The first day they actually held a draft just like the NFL. There were ten previously-appointed managers for the ten teams and they had a lottery for the order in making their choices. There were approximately 150 boys to be picked, all between five and seven years old. I knew not one person, parent, coach or kid except Chuck and Scott! The coach, who won the lottery and had the very first pick, picked Chuck, who was six. Later on in the draft, with his fourth choice, he picked Scott, who was barely five and not too well co-ordinated then. I had never seen or talked to this nice-looking young man, but when the draft finished and all the boys reported to their coaches, I did walk over and listen to their first instructions, which I thought were excellent. Finally, when this ended, I approached the coach and asked with nobody else listening, "Why did you pick Chuck when you could've had anybody?" His reply was, "Well, he's Debbie Meisterlin's younger brother."

**Debbie Meisterlin Keller
"The Natural"
with Arnold Palmer**

Debbie could successfully accomplish anything as a young girl and without coaching. When it came time for her to choose what she wanted to do, it was golf. I didn't waste time trying to teach her myself, so at the age of 11 she began taking golf lessons from the best teaching professionals I could find, and that's how she got started! She was a natural and I always have wondered what she could of accomplished as a gymnast, tennis player, musician or artist. Today, she's a retired standup comedienne and golf pro! She's married to a fine man and seemingly they couldn't be happier!

    In the mid-1970s, my oldest daughter Claudia, an RN, gave birth to her first child, a little girl they named Rebecca, who became "Becky" to the family. It was a long and difficult delivery for Claudia and shortly thereafter, being a nurse, she realized there was a problem. Actually there were several problems—hydrocephalus, diabetes and severe rheumatoid arthritis! They operated on Becky for the hydrocephalus as soon as possible, placing a shunt in her head to drain the water from the brain. Irene and I both didn't believe that little Becky would survive four months. She was truly a medical marvel! Becky not only survived, but with Claudia and Tim as parents, fought her way through life for a period of 36 years! Unfortunately, due to the shunt in her cranium, she didn't grow in height properly, which didn't help. But she had several very positive human traits: intelligence, a strong will to be independent and self-reliant, a wonderful sense of humor and a love of people! I remember visiting Tim and Claudia's home, a two-story house with the bedrooms all on the second floor and Becky crawling up the stairway. She was four at the time and her rheumatoid arthritis was so painful that crawling up the stairs was the only method available to her. I ran to the stairs only to have her reprimand me, stating, "Leave me be, I can do this myself!"

When she graduated from high school, like any normal student she decided to go away to college to be on our own. She finally decided that Cal State Stanislaus, commonly called "Turkey Tech," located in Turlock in the Central Valley of California was where she wanted to be. She joined a national sorority and pursued a degree in education to become a schoolteacher. She accomplished most of her goals in life on her own, but with help always there when needed from Claudia and Tim. Every day she lived was an inspiration to all of us who knew her and touched her life. Yes, she was a medical marvel but more than that, she was a model for how life should be lived! Tragically, at the age of 36, the good Lord decided that Becky should join and help him. I still see and hear her every day. Thank you Becky!

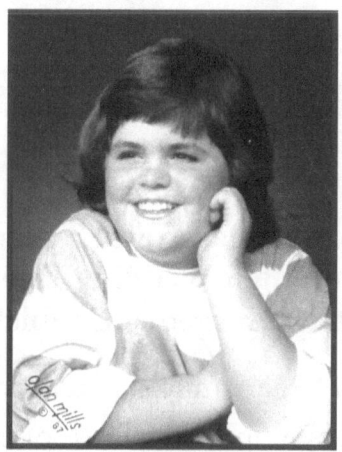

**1988
Granddaughter
Becky Tynan
"The Inspirational"**

"The Adhesive," who has held the Meisterlin family together all these years, is Claudia, my oldest and most revered child! With a somewhat unstable mother, a father anxious to succeed and a bit of a playboy by heritage, and five siblings, Claudia has for 55 years held this clan together, with help from husband, Tim!

**1970
"The Adhesive"
Claudia and Tim Tynan
on their Wedding Day
One Gorgeous Couple!**

In raising a large family, a parent tries to instill the desire for each person individually to prepare to meet and succeed in life without help from anyone. Simply said, I tried to raise children separately to stand on their own two feet. Claudia is the only person in our dysfunctional family, except for Tim, that everybody in the family trusts and believes in. (Unfortunately some members not only won't talk to others, but won't attend family gatherings if certain other family members attend. There are two that feel that way about me. It hurts, but I can live with that.) If there is a problem, Claudia is always front and center working with the family's best interest at heart—and I repeat—always! She's intelligent, has a great sense of humor and empathy to match. She has always had a heart of gold! They just don't make human beings better than my daughter Claudia!

One of the most challenging parts of my life has to do with my daughter Cynthia. She was the middle daughter and from the time she was born, she was a very difficult child. She had colic as a baby and Mildred and I didn't get a decent night's sleep until Cynthia was two. When she became school age, she was always in trouble and barely able to pass to the next grade levels. One moment Cynthia would be full of energy and without a care in the world and the next moment find herself in the total depths of despair. We knew something was wrong, but none of the doctors or psychiatrists back then could identify it with any certainty. We spent more time and money for professional advice for Cynthia than we did on things for all the other children combined.

Mildred's family on her father's side had a history of schizophrenia. Her uncle had been institutionalized in San Jose, California. It wasn't until much later that we realized that Cynthia needed help. By then, she was grown up and on her own.

Cynthia's condition was very difficult then and it continues to be heartbreaking for the entire family, especially her own children. It affected our marriage when our children were growing up and continues to affect us all very deeply today.

**"The Challenge"
Cynthia Meisterlin Mezenski**

Our daughter Julie was 16 when we first met in Palm Springs in 1971. She was a very attractive teenager and active at Palm Springs High School, including being the statistician for the boy's baseball team helping coach Kilgore, which she performed excellently and loved! Coach Kilgore was equally fond of Julie and he and his wife had Julie involved in all of the baseball team activities.

Upon graduating from high school, Julie attended College of the Desert, a junior college located in Palm Desert. She then attended San Diego State University (SDSU) for two years before receiving her B.S. degree in marketing.

In 1986 she married Jamie Wills, also a SDSU grad and along came the two wonderful kids, Michael and Kathryn. Mike, 26 and Kathryn, soon to be 23 are now out of the nest, living and working on their own. Julie and Jamie reside in Escondido.

Below is a picture of Julie with her first-born child Michael. The expression on her face says it all: "Look what I produced!" Irene and I have always believed she was born to be a mother. She continues to be a great mother and wife to Jamie and has grown to be a finer and even better woman with maturity.

From the beginning, my son Chuck became the closest thing to a true son that Irene ever had. At the same time, Julie, in my mind, became a daughter for life and one that I am extremely proud of! Like her mother, she is special!

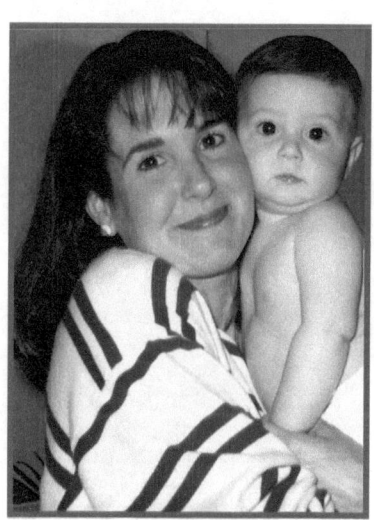

"The Mother"
Julie Wills
and Michael

I could write many more pages just about my sons. The boys were raised to be gentlemen and handle their own lives and be responsible parents. Fortunately, I am proud to say that both my sons Carl Albert and Scott Carl have completely accomplished my wishes. That really says it all!

Chapter 27

The Attitude of Gratitude

According to the story my birth mother told Irene, I was lucky to be born. I was a "blue baby," and she could not have any more children, nor did she desire to be a mother! I was extremely fortunate to have a father and stepmother, Edith, who wanted me. My Grandmother Paprocki, who actually raised me from age one to five, loved me and was intelligent enough to send me to my father and his new wife in California. It was also Grandma Paprocki who set the wheels in motion by teaching me to play cards, both Rummy and Gin Rummy at the age of four. Looking back over 80 years, there's no doubt in my mind that the extreme good fortune and luck due to timing started at that age.

My missing active combat in World War II and the Korean War altogether would never have occurred if I hadn't skipped the first grade—which was entirely due to playing cards! I was even lucky when my first wife Mildred divorced me so when Irene came into my life I appreciated a great lady!

The friends I made in grammar school, the Goodison twins, and my adversary Pat Smith Ramsey, who made me a better student, all helped prepare me for a successful life. In middle school, coach J. P. O'Neill made me confident that I could attain my goals. In high school, my two closest friends, George Alexander and Bob McDonald, always believed in me, right or wrong, and stuck by me to the end of their lives. In college, Dave MacElhatton was always there for me to lean on.

The two most influential men in my life story were Bill Garvai and Dave Hall, who from the very first moment became my two closest friends and confidantes until the day they passed on! Most of the success I've had in life is due to Dave and Bill. The last time Irene and I visited New York, we visited Dave in his office on the 39th floor of the World Trade Center, building number two, with an absolutely perfect view of the Statue of Liberty. We had lunch together on the 56th floor, which is where the plane hit on September 11, 2001! Luckily, David retired many years before. During his stay in New York City, he joined the most famous Bridge club in the world and played for money with the likes of Omar Sharif. When he and Catherine left New York, they moved back to their original area and built a gorgeous home near a private country club. Dave played golf three to four days a week and traveled with his son Deke twice a month to New York to the Bridge club to compete. Dave said to me that Deke was his only Bridge partner in life that came close to being as good as Lloyd Rentsch.

Bill Garvai was my closest friend in my lifetime and like Dave he was always there giving me a boost or calming me down, whatever it took, and I'm proud to say it was a two-way street. A few years after the turn of the century, Bill had knee replacement surgery, which I didn't hear about for over two weeks while he was in a coma. I called Alma and she said, "Don't waste your time as he's just lying there and can't communicate!" I was having a problem at the time, but my grandson R. Scott drove me to the Torrance hospital. We entered Bill's private room to find a nurse sitting by his bedside. We introduced ourselves and I said that Bill was my closest friend in life and I'd come to pay my respects. She replied that for over two weeks he had been completely non-responsive.

    She then leaned over inches from Bill's left ear and said loudly, "Your best friend Carl is here!" To our amazement, his lips moved and I was almost sure that I understood what he said, which was barely audible! I asked my grandson Scott, "Did you understand what he said?" Scott replied, "I thought he said 'I had an 86 last week.'" I looked at the nurse and she nodded yes and that's exactly what I had heard. The nurse then said, "That's the first sign of hope we've noticed!" Three or four nights later early in the morning, I was having a dream about Bill and I playing the fourth hole at Palos Verdes when I holed a sand shot for a Birdie. In the dream, the look on Bill's face was 'what's the big deal!' All of a sudden I woke up. It was 4:36 a.m. I found out later from Anne, Bill's daughter, that the time on the death certificate was identical.

    In our waning years, we've been blessed by many friends and neighbors, and this again helps me in being the luckiest man in the world. Thank you Donna and Stan Rood, Jan and Fred Schudel, Gayle Coover, Pete Kohl, Tommy Morrison, Fanny Freeman, Pat Williams, Betty and Harry Williams, Merv Johnson, Sue and Greg Fahey, Maha and Gus Calderon, Dave and Kelli Sierra Lee Velasco, Billy Peters (my nephew), George Blanda, Chuck Knox, Jack Benny, my Bridge partner Ken Gilbert (and the best Bridge partner I've had in the last 40 years), his wife Sandy and many, many other wonderful people who brought happiness into our lives. We only hope that we reciprocated. We were extremely fortunate and lucky that are lives touched!

January 1979
La Quinta Country Club
Bob Hope Desert Classic
Carl Meisterlin and George Blanda

Probably the most important friends I was lucky to have made in the business world were: E. B. McClure, Mac McBurney, Peter John Tew, Phil Schotsal of Walgreens, Al Zeller of Gilmore Steel, Bear H. Smith, Jerry Norman, Mike Flick (Bill Garvai's prodigy), Willie Shoemaker at Golden Gate Fields, John Brodie (the 49's quarterback), Jack Carlson of Kaiser Steel, George Jones at HMS, Bill Reinheimer and George Ford. All of these men are responsible for my successes in business and life!

Today most of my older friends and associates are up above, hopefully laughing and still attempting to stick needles in my funny bone. My last great friend and golfing buddy Bill Ford, a couple of years older than I, whom I played golf with twice a week for five years until 30 months ago, lost his wife four years ago. Thankfully, he had his three boys and a girl who live locally. Irene and I saw Bill at least once a month, as it was good therapy for all of us, give-and-take. There is absolutely nothing better than having a good laugh! Bill died a happy man on May 11, 2014.

There are a couple hundred friends not mentioned in this story who taught me, were my pals, cared for me and laughed until we cried, and I'm sure I've omitted many, but I'll add just a couple more possibly familiar names: Hoagie Carmichael, Bob and Linda Christiansen, Bill Powers, Spike Jones, Art Spangler, Dr. Stanley Racz, Doug Sanders, Paul Weitmann, Lute Olson, and Spiro Agnew. All are very wonderful human beings that helped me to become the luckiest man in the world!

What holds my life together, of course, is my beloved wife Irene! In our 44 years of being together, she has pushed me, pulled me, and fortunately directed me to be in the right place at the right time. She has always been a help and not a hindrance, making my life less stressful and happier.

Irene Carlson Meisterlin

Irene also brought with her nine Alpha Delta Pi sorority sisters from UCLA that had bonded together in 1946-47. These girls were all married and had children and everything in common. They met twice a year ordinarily and had their own "psychiatry in meetings." Since meeting them 44 years ago, I never knew any of these beautiful intelligent women to use a real psychiatrist! They'd already been together over 20 years before I came on to the scene, but fortunately from day one they accepted me as Irene's significant other! They were all wonderful friends of Irene and by the time we finally were married, I realized that the main motivating member of the group that held it together was Irene. She invited the group to the desert to her house for at least four days and three nights every two years, which I loved and appreciated.

There was Beverly from Los Olivos, Betty from Santa Barbara, Lois from the Valley, June from Brentwood, Nadine from West Hollywood, Bobbi from Torrance and then Palm Springs, Patsy from San Pedro, Margie from Huntington Beach and finally Ruthie from Newport Beach who became a neighbor at La Quinta Country Club. All of these friends of Irene became my close immediate fun-loving pals, to the point of thinking and treating them as sisters. As the years go by we've lost some: Betty, Margie, Nadine, Ruth and now Lois. The remaining few are all widows with the exception of June and Irene, the only two who married younger men.

Both Jerry Norman and myself are just months younger than our wives and for the last few years we have been physically included in the group as we mostly chauffeur and pick up the checks, which is a delight and fun for both of us! Jerry and I have always had a lot in common and enjoyed each other's company, so it's always been a treat for me when we can be together.

There's just been a book published pertaining to Jerry's basketball coaching career as number one assistant to the most famous basketball coach of all time, namely the great John Wooden! The book is "In the Shadow of a Legend" and 100% of the proceeds go to a charity that Jerry created several decades ago. That's the Jerry Norman his close friends know! It also describes what I call class, which all Irene's sorority sisters embody!

All five of the remaining sisters have a myriad of ailments and live one day at a time, but Irene calls each one at least once a week and they all do their best to cheer each other up and have a few laughs together! I'm so proud of her as a truly wonderful lady and friend. To have her as my wife makes me the luckiest man in the world!

All in all, I've been lucky from the day I was born. Because of the timing during my lifespan, I was put in the right place at the right time with the knowledge, friends and family to see me through, as well as a perfect mate and partner, my wife Irene, whom I live for every day! She reciprocates 100%! We jokingly try to give each other Vitamin F (fun) and Vitamin L and L (love and laughter) 24 hours a day!

Due to a myriad of problems, good and bad in 2005, we made the decision to move to our vacation home in Carlsbad, approximately 25 miles north of San Diego near the Pacific Ocean where every day is a "lousy day in paradise." In all our travels covering two thirds of the globe, we've never found a place with weather that compares to the San Diego area, even Los Angeles. It was a major downsizing problem and our family mostly didn't want our treasures—it was junk to them—so we were forced to have a professional garage sale, which was successful but also heartbreaking. We moved into our townhouse in Carlsbad on June 1, 2005 and remain here still today in 2014 fighting going into an assisted living community! Our ailments are many, but our doctors keep us upright and living one day at a time. We consider ourselves lucky every morning to wake up! We walk twice a day a minimum of a half mile, holding hands, recalling Charlie Brown where Sally and Linus state, "love is walking hand-in-hand." And so it is, except for Irene and I, it's also for stability!

Our immediate neighbors in our cul-de-sac of 16 townhouses are mostly young people with growing families. When we first moved into our vacation home in 1984, most of the tenants were older than we were and retirees. Fifteen of the units were owned and we only had one investment owner who rented their unit. It's wonderful having young people surrounding us, and they're forever spoiling us with nourishment and physical and mental assistance; particularly now that we're part of the age of technology! I credit Maha and Gus, who helped with my computer from day one and now my genius guru, James, who makes my computer write my story without losing chapter after chapter somewhere in space!

One of the luckier items in life is having a loving and caring mother-in-law who really likes you. I've had two—Emily and Julia. I loved both! Having 11 grandchildren and having 10 of them turn out superbly is better than one can hope for and I love all of them. When it comes to great-grandchildren, just having them close to you is its own reward. There's nothing better than babies and little children to keep you young! We have eight boys and one beautiful 14-year-old girl named Skylar, the oldest of the nine. Of course I also have my beautiful children: my daughters Claudia, Cynthia, Julie and Debbie; and my sons Chuck and Scott.

We're lucky to have our immediate family close by. We see them throughout the year and always in the summer when the Del Mar Racetrack is open! We love being able to spoil them by either taking them to the private turf club or just lending them our tickets to use at our table on the finish line. Either way we get to enjoy their company and watch them grow both mentally and physically, which is lucky! All these wonderful children gave me purpose. When you're in your late 80s and have a few marbles left it's very comforting! How lucky can any man be to have a family such as this and a woman like Irene at his side!

I was born lucky and Irene and I will eventually die lucky. We both agree daily that we were lucky to be born when we were! We both sincerely hope that we've spread as much goodwill and happiness to those who have touched our lives as we have received from these same people and others, wherever you are! God Bless you all!

Enjoy Life!

Acknowledgments

Thank you to the following people who helped project my stories from my mind onto paper: Karen Mireau for her constant encouragement and professionalism, Michael and Katherine Wills for teaching me how to use my new computer and Dragon 12 software in the beginning, and to Maha Calderon's ongoing assistance. A very special thanks to James Miramontes, Sr. for taking over the computer when I was too frightened to start it and to his lovely wife Laura!

Many, many thanks to those friends whose names appear as characters in my story. For example: Gayle who is everything her character portrays. Thanks, Irene, for your patience! Thank you all for making my life lucky, happy and wonderful.

About the Author

Carl Walter Meisterlin
February 16, 1966

Born in 1928 into a family of aristocrats, Carl Meisterlin realized at an early age that social status is no guarantee of personal or financial success.

Carl's positive life philosophy, his faith in The Lord and the goodness of humanity, and his sense of humor all played pivotal roles in overcoming the challenges life handed him. He discovered that timing (and being open to possibility) is everything. With hard work, a supportive family and good luck, he became a successful real estate entrepreneur until his retirement in 1993.

Carl feels blessed to be a father to six children, grandfather to eleven and great-grandfather to nine! This is just one of the reasons he considers himself "The Luckiest Man in the World."

Carl and the love of his life, his trophy wife Irene, now reside happily in the paradise that is Carlsbad, California. It is their hope and wish that everyone experience the true love and good fortune that they enjoy.

Where there's a will, there's a way!

Contact:

Carl W. Meisterlin
Author
cwmirene@aol.com

Karen Mireau
Publisher
Azalea.Art.Press@gmail.com
http://azaleaartpress.blogspot.com

For Book Orders:
www.Lulu.com